The Family
in the American Economy

The Family
in the American Economy

BY HAZEL KYRK

THE UNIVERSITY OF CHICAGO PRESS

173
K99

39193

THE UNIVERSITY OF CHICAGO PRESS, CHICAGO 37
Cambridge University Press, London, N.W. 1, England
The University of Toronto Press, Toronto 5, Canada

PREFACE

THIS book differs from others on the family in that it is concerned with economic welfare, particularly the economic welfare of American families. In the main it is an analysis of their economic position in terms of incomes, prices, and standards of living. The economic role of the family as a part of the institutional framework is emphasized and the implications of the changes that have occurred in the composition of the group living together and in the family as a system of rights and responsibilities. Attention is directed not only to the economic situation of the families in a given community or group at a given time but to the probable course of events during the family life-span. As a result, the economic position of children, young adults, those in their middle and in their later years comes into prominence and the differences in the economic life-history of men and of women. Throughout the discussion the fact that, according to the "blueprint," the family, not the individual, is the self-relying, self-supporting unit is taken into account as well as the fact that the income-claiming and using unit is usually a family group. It follows that the allocation of income among alternative uses cannot be described as a process by which an individual attempts to maximize his welfare or satisfactions, but as an apportionment by one or more members of a group acting jointly or separately for the joint and several benefit.

This book must also be distinguished from certain others which are concerned with the economic welfare of families. Most similar in general character and purpose are those which analyze market practices and operations from the standpoint of buyers for personal and family use. In this book market process and public policy are viewed not only from the standpoint of families as income-spenders, desirous of maximizing the returns from their expenditures, but as income-recipients, desirous of maximizing income received and assuring its continuous flow. It is broader in scope than those which concentrate upon the consumer interest and, correspondingly, may give scant attention to issues which they intensively explore. Of quite different character and approach are those books designed to help families improve their economic position by the development of greater skill in home production, greater efficiency in budgeting, buying, or management in general. Insofar as these books deal with an

v

economy, rather than with techniques, it is the domestic economy and the use of resources under the conditions thus set. The larger economy within which the domestic economy operates is taken as given, as well as all conditions not under the control of the individual or family. This book, as the title implies, deals primarily with the larger economy and family economic welfare as affected by its nature and functioning. It is addressed to the student who desires to explore certain issues of import for the economic welfare of families as a whole, not to the person who is looking for insights and instructions that will immediately and directly be of profit to him or his family as income recipient or user. The main individual and social benefits that may be hoped for from its study are those that come from an enhanced understanding of the economic world.

This book in fact represents the material prepared for the students in a course offered for many years at the University of Chicago. In its preparation and the use made of it in the classroom two objectives were paramount. One was to acquaint the student with the major sources of factual information when such information was relevant. As an integral part of that process an attempt was made to develop standards for the appraisal and interpretation of such data and to point out gaps and deficiencies. It is expected that students who use this book will supply new data as they currently become available. It is hoped that they will know that least important, even inconsequential, is the item that is simply of recent date but that of basic importance are the results of those studies which show new relationships or trends.

The second and main objective in the preparation of this material, to which the first was purely contributive, was to provide the type of analysis that would disclose the important issues in each area. The assumption was that if the issues were correctly stated the readers would think about the right things and could seek in other sources a more extended discussion than could be given here. Thus, although the reader who weighs and considers may not come to the same conclusion as the author who sets the problems, they are more likely to have thought about the same things.

Those familiar with the author's *Economic Problems of the Family*, published in 1933 and now out of print, will recognize that this book, although the same in character and purpose, is new not only in title but in other respects. What began as a revision became more than a reorganization and a rewriting. The context in which many topics were discussed and their relative emphasis changed. The discussion of many others was completely altered. Entirely new chapters were added. One chapter alone stands substantially as it was in the earlier book, that on "The Standard of Living," and only limited changes were made in the discussion of "Consumer Production," "The Economic Position of Homekeeping Women," and "Income and Property Rights of Husband and Wife under the Law."

HAZEL KYRK

CHICAGO, ILLINOIS
June 1, 1953

CONTENTS

LIST OF CHARTS xv

LIST OF TABLES xvii

I. FORMS AND FUNCTIONS OF THE FAMILY. 1
    What Is a Family? 1
    Changes in the Family 2
    The Family in Other Cultures 5
    Social Changes Shaping Development of the Modern Family . . 10
    Relation of the Modern Family to the Economy as a Whole . . . 12
    Individual and Social Needs Met by the Family 13
    Economic Significance of the Family 15

II. AMERICAN FAMILIES TODAY 18
    Sources of Information 18
    Trend in Marriage Rate and Age 19
    Family Status of the Population 21
    Types of Families 25
    Size of Households and of Families 27
    Families with Children under Eighteen 29
    Maximum Size Usually Attained 30
    Differences between Urban and Farm Households and Families . . 32
    Differences between White and Nonwhite Households and Families 34

III. COMPONENTS OF FAMILY INCOME AND WEALTH 36
    Sources of Information 36
    Defining Income and Income-Recipient 37
    The Family Balance Sheet 41
    Components of Money Income 42
    Components of Nonmoney Income 46
    Calculating the Amount of Nonmoney Income 48
    Impossibility of Making Exact Comparisons of Incomes 50
    Relation between National Income and Personal Incomes . . . 52

IV. CONTRIBUTORS AND CLAIMANTS TO THE FAMILY INCOME 56
    Sources of Information 56
    Contributors and Claimants in the Population as a Whole . . . 57
    Family Status of Contributors and Claimants 60
    Husbands and Wives as Contributors to Money Income 63
    Reasons for Earning by Married Women 67
    Other Family Members as Contributors 74
    Economic Status of Single, Widowed, Divorced, and Separated,
        Eighteen and Over 74
    Who Supports the Nonearning Family Members? 76
    Concentration of Support Burden 78

V. AMOUNT AND ADEQUACY OF FAMILY INCOMES 82
   Factors Affecting Degree of Equality 83
   Money Income as a Measure of Consumption Level 84
   Additions to and Deductions from Money Income 86
   Effect of Price and Other Market Conditions 87
   Effect of Family Size and Composition 88
   Attempts To Devise a Scale of Income Equivalence for Families of
      Different Sizes 89
   Adequacy of Consumption Levels Attainable 92
   Personal Standards as a Measure of Poverty 93
   Scientific Standards as a Measure of Poverty 94
   The Social Standard as a Measure of Poverty 96
   Determination of the Social Standard 97
   Estimation of Number of Families below the Poverty Line . . . 98
   Adequacy of Family Income versus Adequacy of Incomes of Indi-
      vidual Income Recipients 101
   Economic Experience of Families during Their Life-Span 104
   State of the Economy and the Economic Experience of Families . 105
   Economic Experience as a Function of Source of Income 105
   What Is the Usual Course of Income? 108

VI. IMPROVEMENT OF INCOME POSITION 111
   Primary versus Secondary Poverty 111
   Individual Efforts To Reduce Pressure on Income 112
   Individual Efforts To Increase Money Income 114
   Increasing Family Income by Increasing Number of Earners . . 116
   Collective Bargaining as a Means of Improving Economic Position . 117
   Children and Poverty 120
   Poverty and Consumption Standards 122
   Poverty and Inequality 125
   Inequality of Earnings 128

VII. PUBLIC POLICY AND THE INCOME PROBLEM 131
   The Income Tax as an Equalizing Measure 132
   Minimum-Wage Laws 135
   Agricultural Policy and the Problem of Poverty 136
   Public Assistance to the Needy 137
   Family Allowances 141

VIII. FREE GOODS AND SERVICES 145
   Development of the Free Services 145
   Why the Free Services? 146
   Differentiation of Governmental Services 148
   Free Services for Whom? 149
   What Types of Goods and Services Should Be Provided at Public
      Expense? 151
   Cost and Quality of Free Services 152
   Outlays for Free Goods and Services 155
   Future Expansion of Free Services 156

Should the Health Services Be Free Services? 159
Family Use of the Free Services 163

IX. INCOME INSECURITY 165
Forms of Income Insecurity 166
Old Age as an Economic Risk 167
Risk of Unemployment 169
Economic Risks Other than Unemployment 171
Security of Salaried Workers 172
Conflicting and Coincidental Individual and Social Goals . . . 173

X. PROVISION FOR THE FUTURE THROUGH SAVING 174
Debt versus Saving Beforehand 175
Insurance versus Saving 176
Motives for Saving 177
Determinants of Amount Saved 180
Disposition of Saved Funds 181
Assets, Liabilities, and Net Worth of American Families . . . 187

XI. PROVISION FOR THE FUTURE THROUGH INSURANCE 190
Assessment of Insurance Needs 191
Types of Policies 194
Factors Affecting Cost of Insurance 196
Term, Whole-Life, and Limited-Payment Insurance 199
Group Insurance 205
Provision for Old Age 206
Problems in Planning an Insurance Program 209
How Adequate Is Insurance Protection? 210
Insurance against Risk of Illness or Accident 211

XII. SOCIAL SECURITY 215
Possible Scope and Character of Public Policy 215
Aid to Dependent Children 217
Old Age Assistance 220
Assistance to the Blind and Disabled 225
Social Insurance Programs 226
Compulsory Insurance against Risk of Industrial Accident and Occu-
    pational Disease 226
Federal Old Age Insurance 229
Survivors' Benefits 232
Unemployment Compensation 236
Sickness and Disability Benefits 240

XIII. CONSUMER PRODUCTION 243
Differentiation of Consumer Production from Other Activities . . 244
Changes in the Character of Consumer Production 247
Some Characteristics of Modern Household Activities 250
The Choice between Making and Buying 252
Efficiency in Consumer Production 254
Efficiency as a Problem of Reducing Overhead Costs 255

Efficiency as a Problem of Increasing Scientific Management . . 258
Obstacles to Improvement in Management 261
Adequacy of Motivation 263
The Future of Consumer Production 265

XIV. The Economic Position of Homekeeping Women 270
Division of Labor between Men and Women 271
Peculiarities of Economic Status of Women 275
The Vocational Divide in the Life of Women 276
Character of Work and Working Conditions 277
Women and Leisure 279
What Are the Facts? 281
What Forces Are Increasing and What Decreasing the Working Week? 284
The Uneven Distribution of the Burden of Housework 287
The Problem of Overwork 289
The Problem of Underwork 291

XV. Income and Property Rights of Husband and Wife under the Law 297
Are Legal Rights of Importance? 297
What Is the Law? 298
Husband and Wife under the Common Law 298
The Wife's Right to Support 300
Agency of Fact 301
Survivor's Rights 302
Equitable Separate Estates 303
Statutory Removal of Common-Law Disabilities of Married Women 303
Testamentary and Survivor's Rights in the Common-Law States . 306
The Community-Property System 307
Special Problems of the Community-Property System 309
Dissolution of Marriage by Divorce 311
Rights and Responsibilities of Divorcing Spouses 312
What Should the Law Be? 313

XVI. Planning Expenditure of Income 320
Income Receipts versus Outlays through Time 320
Are Expenditures Planned? 321
Budgeting 322
When Is Budgeting Most Important? 323
What Budgeting Does and Does Not Achieve 324
Deterrents to Budgeting 325
Who Determines How the Family Income Is Spent? 326
Children and Money 330
Tools and Techniques of Budgeting 330
Are There Rules To Follow? 332
The Decision-making Process 335
Checking Plan with Performance 336

XVII. The Cost of Living 338
Measurement of Changes in the Cost of Living 338

Place-to-Place Differences 341
The High Cost of Living 342
The Cost of Living Historically Considered 342
Cost of Housing 344
Costs of Distribution 346
Market Structure 347
Changes in Market Structure 349
Special Problem of the Chains 350

XVIII. The Cost of Living—*Continued* 352
Extent of Competition 352
What Is Competition? 353
Public Policy and the Monopoly Problem 355
Antimonopoly Legislation 358
Buying Practices of Consumers 360
Does the Market Facilitate Intelligent Choice? 361
Attempts To Outlaw Misinformation 362
How Secure Informative Labeling and Advertising? 363
Sales Promotion 365
High Cost of Living as a Product of Monetary Inflation . . . 368

XIX. The Standard of Living 373
What Is One's Standard of Living? 373
Significance of the Standard of Living 374
The Standard of Living as an Attitude toward a Given Mode of Living 375
Origin of Our Standards 376
Nature of Our Standards 378
The American Standard of Living 380
Character of Our Wants 386
Necessaries, Decencies, and Luxuries 387
Improvement of Consumptive Choices 389
Education for Wise Consumption 391

References for Further Reading 395

Index 399

LIST OF CHARTS

I. MEDIAN MONEY INCOME OF URBAN AND FARM MEN BY AGE, UNITED STATES, 1947 109

II. MEDIAN ANNUAL EARNINGS OF INDIVIDUALS BY OCCUPATION AND AGE, MINNESOTA, 1938–39 110

III. ANNUAL PREMIUM FOR $1,000 OF (A) ONE-YEAR RENEWABLE, CONVERTIBLE TERM, AND (B) ORDINARY LIFE INSURANCE BEGINNING AT AGE 25, BOTH NONPARTICIPATING 201

LIST OF TABLES

1. DISTRIBUTION OF FAMILIES AND INDIVIDUALS BY TOTAL MONEY-INCOME LEVEL FOR THE UNITED STATES, 1947 83

2. DISTRIBUTION OF FAMILIES BY TOTAL MONEY-INCOME LEVEL, BY SIZE OF FAMILY, FOR THE UNITED STATES, NONFARM AND FARM, 1947 85

3. DISTRIBUTION OF NONFARM POPULATION EIGHTEEN YEARS OF AGE AND OVER BY AMOUNT OF MONEY INCOME IN 1947, CLASSIFIED BY SEX AND MARITAL STATUS 102

4. LENGTH OF HOMEMAKERS' WORKING WEEK 283

5. EFFECT OF CHILDREN IN HOUSEHOLD UPON LENGTH OF HOMEMAKERS' WORKING WEEK AND AMOUNT OF HELP RECEIVED 289

CHAPTER I

FORMS AND FUNCTIONS OF THE FAMILY

WHAT IS A FAMILY?

WHAT are the essential characteristics of the group or institution that may properly be called the "family"—characteristics that identify it whenever or wherever found? A family without question is a group of individuals.[1] There are, however, many kinds of human groupings, in schools, churches, workshops, political organizations, and the like. One essential characteristic of the group of persons who constitute a family is that they are related by blood or by law. In every society some system of tracing relationship is found. Thus each individual as a family member acquires a recognized status. Both child and adult can identify and place himself in these terms. By virtue of a recognized and named relationship he belongs in a particular group. The relationship between family members is more, however, than a means of identification. Family status carries with it specific rights and obligations determined and upheld by custom, law, and ethics. The family, in other words, is not only a group of related persons; it is a system of claims and obligations. Social and economic ends are achieved by tying rights and responsibilities to defined biological and legal relationships. Family status gives the individual certain assurances and certain duties. The family may thus be defined as a unit of mutual responsibilities as well as a group of related persons.

The family may also be defined as a way of living, a form of human association. There is no family from this standpoint unless the related members live together in a common dwelling place, and only the group that so lives may be called a family. The concomitant of such living is usually a common hearth, a common table. Sumner and Keller report that members of the Hindu family are "designated in downright manner as 'those who cook together.' "[2] The group living together are usually those most closely related and those whose claims upon and responsibilities for

---

1. The United States Bureau of the Census until recently included in its count of families persons living alone and thus reported a certain number of one-person "families." Actually the Bureau was counting occupied dwelling units rather than families.

2. W. G. Sumner and A. G. Keller, *The Science of Society* (New Haven: Yale University Press, 1927), I, 196.

one another are prior to those upon and for others. Whether the assumption of responsibilities followed the choice of this way of living or vice versa is inconsequential at this point. Unrelated persons living together are said to live like a family, and, if mutual responsibilities are recognized as among the related, their similarity to the family lacks only the fact of relationship and the obligations and rights it carries.

In our society those living together in a common domicile are usually a married couple with their unmarried children, if any, or a parent with such children.[3] Other relatives or unrelated persons may live with the family so constituted, but without evidence to the contrary their presence is generally regarded as an undesirable deviation from the norm. Conversely most married persons, children, and parents of children live in family groups as described. In our society also it is this nuclear or immediate family that is the primary unit of mutual responsibility. Claims upon other relatives outside this group or responsibilities for them have been progressively lessened and unenforced. In form, then, the modern family is typically a married couple, parents, or a parent with a child or children. This group is usually separately domiciled. The care, nurture, and support of the children are the parents' responsibility. Husband and wife have mutual claims and obligations.

CHANGES IN THE FAMILY

In all respects emphasized, as a way of living, a status-giving arrangement, a system of rights and obligations which serve to supplement those otherwise determined, the family is a well-marked part of the culture pattern of our society as it has been and is in all others. The persistence and universality of the family is a well-established historical fact. In the vast literature dealing with the family in one aspect or another this fact is abundantly emphasized. Equally emphasized is the fact that the modern family differs from the family of yore or that American families differ from those in many other contemporary societies. Along with this statement of differences may go various conclusions: that it has lessened in importance as a social institution, that it has lost many of its once important functions, that it performs its functions less well than the family of earlier days, that the values and arrangements it represents are not in accord with those otherwise prevailing in our society. Whatever conclusions and judgments are valid, the legal and customary arrangements represented by the modern family are the outcome of the developments that made our world in other respects. Perspective and objectivity are

---

3. See chap. ii for statistical evidence to this effect.

best secured by a review of those developments and a contrast of the situation of the family now with what it was in societies differently organized and with different values.

Some of the changes in the family frequently noted are relatively recent, others remote in time, some are most pronounced in American families, others are characteristic of all Western culture, some are in process, and others are complete. One of these changes is that the marriage which marks the beginning of a new family is increasingly a free personal choice of the partners, a freedom consistent with the high value put on personal choice in all realms in our culture. Also consistent and probably an inevitable concomitant of free choice of a mate is increasing freedom to terminate the marriage, a freedom not so happily viewed and more limited. Of the same character, deriving from the same sources and equally in harmony with prevailing values of our culture, is the non-authoritarian character of the American family, and the resulting relations between husband and wife, parents and children.

Another change in the pattern highly characteristic of the American situation is the withdrawal of the married couple into domestic privacy in the form of a home separate from all others. As Ruth Benedict said: "As soon as the wedding is over everybody expects them to have their own latch key and their own possessions around them. If they cannot manage this, they feel cheated and other people think something is wrong. It is the same if they have to give a home to a parent."[4] One of the most well-defined and pervasive patterns for living in our culture is the establishment of an independent household at the time of marriage and its maintenance thereafter. There may be a good reason for failure to do so, but an explanation of such aberrant behavior is usually considered necessary. Economic inability to do so or economic inability of aged parents to live independently is regarded as an enforced deviation from the proper manner of living. The "doubling-up" of families during economic depression or housing shortage is taken as an index of the straits to which some are reduced. Measures of housing "need" start with estimates of the number of married couples and of probable marriage rates in succeeding years.

Along with these changes have been others less visible but of great economic and social importance, changes that are an inseparable part of the technological and institutional character of our society. In the first place, the larger social group of which the nuclear family created by marriage is a part is no longer made up of persons united by a kinship bond

4. "Are Families Passé?" *Saturday Review of Literature,* December 25, 1943, p. 6.

or by generations of close association or by fixed master-slave or lord-serf relations. The small family, which in our society is "the family," always and everywhere has been part of a larger group with the members of which it was associated in obtaining a livelihood and in other ways, to which it had obligations, and upon which it had claims. Davis says: "Although the immediate family is a universal group, it is not instinctive; rather it is a cultural phenomenon, and as such its specific form, and above all its connections with the rest of society, vary tremendously from one social system to another."[5] Today the larger group with which the family is connected in one way or another is a city, a state, a nation, a business concern. The members of these larger groups are unrelated, their relations impersonal. Families living in the same neighborhood are less and less likely to be related. Those who recently came to this country may have left their kindred behind them. Free and frequent movement from place to place has scattered the kindred who live here.

In the second place, as has been indicated, the obligations and rights arising from birth or marriage are more and more closely limited to those between husband and wife and parents and their unmarried children below school-leaving age. The recognized claims of children upon relatives other than their parents are slight and uncertain. Likewise, the sense of obligation of parents for adult children and of such children for their parents has been lessening. Brother feels little obligation to brother or sister to sister. "One of the outstanding peculiarities of Western civilization . . . is the degree to which kinship has lost its social importance."[6] Upon the other hand, the sense of responsibility of parents for dependent children is very strong, and the period of dependency is much longer than ever before. The rights and obligations that go along with marital status are recognized and enforced by law and strong social sanctions.

In the third place, the modern family which is typically urban is not and cannot be as nearly self-sufficing as the older rural family, nor does the rural family have the degree of self-sufficiency that it once had. In many discussions of change in the family's economic position this change is emphasized to the exclusion of all others. Far too sweeping statements have often been made regarding the former degree of self-sufficiency of the husband-wife, parents-children group. Further, the economic functions of the family have been identified with its productive, leading to the conclusion that as its productive activity declined so did its economic

5. Kingsley Davis, "Children of Divorced Parents: Sociological and Statistical Analysis," *Law and Contemporary Problems*, X (summer, 1944), 701.
6. *Ibid.*, p. 704.

significance. Actually the economic significance of the family arises not only from the tasks the members perform for and with one another but from the rights and obligations that the family relationship entails. The family may be less and less a productive unit, but it remains to no less an extent than before a unit of mutual responsibility. The size of the group whose members have mutual claims and obligations may have diminished and their relationship changed, but the family as an institution continues and performs its usual functions in this respect.

THE FAMILY IN OTHER CULTURES

Studies of the family in other cultures support the generalizations that have just been made. In primitive or simple societies of our own or earlier days the small group identical with or similar to our own modern family is a part of a larger group identified by a kinship bond. The kinship grouping in these cases is always on a unilateral basis; that is, lineage is traced either through the mother's line or through the father's, not through both. A unity or undivided allegiance within the group is thus insured. Groups so bound together constitute clans or gens or what may be described as a "great family." In the patrilinear type of grouping, women upon marriage become members of their husband's clan or gens as do their children, and marriage does not alter the sons' position and loyalties. Brothers in such a group have a sense of solidarity with one another as great as that of fathers and sons. Under the matrilinear system the family is least like our own; the father may be eliminated as a member of the household, and his status does not carry with it the same responsibilities. The marriage bond does not have the same significance. The patrilinear system keeps together the father, mother, and children and gives the father authority over and responsibility for his own children.[7]

If the family is defined as a unit of mutual responsibility based upon a recognized relationship, the family in primitive societies is the extended kinship group, and each member has a responsibility for and claims upon a larger group than is the case today. Today the family as a unit of responsibility is created by the marriage bond and by the biological linking of parent and child. Two adults assume in certain respects the same responsibilities as does the larger clan or gens under other systems.[8]

7. It should be noted that divorce, so frequent in our society, and remarriage may create quite complicated lines of authority and responsibility as between families. A man may have responsibility for children not members of his household, or he may assume responsibility for and have as members of his household another man's children whose mother he has married.

8. Under the present bilateral system of tracing descent with both the maternal and the paternal lines given equal recognition, each individual belongs to two families, an impossible situation if membership carried its earlier meaning.

Margaret Mead argues that the family as it now stands is a weak form of organization for the purpose of child nurture and support. She points out that it can be shattered by either death or divorce, leaving the child "in an indeterminate position economically, socially and affectionally."[9] It is true that the parental responsibility remains in spite of divorce, but the power and willingness to meet it grow weak especially if a new family is established of which the children in question are not a part. She also argues:

Were state responsibility for children substituted for the present family organization we would obtain a type of guarantee for children which the present weak bilateral family group fails to give. In the clan, or any of its modifications, a child's status and subsistence is assured as long as there are members of the clan alive. Under the state, a child would again claim a relationship to a large group of adults— a group too large to be dissipated by a single blow. . . . Our present narrow definition of adult responsibility towards children as being limited to own or legally adoptive parents has robbed the child of that security which was assured by all primitive societies not primarily organized about the marriage tie.[10]

Davis makes similar observations. He says:

The decline of kinship has affected the extended, not the immediate, family. The latter has lost some of its erstwhile functions . . . but because it is virtually the sole remaining kinship unit it has acquired some of the functions formerly performed by other kinship relations. Its burden has therefore become heavy—perhaps too heavy for its inherently frail structure.[11]

Not only does the system of complete parental responsibility without claims upon others constitute a threat to the child's security if the marriage between its two adult protectors is broken, but, while it endures, the adequacy of the provision for his needs is entirely a function of their ability, knowledge, foresight, and good fortune.

The modern family is an economic unit in the sense that resources are shared and the members live together. It is not an economic unit in the sense that the members work together to provide their common livelihood. Generally speaking, the nuclear family, the husband and wife, the parents and their children, has never been a completely self-sufficing group. The more accurate generalization is that it always and everywhere has lived in close association with a larger group, with its economic life organized on the basis of co-operation with other members of that group. The basis of the co-operation in simple kinship groups with limited productive powers and resources is different from what it is in a market economy, but in both

9. "Contrasts and Comparisons from Primitive Society," *Annals of the American Academy of Political and Social Science*, CLX (March, 1932), 28.
10. *Ibid.*
11. *Op. cit.*, pp. 704–5.

cases there is an organized system for working together and for sharing the group product, not self-sufficiency of the nuclear family.

Many of those who have emphasized the former self-sufficiency of the family have focused their attention on the situation of many families in the early American settlements or on the frontier as it moved westward. The pioneer family was a marvel of self-sufficiency, but this was only a brief episode in the history of a particular people, incident to the settlement of a new land. As rapidly as it could be achieved, self-sufficiency of the isolated families of the frontier disappeared. Lands were taken up, settlements grew thicker, roads were built, towns grew, production for the market developed. Only on the frontier and in remote districts did the old regime linger. What some regard as the golden day of complete identity of the economic interests of the family group and of the participation of all members according to sex, age, and aptitude in a joint enterprise was over in a relatively short period of time.

Others who emphasize the former self-sufficiency of the family have in mind not the small family of the present day but the extended kinship group so like it in certain respects or the plantation or manorial household which included many persons other than those related. The initial self-sufficing group that the records reveal to us is a kinship group of the sort previously described. Müller-Lyer says:

> On the lowest stage of culture known to us man lives in small hordes or clans, the members of which are bound together by common extraction and ties of blood. The solidarity of the horde . . . leads to economic union and organization of labor. But even in the clan . . . there is found a second form of organization of labor; that is the family, the strong tie which binds together a man, his wife, and their children. . . . The family is a part of the clan and the clan or horde itself produces everything that it needs. We might therefore speak of a self-sufficing clan, although not yet of self-sufficing families.[12]

Malinowski, writing on "Marriage" in the *Encyclopaedia Britannica*, said:

> Each [husband and wife] has to collaborate with other members of the community of the same sex in some wider enterprise, from which the family benefits only partially and indirectly. In spite of repeated theoretical assertions as to the existence of the "closed household economy" . . . we find in every community, however simple, a wider economic collaboration embracing all members and welding the various families into larger cooperative units. The fuller our knowledge of relevant facts, the better we see on the one hand the dependence of the family upon the rest of the community, and on the other hand the duty of each individual to contribute not only to his own household but to those of others as well.[13]

12. F. C. Müller-Lyer, *The History of Social Development* (London: G. Allen & Unwin, Ltd., 1920), pp. 155–58.

13. Bronislaw Malinowski, "Marriage," *Encyclopaedia Britannica* (14th ed.), XIV, 943.

Although primitive peoples are not entirely without specialized workers, as the weaver, the potter, the arrow- or basketmaker, in the main the limits upon the self-sufficiency of the small family are set by the collective activities of the group. Certain tasks by their nature would be performed by the persons living in closest association. Those which center around the hearth—cooking, the care of children, the carrying of wood and water, the making of many tools, utensils, and articles of clothing—would be in this category. The women may gather wild grains and berries for the use of the small family group. But, roughly, it may be said that the supplying of the basic needs of the group, the production of the primary foodstuffs and raw materials, is likely among primitive groups to be a process of labor-in-common under group control and with group ownership of the chief means of production. The advantage of combined action in such activities as hunting, fishing, and defense perpetuates the close association of small families into clans and clans into tribes. When it comes to the working-up of materials, the grinding of corn, the cooking, the sewing, the pottery, the basketry, each household is more likely to meet the requirements of its members with its own labor. If we think only of manufacture or the manifold arts involved in the working-over of materials, we may accurately perhaps set up household economy as the first stage and talk about the passing of the self-sufficient family.

The limitations upon the self-sufficiency of the small family set by collective activities and communal control by no means disappear if we turn our attention from primitive peoples to those of higher cultural levels living in the historic era. The advantages of life in a group whose members work together at tasks beyond the powers of a single small family and share the use of certain resources are evidenced by the persistence of such an arrangement in the recorded history of almost every people. Long after theories of blood relationship had been abandoned and kinship groups had become village communities, long after the peoples of western Europe, for example, had abandoned a nomadic life and taken up the systematic cultivation of the soil, labor in common and, even more important, communal management persisted as the means of providing the group with its foodstuffs, raw materials, and certain other necessaries.

The history of agriculture, whether pastoral husbandry or the cultivation of the soil, is largely a history of communal management and of methods that demand collaboration. Vinogradoff in his study of the growth of the English manor says: "There seems to be hardly anything more certain in the domain of archaic law than the theory that the soil was originally owned by groups and not by individuals, and that its individual appropriation is the result of a slow process of development."[14] Discussing the agrarian arrangements under the open-field system characteristic of agriculture down to a comparatively recent date, he describes the economic position of the households in the local organization as follows:

They had the common and undivided use of the waste land, but this use could be limited and apportioned by the community. . . . The scarce and highly valued meadows were assigned under strict rules of proportionate division and redivision; the arable which formed the most important . . . portion of the whole, lay in scattered strips in the various fields . . . of the village; everybody had to conform to the same rules and methods of cultivation of crops, and when these had been gathered the strips relapsed into the state of an open field for common use. The homesteads and closes around them were kept under separate management, but had been allotted by the community and could in some cases be subject to reallotment. If this is a correct general description of the main system in operation in the course of the thousand years from 500 till 1500 A.D. and extending many of its incidents to even later times, one can scarcely escape the conclusion, that . . . the average English householder of the middle ages lived under conditions in which his power of free disposal and free management was hemmed in on all sides by customs and rules converging towards the conceptions of a community of interests and rights between all the household shares of a village.[15]

The patriarchal household, made up of the father and all his sons, whether married or unmarried, with their wives and children, is described as the center of domestic and economic life in the early history of Greece and Rome. Glotz describes this "great family" of Homeric times united around the same hearth, dwelling under the same roof, eating at the same table, and sharing a common patrimony.[16] The household did not long remain in this simple form: "It was destined to rapid transformation through the existence of the city. . . . The *genos* begins to split up into small families. . . . Individualism is born. . . . In the very bosom of collective property, private property is formed."[17] Furthermore, in the ancient civilizations

the household . . . was strengthened and increased by the introduction of slaves. . . . The nobles introduced slaves in very large numbers as field workers, herdsmen, fishers, bakers, butchers, and so on, so that they were in a position to supply by their own labour almost all the needs of . . . the household. This . . . system attained its fullest development later on in the large pastoral estates of the Roman nobility.[18]

Slavery was the basis of the family autonomy of the ancient civilizations. Although separated in time by hundreds of years, the great feudal

14. Paul Vinogradoff, *The Growth of the Manor* (London: G. Allen & Co., 1911), p. 18.
15. *Ibid.*, pp. 165–66.
16. Gustave Glotz, *Ancient Greece at Work* (New York: A. A. Knopf, Inc., 1926), chap. i.
17. *Ibid.*, pp. 8–9.   18. Müller-Lyer, *op. cit.*, p. 171.

households of the Middle Ages, with their serfs and retainers, were akin to the slave households of the ancient civilizations. The lord's domain was worked by the tenantry; he had his dues in kind; he had his great household with its servants. The families of the vill had their homesteads and their commonalty. They made up small local groups that were largely self-sufficing. Their husbandry, as previously noted, was largely carried on on a collective basis under communal control. Except for the presence of a few specialized craftsmen such as the smith and the miller, the industrial arts were household employment. Each family prepared its own food and drink and provided its own clothing and utensils.

Most accounts of the household organization, the manner of living, and the domestic life of the ancient civilizations and of the great days of the feudal system deal entirely with the ruling class. The enslaved population is subsidiary and out of the picture. Yet it was the base upon which the arts and refinements of these civilizations rested. Division of labor was highly developed in the slave households of Greece and Rome. Skilled crafts developed. The surplus productive powers of the enslaved classes above the amount necessary for their bare existence could be used to expand the manner of living of the superior class. The benefits of a "surplus economy" first became available to a privileged class through the institution of slavery. The arts and learning developed as is possible when some are freed from the burden of providing their daily bread by their own direct toil. Even under the less onerous feudal system the many contributed the fruits of their toil to the few according to a system of hereditary right and custom. The fine arts, ceremony, elaborate codes of manners, the lady, "civilized" ways of living, were the by-products. The great achievement of the Western civilizations from the standpoint of the economic interests of the family was that they were able to bring about a surplus economy without slavery or hereditary bondage.

SOCIAL CHANGES SHAPING DEVELOPMENT OF THE MODERN FAMILY

To understand the economic and social position of the modern family and the setting within which it operates, three familiar lines of development that altered profoundly the lives of the people of the Western world must be reviewed and their significance noted. One of these developments was the emergence of the nation or a centralized system of government. Another was the series of technological changes which changed the place and manner of production and made people members of an economic society wider in scope than the political unit to which they belonged. Third to be listed, but not last to occur or least in importance, were those legal and political changes resulting in democratic procedures and forms of organization and the development of a market economy with its various characteristics.

The character of the modern state may best be seen by contrasting it with the kinship group, the village community or city-state. The modern state is actually or potentially vast in scope, constituting an empire or a commonwealth of minor subdivisions. Few of its members are known to one another. There is no bond of kinship or even of propinquity between most of the members. Membership is determined primarily by place of birth rather than by parentage. The state is conceived as an instrument to promote the welfare of its members, and the measures that will do so are matters of concern and debate.

The story of the great changes in ways and places of production that have taken place in the last two or three centuries has been often told. It is a part of the history of the great industrial nations. The first great step toward our modern economy came with the growth of free towns and a free artisan and merchant class. Town life and the development of trade and commerce made possible division of labor. Skilled craftsmen made superior wares. Retail selling, the use of money, the devices of modern commerce, came into common use. The economic status of the private household in the commercial towns of western Europe differed in degree but not in kind from that of the household today. As opportunity permitted, specialized labor for money was undertaken and purchase was substituted for home production. The opportunity came with a slowness that can scarcely be realized today. It came only with the slow development of means of transportation and of the mechanisms that facilitate trade and commerce; it came with the slow development of new crafts and new wares. As they could, the townspeople gave up the production of their own foodstuffs and raw materials. As their means permitted, they bought on the market the finer fabrics and the more skilfully wrought goods than could be turned out by home production. More and more households participated in the new economy as time went on. More craftsmen and merchants could dispose of their wares. More cottagers could be employed in spinning and weaving for merchant-capitalists.

The marked decrease in the volume of home manufacture and in the self-sufficiency of the local community came, however, with the industrial changes at the end of the eighteenth and beginning of the nineteenth century. At this time came the mechanical inventions, first in the textile and then in other industries, and the application of nonhuman motive power to these mechanical devices. The effective and economical use of these devices was only possible through their concentration in a central place to which the workers came. The concentration of a large number of workers under one roof again made possible a more advantageous use of their labor by specialization and subdivision of process. Other economies of production were possible so that it came to be that a supply of textiles and other goods for thousands of families scattered through many countries was produced in a single establishment. Equally, if not more, important in hastening the coming of the new market economy were the new means of transportation that provided the outlet for the enlarged output of the new means of production. The economic unit was no longer the agricultural village community, the town with its simple crafts and weekly markets, or even the nation with its periodic fairs and slow sailborne commerce. There ceased to be self-sufficing units short of the world itself. The market for many goods became international, even world-wide.

The third series of changes to be noted were of a different order from those just described. They were changes not in the technique of production but in the rights and powers of those who produced. On the political side they were those changes in law and philosophy that transferred authority from those who seized it or who were born to it to those who derived it from the consent of the governed. On the economic side the change is usually described as the coming of free enterprise: free spending on the market and free entry into occupation or business. The earlier regimes of status became in large degree regimes of contract. Societies were transformed from those where a few were born to power and privilege and many to slavery and serfdom to those where all were free men.

RELATION OF THE MODERN FAMILY TO THE ECONOMY AS A WHOLE

The social and economic arrangements that came to characterize the great societies of the Western world inevitably brought changes in the relation of the family to the larger economy of which it is a part. It is now a contractual and pecuniary relationship established by one or more of the family members. In their major work activities individuals are not characteristically associated with persons related to them by blood or law. Few of the goods and services they enjoy are the direct product of their own labors. The increased economic dependence of the family in the form of lessened self-sufficiency that has resulted from changes in technology and in organization of production has often been emphasized. Less emphasized, although perhaps of greater import, are the results of the institutional changes that paralleled or preceded them. The result for the family as we know it was an entirely new kind of economic independence.

The institutional changes briefly described carry with them the assumption that each adult is responsible for his own support and for that of his wife and children not yet of earning age. The modern family is not self-sufficing, but it is supposed to be and ordinarily is largely self-supporting. The presumption is that the members do not look outside the immediate family circle for the wherewithal to purchase food, clothing, and shelter. Correspondingly, the family's responsibility tends to stop with its own members. Sharing with others is not obligatory, except as an act of generosity or charity, very different in character from the discharge of an obligation. Collective responsibility for children, the aged, the disabled, the economically unfortunate, manifests itself largely through the impersonal agency of the state.

The aspect of our modern society that has just been emphasized is usually called "individualism." Freedom of contract, freedom of occupation, freedom to own, accumulate, and use wealth as desired, freedom to move about, had as their correlative individual responsibility for livelihood and fortune. Individualism means self-support, individual reliance upon one's own efforts and resources. Actually the proper name for this economic system is not "individualism" but "familism." The self-relying unit is not the individual but the family, the husband-wife or parent-child group. Adults are responsible not only for themselves but for their dependent children. The wife is supposed to look to her husband for those things not provided by her own efforts. As the self-supporting unit is not the individual but the family, so self-interest is not, as is commonly said, the motivation for economic endeavor but family interest. It is not so much love for self as love for one's own children that is the obstacle to the application of the Golden Rule, a love moreover which society approves and relies upon to insure child nurture and sustenance.

INDIVIDUAL AND SOCIAL NEEDS MET BY THE FAMILY

What are the human needs and social values that account for the persistence and universality of the family? Is the American family system in accord or in conflict with the culture pattern in other respects? Is the dwindling in size to near the basic minimum as a group living together and as a unit of mutual responsibility to be encouraged or discouraged? Does this dwindling foreshadow its disappearance, and what would this disappearance mean in terms of human personality and welfare and in terms of new social arrangements that would be necessary?

A variety of evidence could be assembled to indicate how strongly life in small family groups is intrenched in our standard of living. The assumption is that all individuals, young and old, will live in that way except for special circumstance. Attempts to make other ways of living with a lesser degree of exclusiveness possible and attractive have not been successful. Recognition of its costs, and it has its costs, does not deter us from choosing it. Even when families are forced to live at public expense, this way of living is usually allowed for; even the so-called subsistence budget is drawn up on the basis of life in small family groups.

Is this pattern of living so widespread and persistent because of its economic values in the sense that the family members are thereby better fed, better clothed, and better housed than would otherwise be the case? The economies and diseconomies of life in small family groups will be intensively analyzed later. It is evident that production for small family units is inefficient and wasteful in many respects as compared with production differently organized. The overhead costs of housing, feeding, and otherwise providing for such small groups are relatively high, especially if at least one able-bodied person is withdrawn from the paid labor force to devote full time to the tasks involved. Only a weak case could be made for family living if it were based only on the greater abundance of material goods thereby provided.

The bases of the preference for the family as a way of living could not be adequately arrived at without intensive analysis of human needs and interests. The preference seems to represent both a desire for withdrawal from others, a desire for privacy and exclusiveness, and a desire for close association with a selected group closely bound by affectional and other ties. The place of the individual in this group and the relation of others to him are unlike those in any other. The effect upon personality development is profound. As in all forms of human association, conflicts and tensions are inevitable. In fact, in the modern family they are so great and numerous as to seem to constitute a major source of human misery. Why this is so and what can be done to prevent or alleviate it have become the subject of systematic study and brought into existence diagnosticians and counselors of all levels of competence. Few, however, recommend the abandonment of family living per se, and few would follow the recommendation if made.

The widespread practice of family living is undoubtedly related to the fact that parents are responsible for the care and nurture of their children. Not only do most parents desire close association with their children, but it is generally considered that they best discharge their responsibility by keeping the children with them as members of a small family group. Those who have studied the emotional and physical development of children are of the opinion that both are enhanced by family living. The accepted standard for the care of children dependent upon the community is no longer the orphanage but the foster-home if life with one or both parents is impossible or impracticable. The values of family living to the child are presumably of the same order as its values for the adult. For the young child certain of these values may be intensified, while others become paramount as he grows older and contacts with the outside world multiply and become more complicated.

Not only do the desires of most parents and the needs of most children as now understood indicate that they live together but, since the parents have responsibility for support, the establishment of a family home is an economy measure. As an economy measure also the parents usually assume responsibility for the care of young children, many of the necessary services for those older, and general management and supervision of activities and regimen of all for whom they are responsible. Thus the family is the child-rearing as well as the child-supporting agency. With enhanced knowledge of the physical and emotional needs of children for optimum development, concern arises lest this arrangement make for a great lag between science and practice. Programs for parent education are promoted in the endeavor to make widespread the knowledge of the experts.

ECONOMIC SIGNIFICANCE OF THE FAMILY

The economic significance of the family in our scheme of things arises to large degree from the fact that it is a unit of economic rights and responsibilities. The importance of the family may have lessened as a productive agent, but it is still a part of the system by which claims to social product are established and the maintenance of a large fraction of the community assured. Individuals derive the claims by which they are assured of maintenance in three ways: through contract, through civil status, and through family status. The characteristic method in a market economy is through contract. Rights to receive wages, interest, dividends, and other payments are derived from the promise, express or implied, of a legally responsible individual or firm, the promise made binding by the giving of a consideration. Contractual claims are enforced by the state as well as by the self-interest and integrity of the contracting parties. In a free-enterprise society the primary claims upon national income are mainly of this character. It is essentially a *quid pro quo* arrangement, emphasizing self-reliance, self-support, individual responsibility. Quite different is the claim to money income, goods, or services based upon civil status. An increasing proportion of the population have such claims: those receiving old age assistance, social security benefits, veterans' benefits, and the like. The eligibility of such persons to receive income has been established by statute. Their claims are not upon a particular person or group of persons but upon the state. A third set of claims to maintenance also arises from status, not civil but family status. In this category are those rights that come from blood or legal relationship to a particular person. Behind this system of rights and obligations, as behind those based on contract, lies the authority of the group, the force of law and custom.

The institutional changes in the Western world previously reviewed are often described as a change from a regime of status to one of contract. The obligations and claims that come from contract grew and were extended to a wider and wider group. As contractual rights move with and measure freedom and opportunity, rights due to family and civil status represent security. If the two great demands of our age are for more opportunity and more security, the great problem of our age may be described as how to limit and define the area of contractual rights and of those derived from family relationship and from citizenship. The recurrent question is: What shall the state assure to its members—to the young, to the old, to the sick, to everyone? How far can rights based on civil status be extended without the assumption of controls that decrease various forms of economic and personal freedom? The security represented by the clan or great family system carried with it a high degree of control of the individual by the group.

Another related but unresolved question is: How far should the claims and obligations of family relationship extend? What group should the family comprehend as a system of rights and duties? What does a man "owe" his parents? His brother or his brother's children? What, correspondingly, do they "owe" him? Can the standard for responsibility differ greatly from the standard as to what persons should live under the same roof? Should services given and support provided for others be entirely a matter of affection and free choice? The kinship bond still carries a sense of obligations to and of claims upon others outside the immediate family circle, the degree varying from family to family and from community to community. Should we try to stay its weakening? Or should the ethical emphasis be upon developing solicitude for all children, related or nonrelated, all aged, and all needy?

Those aspects of the family system that have special economic significance might be summarized as follows. The family is a way of living well-nigh universally insisted upon, the most basic and resistant element in our standard of living. Life in such groups is a premise with which we must start in any consideration of the economic position of women and of the cost of living. As a system of rights and obligations the family represents a status system surviving and functioning in what is otherwise largely a regime of contract. A major issue of social policy is at what point and in what degree rights based on civil status shall be substituted for those once based upon family status. A further issue to be later explored is what rights and obligations should attach to marital status. What should be the property rights of each spouse during the marriage and when it is broken? The family system as it now stands makes for a high concentration of the burden of support of children.[19] The social investment in human resources correspondingly is made by a limited group, and the investment itself is correspondingly limited. The family system also makes for inequality in opportunity and wealth in a society attempting to promote equality therein. The family attempts to give its children advantages; society to give all an equivalent chance to get what is desired out of life. The family attempts to accumulate an inheritance for its children, thus further reducing the chance that all will have an even start and that, later, incomes will be equal.

In the following chapters many of the issues that have been raised here will be discussed at greater length. The generalizations made concerning the nature and functions of the modern family will be basic to that discussion.

19. See chap. v.

CHAPTER II

AMERICAN FAMILIES TODAY

W HATEVER the modern family may be in an economic or social sense, as a physical entity it is a group of related persons living under one roof. Other kin residing elsewhere are not counted when an enumeration of families is made or their composition studied. When the group of related persons live together as a separate housekeeping unit, they constitute a private household. Unrelated persons also may live together in private households, but such groups are not families, nor are unrelated persons living in private households as lodgers or helpers, strictly speaking, family members. If a family is narrowly defined as a husband and wife, parents, or a parent with a child or children, two or more may be found in the same dwelling; and, if a count is made and composition noted, the number of families reported will be greater and average size smaller than if "family" is more broadly defined as the whole group of related persons who live together.[1]

Basic to all discussion of the family are the facts about this form of association. To what extent is the sharing of a domicile with other related persons a part of the American pattern for living? What exactly is the family status of the various ages and marital classes that compose the population? Are the related persons living together usually a married couple and their unmarried children, or with what frequency do other relatives and even outsiders live with them? How many families have children, and what is the number most frequently found?

SOURCES OF INFORMATION

Answers to these and similar questions concerning American families can now be found in various reports of the Bureau of the Census. Prior to 1930 this was not the case. Although in the enumeration of the population that has taken place every ten years since 1790 the data were collected by household groups within which "families" of any desired definition might be located, only twice prior to 1930—in 1890 and in 1900—was the com-

---

1. The husband-wife or parent-children group is sometimes called the "biolegal" family; others term it the "nuclear," the "small," or the "immediate" family. The whole group of related persons living together is usually called the "social" family.

position of these households examined and then only with respect to their size.[2] Until fairly recently fewer basic facts were known in regard to the family than any other social institution. Thinking in regard to the family accordingly was based upon limited observation, and supposition was substituted for knowledge of the facts.

As a part of the analysis of the population data collected in 1930, the Bureau of the Census published for the first time a special volume on families.[3] Detailed information concerning American families and the family status of the population first became available, however, through the publication of special analyses of the 1940 census data. Since 1945 the Bureau of the Census has been issuing at frequent intervals special reports giving the results of sample studies.[4] In these reports the composition and characteristics of households and families are intensively analyzed and details given concerning the family status of the population, classified by age, marital status, and in other ways. Similar and additional data are becoming available from the census of 1950.

TREND IN MARRIAGE RATE AND AGE

From statements that are sometimes made it would seem that the facts about marriage, although readily available, are not widely known or properly interpreted. It is sometimes assumed that, since the social and economic penalties for nonmarriage have been lightened or have disappeared, the proportion of persons who never marry must have greatly increased. It is true that marriage is not so necessary for economic reasons or for social status for either men or women as was the case in earlier times or in other cultures, but this does not seem to have affected to any marked extent their willingness to marry. The percentage of women fifteen years of age or over who were married or had previously been married when the

2. In 1909 a special analysis of the returns of the First Census (1790) was published which gave a distribution of families by size (U.S. Bureau of the Census, *A Century of Population Growth, 1790–1900* [Washington: Government Printing Office, 1909]).

3. *Fifteenth Census of the United States, 1930, Population*, Vol. VI. In 1928 the author secured a grant from the American Home Economics Association and the Social Science Research Committee of the University of Chicago to demonstrate the kind of information concerning the family available from the census schedules if the data collected were tabulated and analyzed with the "family" as the statistical unit. The study was made by Day Monroe and the results published in *Chicago Families* (Chicago: University of Chicago Press, 1932). A special analysis of the 1920 census data for Rochester, New York, although primarily a study of the family status of married women, gave the most extensive information available up to that time concerning the families of any community (see B. M. Nienburg, *The Woman Home-maker in the City* [Washington: Government Printing Office, 1923]).

4. U.S. Bureau of the Census, *Current Population Reports*, Series P-20. (Processed.)

census was taken in 1890 and at each successive census date until fifty years later in 1940 was as follows:

Year	Percentage Married or Previously Married
1940	74
1930	74
1920	73
1910	70
1900	69
1890	68

Not only are relatively fewer women remaining unmarried, but even before the war years they were marrying at an earlier age. The percentage of women in various age groups who were married or had previously been married in 1890 and in 1940 was as follows:

AGE GROUP	PERCENTAGE MARRIED OR PREVIOUSLY MARRIED	
	1890	1940
15 and over	68	74
15–19	10	12
20–24	48	53
25–29	75	77
30–34	85	85
35–44	90	90
45–54	93	91
55–64	94	91
65 and over	94	91

The median age of marriage for both men and women lowered during those fifty years. The median age of men at their first marriage was 26.1 years in 1890 and 22.0 for women. A half-century later in 1940 it was 24.3 years for men and 21.6 for women.[5]

Should the degree of nonmarriage and the proportion of late marriages shown by this record surprise or disturb us? The means by which other cultures have insured marriage for all attaining the proper age should be considered before passing judgment. In our society more of the physically handicapped survive; some of these probably should not marry. The fact that nine out of ten do ultimately marry without the strong sanctions and pressures that other cultures have imposed to insure marriage would seem to indicate a satisfactory predisposition toward the marital state.

It is well known that more marriages are now broken by divorce than formerly. The divorce rate in 1890 per 1,000 marriages during that year was 62. In 1940 it was 165, and in 1950, 231.[6] Since divorce usually occurs

5. See Paul C. Glick, "The Family Cycle," *American Sociological Review*, XII (April, 1947), 165.

6. U.S. Bureau of the Census, *Statistical Abstract of the United States, 1952* (Washington: Government Printing Office, 1952), p. 80.

relatively early in the marriage, divorced persons are likely to remarry. By comparison of the number giving their marital status as "divorced" on the day the census was taken in 1940 with the number granted a divorce during the preceding twelve years, it has been estimated that about half of all divorced persons remarry.[7] Thus divorce increases the number of married persons who have been married more than once. The average duration of marriages is lengthened, however, and the proportion of second or third marriages is decreased by the fact that widowhood now ordinarily comes late in the life-span, and remarriage of the survivor is therefore less frequent. A sample study by the Bureau of the Census in 1948 showed that about four-fifths of those fifty-five years of age and over, married and living with their spouses, had been married only once.[8] If the younger age groups had been included, the proportion, of course, would have been higher.

FAMILY STATUS OF THE POPULATION

Few patterns of human behavior are so well marked or followed so well-nigh universally as life in private households with persons related by blood, marriage, or adoption. Well over nine-tenths of the population are so living. Very few family groups are boarding or lodging. Practically all live independently of others in their own homes. The movement of large numbers of men into military establishments alters for most of them this pattern of living, but the civilian population continues to live as before. The over-all picture at the end of the 1940's, according to the sample surveys of the Bureau of the Census, was as follows:[9]

Family and Domicile Status	Percentage of Civilian Noninstitutional Population
Total.......................................	100
Not living with a related person...................	6
Living in own home....................	3
Living in hotel, lodging or boarding house..	1
Living as lodgers in private household....	2
Living with a related person......................	94
As lodger in hotel, lodging or boarding house or in private household.........	1
In private household..................	93

7. W. J. Goode, "Problems in Postdivorce Adjustment," *American Sociological Review*, XIV (December, 1949), 397.

8. *Current Population Reports*, Series P-20, No. 23 (Washington, March, 1949).

9. The data for this distribution, as other statistical data in this chapter unless otherwise indicated, are derived from the U.S. Bureau of the Census, *Current Population Reports*, espe-

About half of those persons who were not living with related persons were living, it will be noted, in their own homes. They were in the main the older members of the population. The Census studies show that about 80 per cent of those so living are forty-five years of age or older, and almost 40 per cent, sixty-five or more. About half are widowed persons, almost two-fifths widowed women. Increase in the frequency of this way of living means a decrease in the proportion of persons living as lodgers, of unmarried persons living with their parents, and of widowed parents living with their children.

More than nine-tenths of the population, as has been noted, live in private households with others related by marriage, birth, or adoption. Their distribution by family and marital status was approximately as follows at the end of the 1940's:

Family and Marital Status	Percentage of Related Persons Living in Private Households
All...	100
Husbands and wives, co-heads of households.........................	45
Widowed, divorced, separated and single heads; over half widowed........	4
Sons and daughters of heads, not married or, if married, spouse absent..	40
Single, about four-fifths under 18............................ 39	
Widowed, divorced, and separated, about half with children under 18.. 1	
Married sons and daughters and their spouses........................	3
Other persons related to household head............................	8
Married, widowed, divorced, and separated; about one-fourth, parents of head...	3
Children under 18; over two-thirds grandchildren of the head and about same proportion with a parent or parents also in household...	3
Single, 18 and over..	2

Special interest attaches to the family status of children. Very few of the 30 per cent of the population under eighteen years of age live other

cially Series P-20. Percentage distributions are given rather than counts, since relative magnitudes are what it is desired to show, and they do not vary from year to year or sample to sample as do the counts. If the absolute magnitude is important, it will be mentioned in the text. Quantities are rounded, not only because the picture is more clearly shown by this procedure, but to avoid an impression of exactness which would be quite unwarranted. It must be remembered that estimates based on samples are subject to sampling error, the error being greater for some items of information than others. Discussion of the sampling variability of the various estimates is found in the publications from which the data are derived. Since the percentages are rounded, the total is not always 100.

than with their parents or other than in a private household. Their family status toward the end of the 1940's was as follows:

Family and Domicile Status		Percentage of Children under Eighteen
All		100
Not in private households*		1
In private households		99
Both parents present†		87
Parents, heads of household	83	
Parents, not heads of household	4	
One parent present		9
Parent, head of household	6	
Parent, not head	3	
Neither parent present		4
Children related to household head	4	
Children not related to head	‡	‡

* About a sixth of this group were with a parent or parents. Children in school living away from home are considered to be temporarily absent and are included with other family members.
† A "parent" might be step or adoptive.
‡ Less than one-half of 1 per cent.

Only 1 per cent of all children were in institutions or living with persons not related to them. As many as 96 per cent were living with one or both parents, and nine-tenths in a home of which a parent was head. Eighty-five per cent of those living with but one parent were living with their mother.

The family status of the population eighteen and over varies with marital status and with age. Since most of those single are young men and women, it is not surprising that three-fourths of them live in the homes of relatives, usually their parents. Many are still in school, and others, although employed, still live at home. About an eighth, however, were living as lodgers toward the end of the 1940's, and about the same proportion were living alone or with an unrelated person in their own housekeeping units or were themselves heads of families.

Two-thirds of the population eighteen and over are married persons domiciled with their spouses. Even in the early postwar period with its housing shortage, over 90 per cent of the married couples were maintaining their own homes. Seven per cent were living with relatives, and the remainder with unrelated persons. Three-fourths of those living with relatives were young persons living with a parent or parents of either the husband or wife, usually the latter. By the end of the 1940's the proportion maintaining their own homes had risen. Only 5 per cent were reported as living with relatives and 1 per cent as living in the households of unrelated persons or in hotels.

The widowed portion of the population are mainly older people, nine-tenths forty-five years of age and over, and approximately half sixty-five and over. Three-fourths of the group are women. Most of the widowed, not far from three-fifths, are either family heads or live alone in their own homes. The next largest group, about a third, live with relatives, the older persons usually with their children. The remainder, about a twelfth, live in the homes of unrelated persons, or in nursing homes, hotels, or institutions.

In age and family status those who are divorced or not living with their spouses fall between the single adults and the widowed. About two-fifths of the women in the group are under thirty-five. A somewhat smaller proportion of men are as young, but half are under forty-five. About two-fifths of the divorced or separated maintain their own homes, a sixth living alone, and a fourth as family heads. Over four-fifths of the family heads are women, and nine-tenths of them have children. The same proportion of the divorced and separated live with relatives as maintain their own homes. The majority of those living with relatives were probably living with their parents. Over two-fifths of the women so living had children under eighteen. Almost half of the divorced and separated women had children of this age as compared with less than a tenth of the widowed. Very few of either the widowed, divorced, or separated men—well under a tenth—had sons and daughters under eighteen living with them. A larger proportion of the divorced and separated—almost one-fifth—were living as lodgers in private households or in hotels than of any other marital group. Over two-thirds of those so living were men.

Special attention might well be given at this point to the widowed, divorced, and separated persons who are the parents of children under eighteen and have such children living with them. As previously noted, about a tenth of all children under eighteen years of age are living with but one parent. The parent in not far from nine-tenths of the cases was the mother. Most of these mothers are women whose husbands are living but absent from the family home. Such separation does not always mean desertion or estrangement. Included here are the wives of men in military service and of those who are employed at a distance from home. Almost as many of these mothers are widowed as are separated from their husbands. About a fourth are divorced. A third of all the one-parent families are living in the homes of related persons, but over three-fifths live in their own homes.

The family status of that part of the population sixty-five years of age and over is often the subject of concern. This part of the population is increasing, thus increasing that part which is nonproductive and supported either by others or by equities built up by the persons concerned in their earning years. About half of this age group were married and domiciled with their spouse in 1949. Over 95 per cent of those married were maintaining their own homes. Only a few aged couples were living in the homes of their children. About half of those widowed, divorced, separated, or still single were also maintaining their own homes, either as heads of families or living alone. Over two-thirds of this group were women. The older people who live with relatives are mainly the widowed, divorced, or separated. Close to two-fifths were in the homes of relatives at the end of the 1940's. The "in-law" problem is much discussed, but it would seem that only about an eighth, at most a seventh, of all families contained a mother- or father-in-law.

TYPES OF FAMILIES

From what has been said it is evident that families may be classified in two groups: those with a married couple and those with a widowed, divorced, separated, or single person as the head. The relative importance of the two types of families at the end of the 1940's was as follows:

Family Head	Percentage of All Families
All	100
Married couple	87
Widowed, divorced, separated, or single person	13
Female	10
Male	3

It will be noted that when the family head is not a married couple it is usually a woman. Almost two-thirds of the female heads were widows. Widowed men also predominate among the male heads, but almost as high a proportion of these heads were single. About 5 per cent of all married couples are not counted here as "families." They were living as "subfamilies," that is, as members of a family to whose head they were related. Less than a twentieth of the families with a married couple at the head included another husband and wife, but a seventh of those with a widowed, divorced, separated, or single person as head included such a subfamily. Almost half of the latter group of family heads were fifty-five years of age or over and thus might well have a married son or daughter living with them.

Another type of subfamily is also found. As defined by the Bureau of the Census, it is a parent with a child or children under eighteen. A sub-family of this type or a husband-wife subfamily is found in one-fifth of the family groups headed by a widowed, divorced, separated, or single person. Since about half of the married couples living as subfamilies have children, and by definition all other subfamilies have one or more, there may be children in the primary family who are not the sons or daughters of the head. This is especially common in those headed by a widowed, divorced, separated, or single person.

The composition of those families headed by a married couple at the end of the 1940's was as follows:

Family Members	Percentage of Husband-Wife Families
All	100
Husband and wife only	29
Husband, wife, and children under 18 only	43
Husband, wife, and related persons 18 and over only	12
Husband, wife, and children under 18, and related persons 18 and over	16

It will be noted that in a high proportion of the families headed by a married couple the "social family," that is, the group living together, was the nuclear family. This was true in at least that 72 per cent of the cases where the family included only the married couple or the married couple and their children under eighteen.

The composition of the families headed by a married couple varies, as would be expected, with the ages of the husband and wife. The children under eighteen are concentrated in the homes of men under forty-five. Three-fourths of the heads of that age had sons and daughters under eighteen living with them. The few subfamilies are the parents or siblings of the heads. When the husband is forty-five or over, the family more frequently consists of husband and wife alone. Only about a third of the men of that age had sons or daughters under eighteen living with them. A large proportion of the subfamilies are in these older families. Here are found also unmarried sons and daughters eighteen and over. Most of the related persons eighteen and over were undoubtedly sons and daughters of the heads, but what proportion is unknown. Practically all of the children under eighteen in husband-wife families were those of the heads. One or both of the parents of those who were not were usually also family members.

In striking contrast with the composition of families headed by a married couple is that of those with a widowed, divorced, separated, or single person as head. Toward the end of the 1940's the composition of families of this type was as follows:

Family Members	Percentage of Other Families
All	100
Head and children under 18 only	19
Head and related persons 18 and over only	57
Head, children under 18, and related persons 18 and over	24

The membership of these families was predominantly adult. Not far from three-fifths had no member under eighteen. Although over two-fifths of these families had children among their members, in almost a third of the cases they were not the children of the head.[10] In these families grandchildren are relatively numerous, as are subfamilies and unmarried sons and daughters eighteen and over. These families are smaller than those headed by a married couple. Forty-five per cent were reported as having only two members in 1949, but only 29 per cent of the husband-wife families.

SIZE OF HOUSEHOLDS AND OF FAMILIES

Average size of households and of families and their distribution by number of members will vary with the definition of these units as well as with changes in birth rates and ways of living. The reported size of households will be largest if institutions, hotels, and boarding houses are included as well as private households. Family size will be largest if all related persons living together are counted, and smallest if the term "family" includes only husband and wife, parents or parent and their own children. The average number of persons related and unrelated in all types of households in 1940 was 3.76 and in private households 3.67.

Everyone knows that the size of both households and families has been growing smaller in the United States. In 1850 the average number of persons per household of all types, counting all members, was 5.6 as compared with 3.76 in 1940. Averages, however, tell nothing concerning the frequency of households of different sizes. The following comparison, fortunately possible, shows how much more frequent those with only one, two, or three persons have become during the course of our national history and how much less frequent those with six, seven, eight, or more.[11]

10. About 30 per cent of the heads had own children under eighteen living with them.

11. Only private households are included in the 1940 and 1949 distributions. In 1790 all the "free" members of private households were counted. The 1890 distribution includes all types of households, but, if all quasi-households were assumed to have at least seven members and subtracted, the proportion of households with seven or more members would change only from 20.2 to 19.2 per cent.

In the hundred years from 1790 to 1890 the percentage of households with fewer than five members rose from 37 to 50 and in the next fifty years to 73.

NUMBER OF MEMBERS	PERCENTAGE DISTRIBUTION OF HOUSEHOLDS			
	1790	1890	1940	1949
All............	100.0	100.0	100.0	100.0
One..............	3.7	3.6	7.7	8.0
Two..............	7.8	13.2	24.8	27.2
Three............	11.7	16.7	22.4	24.1
Four.............	13.8	16.8	18.1	19.2
Five.............	13.9	15.1	11.5	10.4
Six..............	13.2	11.5	6.8	5.5
Seven............	11.2	8.5	3.8	2.7
Eight............	9.0	5.9	2.2	1.3
Nine.............	6.5⎫	3.8⎫		
Ten..............	4.2⎬	2.8⎬	2.7	1.5
Eleven and over....	4.9⎭	2.1⎭		

The increase in the proportion of one-, two-, and three-person households is a reflection of changes other than the decline in the birth rate. It is also a result of circumstances previously discussed. More of the older people, the widowed, divorced, and even young single adults live independently and not with their kinfolk. If the same number of people distribute themselves among more households, the average size of the household decreases. That this has been happening is shown by the fact that from 1930 to 1940 the population increased 7 per cent, but the number of households increased 17 per cent. The same process continued during the 1940's. The Bureau of the Census notes, "Although there was an increase in the civilian population of 12 percent during the nine years (1940–1949), the number of households increased by 21 percent."[12] Sons and daughters marry at an earlier age, and many work and live away from home after they leave school. Raising of the school-leaving age operates, of course, to increase the size of families and of households.

Basic, however, in reducing family and household size is the fall in the birth rate. A special study by the Bureau of the Census, *Differential Fertility, 1940 and 1910*, gives quantitative evidence of the change during that period:[13]

WOMEN, FIFTEEN TO SEVENTY-FOUR	NUMBER OF CHILDREN BORN PER 1,000 WOMEN	
	1910	1940
All women...............................	2,465	1,796
All women ever married..................	3,626	2,532
All mothers.............................	4,196	3,177
Percentage of women ever married to whom children had been born.................	86.4	79.7

12. *Current Population Reports*, Series P-20, No. 26, p. 3.

13. *Sixteenth Census of the United States, 1940, Population, Differential Fertility, 1940 and 1910* (Washington: Government Printing Office, 1943).

The birth rate was relatively low in the 1930's, as always in a depression period, and shot upward in the 1940's. Whether a new level has been established that will persist for some time can only be conjectured, or how the number of births reported by women, fifteen to seventy-four, in 1970 will compare with the number reported in 1940.

The change in the size of the family as distinguished from the household cannot be traced over as long a period as the latter. The average size of the family will be larger than that of the household, since no family can include less than two persons. In 1949 the Bureau of the Census reported 3.42 persons as the average size of household and 3.58 as that of the family. In 1930 the median size of the families living in private households was 3.61; in 1940, 3.38; and in 1947, 3.28.[14] If the median size for all families at these dates were taken, it would be slightly smaller, since families maintaining their own homes are somewhat larger than others.

The distribution of families by the total number of members in 1949 was reported as follows by the Bureau of the Census:

		PERCENTAGE DISTRIBUTION OF FAMILIES	
NUMBER OF MEMBERS	All	With Married Couple as Head	With Other Head
All........	100	100	100
Two..........	31	29	45
Three.........	26	26	24
Four..........	21	22	14
Five..........	11	11	8
Six...........	6	6	5
Seven or more...	6	6	4

FAMILIES WITH CHILDREN UNDER EIGHTEEN

More important than the total number of family members are their ages and the distribution of the burden of the care and support of those in the nonproductive years. The proportion of family heads having sons or daughters of their own living with them was as follows in 1949:

		PERCENTAGE DISTRIBUTION OF FAMILY HEADS	
NUMBER OF SONS OR DAUGHTERS UNDER EIGHTEEN	All	Married Couple	Other Head
All........	100	100	100
None..........	48	44	70
One..........	22	23	15
Two..........	16	18	8
Three or more...	14	15	8

14. The median size in 1940 here given is smaller than the average (mean) previously noted, 3.8.

About half of the married couples living as subfamilies had children under eighteen; 6 per cent had three or more.

Although relatively few of the families at recent census dates, even those of married couples, included as many as three sons and daughters under eighteen, the distribution of the children themselves presents a different picture. About half of the children are in families having three or more children under eighteen to support. The distribution of the children living with both or one parent by the number of children those parents were caring for was as follows in 1948:

NUMBER OF CHILDREN UNDER EIGHTEEN	All	PERCENTAGE DISTRIBUTION OF CHILDREN LIVING WITH BOTH OR ONE PARENTS	
		With Both Parents	With One Parent
All.........	100	100	100
One...........	21	20	29
Two...........	30	30	32
Three or more...	49	50	39

The parents who were caring for one or more children under eighteen represented a little over two-fifths of the total population eighteen to sixty-four years of age, and slightly more than one-half of those of that age who had ever been married. Actually, the parents were not evenly scattered among the latter group, seven out of ten of them being under forty-five years of age.

MAXIMUM SIZE USUALLY ATTAINED

The picture of the family as an agency for the care and maintenance of children is somewhat distorted if only cross-section views of the composition at a particular time are examined. The most significant fact about family size is that it waxes and wanes in the course of the family life-span. Starting with two adults, as children are born, the family moves from one size category to another. Infants become school-age children, then adolescents, then young adults who leave school, become self-supporting, marry, and leave home. Unless the family has been broken by death or divorce before the child-rearing cycle was complete, the family composition is again two adults, probably twenty or more years older than at the beginning of the family life-span. The most significant questions about family size are: What is the number of members when most families are at their maximum? How long do families have one or more children under school age? One or more dependent upon them for support? Such questions are of special importance when the adequacy of earnings for family support and the gainful employment of women are under discussion.

The cycle of growth and decline in family size is suggested by the change in number of sons and daughters under eighteen in the homes of married couples when classified by the age of the husband. In 1947 the Census estimate was as follows:

PERCENTAGE DISTRIBUTION OF MARRIED
COUPLES WITH SPECIFIED NUMBER OF
OWN CHILDREN UNDER EIGHTEEN*

AGE OF HUSBAND	All Couples	None	One	Two	Three or More
Under 25.......	100	42	41	14	3
25–34..........	100	24	31	25	20
35–44..........	100	23	24	27	27
45–54..........	100	49	23	14	14
55–64..........	100	79	13	4	4
65 and over.....	100	94	3	2	1
All ages.......	100	46	22	17	15

* Only married couples who were heads of households are included.

In most of the younger families shown in this distribution more children will be born. In the older some or all of the children have left home. No one of these groups of families represents those completed and thus shows the maximum size usually attained. The nearest approximation to it are those where the husband is thirty-five to forty-four years of age, but about two-fifths of these men had wives under thirty-five and some will have more children. It should be noted, however, that if this were the maximum size usually attained, about three-fifths of the children would be reared in families having three or more to support, although at any one time only about a seventh of all married couples have that many children.

The Census report, *Differential Fertility, 1940 and 1910*, throws some light on the usual size of the completed family and its change over time. The reported number of children ever born to all women ever married, and to all mothers forty-five to forty-nine whose families may be considered completed, was as follows in 1910 and 1940:

NUMBER OF CHILDREN
PER 1,000 WOMEN
FORTY-FIVE TO
FORTY-NINE

CLASS	1910	1940
All ever married........	4,744	3,052
All mothers............	5,241	3,606

The proportion of women ever married, forty-five to forty-nine years of age, who reported no children, only one, two, three or more was as follows at the two dates:

PERCENTAGE DISTRIBU-
TION OF WOMEN EVER
MARRIED FOFTY-FIVE
TO FORTY-NINE

NUMBER OF CHILDREN EVER BORN	1910	1940
All...............	100	100
None................	10	15
One.................	10	17
Two.................	12	19
Three or more........	68	49

More of the children born to women reporting in 1940 survived than of those born to those reporting in 1910, thus minimizing the difference in the size of the family at its maximum, but the data indicate a marked change. During the depression period in the thirties the birth rate fell below the level of the 1920's, but in the next decade there was an upsurge that threw askew all the predictions earlier made as to rates of population growth. The percentages of preschool and of school-age children in the population increased greatly. Not only was the birth rate in 1941–45 above the low level of 1930–34 but the postwar rate was well above the 1941–45 average.[15] Various theories have been propounded as to the causes of this unexpected change. Whether the birth rate will stabilize at the new level, decline, or continue to rise is unknown. To the degree it continues, the proportion of children who are reared in families of three, four, or more will also increase.

DIFFERENCES BETWEEN URBAN AND FARM HOUSEHOLDS AND FAMILIES

The frequency of the various types of households and families and their composition vary with the degree of urbanization of the communities in which they are found. The household headed by a married couple is more frequent in farm than in nonfarm communities, and the person living alone or with no related person is less frequent. The extent of the differences in these respects in 1949 was as follows:[16]

| | PERCENTAGE DISTRIBUTION OF HOUSEHOLDS | | |
TYPE OF HOUSEHOLD	Urban	Rural Nonfarm	Rural Farm
All households.............	100	100	100
Households of one or of two or more unrelated persons.......	11	8	5
Households of two or more related persons................	89	92	95
Married couple as head.......	76	82	86
Other heads.................	13	10	9

Farm families represent an occupational group as well as a group living in the open country. Their special characteristics are affected by the way they make their living as well as by their place of residence.

15. J. S. Davis, *The Population Upsurge in the United States* (Stanford, Calif.: Stanford University Press, 1949), p. 12. See *ibid.*, pp. 56–59, for discussion of possible causes for the increase.

16. Urban population, as here defined by the Bureau of the Census, is in general that residing in cities and other incorporated places having 2,500 inhabitants or more. The rural nonfarm population includes those living in the open country and in small villages as well as the suburban population of large cities.

The most significant fact in regard to farm families from the standpoint of long-run social welfare is the proportion of the nation's children for which they have responsibility. The fact that farm families have been supporting a disproportionate share of the nation's children has been noted again and again in various connections. In 1949 only 17 per cent of the civilian noninstitutional population eighteen years of age and over lived on farms, but 25 per cent of those under eighteen. The respective proportions of farm and nonfarm married couples with no children under eighteen and with one, two, three, or more were then as follows:

NUMBER OF OWN CHILDREN	PERCENTAGE DISTRIBUTION OF HUSBAND-WIFE FAMILIES	
	Farm	Nonfarm
All	100	100
None	40	45
One	19	24
Two	16	18
Three	10	8
Four or more	14	5

The concentration of farm children in families rearing three or more is evident. About two-thirds are in such families at a given time, but probably close to three-fourths are reared in families with this heavy responsibility.[17]

The difference between farm and nonfarm families in the number of children is not due to the fact that the farm married couples are the more youthful. In fact, a larger proportion of the husbands in nonfarm families are under forty-five than in farm families. There has been a marked difference in the birth rate as between farm and nonfarm families. The Census study in 1940 showed the following difference in the fertility of women forty-five to forty-nine classified by the degree of urbanization of their residence:

AREA	NUMBER OF CHILDREN BORN PER 1,000 WOMEN FORTY-FIVE TO FORTY-NINE	
	Ever Married	Mothers
Urban	2,604	3,169
Rural nonfarm	3,286	3,806
Farm	4,234	4,666

Less than a tenth of the farm women of this age ever married, as compared with about a sixth of the urban, reported that no child had ever been born to them. Two-thirds of the farm women had borne three or more children,

17. Around 45 per cent of the urban children are in families with three or more children under eighteen.

but only slightly over two-fifths of the urban. During the 1940's the difference between the urban and the farm birth rates tended to diminish The urban rate accelerated more than the farm and approached it more closely. The farm family's responsibility for the rearing and support of children therefore does not exceed that of the urban family as much as it did in the past.

DIFFERENCES BETWEEN WHITE AND NONWHITE
HOUSEHOLDS AND FAMILIES

The 9 per cent of American households with nonwhite members, mainly Negroes, differed from those of the white population in certain respects. The differences are those that would doubtless be found if a group of the white population were placed under similar economic and social disabilities. In 1940 a larger proportion of the nonwhite households included lodgers. The percentages for the two groups were as follows:[18]

| | PERCENTAGE OF HOUSE- HOLD MEMBERS WHO WERE LODGERS | |
AREA	White	Nonwhite
Urban	3.9	12.1
Rural nonfarm	2.4	4.7
Rural farm	1.5	2.1

A larger proportion of nonwhite families also live as lodgers in private households or in hotels or boarding houses. In 1947 over a fourth of all families with this domicile status were nonwhite. A larger proportion of the nonwhite families includes subfamilies. An eighth of all married couples living with relatives in 1947 were nonwhite and almost a fourth of the parent-child subfamilies. The proportion of nonwhite women whose husbands are living but absent from the home is disproportionately large. Less than a twentieth of all white married women were living separately from their husbands in 1947, but a seventh of all nonwhite. The proportion of all nonwhite families with a married couple at the head is therefore smaller than among the white. In the South, where over three-fifths of the nonwhite families are found, over a fifth of the nonwhite families had a widowed, divorced, separated, or single person at the head, but only an eighth of the white families.

The composition of nonwhite families clearly varies somewhat from that of the white. They contain more subfamilies and other relatives. The number of children born to nonwhite mothers exceeds the number born to

18. Data were not available for a later date.

white. In the southern region in 1940 the reported number born to each group forty-five to forty-nine years of age was as follows:

COLOR	NUMBER OF CHILDREN PER 1,000 WOMEN FORTY-FIVE TO FORTY-NINE	
	Ever Married	Mothers
White	3,567	4,062
Nonwhite	3,795	4,511

In spite of the somewhat higher birth rate, the proportion of nonwhite husband-wife families without sons and daughters under eighteen in the household was larger in 1947 in that region than that of the white. Half of the nonwhite couples maintaining homes had no children of their own of that age among the family members, but only two-fifths of the white couples. A higher death rate among nonwhite children and a lower school- and home-leaving age may account for the difference.

CHAPTER III

COMPONENTS OF FAMILY INCOME AND WEALTH

THE family's chief economic concern is its income, its size and security. The road to improvement in economic position, as most people see it, is increase in rates of pay or profit. Wiser and more economical spending will also improve the level of living, as will alterations in market conditions, particularly in prices, but, for reasons to be explored later, advancement in the income scale is the common measure of advancement in economic welfare.

In succeeding chapters data on the distribution of families by the amount of their incomes will be analyzed and their adequacy to provide a satisfactory level of living for the family appraised. Public policies in effect and proposed to reduce inadquacy and insecurity of income, as well as private practices with the same objectives, will be discussed in detail. Basic to this analysis is understanding of the sources of income today, their economic character and relative importance, and the items that must be taken into account if a true measure of income is to be obtained.

SOURCES OF INFORMATION

The first large-scale studies of income in the United States were those of a private organization, the National Bureau of Economic Research. The subject of their investigation was the aggregate national income. Their first publication in 1921, *Income in the United States, Its Amount and Distribution, 1909 to 1919*, gave estimates of the national total for each year by major sources of production and by major classes of income received. In later publications, beginning in 1937, the earlier estimates were revised, and the components from 1919 on given in greater detail. In 1934 the United States Department of Commerce made available estimates of national income from 1929 to 1932. It now publishes annual estimates, the series starting with 1929.[1]

Studies of the distribution of personal income among recipients came later than the studies of the aggregate, owing not to lack of interest but to lack of the necessary data. In its first publication the National Bureau of Economic Research gave an estimated distribution of income recipients

1. Published as a supplement to the July issue of the *Survey of Current Business*.

36

by the amount they received in 1918, an estimate admittedly based upon inadequate data. The income recipient in this estimate was the individual who by virtue of ownership or contract for services was the legal claimant, not the family that in most cases actually made use of it. The first comprehensive estimate of the distribution of families by income was made by the National Resources Committee for the year 1935–36 on the basis primarily of field studies conducted by the Bureau of Labor Statistics and the Bureau of Home Economics.[2] A later canvass of a sample cross-section of families by the latter two agencies provided estimates for 1941 as well as some information on the components of family income.[3] The Bureau of the Census now publishes annual estimates of the distribution of families by the amount of their money income, based on sample studies, the first for the year 1945.[4] As a part of an annual survey of consumer finances for the Board of Governors of the Federal Reserve System, estimates of such distributions are also available.[5] This series also begins with 1945.

DEFINING INCOME AND INCOME-RECIPIENT

Whether the income concerning which information is sought is the national, the individual, or the family income, difficult questions of definition arise. What precisely is income? The term is freely used in general discourse without serious misunderstanding, but what is included and what excluded from the sum so called may alter the results appreciably. Quite aside from the problems involved in the definition of income each modifier, as "national," "individual," or "family," raises its own questions. Is national income, for example, the commodities and services produced within a given country during a period of time to whomever they may go, or is it the total enjoyed by the residents in that area wherever the goods have been produced? Individual income clearly includes wages, salaries, interest, dividends, benefits, and the like, to which specific individuals have a claim. Such claims would include not only money payments but pay in kind, that is, in food, clothing, or housing. The allocation of the total money income from a farm or other business to the head of the

2. *Consumer Incomes in the United States, Their Distribution in 1935–1936* (Washington: Government Printing Office, 1938). The field study was a Federal Works Project.

3. U.S. Bureau of Labor Statistics, *Family Spending and Saving in Wartime* (Bull. No. 822 [Washington: Government Printing Office, 1945]); U.S. Department of Agriculture, *Rural Family Spending and Saving in Wartime* (Misc. Pub. 520 [Washington: Government Printing Office, 1943]).

4. *Current Population Reports*, Series P-60. (Processed.)

5. These surveys are now made by the Survey Research Center of the University of Michigan and the results published first in the *Federal Reserve Bulletin* and later as "separates" which are available upon request from the Board.

family even if other members assisted in the enterprise seems more questionable, although he may have legal claim to it.[6] If the family is taken
as the income-recipient unit, this problem does not arise. Estimates of
family income may also include the value of home-produced food, the use
of an owned home, and similar items without raising questions concerning
who provides or who has the disposal of it. When consumption studies
parallel income studies, since the family is the consuming unit, it must be
the income unit as well. For some purposes, however, data on individual
incomes, although limited to money receipts and possibly pay in kind, are
more useful than those on family incomes, especially if the individuals are
classified by age, sex, and family status.

If family incomes are sought, "family" must be defined for this purpose,
that is, the persons whose incomes are to be added together to arrive at
the figure desired. The amount of the family income, the size of the family
receiving the income, and the number of one-person income units will
clearly vary with each investigator's method of determining whose income
is to be included in the total and whose separately given. Difficulties arise
when two or more married couples live together in one household or when,
as is more frequent, the household includes earning sons or daughters or
other income-receiving relatives of the married couple or household head.
The Bureau of the Census includes in the family income the income of all
related persons living in the same household. Other agencies attempt to
exclude those who, though related, are living as would unrelated boarders
or lodgers. The family members excluded are sometimes described as those
who do not pool their incomes with those of other family members. Pooling of incomes literally would imply that the total fund was subject to
whatever patriarchal, matriarchal, or other system of allocation prevails
when there is but one income contributor. Pooling of the incomes of the
adult family members other than husband and wife is probably infrequent
except at very low-income levels, where the total scarcely covers minimum
needs.

Even though many families may have members who do not pool their
incomes, there are probably few such members who live as would unrelated boarders or lodgers. They may receive services and privileges beyond
those to which their contributions to the family purse would entitle them,
or make contributions beyond the market value of what they receive.
Only infrequently would the use of the family car and living quarters, the
food provided, or the services rendered by the mother be conditional upon

6. If these family members work at least fifteen hours per week, they will be counted as
part of the labor force but, in an income distribution, will appear as persons without income.

or proportional to the money contribution of the earning son or daughter. The expenditure pattern and the consumption level of a person living as a family member are likely to be quite different from those of one with the same income who is not so living. There are, therefore, strong arguments for defining family income as the income of all related persons living together.

If family incomes are sought, a further problem arises. The income recipients in some families at the date of the study may not be identical with those in that position during the year for which information is sought. An earning son or other relative of the head, now a family member, may have lived elsewhere for all or part of the preceding year. A family member who contributed to the family income during the year may have died or left the family group before the date of the study. Should the family membership be re-created to allow for these changes during the year or should the family income be the sum of the incomes of those who are members at the time the inquiry is made? The Bureau of Labor Statistics and the Bureau of Human Nutrition and Home Economics have followed the former procedure; the Bureau of the Census, the latter.[7]

The problems involved in defining income exceed in number and difficulty those involved in giving a precise meaning to individual, family, or nation as the income unit. The basic criterion to be used in deciding what is to be included or excluded is the purpose for which the income is to be calculated. Income as a base for tax assessment may be defined in one way, income as that to which savings or expenditures are most closely related in another, and income as that which measures the attainable level of living in still another. Expediency and practicability may also determine the definition, since the cost of securing valid estimates of certain constituents may outweigh their importance. Others will not be voluntarily disclosed by their recipients or may be grossly over- or under-estimated. Still other components cannot be reduced to monetary terms for summation. Omissions, however, on the ground of expediency and practicality are omissions. They are constituents of the income that ideally would be included. Their omission distorts the results to some degree and must be taken into account in conclusions based on income data.

So important today is income in money in enabling people to live as

7. If consumption data are being secured, a family nucleus must have been in existence for the full period and the number of full- and part-period consumers during the period counted. From among them the number of income recipients would then be counted for the full period or part of it. Thus the family is re-created as an income-receiving and income-spending unit.

they desire that the term "income" is often used to mean money income alone. Actually income as a measure of economic welfare includes rights to consumption goods and services other than those represented by the money income during the period in question. Total income or power to consume is greater than that given by money income alone. Ownership of such assets as houses, furniture, equipment, and automobiles gives the owner the right to their services without rental payment. From the unpaid productive efforts of family members come commodities and services that expand consumption possibilities. The state or other organized group may provide "free" services and facilities. Differences from time to time and from group to group in the relative importance of such sources of income will obviously lessen the exactness of comparisons of relative economic well-being based upon money income alone.

Money income alone may appear in the estimates of national income or be made the basis of distributions of individuals or families by income size for various reasons. One is the impracticality or impossibility of measuring items of nonmoney income, more particularly of measuring their money value as is necessary if an income total is to be secured. Since the various components of nonmoney income vary greatly in the difficulty of this measurement and reduction to monetary terms, certain items may be included and others omitted. It is possible and practicable to include some in the national account but not in the account of the individual or family, the value of the goods and services furnished free at public expense, for example. Money income only may be taken into account for another reason. It may best serve the purpose of the investigator. If the purpose is to describe the relation between income and savings or expenditure, money income may be that with which these items vary, not the total income, money and nonmoney. Nonmoney income is not disposable as between savings and consumption or as between different forms of consumption, as is money income. Nonmoney income in the form of food or housing must appear on the consumption side of the household account as food and housing. The family with a money income of $5,000 has greater freedom of choice among consumption alternatives than has the one with a money income of $4,000 and nonmoney income of an estimated value of $1,000. Yet it still remains true that, of two families with money incomes of $5,000, the one that owns a home, has some home-produced food, and lives in a community with diversified free services is in a better economic position than the other, if price levels and tax deductions are the same.

THE FAMILY BALANCE SHEET

Income and wealth are essentially accounting concepts, ways of measuring economic position. In its most generalized form personal income during a period may be defined as the amount by which rights to goods and services would have increased between the beginning and end of that period if nothing had been used up, destroyed, or stolen, or, put in another way, as the rights which might have been exercised in consumption without altering the recipient's rights or obligations from what they were at the beginning of the period. During a period consumption may exceed income at the expense of assets on hand at the beginning of the period or through credit purchases or cash borrowing. In either case net worth at the end of the period is less than at the beginning. Assets have decreased, liabilities increased, or both may have happened. Thus we have the formula: consumption = income ± change in net worth. A positive change in net worth in the form of an increase in assets or decrease in indebtedness represents savings; a negative change, dissaving. Most agencies making studies of family income and consumption seek data also on the change in net worth of the families during the period of study. Thus the family's complete financial history during the period is secured. The estimate of change in net worth is a check upon the accuracy of the consumption and income figures, since the difference between the two is the change in net worth. Data on the form in which savings are made and the character of the liabilities incurred are also thereby provided.

Family assets today fall into one or more of three main classes: (1) those that are money-income-earning; (2) such completely liquid assets as cash on hand and checking-account balances; and (3) those yielding only income in use. Money-income-earning assets include those represented by investments in farms and other business enterprises, rental property, corporate securities, notes receivable, and bank deposits upon which interest is paid. The liquidity of money-earning assets varies, that is, the quickness with which they can be turned into cash of known amount. Series E government bonds are payable upon demand, as are usually savings-bank deposits. The cash-surrender value of life-insurance policies and the accumulations of those buying deferred annuities are also payable upon surrender of the policies. Interest accrues annually on the Series E bonds and on the funds in the hands of insurance companies, but it is not paid separately from the principal.

The assets that yield only an income in use are of two kinds: one, relatively unimportant, includes stocks of food, fuel, and supplies that disappear upon use; the other, increasingly important, durable consumption goods, the useful life of which may extend over several years. The most important in this category is the family home or homes if the family owns more than one. To the family home has been added in recent decades an increasing variety of durable goods that represent an investment of increasing amount: automobiles, household furniture, furnishings, and equipment, radios, television sets, and the like as well as clothing and jewelry. Many of these goods were unknown a few years ago, and many are substitutes for low-cost items that served in an inferior fashion the same general purpose or were formerly found in few homes. This class of assets is the least liquid of all assets. There is a fairly well-organized market for residential property and automobiles but not for the other consumer durables. Accurate estimates of their current value are therefore difficult to make.

Assets of the character just described depreciate both in money value and in usefulness from wear and tear and from obsolescence. Thus the net worth of the owner declines unless equivalent additions to holdings in the form of other assets are made. All money-earning assets do not suffer physical depreciation or become obsolete, but all that are transferable fluctuate in market value. Only when, through sale, capital gains or losses are realized is the income available for consumption or savings thereby affected. The market value of the family home (rarely other consumer durables) may also be greater or less than the equity therein after allowance for depreciation. In this case also a capital gain or loss may be realized.

COMPONENTS OF MONEY INCOME

The diversity of the sources from which families may derive their money income is shown by the items commonly listed on the schedules used in income studies. In the study of money incomes and expenditures in 1941 the list included wages, salaries, earnings from independent business or professions, receipts from roomers and boarders, interest and dividends, profits from enterprises owned but not operated, net rent and royalties, unemployment-insurance benefits, federal old age and survivors' insurance benefits, other retirement benefits and industrial pensions, income from annuities, regular contributions from persons not in the family, and direct-relief payments. Wages and salaries included tips and bonuses. Entrepreneurial earnings from farm operation included government cash subsidies. Direct-relief payments included old age assistance, aid to dependent children and to the blind, and all other similar public and private payments to individuals. Other possible sources of money income to be reported if received included such items as benefits received by those insured against accident or illness, allowances to the dependents of military personnel, alimony, prizes, rewards, and net gambling gains.[8]

Most of these types of money income represent contractual claims established through market transactions. The rights represented arose from sale of services, from loan of funds to business enterprises or government, from investment in corporate enterprise, from independent business enterprise, from private contract with insurance companies, and the like. Roughly, contract income falls into two main classes: earnings, or labor income, and income arising by virtue of ownership of assets, loaned or invested, directly or indirectly. Wages and salaries clearly belong in the first category, interest and dividends in the second. Entrepreneurial earnings, however, as those of farmers, retail merchants, and other independent business operators, are a combination of personal earnings and income from ownership, as are those in less degree of physicians and lawyers engaged in private practice. In various respects they are a class of income distinct from wages and salaries and income from investments.

Other types of money income growing in importance, especially in terms of the number of recipients, are what might be called "civil rights" income, since the claims represented were established by statute. Such are the benefits paid under the Social Security Act, state unemployment compensation, old age assistance, aid to dependent children, and other similar forms of money payments.[9] The proper classification of certain forms of income would be difficult and disputed, allowances going to servicemen's dependents, for example. It seems highly desirable, however, to note that the rights represented by certain forms of income unmistakably arise from a contract; others arise from status in a quite different sense. The social implications of the two are quite different. Contract income in the main is derived from the productive activity of persons or use of their property. Civil rights income, as the name implies, is an expression of public policy based upon welfare considerations. To be distinguished both from income based on civil status and that derived from

8. U.S. Bureau of Labor Statistics Bull. No. 822, pp. 13–14.

9. Eligibility, or the right to receive those payments called "benefits," is defined quite precisely by statute. Eligibility of special groups to receive assistance is defined in more general terms. The statute providing for federal supplementation of state payments to special groups of the needy forbids such supplementation unless the state provides for a fair hearing, before the single state agency administering the plan, of those whose claims are not acted upon with "reasonable promptness." The claims of the other needy are far less precise. The public agencies set up to provide general assistance are charged only with the general responsibility to relieve economic distress.

contractual rights is that which is purely a matter of individual discretion, not only the amount but any payment at all. Such income is a gift pure and simple, a transfer directly from one person to another. Civil rights income is transfer income of a different sort. Usually it represents a compulsory transfer from individuals to public agencies and from them in turn to the recipients.

The relative importance of the various forms of contract income tends to change over time, as does that of the income which comes from the state or federal treasury. Urbanization, large-scale business enterprise, and the corporate form of business organization make wages and salaries the sole or the major source of the income of more and more families. At any one time the relative importance of various sources will vary with the occupation and age of the recipient. The sources will vary between the farm and the nonfarm population and between those with low and those with high incomes.

It is not known with any exactness how many individuals in recent years have had income only from earnings, how many derived their income mainly or wholly from investments or similar sources, or how many had appreciable amounts both from earnings and ownership. The largest group of income recipients is undoubtedly those whose income is wholly or mainly in the form of wage or salary or derived from self-employment. The number living wholly on income from investments is also undoubtedly small. Analysis of income-tax returns confirms these assumptions. These returns indicate only the sources of contractual income, since the civil rights income is not taxed.

Analysis of the state income-tax returns filed in Wisconsin for the year 1936 gave some quantitative indication of the situation in that state in that year. After allowance for those not required under Wisconsin law to file a return, it was estimated that the income of 77 per cent of those receiving "contract" income was primarily or wholly wage or salary, of 20 per cent primarily or wholly entrepreneurial earnings, and that the income of only 3 per cent came primarily or wholly from investments.[10] These data also indicate that more than two-thirds derived their income in that year from but one source. The Wisconsin study showed

a striking variation in composition over the income scale. . . . Interest, dividends and capital gains are relatively minor sources of income for persons in the lower groups, but become larger sources as individual incomes increase. At the higher levels dividends are the largest of these three receipts. . . . Rent is a small percentage at all levels.[11]

10. F. A. Hanna, J. A. Pechman, and S. M. Lerner, *Analysis of Wisconsin Incomes* (New York: National Bureau of Economic Research, 1948), II, 24.

11. *Ibid.*, pp. 17–18.

The property income of persons with low incomes was found to be mainly rent and interest; of those with high incomes, mainly dividends and capital gains. Property income was found to be of greatest importance at the higher income levels, constituting 7 per cent of the total income of persons with incomes between $1,000 and $2,000 and 88 per cent of the income of those with incomes of $100,000 and over.[12] But property income was relatively important at the very lowest income level, more so than at intermediate, since here are many widows and aged who have income from small investments and no or little income from other sources.

A special analysis of the amounts of income from various sources reported on federal income-tax returns for the year 1935 gave the following percentages derived by various income classes from property:[13]

Income Class	Percentage of Money Income from Property
All classes	17.8
Under $5,000	13.6
$ 5,000–$10,000	28.6
$ 10,000–$25,000	44.7
$ 25,000–$50,000	59.6
$ 50,000–$100,000	67.6
$ 100,000–$500,000	78.6
$ 500,000–$1,000,000	94.2
$1,000,000 and over	98.5

The number of persons receiving benefits or assistance in the form of monthly money payments from the public treasury is reported by the responsible agencies. In 1950 the average monthly number receiving income of this type was as follows:[14]

Type of Income	Average Monthly Number Receiving, 1950
Benefits*	
Old age retirement	2,146,000
Survivors, mainly widows and their children	2,222,000
Disability, mainly workmen's compensation	2,439,000
Unemployment	1,434,000
Assistance	
Old age	2,783,000
Dependent children (families)†	644,000
Blind	966,000
Permanently and totally disabled	61,000
General	521,000

* Government employees are excluded, veterans included.
† The children on whose behalf these payments were made numbered about 1,637,000.

12. *Ibid.*, Foreword, p. 15.

13. Temporary National Economic Committee (76th Cong., 3d sess.), Monograph No. 4: *Concentration and Composition of Individual Incomes, 1918–1937* (Washington: Government Printing Office, 1941), p. 48.

14. *Social Security Bulletin*, September, 1951.

The average monthly number receiving was lower than the number who received income of this sort in the course of the year. Especially is this true for unemployment compensation, since the period of receipt is limited, and, when conditions are favorable, many will draw for only part of the period during which they are eligible and then resume employment. Those who are beneficiaries in one month tend to be replaced by others in the succeeding month. There is high turnover also in the group receiving general assistance. They tend to be short-period recipients in contrast to most of those receiving old age assistance, whose payments terminate only at death. Many of the individuals not living in families who reported incomes under $1,000 in 1950 were undoubtedly living on "civil rights" income as well as many families at low-income levels.

Families are more likely to have money income from two or more economic sources than are individuals, since among the members may be both wage-earners and the self-employed: those who are earners and those who receive income from property or from pensions, assistance, or benefits. Wage or salary was the only form of money income reported by 44 per cent of American families in 1950.[15] About half of the urban families reported only this one source of income. About a fourth of the farm families had only incomes from self-employment, mainly farm operation, and a fifth had wage or salary income as well. About three-fifths of all families reported money income from earnings only, either wages, salaries, business operation, professional practice, or two or more of such sources. Slightly over a third reported income both from earnings and from such sources as investments, pensions, assistance, benefits, and the like. Only a twentieth reported no income from earnings. The median income of this last group was only a third of that of the families with income only from earnings and an even smaller proportion of that of families with income from both earnings and other sources.

COMPONENTS OF NONMONEY INCOME

Nonmoney income is made up of those consumption goods and services available for use during the period in question, not through purchase but otherwise. As has been indicated, there are four sources of such income. One is pay for services in the form of food, clothing, housing, or similar items. A second, much more important, is production of goods or provision of services by one or more members of a consuming unit for the use and

15. U.S. Bureau of the Census, *Current Population Reports*, Series P-60, No. 9 (Washington, March, 1952).

benefit of the members of that unit. If all goods were so produced, the consuming unit would be completely self-sufficing.

"Consumer production" is the source of two groups of commodities and services ordinarily distinguished as components of nonmoney income. One is made up of those products of the farm, the garden, and the woodlot that are used by the family; the other, the domestic and personal services rendered by the wife and to smaller extent by other family members. Consumer-produced food, fuel, ice, etc., are important elements of the income of farm families, less of the town or village, and insignificant or nonexistent in large urban communities. These items are often described as the "farm-furnished" part of the income of the farm family, emphasizing the part of the farm in their production as well as distinguishing them from purchased items of similar nature. These products used for home consumption involve a labor cost, as well as possibly some current money outlay in the way of seeds, feed, and other supplies. They are unique among consumer-produced goods in that an acreage is necessary to provide them. The bulk of consumer production, however, is represented by the utilities provided by the unpaid activities of the family members for the family members. All families, both urban and rural, have income from this source.

A third component of nonmoney income is the service income from house, furniture, equipment, automobile, and similar consumers' goods owned by the family and available for use during the period in question. This service income results from the practice of owning rather than renting the durable consumers' goods used; since owner and user are the same, no payment is necessary for their services. If all such goods were rented or hired, or if families used no goods with a life longer than a year, there would be no problem of the sort under discussion in estimating national or family income. As income from money-earning assets is an addition to money income, so the service income from consumer durables is an addition to nonmoney income.

There is a fourth source of consumption goods and services other than through use of the money income. In every community some services are provided "free" or for a payment that is only a fraction of the cost. Such services are "free" in the sense that they are free or partly free to their users or beneficiaries. They are paid for from the public treasury or in some cases from private endowment or subscription. Among the "free" goods, but a minor and decreasing part of the whole, are the food, clothing, and medical services supplied to those dependent upon public or private assistance.

CALCULATING THE AMOUNT OF NONMONEY INCOME

If family income is to be a gauge of the consumption level attained or attainable, or if national income is to measure commodities and services produced, account must be taken of the more important items of non-money income. Comparisons over time, among communities, or even among families of the same place and time would otherwise be inexact. The problem is that of reducing all the items involved to a common denominator in order that they may be summated and the relative importance of the various constituents may be known. Similarly, also, when comparisons over time or from place to place are made, money income must be expressed in dollars of the same purchasing power. Both present difficult problems, at some points impossible of solution.

Commodity income, or the food and fuel furnished by the employer or by the farm, home garden, or poultry lot, is relatively least difficult to value in money once the physical quantities have been estimated. Most of the items included here are bought and sold on the market, and the main problem is to decide whether they should be valued at the price that would be received if they were sold or the price that would be paid if they were purchased. Pay in kind, that is, food or clothing furnished by the employer, clearly would be valued at its purchase price, since the recipient could not or rarely would sell it. The farm family in whose income and consumption consumer-produced items are frequent and sizable is in a different position.

Commodities produced and consumed by farm families fall into two classes: those that are a part of the crop or livestock produced for sale and those that are produced wholly for home consumption. The value of the former at the possible sale price represents money income foregone because of home consumption; the value of the latter at purchase price represents money income saved by home production. For specific purposes each mode of valuation has its usefulness. The farm family may use the first as a basis for deciding whether to consume or sell a certain product. If, on the other hand, the family wishes to discover what it has saved by home production, it would use the latter. For the purpose of arriving at an estimate of the family's total income as an index of possible consumption level comparable with others elsewhere, valuation at the purchase price seems desirable. There is, in fact, little difference between the local sale and purchase price.

Next to commodity income, whether "pay in kind" or the result of consumer production, comes "use income" in relative ease of arriving at its approximate money value. When most families owned few durable goods other than a house, the problem was simpler than at present. Now in the list of such goods frequently owned are automobiles, television sets, electrical equipment, and numerous articles of furniture and clothing, the value of whose services to the owner-user is not represented by an outlay during the period. The first question is, therefore, how exhaustive to make the inventory of "durable" goods. The next is how to value their use during the period in question.

In nonfarm communities, where some families own their homes and many others rent, the rental value of each type can be taken as a basis for calculating the occupancy value of the owned home. As usually estimated, the difference between the rental value and the owner-user's outlays for taxes, insurance, and repairs is considered the occupancy value.[16] No allowance is made for depreciation from wear and tear and obsolescence, although the rent paid to a landlord must cover this loss in asset value. Since farm homes are not usually rented apart from the farm, the rental value for both renters and owners must be calculated as a percentage of the capital value, a value not easy to estimate. Even with capital value given, the occupancy value of the owned farm home is difficult to calculate, since some outlays such as taxes cover the farm and farm buildings as well as the house.

Durable consumer goods other than the family home are not ordinarily rented, so the procedure used in arriving at the service income derived from home ownership is not feasible. If the task of calculating the income from the use of all or part of such goods is undertaken, a possible procedure is to consider the interest on the investment, which represents money income foregone in order to have their use. A reserve for replacement of consumer durables in an amount equivalent to the depreciation must be set aside from the money income if the net-worth status of the family is to be maintained.

With the other two classes of items that enter into nonmoney income, the "free" goods made available largely at public expense and the unpaid services rendered by family members, we come to a much more difficult problem of valuation. Although these items constitute important additions to income defined as rights to consumption goods, there is no satisfactory way of arriving at their proper money value to the family enjoying them. The total current outlay by organized groups in the community

16. The occupancy value so calculated will be high when rental values are high or when outlays for upkeep are relatively low. During a year when major repairs are made, the estimated income from ownership may be negative. For a group, differences in outlays for repairs will cancel out unless in the year of study a large proportion are postponing or are making extensive repairs and replacements.

and by governmental units for the provision of free services of one kind or another may be discovered. The amounts may appear in estimates of national income and consumption. There is no way, however, of estimating the money value to the individual or family of the services of which they may have the advantage. There is no relation between a family's tax payments and the public facilities used or services enjoyed.

Even more difficult than the valuation of "free" services is the problem of placing a monetary value on the services rendered by the family members. In its first study of national income the National Bureau of Economic Research pointed out the impracticability of attempting to set a market value on these services. "Following common practice," they said, "we do not count as part of National Income anything for which a price is commonly not paid."[17] If the market-valuation process does not take place for the services of some group, as is the case with housewives, there is in fact no market value. There is neither market demand nor market supply. The number of workers in the group, their output, and their remuneration lie entirely outside the process of market determination. There is no competitive process, no employer or employee, no movement from job to job, such as operate to establish money values of the services of other workers.

IMPOSSIBILITY OF MAKING EXACT COMPARISONS OF INCOMES

It thus appears that there is no practicable method of reducing all the items of income to a common denominator. The Department of Commerce has found it feasible to include only certain classes of nonmoney income in its estimates of national income. Their inclusion increases the estimate in recent years by only about 5 per cent. They include neither the services of housewives nor of any consumer durables except the owned home. In a Swedish study of the movement of national income from 1861 to 1930, estimates were made of the value of the use of all consumer durables owned and of unpaid domestic labor. The latter was valued at the average annual wage of servants. Almost 30 per cent of the total national income in 1930 when made so broadly inclusive was the estimated value of the consumer durables (including owned homes) and of unpaid domestic work.[18]

Some of the results of our inability to reduce to monetary terms all the items that actually make up a part of the income of the family or nation should be noted. Total incomes can be only roughly compared from

17. W. C. Mitchell *et al.*, *Income in the United States, Its Amount and Distribution, 1909 to 1919* (New York: Harcourt, Brace & Co., 1921), I, 57.

18. E. R. Lindahl *et al.*, *National Income of Sweden, 1861–1930* ("University of Stockholm, Stockholm Economic Studies" [London: P. S. King & Sons, 1937]), III, Part I, 234–35.

family to family, place to place, and time to time. Figures giving the money income alone, or even the estimates in monetary terms of all items that can be so expressed, are not adequate indexes of the volume of commodities and services actually enjoyed by the families or communities in question. When a money value is placed upon the use of the family home and upon the home-produced food, fuel, and certain other items that farm families have at no or little cost, and these values are added to money income, farm families make a much better showing relative to urban families than when money incomes alone are compared. Likewise the inclusion of the omitted elements of real income would bring up the incomes of those with low money incomes relatively more than they do the total for those with high, thus operating as an equalizing factor. The relative importance of the nonmoney items considered in the 1941 study of family incomes among farm and nonfarm families at various money-income levels was as follows:[19]

ANNUAL MONEY INCOME CLASS	RATIO OF NONMONEY TO MONEY INCOME		
	Urban Families	Rural Nonfarm Families	Rural Farm Families
Under $500	59	63	156
$ 500–$1,000	21	33	72
$1,000–$1,500	11	16	45
$1,500–$2,000	7	14	36
$2,000–$3,000	7	12	26
$3,000–$5,000	6	8	19

Comparisons of income between one country or period and another may also be thrown askew by changes in the proportion of women who work at home and those who work for money.

If we suppose that in one country one million wives remain at home and one million wives work in industry, and there are no domestic servants, the total "income" will differ from that of a country where half the wives work in industry and half the other women are domestic servants in the homes of the absent wives, despite the fact that the total "work" being done is the same in both cases.[20]

As decade by decade housewives buy more commodities and services which their mothers produced at home *and themselves seek outside employment at a money wage*, the range of goods not commonly paid for in money shrinks. Hence figures such as we get for the National Income in successive years tend to exaggerate the increases in economic welfare.[21]

Differences in the "free" goods available may also bring about differences in the attainable level of living of families at different times and places that are not shown by their relative money incomes. Public schools,

19. U.S. Bureau of Labor Statistics, Bull. No. 822.
20. Sir Josiah Stamp, "The Wealth and Income of the Chief Powers," *Journal of the Royal Statistical Society*, LXXXII (1919), 477–78.
21. Mitchell *et al.*, *op. cit.*, I, 58.

libraries, and recreational facilities may reduce greatly the demands that would otherwise be made upon the family's money income and increase the sum total of the commodities and services that it may enjoy. In comparing consumption levels, adequate notice is rarely taken of the "free" income of the family.

It has been noted that differences in price levels from community to community and from time to time alter the volume and variety of goods that can be secured with a given money income. There are other closely related differences more difficult if not impossible to allow for. How make allowances, for example, for the fact that in one community it requires less fuel to maintain a given temperature than in another? Or that in an industrial community coal smoke may so pollute the atmosphere that increased expenditure of time and money is necessary in order to have the same cleanliness of person and surroundings that was possible in a non-industrial community? A research worker at the Mellon Institute in Pittsburgh estimated many years ago that "the average family spends $100 a year more for house cleaning, depreciation and additional laundry as a result of the smoke nuisance."[22] Greater expenditures for health purposes may also be necessary. Recreation, quiet, light, air, and beauty of surroundings that are literally free goods at one time or place may be economic goods of relatively high price at other times or places. Many factors of this sort are not shown in an accounting in monetary terms, since only those things for which money is paid are counted as satisfactions secured.

RELATION BETWEEN NATIONAL INCOME AND PERSONAL INCOMES

The Department of Commerce defines national income as "the aggregate earnings of labor and property which arise from the current production of goods and services of the Nation's economy."[23] This concept of national income is a highly defensible one, and the aggregate defined is one that it is important to measure. The total income received by persons during the same period will not be the same as the total national income so defined. One reason for the difference between the two totals is that the whole national income is not currently distributed among earners and investors. Corporate profits are not ordinarily paid out in their entirety. Taxes are levied upon corporate income and employers' payrolls and compulsory deductions made from paychecks. Further, some families and individuals receive income which does not represent current earnings or current production. Interest on the government debt is an outstanding

22. S. S. Wyer in *Proceedings of Tenth National Conference on Housing, 1929* (New York: National Housing Association, 1929) p. 121.

23. *Supplement, Survey of Current Business*, July 1, 1947, p. 8.

example, as well as social security benefits, public assistance, and similar claims.

The relation between national income as defined and the sum of personal incomes or income receipts by persons in 1947 and in 1950 as shown by the figures of the Department of Commerce is as follows:[24]

	NATIONAL INCOME (IN MILLIONS)	
	1947	1950
Total national income........................	$198,604	$238,963
Less:		
Undistributed corporate profits less adjustment of inventory value downward.......................	$ 6,231	$ 8,479
Corporate profits tax liability....................	11,940	18,593
Contributions for social insurance by employers and employees.....................................	5,683	6,962
Excess of wage accruals over payments.............	15	....
Equals: amounts distributed to persons*..............	$174,735	$204,929
Plus:		
Net interest paid by government...................	$ 4,378	$ 4,710
Benefits, assistance and similar payments by government..	11,129	14,330
Consumer bad debts and other transfer income from business concerns............................	674	752
Equals: personal income...........................	$190,916	$224,721

* Includes payments to nonprofit institutions, trust funds, and the like.

The relative importance of various classes of personal income is also shown by the Commerce estimates of the amount in each category. In 1947 and in 1950 their estimates were as follows:

	PERSONAL INCOME (IN MILLIONS)	
	1947	1950
Total..	$190,916	$224,721
Wages and salaries.............................	$119,926	$142,899
Other labor income*............................	2,364	3,472
Proprietors' income.............................	$ 35,365	$ 35,964
Business and professional.......................	$ 19,776	$ 22,277
Farm..	15,589	13,687
Rental income†................................	6,975	8,039
Dividends....................................	6,561	9,169
Interest......................................	$ 7,922	$ 10,096
From government.............................	$ 4,378	$ 4,710
From business and persons......................	3,544	5,386
Transfer payments..............................	$ 11,803	$ 15,082
From government.............................	$ 11,129	$ 14,330
From business‡................................	674	752

* The largest item included is employer contributions to private pension and welfare funds. Also included are compensation for injuries and pay for military reservists.

† Amount adjusted to correspond with that given in *National Income and Product of the United States, 1929–1950* (Washington: Government Printing Office, 1951), p. 79.

‡ Includes consumer bad debts, cash prizes, donations, thefts, personal injury payments to non-employees, etc.

24. *Survey of Current Business*, July, 1949, and July, 1951.

Wages and salaries were far and away the most important class of income, the amount received decidedly greater than all other forms of personal income combined. Interest, dividends, and rent, that is, income wholly from investment, were less than an eighth of the total in 1950. The transfer payments shown were about a fourteenth. If interest on government debt is considered a transfer payment and the $300-million cash subsidy included in farm income were added, the proportion of aggregate personal income of this character would rise appreciably. Such was the relative importance of various classes of personal income in prosperity years. In a depression year, when proprietors' income and dividends would shrink greatly, labor's share in spite of unemployment would be a larger proportion of the total.

As was previously noted, about 5 per cent of the total personal income consisted of consumption goods and services, consumer produced, received as pay, the result of home ownership, or from other sources. Such items increased the total of some classes of personal income appreciably. Over a fifth of the farm proprietors' income was of this character, and the occupancy value of nonfarm owned homes was almost two-fifths of the total rental income. All interest from government was in money, but not that designated as from business or persons. Over two-fifths of the latter was the estimated value of services rendered without pay by financial intermediaries other than insurance companies.[25]

Transfer payments must be itemized if the purpose of these payments is to be understood. The major classes in 1947 and in 1950 were as follows:

	TRANSFER PAYMENTS (IN MILLIONS)	
	1947	1950
Total..............................	$11,803	$15,082
From government........................	$11,129	$14,330
Social Security benefits.................	$ 1,527	$ 2,781
Pensions of federal, state, and local civilian employees...........................	557	627
Public assistance.......................	$ 1,478	$ 2,360
Special types.........................	$ 1,314	$ 2,069
General assistance....................	164	291
Veterans' benefits and pensions..........	6,721	7,407
Other, including veterans' bonuses.......	846	1,155
From business..........................	674	752

About half of the transfer payments in each year went to veterans and their dependents and must therefore be charged to warfare, as must the

25. Included also in the interest total are the amounts accrued on accounts with insurance companies and the like. Only about 15 per cent of the interest from nongovernmental sources in 1947 was money income actually paid out currently.

greater part of the interest paid by government, rather than to welfare in a more restricted sense.

To round out the national account, the disposition of personal income may be noted. It was as follows in 1947 and 1950:

	PERSONAL INCOME (IN MILLIONS)	
	1947	1950
Total..	$190,916	$224,721
Personal tax and nontax payments...................	$ 21,506	$ 20,460
Personal consumption expenditures...................	165,486	193,568
Personal savings...................................	3,924	10,693

Included in personal consumption expenditures is a charge for depreciation on owned homes. Included in personal savings are the increases in reserves of insurance companies, the increase in the cash-surrender value of policies held by individuals. To savings must be added undistributed corporate profits to secure the total amount.

CHAPTER IV

CONTRIBUTORS AND CLAIMANTS TO
THE FAMILY INCOME

THE family's money income, as was emphasized in the preceding chapter, may come entirely from one family member, or it may be the sum of amounts received by several. Likewise, the group depending upon a given income for support may include no one who is not an income contributor, or it may include several who are not. The situation will obviously depend upon the age of the family members, their relationship, and the responsibility each is expected or has been willing and able to assume. The purpose of this chapter is to examine the relative size and composition of the two groups, to describe how both contributors and claimants are currently distributed among families, and to note typical changes in earners and dependents during the family life-span.

SOURCES OF INFORMATION

There are three sets of data that throw light upon the age, sex, and family status of the contributors and claimants to family income and the relative size of the two groups. One gives data on money-income recipients in a particular year.[1] The second gives data on those who worked for pay or profit during a particular year; the third, on the number employed or in the labor market in a particular survey week.[2] The total number of money-income recipients during a year will exceed the number who worked for pay or profit during the year, since there are forms of money income other than pay or profit. The number employed in a particular week will be smaller than the number who have worked for pay or profit at some time during the year. The number of young people and married women who have worked at some time during the year is especially likely to exceed the number working at a particular date. Many of the former

1. See, e.g., U.S. Bureau of the Census, *Current Population Reports, Consumer Income*, Series P-60, No. 5 (Washington, February, 1949), and No. 9 (Washington, March, 1952). (Processed.) The details given in these reports concerning the personal characteristics and family status of persons with and without money income during the year of study, and concerning family size and composition, are far greater than in other income studies.

2. See U.S. Bureau of the Census, *Current Population Reports, Labor Force*, Series P-50, No. 8 (Washington, August, 1948); No. 13 (Washington, February, 1949); No. 22 (Washington, April, 1950). (Processed.)

work only during vacations; many of the latter move from the labor market to housekeeping and then back again. We have data over a longer period of time and more detailed data concerning the "labor force," that is, those employed or seeking work at a particular time, than for those who have earned at some time during the year or those who have received some money income. It is therefore upon these data that we must largely rely for information concerning changes in the contributors and claimants to income in our economy.

CONTRIBUTORS AND CLAIMANTS IN THE POPULATION AS A WHOLE

According to the data available, slightly under half of the civilian non-institutional population in early 1948 had received some money income in the previous year.[3] Two-thirds of those eighteen and over were money-income recipients. If all under eighteen who had earned occasionally had reported such earning, the proportion of these young people who had been income recipients might have been close to a tenth. Their earnings, however, as well as the incomes of others not reporting, were undoubtedly small. Nine-tenths of all those reporting earnings in 1947 were eighteen to sixty-four. A slightly lower proportion of those who reported money income of any kind were of this age.

Those in the population who are income recipients and those who are not are more precisely shown if the two groups are distributed by age and sex. In 1947 the composition of the two groups was as follows:

| | | PERCENTAGE OF CIVILIAN NONINSTITUTIONAL POPULATION | |
| | | Without Money | With Money |
AGE GROUP	All	Income	Income
All...........	100	100	100
Under 14*........	25	48	...
14–19...........	9	10	7
20–64...........	59	37	83
Men...........	29	2	58
Women........	30	35	25
65 and over.......	7	5	10
Men...........	3	1	6
Women........	4	4	4

* Assumed that proportion receiving any money income was negligible.

3. All data in this chapter concerning earners or money-income recipients in the population in 1947 come, unless otherwise indicated, from Census reports previously noted. Reports for later years show little change except the continuation of such trends as increase in proportion of married women earning and of persons sixty-five and over in receipt of money income. The proportion of the population fourteen to seventeen with and without money income in year of study was estimated, since reports give data only for those fourteen to nineteen.

These distributions give quantitative expression to what is commonly known. Almost three-fifths of those making no contribution to money income are children and young people under twenty, a little over a third are women twenty to sixty-four, and the remainder are largely old people. Those in the population who were not in the labor force in 1947, a somewhat smaller group than those without money income, were occupied as follows according to the Census data:[4]

Age and Employment Status	Percentage of Population Not in Labor Force
All	100
Under 14, in nursery or school	45
14 and over	55
Going to school	8
Keeping house	39
Unable to work, or voluntarily idle	8
Men	6
Women	2

Also as would be expected, most of the money-income recipients are men twenty to sixty-four years of age, close to three-fifths of the total. Only 3 per cent of the men in that age group early in 1948 reported no money income in 1947. Although only a little over half of the men sixty-five and over reported work for pay or profit in 1947, about 85 per cent reported the receipt of money income. For the proportion of women who contribute to money income we must look at the nonfarm population, since those who work without pay on the family farm are not included among the money-income recipients.[5] A third of the nonfarm women, eighteen to sixty-four, reported money income in 1947 and almost half of those sixty-five and over. Many of the latter group as well as many of the men of that age were receiving old age assistance, Social Security benefits, or other types of pensions.

If the steady full-time earners could be separated from those who work irregularly or only part time, the relative importance of men twenty to sixty-four as contributors of money income could be more accurately shown. They undoubtedly constitute the bulk of the steady, regular earners. In 1947, for example, 9 per cent of all of any age, male or female, who reported earning at some time during the year were not doing so in December. Some of the younger group had gone back to school; some of

4. Based upon annual average as given in U.S. Bureau of the Census, *Current Population Reports*, Series P-50, No. 13.

5. They are included in the labor force if they work fifteen hours or more per week.

the older had reached the age for retirement; some regular workers were seasonally unemployed; some of the women had married and left the labor market; others already married had also decided to leave. Half of the withdrawals were women forty-five or over, and a fifth were young persons fourteeen to seventeen years of age. A third of all who had earned earlier in the year but were not earning in December were in school, slightly less than half were keeping house, and a fifth were unable to work, experiencing a period of seasonal unemployment, retired, or otherwise voluntarily idle. The proportion of the various groups of earners at some time during the year not earning in December was as follows:

Age Groups	Percentage of Earners during Year Not Earning in December
14–17	39
18–64: all	7
Men	3
Women	16
65 and over: all	15
Men	13
Women	23

Not only do a large proportion of those of high-school and college age leave the labor market when school is in session, but others still employed are only part-time workers. Those sixty-five and over are also likely to be part-time workers and to be an impermanent part of the labor force. Women as workers show the same characteristics. In 1948 an eighth of all male workers in nonagricultural industries worked on the average only fifteen hours per week or less, but more than a fourth of all the female workers worked these short hours. It was probably the married women, especially those with the larger families and younger children, who were working part time.

Taking the year 1948 as a whole, that is, allowing for movements from school and home to labor market, from employment to retirement, for voluntary idleness and the like, the population as a whole seems to have been distributed on the average approximately as shown on page 60. At any one time during the year these proportions would be slightly different. During school months the proportion in school would be larger and in the labor force slightly smaller, and there would be other slight shifts of the nature previously indicated. The general picture during this year of full employment is that, on the average, month by month, slightly over two-fifths of the population were in the labor force,[6] a fifth or slightly

6. About 3 per cent of the labor force were unpaid family workers working more than fifteen hours per week, three-fifths women and girls.

over were caring for children and performing other household tasks, and the remainder, about one-third, were in the nursery, in school, in institutions, retired, unable to work, or idle either voluntarily or because of the seasonal character of their work. With recession or depression the proportion actually at work would decline and that seeking work increase (both are included in the labor force). The trend over time has been a concentration of those in the labor force more and more in the age group eighteen to sixty-four and an increase in the proportion of women of those

Age and Employment Status	Percentage of Total Population
All..	100
In institutions.....................................	1
In armed forces....................................	1
Civilian noninstitutional population...............	98
Under 18..	31
In school...................... 16.5	
In labor force................. 2	
Other, about 90 per cent preschool	
children.................. 12.5	
18–64...	60
In school...................... 1	
In labor force................. 38	
Men............... 27	
Women............ 11	
Keeping house, almost entirely	
women................... 20	
Unable to work, seasonally unem-	
ployed, voluntarily idle... 1	
65 and over.......................................	7
In labor force, over four-fifths men... 2	
Keeping house, almost entirely	
women................... 2	
Retired, unable to work, etc.......... 3	

ages in the labor force. The proportion of the population in school and the proportion of the population over sixty-five have been growing. If no one under eighteen or over sixty-five worked for pay or profit and if the number eighteen and over in school should be doubled, the concentration of those currently earning would be even more marked; and, unless increase in paid work by women offset the decrease by young people and those over sixty-five, the proportion of earners in the population would decline below its present level of between 40 and 45 per cent.

FAMILY STATUS OF CONTRIBUTORS AND CLAIMANTS

More important than sex or age of earners or other income recipients is their family status, since this determines their presumptive dependents, that is, those with whom they must share the income they receive. Presumptive dependents are to be distinguished from actual dependents.

The former are those that by law or community standards a person is supposed to support; the latter those he may actually be supporting. The former are defined by income-tax exemptions, Social Security provisions, statutory and administrative rules governing public assistance, and by other social judgments variously expressed. The law is by no means consistent in the definition formulated or implied and may lag behind approved practice. We have here one of those realms of changing social sanctions, with both law and ethics uncertain as to the economic responsibility involved in certain relationships.

About a tenth of those reporting the receipt of money income in 1947 were persons who lived alone or with unrelated persons. Some probably contributed to the support of relatives not living with them, and part of the income of others undoubtedly came from relatives living elsewhere. In the main, however, this tenth of the income recipients probably used their incomes wholly for their own support.

Since well over nine-tenths of the civilian noninstitutional population live in family groups, the proportion of all family members who are income recipients and their age and sex distribution are very similar to what exists among the population as a whole. The relative importance of various family members among contributors and noncontributors was as follows in 1947:[7]

FAMILY STATUS	PERCENTAGE OF ALL LIVING IN FAMILIES	
	Money-Income Recipients	Not Money-Income Recipients
All............................	100	100
Married men, wife present*..........	55	1
Wives, husband present..............	15	34
Widowed, divorced, separated, or single persons who were family heads†....	6	1
Other family members...............	24	64
Under 18‡.......................	5	56
18 and over......................	19	8

* Proportion of married persons, living with relatives, who were income recipients is estimated on the basis of the percentage of these husbands and wives in the labor force.

† Over nine-tenths of these family heads without income were women. About four-fifths of those with income were women.

‡ The income study gives the number of income recipients that were fourteen to nineteen. The number fourteen to seventeen was estimated.

Nine-tenths of the family members without income were wives of the head or children under eighteen. If to these were added persons eighteen and over in school, and older women keeping house for a son or other

7. The age and family status of income recipients in 1947 were recorded as they stood at the date of inquiry, April, 1948.

relative, practically the whole group would be accounted for. If nonfarm families alone were considered, the proportion of married men among the income recipients would be slightly less, and of their wives and other family heads slightly more, the difference increasing with degree of urbanization. The number of "other" family members eighteen and over who were income recipients was more than twice those who were not. Most of them were undoubtedly sons and daughters of the family head who had not yet married or had not left the family home for a job in another location. In April, 1949, the frequency of one or more earning family members varied as between families with a married couple at the head and those of other types as follows:[8]

NUMBER OF EARNING FAMILY MEMBERS	PERCENTAGE DISTRIBU- OF FAMILIES	
	Married Couple as Head	Other Head*
All.	100	100
None.	5	14
One.	58	43
Two.	28	30
Three or more.	9	13

* The percentage of these families with no earner and with only one is estimated, since heads of one-person households are included in the data given in the Census report.

It is clear that many families have more than one income recipient. The average number reported in 1947 by nonfarm families was 1.67; by farm families, 1.56. The income reports do not indicate what proportion of families have money income from only one member, but it is probable that not far from half fell in this group. The number of earners and of all other income contributors will vary with the type of family and its composition. In families consisting only of husband and wife there can be no more than two earners, and the wife over sixty-five is less likely to earn than the one under twenty-five. If there are young children the chances are great that there will be but one earner, but if there are sons or daughters above school age still living at home they will probably have joined the father in the labor force. During its life-span the family may start with two earners, drop to one while the children are young, rise to two or more when the children go to work, become a two-earner family again if the wife takes a job after the children leave home, possibly drop

8. U.S. Bureau of the Census, *Current Population Reports*, Series P-50, No. 22. Families who are lodging or living in quasi-households are not included in the distribution and subfamilies are included among the family members.

again to one earner, and then to reliance wholly upon income from other sources.

Families with a widowed, divorced, or separated person at their head have great variety in their composition. Three-fourths of the heads of such families are women, the great majority older women. The households of the older heads often include married children and others eighteen and over. Some households are those of younger women, and the children are all under eighteen. In some families of this type the entire income is derived from sources other than earning.

HUSBANDS AND WIVES AS CONTRIBUTORS TO MONEY INCOME

The role of the husband as contributor of money income is indicated by what has been said in regard to the relative importance of men in the labor force and among income recipients. Married men whose wives were members of the same household constituted well over half of all the money-income recipients living in families in 1947. The husband was the sole earner in three-fifths of the households with any earner early in 1949, and only 8 per cent of all married men were not at that date in the labor force.[9] From ages twenty-five to forty-five their voluntary absence from the labor force or inability to work is insignificant. The percentage at various ages in the labor force, April, 1949, was as follows:[10]

Age	Percentage of Married Men, Wife Present, in Labor Force
Under 25	95
25–34	98
35–44	99
45–64	94
65 and over	52
All	92

Only about 2 per cent did not report the receipt of money income from some source in 1947.

Both in steadiness and in amount the husband's income is usually the permanent, substantial core, even when it is not the whole, of the family's money income. Even when there are other earners, their incomes only supplement, rarely exceed, his, partly because he is more likely to be a full-time earner, partly because he is a more skilled, experienced, and continuous worker. The incomes of married men are substantially higher than those of other marital groups as well as those of women. The median

9. U.S. Bureau of the Census, *Current Population Reports*, Series P-50, No. 22.
10. *Ibid.*

money incomes reported by the various groups in the nonfarm population eighteen years of age and over were as follows in 1947:[11]

| | MEDIAN MONEY INCOME | |
MARITAL STATUS	Male	Female
Single..................	$1,641	$1,603
Widowed..............	1,291	875
Divorced..............	2,171	1,325
Separated..............	2,028	1,019
Married, living with spouse	2,708	1,009

The role of wives and mothers as contributors to money incomes is not to the same extent common knowledge as that of husbands and fathers. Even less is there common agreement as to what their role should be. Husbands and fathers are supposed to be the "providers," and they well-nigh universally make some effort to discharge the responsibility expected. Since many wives and mothers do not earn, the basic question is: Why and under what conditions do they join the labor force?

Slightly over 30 per cent of the married women living with their husbands reported receipt of money income in 1950.[12] The latter percentage would have been higher if those who helped to earn the money income from a family farm or other family business could have been included among the income recipients as they are in the surveys of the labor force during a specified week. The proportion who receive some money income during the year will, in spite of that exclusion, be larger than the proportion reported as paid and unpaid workers at a specific date, since, as previously noted, many women work for a few months during the year and then withdraw to give full attention to housekeeping. The proportion of women who though married and living with their husbands are earning has been rising steadily in this country decade by decade. From April, 1940, to April, 1949, the number so engaged increased about 90 per cent. In early 1940 only about 15 per cent were earning; in 1949, 22.5 per cent.[13]

The correctness of the count of married women who should be considered as having a "gainful occupation," the objective prior to 1940, or of those who during the survey week in 1940 and at later dates were employed or in the labor market, has always been problematical. At early dates, when it was relatively infrequent for the wife in the family to be

11. U.S. Bureau of the Census, *Current Population Reports*, Series P-20, No. 23 (Washington, March, 1949). (Processed.) All income recipients fourteen to seventeen were assumed to be single and to have incomes under $1,000.

12. U.S. Bureau of the Census, *Current Population Reports*, Series P-60, No. 9.

13. U.S. Bureau of the Census, *Current Population Reports*, Series P-50, No. 22.

earning, the question concerning "gainful occupation" was probably not even asked by many enumerators. The Bureau of the Census, especially since 1945, has made several changes in its interviewing technique with a view to insuring that all married women and others who should be counted as a part of the current "labor force" be so reported.

Even after all allowances are made for the underreporting of married women who were contributors to money income at early census dates, the marked increase in the proportion assuming this role is apparent. Only about 5 per cent of all married women in the United States were reported as having a "gainful occupation" in 1890 as compared with 24 per cent "in the labor force" in April, 1949.[14] Married women have become a more important part of the labor force as a result not only of this increased frequency of their earning but also because of the decline in the relative importance of young single women as the age of leaving school has been raised and the age of marriage lowered. Many of those working are mothers of children under eighteen. Over two-fifths of the working wives living with their husbands in April, 1949, had children under eighteen, and a sixth had children under six.

The married women who earn are by no means a random sample of their population group. Those who are living with their husbands as co-heads of households, those with young children, those in the upper-income groups, those who live on farms, and those over forty-five earn less frequently than their opposites. The differences in some of these respects in April, 1949, were as follows:

Household Status of Husband	Percentage of Married Women in the Labor Force
All	24
Husband present	22
Husband head of household	22
Urban	24
Rural-farm	20
Husband not head of household	33
Husband absent	46

The married women living with their husbands as subfamilies were younger and, more important, were less likely to have children and household responsibilities than those (the predominant group) who were co-heads of households. The effect of the presence of children, especially those not of school age, is shown by the following variations in frequency of earning in April, 1949:[15]

14. All married women are here compared. Those living separately from their husbands were not differentiated in 1890.

15. U.S. Bureau of the Census, *Current Population Reports*, Series P-50, No. 22.

	Percentage of Married Women, Husband Present, in Labor Force
Number and Age of Children	
All............................	22
No children under 18...................	29
One or more children under 18..........	17
All under 6...................	10
Some under 6 and others 6–17..	12
All 6–17.....................	27

The fact that almost as large a proportion of those with all children of school age were in the labor force as of those without any children under eighteen should not be misinterpreted. The former were a much younger group of women. Age, as well as the responsibility for young children, is a deterrent to earning. Furthermore, some of the women without children under eighteen had older, earning sons and daughters in their households, and their need to earn was less pressing than that of the younger women. In almost three-fourths of the families in which the wife worked in April, 1947, the husband and wife were the only earners.[16] The wife earns rather frequently, we might conjecture, early in the marriage before there are children. When all the children are under six, in nine-tenths of the families the husband is the only earner. As the children enter school, the wife earns more frequently, until about a fourth of the wives are earning when all are of school age. But, as the children leave school and join the father in the labor force, the frequency of her earning diminishes. In only a sixth of the families with another earner besides the husband was she working in April, 1947. After the children leave home and household duties diminish, the wife may again supplement the husband's earnings until her increasing age operates as a deterrent.

For the effect of age and the size of the husband's income upon married women's employment, we must go back to the 1940 data.[17] To remove the effect of certain factors affecting rate of employment, only those married women living in metropolitan districts of 100,000 and over who had no children under ten in their households will be considered. Over two-fifths of those aged twenty-five to twenty-nine were in the labor force but only a tenth of those forty-five to sixty-four. That the income of the husband is also an important factor in determining the employment status of the wife is shown by the same data. About half of the younger age group without children under ten were earning when the husband's wage or salary was

16. U.S. Bureau of the Census, *Current Population Reports*, Series P-50, No. 5.
17. U.S. Bureau of the Census, *Sixteenth Census of the United States: 1940, Population: The Labor Force, Employment and Family Characteristics of Women* (Washington: Government Printing Office, 1943).

under $1,000, but only about a fifth of those whose husbands' earnings were $3,000 and over. Low earnings by the husband did not, however, bring the older women into the labor market to the same extent. Only about a seventh of the equivalent group aged forty-five to sixty-four whose husbands earned under $1,000 were themselves in the labor force.

REASONS FOR EARNING BY MARRIED WOMEN

The more intensive the analysis of which married women are working, the more apparent are the conditions under which they will appear in the labor force and the reasons for their presence there. Making for an increase in the proportion who are earning are the circumstances and forces usually enumerated: increase in the proportion of families living in cities, growing importance of money income, rising standards of living, decline in the birth rate, decline in household production, access to markets well stocked with consumers' goods and services, labor-saving equipment, a generally lessened burden of housework, improved education of women, and lessening of ancient prejudices against their earning. Such a listing does not, however, account for the absence of large groups of women from the labor market or explain precisely why others are there. Some of the circumstances listed merely facilitate earning by married women, but their existence by no means insures it. If there were little economic pressure to earn or if the opportunities for earning were not attractive, the proportion of married women employed would be relatively small.

What has been suggested is that there are circumstances in home, family, and environment that facilitate, and there are those that deter, the employment of married women but that they are actually brought into the labor market either by the push of economic necessity or by the pull of attractive opportunities for earning. If the pressure is great enough, it will override circumstances that would ordinarily deter. If home and other conditions facilitate, neither the push nor the pull need be so great as they must otherwise be.

The conditions which facilitate full- or part-time employment of married women fall roughly into two classes: those which reduce the time and effort required for caring for children, maintaining homes, and performing other housekeeping services at an acceptable standard and those that break down unfavorable attitudes toward their earning, especially those of the women themselves, their husbands, kinfolk, and friends. Ready-to-serve foods, electrical equipment, convenient kitchens, commercial laundries, nursery schools, small families, and a favorable climate of opinion, only in a limited sense, however, explain the increased appearance of married women in the labor market. As was said, without either the pull of an attractive opportunity for employment or the push of economic necessity, married women do not usually become earners. Whether an opportunity for employment is attractive or not will depend upon the woman herself and the general economic level of the family. The kind of work represented may be more attractive than housekeeping, it may give opportunity for employment of special skills or special knowledge, or it may attract primarily because it offers an income that will appreciably raise the family level of living. Ideally all employed married women would have been drawn into the labor market because of such inducements. Actually many are employed for reasons that are midway between that situation and economic necessity, and many for reasons close to, if not absolute, economic necessity.[18] The economic necessity that impels married women into the labor market is not lack of another income recipient in the family. Very few married women living with their husbands are the only earners in their families. In April, 1947, in only 1 per cent of the families with a married couple as head was the wife the sole earner in the survey week, about 3 per cent of all married women who were earners. The economic necessity that pushes the wife into earning is inadequate money income from other sources—inadequate, that is, to provide those things considered essential that cannot be obtained without money.

Decade by decade not only have prevailing standards for food, housing, clothing, medical care, recreation, and other goods and services risen, but at the same time it has become increasingly impossible to have what is currently considered necessary without money income. The urban family without money does not have food. In sickness, home doctoring and nursing are insufficient. Shelter, shoes, movies, as well as milk, take money. With all the will in the world, the wife and mother could not provide what is considered essential by laboring at home. Strict economic necessity means that the family, the wife included, would suffer what would be generally considered privation or poverty if the husband's earnings were not supplemented from another source. Under these circumstances the wife may earn even if home and community conditions do not facilitate and even if she has young children for whose care during her absence she can make no proper provision. She will take whatever

18. The economic and social reasons for the presence in the labor force of single women and other unmarried women without children are very different from those operative upon most married women. The former work for the same reasons that men do. It is expected and taken for granted. There is no presumption that responsibility for their support lies elsewhere.

employment presents itself without reference to wages, hours, and working conditions.

A major deterrent to paid employment by married women is the presence in the home of preschool children. It takes strong pressure to push most mothers of young children into employment outside the home or an opportunity to earn an amount fully sufficient to pay for their care. When money income from other sources is adequate, the proportion of such mothers in the labor force is small. In metropolitan districts in 1940 the differences in proportions among women twenty-five to twenty-nine were as follows:

	PERCENTAGE OF MARRIED WOMEN TWENTY-FIVE TO TWENTY-NINE IN LABOR FORCE	
	Children under Ten	
HUSBAND'S WAGE OR SALARY	None	One or More
All incomes............	41	9
$1–$999..............	49	14
...		
$3,000 and over........	21	3

It is the married women who enter the labor market because of strict economic necessity, in spite of conditions that would ordinarily deter such action, whose situation should cause social concern. Their families would suffer from the loss of their income, but they also may suffer from the loss of their services. If the latter does not happen, it is because in many cases these women do their housework before their paid employment begins or after it ends. They carry in effect two jobs. The eight-hour day and the five-day week may have altered the effect of employment upon the total working time of married women. But from a study of working mothers, all industrial wage-earners, made in Philadelphia twenty-five years ago the investigator reports:

> Most of the visits to the wage-earning mothers were made in the late afternoon or evening. . . . Late afternoon calls found her just back from work preparing supper; evening visits found her cooking, washing dishes, ironing, putting the children to bed. Saturday afternoon she was scrubbing, washing clothes, or marketing. It was only on Sunday afternoon that she might be away from home.[19]

Kingsbury and Fairchild reported the results of an interesting study made in the Soviet Union of the total working time of men and women with identical hours of paid employment.[20] The women with a 7-hour work

19. G. S. Hughes, *Mothers in Industry* (New York: New Republic, Inc., 1925), pp. 176–77.

20. S. M. Kingsbury and M. Fairchild, *Factory, Family and Women in the Soviet Union* (New York: G. P. Putnam's Sons, 1935), p. 251.

day spent on the average 3.7 hours more per day on "indispensable labor" than did the men, with of course the same amount of time less in rest, recreation, self-education, and public activities. The women spent on the average 12.6 hours per day per week in indispensable labor, and the men 8.9. The ideal study for our purposes would be a similar analysis of the time budget of American working couples.

Some of the mothers both of preschool and of school-age children who are working away from home have paid assistance. How many do so is unknown, but knowledge of the earnings of most married women relative to that of household workers, many of whom also are married women with children, would indicate that relatively few could afford to do so— only those who have been drawn into employment by an opportunity to earn a relatively high salary. Some may have in their households non-earning family members who look after the children when the parents are absent. Monroe's conclusion in regard to the earning mothers in Chicago in 1920 was:

> Non-earning related women in the household seem to have helped solve the problem of child care for approximately one-fourth of the mothers earning away from home and having children under two, for fewer than one-third of those having children of two to seven (and none younger) and for fewer than one-sixth of the mothers of children seven to fourteen.[21]

By 1950 nonearning adults were less frequent among the family members than in 1920. They are more likely to be employed themselves or to be living independently. Offsetting this to some extent so far as the pre-school children are concerned is the increase in nurseries and nursery schools providing care for all or part of the day. So far as the preschool children are concerned, it is to be hoped that the findings of the Women's Bureau in regard to the care provided by wage-earning mothers in Passaic, New Jersey, in 1920 would now be of very limited application. The Bureau's conclusion at that time was:

> The care provided seems in great measure to have been casual and inadequate. It is difficult to fix the line of demarcation between the conditions confronting women who said they depended on neighbors to care for their children and those who frankly stated that the children cared for themselves or that "God took care of them."[22]

Young children, it may be assumed, are most frequently left unsupervised when the mothers are under great pressure to earn. The increase in employment during the 1940's was presumably not for that reason, since it was a time of full employment and relatively high earnings for men.

21. Day Monroe, *Chicago Families* (Chicago: University of Chicago Press, 1932), p. 221.
22. U.S. Women's Bureau, Bull. No. 41 (Washington: Government Printing Office, 1925), pp. 136–37.

The situation with respect to the school-age children of working mothers must remain an open question. They themselves are sometimes the "older relatives" who look after the younger children. Mothers of children under six are more likely to work if they have children six to seventeen and when all are of school age the proportion employed increases greatly. The observation made by Hughes in 1925 on the basis of her study of earning mothers in Philadelphia may still be true and generally applicable.

Wage-earning mothers not only leave children five years and over more often than younger children, but they also make less adequate provision for their care and supervision. . . . More than a third of the children between five and sixteen . . . are left to their own devices after school and Saturday. . . . The real problem of child care in the home of the wage-earning mother comes up in later childhood. Generally the mother does not work while her children are in infancy or early childhood. When she does, she usually arranges for their care by a relative or other adult living in the household. It is the child of five years and older who is in danger of being neglected while she is at work.[23]

Study of the effect of age upon the employment of married women suggests that "gray hair" or what it represents is a second major deterrent to earning. As has already been noted, women forty-five and over are employed with less frequency than younger women, although a negligible number have preschool children and relatively few even children under eighteen. There would seem to be nothing in their home situation to deter and much to facilitate their employment. The lag in their employment is probably due to the fact that they are subject to less economic pressure and have less economic incentive in the form of good opportunities for employment than the younger women. The total family income of women around forty-five is likely to be greater than of women somewhat younger. Married men's incomes reach their peak about that time, and, in addition, the children are passing from dependency to self-support. Although by fifty husbands' incomes on the average are declining, the children are leaving or have left home, and there are fewer to support. The major factor preventing employment is probably the lack of attractive income possibilities. Some of these women may never have earned; many more have not earned continuously, some not since their marriage or shortly thereafter. As is true of all married women living with their husbands, they must find their jobs in the locality where the husbands' earnings are highest. Skills they once possessed may be rusty and knowledge outmoded. If they must enter the market as unskilled or semiskilled workers, the possible earnings may not be an adequate inducement when set over against the need for more money, the leisure sacrificed, the effort involved.

23. Hughes, *op. cit.*, pp. 198, 209–10.

During the 1940's the rate of increase in employment of married women was greatest for those forty-five to sixty-four. The number in the labor force more than doubled from 1940 to 1949. The proportion employed went from a tenth to a fifth. This increase represents, it would seem, a clear social gain, a more complete employment of productive resources. With the present marriage age and life-expectation, if few women over forty-five are employed, an important fraction of the able-bodied population is contributing relatively little to the total national income either in salable goods or in unpaid services. For about twenty years the average woman's workday would be far below that of the employed population. The increased frequency of employment of this age group in a time of full employment and high earnings means the appearance in the labor force of married women whose home conditions facilitate this employment and whose employment is a positive good. They are there presumably not because of economic pressure in the strict sense but because of the existence of attractive opportunities for the sale of what they have to offer.

There are undoubtedly some married women employed for other than economic reasons. The push in their case is their dislike of housework; the pull, the attractions other than financial of the work itself, the belief that their social usefulness is thereby enhanced, their desire to utilize special skills, experience, and competence. Any survey of the employments in which married women are found will convince one that this group is relatively small. For most there is also some degree of economic pressure—pressure which in some cases overrides their own preferences. This pressure may be great or relatively small. When great, they work at whatever they can find. Some find what are relatively good jobs, others those that are not generally desired. Some because of their earning are obliged to alter the family's manner of living and lessen supervision of children and resort to makeshift arrangements; some struggle to carry two jobs, and others are able to make the income supplementation without undue strain or impairment of essential services. When the economic pressure is not great, they are likely to earn only when the job is attractive in working conditions or financial rewards and when there are no losses and some gains to themselves and their families.

Married women are probably a more shifting part of the labor force than any other group except those who are still of school age. Those found employed during one survey week are not so likely as men to be employed at another even in the same year. They are more frequently part-time workers and for this as well as other reasons are supplementary rather than principal contributors to the family income. Of all women married and unmarried eighteen to sixty-four reporting some work for pay or profit in 1947, a sixth were neither employed nor in the labor market in December. If married women had been isolated, the proportion would probably have been greater. Eight per cent of all women keeping house in December had worked for pay or profit sometime during the year. Only 3 per cent of the men eighteen to sixty-four who worked during the year were not working or in the market in December. Fifteen per cent of the urban wage-earning wives worked fewer than six months in 1939, but only 5 per cent of the urban wage-earning husbands. In 1928 the Children's Bureau studied 12,227 representative wage-earning families with one or more children under sixteen. Half of the mothers had been employed since their marriage, but only about a fifth in the six months preceding the study. Twenty-nine per cent of those who had earned since marriage had been employed less than 30 per cent of the time, and only an eighth had been employed 50 per cent or more of the time.[24]

The variations in the employment of married women from place to place and from time to time can generally be explained in terms of the foregoing analysis. Employment rates are relatively high when and where the opportunities for working are good and the practice well established. It is high in areas with a high proportion of low-income families, as is the case where the Negro population is high. In 1940 over a third of the wives in Washington, D.C., eighteen to sixty-four years of age without children under ten in their households were earning as compared with a fifth in all metropolitan districts. The government service offers opportunity for employment to married women, and the proportion of Negroes is higher than the average in all metropolitan areas. The proportion employed in Buffalo was 14 per cent and in Binghamton, New York, 29, a reflection of the presence of women's industries in the latter city. Even more striking was the difference between Duluth and Dallas, with 13 per cent employed in the former and 31 in the latter; and the difference between Scranton and Shreveport, with only 9 per cent employed in the former and 32 in the latter. It was the Negro population that brought up employment in Dallas and Shreveport. The percentage employed in Fall River–New Bedford was, however, just as high, 32.5, as in Shreveport, owing to the textile mills there, a historic field for the employment of women. To similar factors may be ascribed the high percentage of employment, 43 per cent, in Winston-Salem, North Carolina. The same forces affect the employment of nonwhite as white married women. The presence of chil-

24. U.S. Children's Bureau, Pub. No. 204 (Washington: Government Printing Office, 1931).

dren, especially young children, lessens the frequency of employment, as do age and a relatively high income from other sources. Yet at any income level or family situation a larger proportion of nonwhite than of white women is employed, showing the effect of what is customary, even possibly expected, within the subgroup in question.

OTHER FAMILY MEMBERS AS CONTRIBUTORS

About a fourth of all money-income recipients in 1947 who were living in families were persons other than the head or the wife of the head. About a fifth of this group were young earners under eighteen. They were almost without exception single, living in the homes of their parents. Many worked only part time or when school was not in session. If those eighteen and over had been evenly divided among families, about a third would have had a member other than the head or the wife of the head to swell the family income total. They were not, of course, evenly distributed, some families having two or more. At the end of the 1940's only about a fourth of the husband-wife families had a member eighteen years of age and over as either a potential or an actual contributor. Many, however, have one or more such actual contributors during their life-span, especially at that period when the children join the father in the labor force. In families with a widowed, divorced, separated, or single person at the head, contributors other than the head are more frequent. Two-thirds of the families of this type at the end of the 1940's had such a potential or actual contributor eighteen or over, not counting the married couples frequently found living as subfamilies in these households. These potential contributors were usually sons or daughters of the head, although an occasional contributor to the family income in families of all types is the parent or more distant relative of the head.

ECONOMIC STATUS OF SINGLE, WIDOWED, DIVORCED, AND SEPARATED, EIGHTEEN AND OVER

Unmarried persons eighteen years of age and over who live in families as what the census calls "relatives of the head" constitute only a little over half of this marital group. About 30 per cent of the unmarried, including therein those separated from their spouses, were living alone or with an unrelated person in their own housekeeping units or as lodgers at the end of the 1940's. The remainder, about a sixth, were themselves family heads.

Practically all the men not living with related persons in a family group reported money income in 1947. About a sixth of the women did not.

They were presumably unpaid workers or were supported by unrelated persons in whose households they were living. Very few of the male family heads were without income, but about a fourth of the female heads were in this position. Those without income presumably were supported by the sons or daughters living with them. Possibly they were contributing services or the use of a family home.

A much higher proportion of women than men in this population group were without money income, the proportion varying with marital status. The percentage of each of these marital groups in the nonfarm population, both those living in families and those not so living, with money income in 1947 was as follows:[25]

MARITAL CLASS	PERCENTAGE WITH MONEY INCOME	
	Men	Women
Single................	83	68
Widowed.............	82	63
Divorced.............	99	81
Separated.............	98	73

One sees here the indirect effect of age as well as sex upon economic status. Many of the widowed were aged and unable to earn, and many of the women would have found it difficult to return to the labor market. Many of the divorced and separated women without income were doubtless young and with a family status similar to that of the single.

The economic position of widowed, divorced, or separated women with children warrants special attention. Only about a fifth of the group had children under eighteen, and about a twelfth had children under six.[26] Over half of the former and over two-fifths of the latter group of mothers are reported as earning. The percentage of each marital class with children under six who were in the labor force in April, 1948, was as follows:[27]

Marital Class and Number and Age of Children	Percentage of Women in Labor Force
All widowed, divorced, and separated........	39
With children under 6....................	45
Without children under 6................	38

25. U.S. Bureau of the Census, *Current Population Reports*, Series P-20, No. 23. The base for these percentages was the civilian noninstitutional nonfarm population as nearly as it could be estimated. The exclusion of the 15 per cent living on farms gives a clearer picture of the economic status of these population classes, since many of those living on farms, although working, were unpaid. The number fourteen to seventeen with money income was estimated on the basis of data in other reports and excluded from the totals.

26. Two per cent of the widowed, 15 per cent of the divorced, and 27 per cent of the separated had children under six (see U.S. Bureau of the Census, *Current Population Reports*, Series P-20, No. 23).

27. U.S. Bureau of the Census, *Current Population Reports*, Series P-50, No. 11, and Series P-20, No. 23.

Marital Class and Number and Age of Children	Percentage of Women in Labor Force
Widowed: all	31
With children under 6	48
Without children under 6	30
Divorced: all	70
With children under 6	67
Without children under 6	70
Separated: all	49
With children under 6	36
Without children under 6	54

Clearly the presence of preschool children was not the deterrent to earning that it was in the case of married women living with their husbands. Over a fifth of all women with children under six in the labor force were widowed, separated, or divorced, although they were only about 6 per cent of all such mothers. Economic pressure was clearly operative here.

The following comparison makes clear the effect of a father living and present in the family group upon the earning of mothers:[28]

	PERCENTAGE OF MOTHERS IN LABOR FORCE	
	Married, Husband	Widowed, Divorced,
AGE OF CHILDREN	Present	Separated
Under 18	17	51
All under 6	10	47
Some under 6 and others 6–17	12	38
All 6–17	27	66

WHO SUPPORTS THE NONEARNING FAMILY MEMBERS?

When there is but one income recipient in a family, there is no question as to who supports whom. All members rely upon the income from this single source. Nor when husband and wife are the only sources of money income does this problem arise. Both are jointly responsible for the money and services necessary for their own maintenance and that of their children below school-leaving age. Their joint income is probably allocated much as it would have been if only one had been responsible for it.[29] It is the economic relation of other income recipients and other family members that poses the problem; for example, the economic relation of earning sons and daughters to their parents or dependent siblings.

We are asking here, not who are a person's presumptive dependents, but whom does he actually support? He may be supporting in whole or in part those for whom by prevailing standards he should not be responsible. Conversely, a person may not be meeting a responsibility for support that according to these standards is his. The social judgment concerning a giv-

---

28. U.S. Bureau of the Census, *Current Population Reports*, Series P-50, No. 22.

29. This assumption may be disputed, and we have no evidence bearing upon it. The earning wife may, of course, have expenses that the nonearning does not.

en economic relation between family members varies with the blood or legal relationship. Clearly we are satisfied with and not striving to change the dependency of children upon their parents. The compulsory school age in a sense defines the minimum period of this dependency. Dependency beyond that point would be judged by the benefits to the dependent versus the adverse effects upon other family members. Extension of dependency of able-bodied sons or daughters for any reason except to secure education of individual and social benefit is generally disapproved. If the parents' income is inadequate to maintain children below school-leaving age at an acceptable level, the situation calls forth social concern. We are not satisfied if the mother must supplement the father's money income unless it does not affect the family adversely and does not increase her total working time beyond that of other workers. If older children must supplement the father's money income to make it adequate to support younger children, that again is considered unsatisfactory. Their recognized responsibility if beyond school-leaving age is self-maintenance. Economically independent old age is also clearly the desired arrangement, as well as arrangements by which the support of the orphaned or the disabled does not pass, except on a voluntary basis to the nearest of kin. Supplementation of the income of adult children, of parents, or other relatives, young and old, ideally would come after primary responsibilities are met, would represent something over and above the minimum necessary for their maintenance, and would be an expression of affection and generosity rather than a duty.

In a family with several income recipients other than husband and wife, any one of these recipients may be partially supported by one or more of the others, he may be self-supporting, or he may not only maintain himself but contribute to the support of others. It is by no means a simple problem to determine which is the case. Statements that a family member who is one of several income recipients places all or a specified proportion of his income in the family fund do not throw light upon the question at issue. They indicate something about the control of the income—who determines its allocation—but not whether the person's income is sufficient to pay for all the goods and services he enjoys. Family members cannot be said to be contributing to the support of others unless they are meeting all their own personal expenses for clothing, recreation, and the like and turning over to their families more than their proportionate share of the common expenses. It is difficult to find a satisfactory formula for determining each member's "proportionate share" of the outlays for housing, household operation, and similar overhead household costs. Mrs. Douglas has suggested that the son's or daughter's share of the general household expense may be found by dividing the total by the number of "equivalent adult males" in the family, and that to this should be added a proportionate share, similarly determined, of the mother's expenses. She argues:

> If the working daughter is to share evenly in the necessary household expenses she must bear her share of the mother's costs just as much as her share of the rent or of the fuel bill. An argument that is based on purely supplementary costs that would assign her no share in the mother's expenses should logically assign her no share in the other relatively "fixed" costs of the household such as rent, fuel, kitchen furnishings, plumbing. These costs would go on in her absence just as inevitably as would the services of the mother.[30]

The proportionate share of each member so determined will vary with the size of the family and their level of living. The larger the family, the smaller the proportionate share of any one member. But the higher the level of living, the larger each one's share. Mrs. Douglas points out that if the earning daughter wants to improve her standards of food, houseroom, furnishings—those items shared by the whole group—she can do so only by raising the standard of the whole family. Her dress and recreational expenditures may be disproportionate to the standard of living of the family, but she cannot easily provide herself with better food without providing it also for her parents and her younger brothers and sisters. The girl in the working-class family may actually contribute to the support of others in the attempt to improve her own living conditions. A contrary situation arises for the sons and daughters living at home as members of families whose standards of living are set by the relatively large earnings of the father. These sons and daughters could not usually pay their proportionate share.

CONCENTRATION OF SUPPORT BURDEN

Whether one looks at the actual number of persons who share the family income or the number each individual's income is presumed by prevailing standards to support, the concentration of support burden at any moment of time is apparent. As already pointed out, a tenth of the income recipients in 1947 were persons not living as family members. Any contributions they made to the support of others were probably offset by contributions from others to them. The burden of support of that part of the population without money income, well over half of the total, fell upon the other nine-tenths of the income recipients. Each family had on the

---

30. Dorothy Douglas, "The Cost of Living for Working Women," *Quarterly Journal of Economics*, XXXIV (1919–20), 239–40.

average two members without income. The wives without income shared, of course, the income of their husbands and the children that of their parents or parent. Whether husbands and parents bore the whole burden of their support is unknown. About a tenth of all family members without income were unmarried or separated persons eighteen and over.[31] Some of this dependent group, probably close to half, were undoubtedly young persons in school supported by their parents. If all dependent relatives of this age had been distributed evenly among families, about one-fifth would have had one to support.

The major burden of support of the nonearners in the population falls upon those responsible for the maintenance of children under eighteen. At least three-fifths of the money-income recipients eighteen and over in 1947 had no such responsibility. If they carried such a responsibility, it was not for their own children.[32] The full picture of the concentration at any one time of the burden of support of children is not seen simply by noting that it is carried by two-fifths of the income recipients. The uneven distribution of the children themselves among those having children must also be taken into account. About half of the children under eighteen in April, 1948, were in the one-seventh of the families having three or more. Thirty per cent were in the 7 per cent of the families having four or more. Thus it would appear that, if the parents or a parent were wholly responsible for the support of their children under eighteen, about a tenth of the income recipients nineteen to sixty-four years of age would provide the money income for half of the children. In some of the families in which both parents were present the mother supplemented the income of the father.[33] Such mothers helped to support about a sixth of the children living with both parents. If the fathers in the families in which the mother did not earn had no aid from another source, they were the sole support of five-sixths of the children living with both parents, or about three-fourths of all those under eighteen. Such fathers were only a little over a fifth of all income recipients.

The question still remains: In multi-earner families how many parents received assistance in the support of their children as well as how many supported or helped to support older children or other relatives? From

31. About seven-tenths of all unmarried or separated family members eighteen and over were income recipients.
32. Included in those having such responsibility are married men and women living with their spouses who had such children and widowed, divorced, and separated parents. A liberal allowance was made for possible parents not living with their children who were contributing to their support.
33. "Parents," here as elsewhere, include adoptive and stepfathers and stepmothers.

the 1940 census data certain minimums can be established. At least a fifth of all earners at that time were the sole earners in families in which were found almost three-fifths of the children. Since there was the usual uneven distribution of children in these one-earner households, it also appears that at least one-eighth of all earners at that time were the sole earners in families in which were found over half of the children.

It has already been indicated that one expression of the community's concept of a person's responsibility for the support of others may be found in the deductions permitted in personal income-tax laws. Data available from the income-tax returns of the state of Delaware show the distribution of the dependents of those filing returns in certain years. In Delaware the general rule is that all persons twenty-one years of age and over, citizens or residents of the state during any part of the income year, must file a return. A specified deduction from income may be made for "each person (other than husband or wife) dependent upon and receiving his or her chief support from the taxpayer if such dependent person is under twenty years of age or is incapable of self-support because mentally or physically defective."[34] Actual dependency of persons under twenty and those incapable of self-support is here the test of an allowable deduction. The dependents claimed were distributed among married couples and others as follows in 1938:

Class of Claimant	Percentage of Dependents Claimed
All	100
Married couples	87
Others	13
Heads of families*	11
Not heads of families	2

* "A head of a family maintains a home for himself and others who are chiefly dependent upon him for support" (Bureau of Economic and Business Research, University of Delaware, *Delaware Income Statistics . . . 1936, 1937, 1938* [Newark, Del., 1941], p. xxxvi).

The same concentration of the burden of support of these dependents is found as in the case of children under eighteen in the country as a whole. The percentage of all married couples and others claiming three or more dependents and the percentage of all dependents claimed by each class of claimant were as follows:[35]

34. Bureau of Economic and Business Research, University of Delaware, *Delaware Income Statistics, Compiled from Income Tax Returns for 1936, 1937 and 1938* (Newark, Del., 1941), I, 190.

35. Only married couples making joint returns are included here. Unmarried or separated persons with no income and no dependents were assumed to be themselves dependents and are not included among those with returnable or other income. These persons twenty-one and over and presumably dependent were about 5 per cent of all filing returns.

CLASS OF CLAIMANT	PERCENTAGE OF RETURNS CLAIMING		PERCENTAGE OF DEPENDENTS IN FAMILIES WITH	
	Three or More Dependents	Four or More Dependents	Three or More	Four or More
Married couples........	16	8	54	33
All others.............	3	1	31	15
All income recipients....	11	6	50	31

On the basis of these returns, about one-sixth of the married couples claimed that they were supporting over half of the dependents found in such families, and about a twelfth claimed the responsibility for a third. About a tenth of all the economic units in the state claimed responsibility for half of the dependents, and about a sixteenth for a little under a third.

CHAPTER V

AMOUNT AND ADEQUACY OF FAMILY INCOMES

INTEREST in the distribution of families by the amount of their incomes arises from one or both of two sources. One, the most recent, is in the economic effects of the distribution, its implications with respect to aggregate consumption and savings, and hence to the functioning of the economy, the level of production, employment, and income. A second and much older interest is in its immediate implications with respect to the welfare of the population represented. Again attention may center on either of two aspects of the distribution. One is the degree of equality shown, whether a large proportion of the total income goes to a small proportion of the people. A second and different question concerns not the relative economic welfare of the population but the adequacy of the consumption levels attainable, the proportion of the population whose incomes are sufficient to provide a level which in some specified sense could be called satisfactory. In the one case the welfare of a family or group of families is measured by its command over goods as compared with that of another; in the second case welfare is measured by the family's ability to attain a defined standard.

Table 1 shows the distribution of families and individuals not in families by the amount of their money incomes in 1947 as reported by the Bureau of the Census.[1] Incorrect interpretation of the welfare implications of such distributions is common. Before a money-income distribution for a particular year is taken as a measure of economic welfare, or the degree of equality shown compared with that of an earlier distribution, a variety of questions must be raised. One set of questions would have to do with distortions and inaccuracies introduced by defects in the sample design and in the collection and handling of the data. There is probably in all field studies an underreporting of small and sporadic sources of income, for example, and an underreporting of families with large incomes. These are not, however, the questions that concern us here. Rather they are those that would arise if both design and execution of the study had been perfect.

1. "Family" in this study includes all related persons living together; "individuals," all members of the civilian, noninstitutional population not so living. To the latter group some investigators add those who, although they were living with related persons, were considered to be independent economic units.

82

FACTORS AFFECTING DEGREE OF EQUALITY

The welfare implications of a change in the degree of equality in family incomes between two points of time cannot be determined without consideration of the many factors that may cause changes in the equality of income distributions. We cannot deduce from changes in the equality of the distribution of families that individual rates of pay and profit have changed in the same direction or to the same degree. A better measure of the equalizing character of economic forces would be the changes in the

TABLE 1*

DISTRIBUTION OF FAMILIES AND INDIVIDUALS BY TOTAL
MONEY-INCOME LEVEL FOR THE UNITED STATES, 1947

Money-Income Level	Families and Individuals	Families	Individuals
Number (thousands).....	44,372	37,279	7,092
Per cent...........	100.0	100.0	100.0
Under $500...........	7.4	4.4	22.5
$ 500–$999..........	8.7	6.4	21.5
$ 1,000–$1,499........	8.9	7.8	14.7
$ 1,500–$1,999........	9.3	8.8	12.0
$ 2,000–$2,499........	11.0	11.3	10.7
$ 2,500–$2,999........	10.1	10.7	6.7
$ 3,000–$3,499........	10.0	11.3	3.9
$ 3,500–$3,999........	7.5	8.4	2.7
$ 4,000–$4,499........	6.0	6.9	1.3
$ 4,500–$4,999........	4.2	4.7	0.8
$ 5,000–$5,999........	6.6	7.7	1.0
$ 6,000–$9,999........	7.8	8.9	1.1
$10,000 and over......	2.5	2.7	1.1

* Source: U.S. Bureau of the Census, *Current Population Reports*, Series P-60, No. 5, Table 2, recalculated omitting individuals without money income (see Table 16, p. 23). About one-eighth of the individuals are reported as without money income. About a twentieth of the family heads are also so reported, but in most if not all cases other family members had money income.

distribution of men eighteen to sixty-four by the amount of their contract income. The income distribution of families will be affected not only by changes in rates of pay and profit but by changes in size and composition of the social family, that is, the related persons who live together in the same dwelling unit. It is also affected by the number of family members in receipt of income, whether it be contract or civil rights income. Along with a rise in the number of persons receiving income of either character or in the amount of such income may come the establishment of a separate residence and a consequent increase in the number of families. Thus average family income and the proportion above a given level might decline, although there had been no decline and possibly an improvement in the economic welfare of the persons represented. The average family income and the degree of equality may rise from the employment of children at an earlier age than before or from an increase in the employment of wives and mothers. Again, if the period between school-leaving and marriage declines, the number of families, their size, and their distribution by income will alter, although there has been no change in population or income per person. So also would they alter if the proportion of subfamilies declined, whether the subfamilies were young married couples, widowed daughters with children, or aged parents of the family head.

MONEY INCOME AS A MEASURE OF CONSUMPTION LEVEL

The limitations of such distributions as those shown in Tables 1 and 2 as measures of relative economic welfare during the year of study must also be noted. These limitations are set by the answers to such questions as these: How accurately does current money income measure consumption level attainable or attained by the various income classes? May equality in consumption levels attained be greater than the equality in income? Do the differences in the money incomes of urban and farm families measure accurately differences in consumption levels attainable? Does the equivalence of the money incomes of families in the same income bracket mean equivalence in attainable consumption level for the persons represented in those families?

If the welfare implications of these distributions are to be correctly understood, it must first be noted that the income which serves as the basis of classification is current income; that is, it is that received or accruing during the year of study. For some families this is about the same as that received in previous years and approximately what they expect for at least a few years to come. For others, the current income is considerably above or considerably below their future expectations or their immediately preceding financial position. Thus in the same income class are families varying greatly in their anticipations and in their previous economic status. In good times the proportion enjoying incomes better than previously will be high; in bad times, the reverse. At all times some during the year of study will have experienced illness or other misfortune; some will have had good fortune and some bad in their economic enterprises. In other words, some of those currently with low incomes formerly were at higher levels and will be again. Likewise some of those currently with relatively high incomes will next year have moved downward. Not all those at the bottom of the distribution are members of a class that may be designated as "the poor."

Common knowledge as well as statistical evidence makes us certain that
the consumption and savings levels attained by families with the same current income will be different because of the differences in past experiences
and future expectations. Those for whom this is a bad year will use savings
previously accumulated or go into debt to maintain something approaching their usual consumption level. Similarly those for whom it is a good
year will, if they anticipate future reverses, make greater savings and
alter their consumption level less than if they anticipated a succession of

TABLE 2*

DISTRIBUTION OF FAMILIES BY TOTAL MONEY-INCOME LEVEL, BY SIZE OF FAMILY,
FOR THE UNITED STATES, NONFARM AND FARM, 1947

MONEY-INCOME LEVEL	ALL FAMILIES	FAMILIES OF SPECIFIED NUMBER OF RELATED PERSONS					
		2	3	4	5	6	7 or More
Nonfarm							
Number (thousands)....	30,759	9,928	8,104	6,215	3,330	1,596	1,586
Per cent..........	100.0	100.0	100.0	100.0	100.0	100.0	100.0
Under $1,000.........	7.7	14.7	5.1	4.3	2.4	3.5	5.1
$ 1,000–$1,999.......	14.7	19.5	15.8	10.9	8.7	9.5	11.6
$ 2,000–$2,999.......	22.8	24.0	24.5	22.2	20.8	17.0	19.6
$ 3,000–$3,999.......	21.6	18.8	22.4	25.1	23.5	20.4	18.9
$ 4,000–$4,999.......	13.0	10.3	14.1	15.3	13.6	14.9	12.4
$ 5,000–$5,999.......	8.2	6.1	8.1	8.8	11.4	12.3	8.3
$ 6,000–$9,999.......	9.4	5.0	7.9	10.3	15.7	18.4	18.3
$10,000 and over......	2.6	1.6	2.1	3.1	3.9	4.0	5.8
Median income........	$3,198	$2,629	$3,180	$3,419	$3,756	$3,977	$3,748
Rural Farm							
Number (thousands)....	6,520	1,751	1,452	1,178	826	566	746
Per cent..........	100.0	100.0	100.0	100.0	100.0	100.0	100.0
Under $1,000.........	25.1	40.1	23.7	15.8	20.1	18.0	19.4
$ 1,000–$1,999.......	25.8	23.4	25.3	29.8	23.2	25.2	29.8
$ 2,000–$2,999.......	18.5	14.9	18.1	18.9	21.9	24.0	19.0
$ 3,000–$3,999.......	10.8	8.9	11.7	12.1	9.6	13.8	10.5
$ 4,000–$4,999.......	5.5	3.8	6.7	6.6	6.6	6.0	4.0
$ 5,000–$5,999.......	5.1	3.0	4.5	7.8	5.7	4.8	6.5
$ 6,000–$9,999.......	6.2	4.5	7.4	6.5	6.1	6.6	7.5
$10,000 and over......	2.9	1.5	2.6	2.5	7.0	1.8	3.5
Median income........	$1,963	$1,358	$2,054	$2,167	$2,298	$2,274	$2,039

* Source: U.S. Bureau of the Census, *Current Population Reports*, Series P-60, No. 5, Table 3.

such years. What is suggested is that the true economic position of families with respect to levels of consumption or savings generally attained or attainable is imperfectly indicated by their incomes for a single year. Relatively large savings or debt payments in one year may be followed by the use of savings or incurring of debt. Consumption levels *attained* tend for these and other reasons to be more equal than current incomes and levels of saving less equal.

ADDITIONS TO AND DEDUCTIONS FROM MONEY INCOME

Money income may imperfectly represent the level of consumption or savings currently attainable or attained for other reasons than those noted. If personal tax levies are large and progressive and have not been deducted from income, as they have not in Tables 1 and 2, the income shown is not the income disposable for consumption goods or for savings.[2] Further, if incomes reported are to measure consumption levels attainable, not only deductions from, but additions to, money income are necessary as discussed at length in chapter iii. To measure the true consumption level attainable, it would be necessary to take account of the goods and services provided wholly or in part at public expense, of those provided without pay by family members, provided as pay by the employer, or available because of ownership acquired prior to the period in question. Wide differences will exist in these respects between families, differences especially between farm and urban families, home-owning and home-renting, those benefiting largely and those relatively little from free public services, those with a wide range of services performed by the wife or mother, and those with few from such a source.

All these possible supplements to the command over goods given by money income are, it should be noted, consumption goods and services of specific kinds, the character determined in some cases by public authority, in others by decisions made earlier with respect to home ownership or the acquisition of other consumer durables, in others by what family members with the resources at hand were able to provide. There is some evidence that, although such goods and services raise the consumption level in the category in which they fall, the level in other categories is determined primarily by money income. That is, families with home-produced food have a higher level of food consumption than do those with the same money income but without home-produced food, but their clothing level is about the

2. If the tax as under the Social Security program confers upon the payee or his dependents the right to receive a future income under certain conditions, the amount may be considered as compulsory savings and the remainder as disposable for consumption or additional savings.

same. Home-owning families have a higher housing level than renters with the same money income, but in other respects their level is about the same. Money income alone is freely disposable among the alternatives the market offers. Although money income alone does not measure the consumption level attainable, the level of living generally desired or even that considered essential cannot be attained or long maintained without a minimum income in the form of money.

EFFECT OF PRICE AND OTHER MARKET CONDITIONS

Equivalent money incomes do not always mean equivalent command over goods and services in the market. As is well known, dollars vary from time to time in purchasing power. The money income distribution in 1950 differs from that found in 1947. The median income in dollars is higher and the percentage of families with incomes under $2,000 is lower. But unless account is taken of changes in prices between these two years, a feat not easily accomplished, it is impossible to say whether the consumption level attainable by most families is higher, lower, or the same as before even if proper allowance has been made for changes in tax deductions and nonmoney income. Prices tend to vary not only from time to time but also from place to place, especially for items like housing, which cannot be moved from one place to another, and for those that are of local origin. The character of the goods found in the market will vary as between communities, since the market supply reflects the demand of those who buy in that market. Items found in one market may be missing in another. The relative price structure of one market as well as its general price level may also vary from that of another, with inevitable results upon the consumption pattern in the two markets. The specific respects in which the attained level is inadequate or adequate, whether food, housing, or other respect, will therefore vary as between families with the same money income. Climatic and other environmental conditions may alter also the resource cost of attaining a given standard, of warmth or of cleanliness, for example.

Even in the same market, families with the same money income do not always have the same command over goods. In time of war or other period of prolonged shortage, rationing schemes may be instituted which deny certain goods to some but make them available to others. The maximum allocations may vary with age or occupation. Patterns of consumption are thereby changed, although not necessarily the total outlay on all consumption items. In the ordinary peacetime American market Negroes rarely have the same range of choice as does the white population. They buy or rent such an important item as housing in a restricted market and consequently must pay a higher price for the same quality than do the whites. Since in many communities many of both the publicly and the commercially provided utilities and services are inferior to those provided for the white population, the consumption level attainable cannot be said to be identical with that attainable by others with the same income.

EFFECT OF FAMILY SIZE AND COMPOSITION

Even among families with access to the same market and with the same nonmoney income, equivalent money income does not mean equivalent economic welfare for their members because of the variations in family size. If all families had the same income, there would still be inequality among the members because of differences in their number and age. When the income-receiving units include both "individuals" and families, the former will constitute a disproportionate part of the lower end of the distribution. Well over two-fifths of the lowest tenth of the units shown in Table 1 were individuals. Correspondingly they were only an insignificant part of the highest tenth. If the poor were defined as the lowest tenth of such a distribution, the economic situation of persons not living in families would be the object of special concern. Such an identification of the poorest group in the population would obviously fail to take account of the fact that the income of those units which were families must support at least two persons and in many cases four or more. Similarly, in a distribution of families by income the least well off in terms of the consumption level attainable by the family members are not necessarily those at the bottom of the distribution. Families with only two members are disproportionately numerous at the low-income levels. Over half of the lowest tenth of the families shown in Table 2 were of this size, but less than a fifth of the highest tenth. Conversely, less than a seventh of the lowest tenth of the families had five or more members, but a fourth of the highest tenth. The incomes of the two-person families tend to be low, not only because there can be no more than two income recipients but because heavily represented here are the young, recently married couples, and, even to greater degree, the elderly whose children have left home. The larger families at the low-income levels are usually a parent or parents with young children; at the high levels they include in greater proportion grown children or other adults in addition to the family head. In the lowest tenth of the families a third of the members were in families of five or more; in the upper tenth, well over half were in families of this size. Three-fourths of the members of the families in the upper tenth of the distribution were eighteen or over. Thus the proportion of potential income recipients was high. In the middle-income ranges covering two-fifths of the families, less than two-thirds were of this age.

Can account be taken of the variations in family size and composition and a distribution effected in which those grouped together are approximately equal in consumption level if they have access to the same market and have the same nonmoney income? The population might be distributed on the basis of income per person, that is, the family income divided by the number who shared it. Many of those at the bottom of the income distribution shown in Table 1 would be found nearer the top in the new distribution, and many of those at the top would be shifted downward. Members of small families move up and of large families move down when the income scale changes from a per-family to a per-person basis. Who, then, were the persons lowest in the economic level? Those found in the lowest tenth of the "recipient units" which included both individuals and families? More than 50 per cent of the persons therein represented were not living in families or were members of two-person families. Or were they that tenth of the population whose economic position is lowest if measured by family income per member? Three-fifths in that case would have been members of families with five or more members.

Income per person, however, is clearly only a rough measure of the relative economic position of the population. Nor is the consumption level attainable by members of families of different size but the same age and sex composition indicated by division of the family income by the number of members. The family of four adults, for example, does not need twice the income of a family of two to enjoy the same consumption level. This is but another way of saying that there are economies in family living. Some costs are incurred for the joint benefit of all family members. The family of four does not need to spend twice as much for housing or equipment or reading material as the family of two in order to attain the same level of enjoyment for its members.

ATTEMPTS TO DEVISE A SCALE OF INCOME EQUIVALENCE
FOR FAMILIES OF DIFFERENT SIZES

Attempts to solve this problem by expressing family size in number of "consumption units" rather than number of persons go back as far as Engel, pioneer in the analysis of data on family incomes and expenditures. For the reduction of persons to consumption units a scale is necessary, a representation of the consumption of the various family members relative to that of one chosen as unity. Engel chose the infant as his consumption unit, which he called a "quet," but those who later dealt with the problem have used the adult male. Thus if the cost of the father's food is taken as unity, that of the child under two might be .5, of the mother .9, and a family of three persons be composed of 2.4 food consumption units. The first work in this country on the problem of consumption units was that of Sydenstricker and King. From the analysis of data on family expenditures collected for the Public Health Service they developed what they called an "ammain" scale. The "ammain," or consumption unit, on their scale was the expenditure for "adult male maintenance." A distribution of families by income per ammain they argued would correctly show the relative economic position of the population.[3] In the thirties Faith Williams attacked the problem anew as a part of a study made by the Bureau of Labor Statistics of the money incomes and disbursements of wage-earning and lower-salaried families living in cities. In the reports of this study families were classified by their disbursements per consumption unit, using scales developed by Miss Williams and her staff.[4] Thus at the same economic level appeared families with quite different total incomes, the smaller incomes in the group being those of small families, the larger those of families with many members among whom to divide the larger amounts.[5]

The difficulty in devising a scale that will represent correctly the economic position of persons of different age and sex arises in connection with those goods used jointly. Their relative shares of those goods which by their nature are individually consumed—food, clothing, and the like— may fairly readily be determined. The shares are likely to alter somewhat with income, but only slightly and slowly. But how determine each person's share of the benefits and services from housing, furnishings and equipment, automobile, reading material, certain recreational equipment? Sydenstricker and King assumed it would be the same as in the case of the goods individually consumed, and Miss Williams that each person's share was the same, thus returning to a per-person division.

Another approach to the problem was made later by the Bureau of

3. See E. Sydenstricker and W. I. King, "The Measurement of the Relative Economic Status of Families," *Quarterly Publication of the American Statistical Association*, XVII (new ser., 1921), 842–57. W. F. Ogburn presents an excellent analysis of their problem and its solution in *Methods in Social Science*, ed. Stuart A. Rice (Chicago: University of Chicago Press, 1931), pp. 210–19.

4. See U.S. Bureau of Labor Statistics, Bull. No. 637 (Washington: Government Printing Office, 1939), Appendix G.

5. If the consumption units instead of the families had been distributed by disbursement per unit, the results would have been different in degree of equality shown.

Labor Statistics.[6] The question posed was, What ratio must the income of families of two or other number bear to that of families of four if they are to be able to live at the same level? The data available on family incomes, expenditures, and savings were analyzed to discover at what income families of differing size met certain tests of equivalent welfare. It was assumed that "families attaining the same degree of adequacy of diet, housing or medical care may be considered as at the same level of living."[7] Two separate scales were ultimately developed, one based on the percentage of families with good or fair diets from the nutritive standpoint and one based on the percentage of income allocated to savings. The two indexes of degree of economic well-being gave quite similar scales. The relative costs of providing the same level for families of various sizes were as follows, taking as the base the cost for a family of four:

Number of Persons	Adequacy of Diets	Amount of Savings
1	......	46.0
2	65.1	66.4
3	83.7	84.4
4	100.0	100.0
5	114.8	114.1
6	128.62	127.0

It should be noted that all types of families were included among those of each size in arriving at these relatives. Families of two include both the young and the old married couple; families of five, those with all children of high-school age and those with all under six. On the basis of these relatives the money incomes that would have given families of varying size the same consumption level as families of four with an income of $3,000 would have been approximately as follows in 1947 after allowance for tax deductions in all cases:

Size of Family	Income
Two	$1,980
Three	2,580
Four	3,000
Five	3,420
Six	3,840

The conclusion to be drawn from the preceding discussion is that families at the lowest economic level are not those with money incomes below $500 or $1,000 or other designated amount. Some with money incomes above the amount chosen cannot provide as high a consumption level for their members as others with money incomes below. If differences in price

6. See *Monthly Labor Review*, LXVI (February, 1948), 179.
7. *Ibid.*, p. 180.

levels from place to place and in goods available without money outlay could be allowed for, further shifting would take place. Farm families at least must be segregated from the nonfarm in any attempt to distinguish those at the lowest economic level. Farm families with money incomes of $500 can undoubtedly attain a higher consumption level than those in large urban centers, although how much higher when all factors are allowed for we are at present unable to determine. In a particular community, except for differences in family size, the relatively poor correspond more closely with those with lowest money income. In a nation-wide distribution the poor are not so easily identified.

The imperfections of money income, or in fact of any income expressible in monetary terms, as a measure of relative economic welfare among families diversely situated have led to the attempt to distribute families or groups of families by a level-of-living score or index computed directly on the basis of their possession or use of specific consumption goods and services. These goods are so chosen that their possession is an indication of the possession of others, both those complementary and those designed for quite different uses. If the methodological problems involved are satisfactorily solved, what results is a distribution of families on the basis of their degree of attainment of the consumption pattern that is generally sought. Degree of attainment would be the product of market situation, family composition, the nonmoney as well as the money income. Economic welfare would be measured directly by attained consumption level, and the difficulties of using current incomes of families and individuals not in families would be by-passed.[8]

ADEQUACY OF CONSUMPTION LEVELS ATTAINABLE

What has been emphasized up to this point is that current money income of families or other recipient units is an imperfect measure of the level both of consumption and of saving attained or attainable. Now it must be noted that, even if it were a perfect measure, we would know only how the command over goods of one family or group of families compared with another. We would not know whether the level attained or attainable by all, or all but a few, was that which by appropriate standards could be considered adequate. The question with which we must now concern ourselves is: What proportion of the population is not able to attain an ade-

8. No method has yet been devised of placing urban and farm families on the same scale with respect to their attained consumption level. Various attempts have been made, however, to distribute farm families on the basis of a level-of-living score or index (see Oklahoma Agricultural Experiment Station, Technical Bull., No. 9 [April, 1940]; Ohio Agricultural Experiment Station, Bull. 624 [September, 1941]).

quate level of consumption and saving? The problem may be defined as the measurement of the extent of poverty. Poverty in the sense that some have less than others is an inevitable accompaniment of inequality in income. Poverty in the sense that the incomes of some are insufficient to feed, clothe, house, or otherwise provide for themselves and their dependents in an acceptable manner is a different matter.

Zweig, in his report of an inquiry made in London in 1946–47, observes:

> It is easier to speak about poverty than to define it. Any definition . . . must be evaluative, i.e., based on a value judgment although not necessarily arbitrary and subjective. . . . We have at least . . . three different standards for denoting poverty, one based on the judgment of society, the second on the judgment of the individual, and the third on the impersonal judgment of science.[9]

Whether or not Zweig's classification of the types of standards from which come judgments of poverty can be accepted without modification, they provide a useful starting point for discussion.

PERSONAL STANDARDS AS A MEASURE OF POVERTY

There is a poverty, says Zweig, that is the product of personal standards of what constitutes healthy and decent living. Such poverty is "felt poverty." "It is an acute sensation of ill-being which finds expression in different ways."[10] This personal standard for tolerable family living

> is very differentiated and graded. It depends on the station in life of the individual, his upbringing, his occupation, his environment and his personal relations. At times it may attain a high level. The individual feels his poverty if he cannot maintain the level to which he is used as a result both of his upbringing and of his former position. Any decline from the position to which he has been accustomed he regards as poverty. . . . Felt poverty is acute in countries with great social contrasts, especially where there is a display of luxury. On the other hand, if a man sees that his fellow-countrymen are also enduring privation, the stress of his felt poverty is less, as, for instance, during war, or during a period of general food scarcity. The stress of felt poverty also increases when the poor think that their poverty is unjustified.[11]

The extent of felt poverty is something that could scarcely be measured. Felt poverty could be greater or less than poverty measured by other criteria. A person or a group may feel poor when their consumption is far above that of the majority of the same community or nation. They may even speak of their "requirements" as if they were other and greater than

9. F. Zweig, *Life, Labour and Poverty* (London: Victor Gollancz, 1948), p. 96.
10. *Ibid.*, p. 98.
11. *Ibid.*, pp. 98–99.

those of others of the same community and time, when in fact the only difference is that they have customarily enjoyed the goods in question and others have not.[12]

SCIENTIFIC STANDARDS AS A MEASURE OF POVERTY

A second standard suggested by Zweig for the demarcation of poverty, the impersonal judgment of science, is one that is rather widely accepted. By this view poverty can be measured by standards as objective and outside the measurer as those by which other phenomena are commonly measured. The assumption underlying it is that human requirements can be determined by scientific methods and the current cost of meeting them estimated. Thus those with incomes inadequate to provide what is required could be discovered and counted. It would also be possible to determine families with sufficient incomes to meet the requirements of their members who were not doing so. The first situation, which Rowntree called "primary poverty," poses an economic problem; the second, which he called "secondary poverty," might be considered an educational problem—at least its reduction would involve a change in personal consumption standards.

The fact is, however, that not only is scientific knowledge of the specific items and quantities of consumption goods and services that human beings require very limited but there are difficulties in extending it. Requirements, that is, means for achieving given ends, can never be scientifically established unless the ends sought are clearly defined. But we do not know, and have scarcely considered other than in rather general terms, the interests or purposes that many consumption goods or certain qualities of these goods are supposed to serve. Yet their use or possession may be urgently desired by all within a given community. They may be highly pleasing and add greatly to the sense of satisfaction, comfort, and happiness. Few consumers' goods are functional in the sense that are producers' goods. Among the most truly functional are medical and hospital services, drugs, and the like. What is required may therefore be stated with some exactitude.[13] In the same category come the nutrients found in food. If longevity, health, and a satisfactory rate of growth in children are taken as ends, these nutrients become requirements in the sense that they are necessary to achieve these ends. It is one thing, however, to say that in

12. See especially Y. Henderson and M. R. Davie, *Income and Living Costs of a University Faculty* (New Haven: Yale University Press, 1928), and review by J. B. Peixotto, *American Economic Review*, XIX (1929), 330; also Peixotto, *Getting and Spending at the Professional Standard of Living* (New York: Macmillan Co., 1927).

13. Dental care falls in a somewhat different class, since the realignment or preservation of teeth is desired for aesthetic as well as health reasons.

the light of current nutritional knowledge the average active male requires on the average 70 grams of protein or 3,000 calories daily, and another to say from what specific foods these must be derived. They may be derived from various sources of widely varying palatability and cost. A list of foods that meet nutritive requirements may not provide meals fit to eat in the judgment of the community and as a diet would be considered totally inadequate.

It may be granted that food serves other needs than nutrition, but can the specific foods that meet them and the amount that is required be scientifically established? During World War II some attention was given to this problem, but the results can scarcely be described as having scientific precision. The National Research Council gave its Committee on Food Habits the task of drawing up a list of those foods essential for morale. This group, whose members were drawn largely from psychology and cultural anthropology, set up ten criteria of the morale value of specific foods and food groups. The foods and beverages held most essential to morale were those popularly regarded as essential, those generally liked or which give consumers the sense of being well fed. The list of "essentials for morale" included many items not among the "essentials for nutrition" chosen by the Food and Nutrition Board from foods commonly used in American communities. Free use of sugar, expensive cuts of meat, white bread, and butter were judged essential as "symbols of status"; coffee and tea for "giving a lift"; soft drinks and alcoholic beverages as essential for recreational occasions, which would fall flat without them; condiments, including sugar, to insure consumption of food nutritionally important; etc. The committee emphasized, however, that it is not the presence or absence of these specific foods which affects morale but something far more subtle, the meaning attached to and the degree of acceptance of their absence.[14] It is clear that, when we seek the requirements for morale, self-respect, or similar values, the specific items arrived at, whether judged to be "scientifically" established or not, are relative to social situations, and the sense in which they are requirements is quite different from those established as necessary to meet biological needs.

The problems involved in establishing what is required in the way of food are magnified and extended when one passes to clothing, housing, furnishings, transportation, recreation, reading matter, and other categories where the interests and purposes served are largely unformulated and are wholly or mainly other than the strictly biological.

14. National Research Council, Committee on Food Habits, *Report on the Morale Building Value of Specific Foods in the American Diet* (Washington, 1942). (Processed.)

THE SOCIAL STANDARD AS A MEASURE OF POVERTY

The third standard that Zweig suggests for distinguishing the poverty level he calls the "social standard."

This standard finds expression in the activities of charitable institutions, welfare measures and legislation, as, for instance, in the rates of old age or widows' pensions, or unemployment benefits. . . . The social standard of poverty expresses to what extent the community is ready to extend its help. . . . This . . . standard . . . will depend on the wealth of the community (size of national income), its sense of solidarity, the extent of help needed (whether a smaller or greater section of the community is affected by poverty) and finally the prevailing ideas about poverty, its causes and results, and the effect of relief measures on national output.[15]

It is true that judgments of what is necessary for individual and family maintenance are implicit in many of the rulings of legislative and administrative bodies in modern communities. Such judgments lie behind the personal exemptions allowed in computing taxable income; they lie behind minimum-wage orders and the allowances given under all types of private and public assistance. It is also true, as he suggests, that there may be a gap between social judgment of need and willingness or ability to support those without income at that level. This would mean that the generality of the community would consider themselves in want if they were not able to live at a level somewhat above that provided the needy.

If there is a standard below which the generality of the community would consider they were experiencing privation, its cost might be considered to represent the dividing line between adequate and inadequate incomes. The group at the poverty level or below might then include not only those supported by the community and those with contract income no greater but some at higher income levels. Poverty would mean income insufficient to secure things commonly desired with a degree of urgency sufficient to warrant describing them as essentials according to prevailing standards. These standards would vary from place to place and time to time and with the general level of income and consumption. Thus poverty would be a relative matter, and the family below the poverty line in one society and at one time might with the same resources be above it in another.

The first question concerning this approach to the problem is one of fact. Is there a prevailing standard with respect to what is essential? Observation, the statistical evidence, and the conclusions of the psychologists indicate that there is and that standards vary not from individual to

15. *Op. cit.,* p. 97.

individual but from group to group. If wants are culture products, then a similarity in judgments of consumption levels, not unique sets of values, is to be expected.

DETERMINATION OF THE SOCIAL STANDARD

If there is a consumption level of such a degree of urgency according to prevailing standards that its cost may serve as the dividing line between incomes to be judged inadequate and those judged adequate, how can it be found? One hypothesis that has been advanced is that it will be found at that point on the income scale where net savings begin to appear; that is, where savers and their savings exceed the dissavers and their use of past savings or the amount they go into debt. The argument is that below that point the urgency of the need for consumption goods is so great that assets are used, credit sought, or families disappear as distinct entities, with their members merged into other groups. By this procedure a single figure would be directly secured, which would be the income necessary to provide the minimum standard of living.

The Bureau of Labor Statistics in 1947 followed a different procedure to attain this end. Its aim was to construct a budget in form suitable for pricing that would represent the goods and services generally considered essential. The procedure adopted was based on the theory that an analysis of families' spending behavior as incomes increased or decreased would disclose which goods and services, in what quantity and of what quality, had such a degree of urgency that in a real sense they could be called necessary. The assumption was that, if a satisfaction point existed which could be considered the dividing line between the more and less urgent needs, it would show itself in the relation between the incomes and the purchases in each consumption category. The records obtained in various field surveys of urban families were therefore analyzed for families of a chosen type and size. As described by the Bureau:

> The relation between amounts bought and changes in income were charted, and that point where the increase in buying showed a tendency to decline relatively was interpreted as the point to be used as the budget level. . . . If families continued to increase the rate of buying as incomes went up, they obviously had an urgent and unfilled need for more of a particular group of articles. At that point where they started to buy in decreasing proportions with larger incomes the budget level was determined.[16]

Thus the items selected for pricing and their quantity and quality were those purchased by families in the income group defined by the point of maximum income elasticity. It is clear that the items so defined are not "needs" in any absolute sense. Some might well be of dubious value from

16. *Monthly Labor Review*, LXVI (February, 1948), 143.

the standpoint of their contribution to well-being. A budget so constructed does not define the requirements for the good life. Rather it represents an attempt to define community standards as expressed in the use of income.

The procedure for budget construction that has been described may not be the answer to the problem, but it is noteworthy in that it represented a search for an objective method of determining items and quantities that should be included. Prior to this time many family budgets had been constructed as necessary tools for the equitable administration of public and private assistance programs. These budgets developed to serve as a guide in determining individual or family allotments have represented the considered judgment of an individual or group of individuals as to the essential items and quantities. Since those constructing the budget were themselves a part of the community, and since they usually examined the data showing the spending habits, their judgments undoubtedly reflected to some degree the prevailing standards of the community. These budgets, however, were not constructed by a systematic procedure and were essentially works of discretion.[17] They were often referred to as authoritative or as based upon expert knowledge of needs. Actually they represented the judgment of those who had given thought to the problem, but not the "impersonal judgment of science." As the science of nutrition developed, care was taken to insure that the foods listed in these budgets would if purchased in the appropriate quantities yield the nutrients recommended by some accepted authority. Thus the budget-makers could say that it would be possible for families receiving income equivalent to the budget total to have fair or good diets.

ESTIMATION OF NUMBER OF FAMILIES BELOW THE POVERTY LINE

Once the difficult problems involved in determining the level of living that meets minimum standards are solved and, if the result is expressed in a commodity-quantity budget, the items are priced and the total cost computed, the next step in the measurement of "poverty" is to compare that cost with the money incomes received in the community in question, either families classified by the number of members or individuals classified by the number of their presumptive dependents. The budget cost and the income necessary to attain the defined level will of course vary with the

17. In the discussion of the budget developed by the Bureau of Labor Statistics in the February, 1948, issue of *Monthly Labor Review* it is repeatedly pointed out that the earlier budgets "involved reliance on the judgment of a person or a group of people" and were therefore in the last analysis subjective, whereas the new budget was determined by objective methods, so that any group of workers using the same data would arrive at a similar conclusion (*ibid.*, p. 131).

number and possibly with the age and sex of those who are to live at that level. In discussing this problem, the Bureau of Labor Statistics says:

To determine accurately a scale of the cost of maintaining families of different sizes at the same level of material well-being, budgets . . . should be prepared for the most representative types of each family size. These should include, at least, the single individual, both under and over 60 years of age, perhaps separately for men and women; the couple under and over 60; the husband-wife family with two children and with three children; and the broken family with one and with two children.[18]

In lieu of such budgets the Bureau developed the scale previously discussed for measuring the budget cost for families of different sizes.

Several studies of the sort here suggested have been made in Great Britain. The first comprehensive attempt to measure the extent of poverty in a community was that made by Charles Booth in 1886–92. The results of his study were published in several volumes entitled *Life and Labour of the People in London*. About forty years later a *New Survey of London Life and Labour* was made and the results published under the title given. Following Booth's pioneer investigations similar studies were made in other British towns. In these later studies the cost of a carefully prepared budget was compared with the results of a field survey of families and their incomes. The first study of this character was made by Rowntree in York for the year 1899 and published under the title, *Poverty: A Study of Town Life*. In 1935–36 and again in 1950 he repeated this study and compared the results with those of the earlier survey.[19] Bowley made similar studies in four other English cities, the first in 1913, the second in 1924.[20] Ford added to this series a similar investigation in Southampton for the year 1931.[21]

No studies have been made in American communities of the character of the British studies described. Nor do we have the distribution of families by number of members and income in any community on the basis of which, if we had an acceptable standard, we could draw a "poverty line." One can, however, use the data available to illustrate certain of the results of such a measurement. Let us assume that the distribution of families of various sizes by income in a certain urban community was as shown in the Census report for all nonfarm communities in 1947. The proportion

18. *Ibid.*, p. 179.
19. B. S. Rowntree, *Poverty: A Study of Town Life* (London: Macmillan & Co., 1901); *Poverty and Progress* (London: Longmans, Green & Co., 1941); *Poverty and the Welfare State* (London: Longmans, Green & Co., 1951).
20. A. L. Bowley, *Poverty and Livelihood* (London: G. Bell & Sons, 1915); *Has Poverty Diminished?* (London: P. S. King & Sons, Ltd., 1925).
21. Percy Ford, *Life and Work in a Modern Port* (London: George Allen & Unwin, Ltd., 1934).

of families with incomes under $2,000, $2,500, and $3,000 would then have been as follows:

Money Income	Percentage of Families
ˮUnder $2,000	22
Under $2,500	34
Under $3,000	45

If now adjustments are made in these incomes for federal income-tax deductions and for differences in budget cost due to differences in family size, the following proportions of these families would have been unable to attain a consumption level costing a family of four $2,000, $2,500, and $3,000.[22]

Cost of Level for Family of Four	Percentage of Families Unable to Attain Level
$2,000	19
$2,500	29
$3,000	41

Thus if the budget that cost a family of four $2,000 were the poverty line, about a fifth would have been below it; if $2,500, a tenth more; and if $3,000, another eighth, not far from the proportions if family income without any adjustments had been taken as the criterion of poverty. The great change is not in the proportion in "poverty" but in the composition of the group placed below (and above) the dividing line as one or the other measure is used. The proportion of families with two, three, four, and five or more members in poverty in each case would be as follows if $2,000 as family income or as cost of a given consumption level for a family of four is taken as the measure:

	PERCENTAGE DISTRIBUTION OF FAMILIES	
SIZE OF FAMILY	Income below $2,000	Income Insufficient To Attain Level Costing Family of Four $2,000
All sizes	100	100
Two	50	38
Three	24	21
Four	14	16
Five or more	12	25

22. The income tax paid by a given family depends upon the age composition of the family as well as its size and upon the number of income recipients other than husband and wife and the number of dependents each may claim. Income from earnings in an employment covered by the Social Security Act is also subject to a tax deduction. The percentages given are only approximate.

If the identification of the poor is important, the measure used to determine who falls below the poverty line is important. The one measure shows a relatively high proportion of two-person families in poverty; the other, a relatively high proportion of those with many members.

ADEQUACY OF FAMILY INCOME VERSUS ADEQUACY OF INCOMES OF INDIVIDUAL INCOME RECIPIENTS

Up to this point attention has been given only to the total money incomes of families, the sum of the earnings or other income of all members. Implicitly the question raised was, If all income from all family members were pooled, could a satisfactory level of living for all members be attained? The character of the benefits derived by all family members from the fact that two or more of those members are income recipients depends on the method of allocation of the several incomes. If the income of one is kept in large part for his exclusive use, the other family members may be living at a level determined by income from other sources. We do not know the extent to which incomes are pooled, or the extent to which earning sons and daughters or other relatives pay their proportionate share of the joint family expenses, or the extent to which they receive from other family members contributions toward their personal expenses. Pooling would mean, as was noted in chapter iii, that the total income from all sources is allocated for the joint and separate benefit of the members, as it would be if it were derived from a single source. The earnings of young children, especially those not yet full-time earners, are probably pooled. The British investigators who have attempted to measure the adequacy of family incomes have advanced the opinion, based upon their observations, that, the lower the total income, the more likely it is that incomes from all sources will be pooled. Only infrequently would one member retain for his exclusive use an amount disproportionate to the needs of other family members when those needs were great.

Even if the incomes of all family members are pooled and a family income from several sources measures as accurately the attainable consumption level for all members as a family income to which there is but one contributor, situations of import if welfare judgments are to be made may remain undisclosed. Is the income raised to the adequacy level only by virtue of the wife's earnings to be accepted as satisfactory without further question? Are the earnings of the older sons or daughters to be considered in determining whether incomes are adequate for the maintenance of young children? If so, in how many families are adequate consumption levels attained only by virtue of contributions from members who, by ac-

cepted standards, should not be earning or who have assumed a responsibility that is not properly theirs?

Questions concerning income adequacy might therefore well center not
on total family incomes but on the incomes of individuals in relation to
their family status and the number of their presumptive dependents. How
many married men, for example, are able to maintain their wives and
children at an adequate level without the assistance of others? How many
of the widowed and divorced men and women with children are in a similar situation? How many of the widowed, divorced, or single who have no
dependent children have adequate means for self-maintenance? If the in-

TABLE 3*

DISTRIBUTION OF NONFARM POPULATION EIGHTEEN YEARS OF AGE AND OVER
BY AMOUNT OF MONEY INCOME IN 1947, CLASSIFIED
BY SEX AND MARITAL STATUS

MONEY-INCOME LEVEL	SINGLE†		WIDOWED		DIVORCED		SEPARATED		MARRIED, LIVING WITH SPOUSE	
	Male	Female	Male	Female	Male	Female	Male	Female	Male‡	Female
Under $1,000....	27	21	44	56	24	38	20	49	10	50
$1,000–$1,999...	35	48	21	26	20	35	29	34	18	32
$2,000–$2,999...	25	24	18	11	33	21	31	11	31	14
$3,000–$3,999...	9	4	10	4	15	3	13	4	23	3
$4,000 and over..	4	3	7	3	8	2	7	2	18	1
Median income	$1,641	$1,603	$1,291	$875	$2,171	$1,325	$2,028	$1,019	$2,708	$1,009

* Source: U.S. Bureau of the Census, *Current Population Reports*, Series P-20, No. 23, Table 10.
† All income recipients 14–17 were assumed to be single and to have had in 1947 money incomes under $1,000.
‡ Those not reporting any money income in 1947, about 3 per cent, are excluded.

comes of all married men met the adequacy test, one could be assured that
the wives who earned did so from choice, not necessity, and that their
earnings raised the family level of living above the minimum. Similarly,
if adults without dependents had incomes sufficient for self-support, contributions from others would likewise be voluntary in a sense they would
not otherwise be, and the sharing of a home with others would be chosen
because of a desire for the association involved, or to lessen certain costs
of living for all concerned, rather than from economic necessity.

Data on the incomes of individuals classified both by their marital and
their parental status do not exist either for a particular community or for
the nation as a whole. The income distribution of nonfarm income recipients in 1947 classified by their marital status is shown in Table 3. It will
be noted that about 28 per cent of the married men reported money in-

comes under $2,000, and 59 per cent under $3,000. But what percentage had incomes adequate to provide a specified level of living for their wives and children if they were dependent entirely upon the income currently received? If we assume that the distribution shown was that in a particular community, and, further, that the parental status of married men in each income group was the same as that of all nonfarm men, the same calculations can be made as were made for families taking into account the entire family income.[23] The percentage of all nonfarm married men having no children under eighteen and having one, two, three, or more was as follows in 1947:

Number of Own Children	Percentage of Non-farm Married Men
All	100
None	46
One	24
Two	17
Three or more	13

In a community with the married men and their children distributed by income, as indicated, after allowance for federal income tax, the percentage able to attain the consumption levels costing $2,000, $2,500, and $3,000 for a family of four would have been as follows:

Cost of Level for Family of Four	Percentage of Married Men with Income Insufficient To Provide Specified Level
$2,000	23
$2,500	35
$3,000	49

About a fifth of those without children would not have been able with current income to attain the level costing a family of four $2,000, but well over two-fifths of those with four or more children would not have been able to do so. Over a third of those without children would not have been able to attain the level costing the family of four $3,000, but more than four-fifths of those with four or more children would have fallen short. It must be remembered that if a Social Security tax had been taken from these incomes, if savings had been allowed for, if the standard for child dependency had been raised to age eighteen or above, or if children were more numerous at the lower income levels than was assumed, the propor-

23. In making the calculation that follows, allowance was made for the probability that among the 46 per cent without children were most of the married men without income and that the lowest income group was heavily weighted with the relatively old and the relatively young without children, thus making the percentage without children more than 46 at the bottom of the distribution.

tion with inadequate incomes by one of these standards would have been greater. It should also be noted how the results are affected by the choice of the standard that defines the poverty line. If the cost of the level of living chosen was $3,000 for a family of four in this hypothetical urban community, about half of the married men would have had, under the conditions assumed, incomes insufficient to provide it. If the consumption level used as the yardstick could be attained by a family of four for $2,000, the proportion below the poverty line falls to less than a fourth.

Whatever standard is chosen, the proportion of children whose fathers' incomes would have been insufficient without supplementation to provide a specified level would be higher than the proportion of married men with incomes below the adequacy line. Under the conditions assumed, about 30 per cent of the children under eighteen living with both parents would have been in families where the father's current money income would not provide the equivalent of a $2,000 level for a family of four, between 45 and 50 per cent where it would not provide the equivalent of a $2,500 level, and over 75 per cent where it would not provide the $3,000. More than half of the children (not far from three-fifths) whose father's income could not provide the consumption levels described would have been in families with three or more children. About one-tenth of the children in all nonfarm communities were living with but one parent, usually their mothers. If the incomes of these mothers were similar to those of the divorced and separated women shown in Table 3, many would fall below the poverty line.

ECONOMIC EXPERIENCE OF FAMILIES
DURING THEIR LIFE-SPAN

We now turn to a question probably more important than the situation of families at a particular time, that is, their economic experience during their life-span. From the data now available it is possible to recapitulate fairly accurately their history in other respects, the ages of husband and wife when they are first married, their domicile status after their marriage, the period that elapses before the first child is born, the maximum size the family usually attains, the length of time one or more children must be cared for and supported, the age of the parents when the last child leaves the home, the period before the marriage is broken by death, and the subsequent experience of the one widowed. Of the economic history of families far less is known. It is certain, however, that the economic history of families will reflect the economic history of the time and place in which their lives are spent. Their economic experiences will vary with the particular employment or group of employments from which the income is derived, and, as the size of the family waxes and wanes, as the children pass from infancy to adulthood, and the parents from youth to old age, the demands upon income will first increase, then decline.

STATE OF THE ECONOMY AND THE ECONOMIC EXPERIENCE OF FAMILIES

Families of the typical pattern formed in 1900 experienced the depression of 1907 when they had only preschool children, the prosperity period of World War I when their burden of support was toward its maximum, and the high-income period of the later twenties when their children were young adults. The Great Depression of the thirties would have hit the parents, or the surviving parent, when they were elderly, possibly sweeping away their savings and making economic independence impossible. Upon the other hand, families formed in 1910 experienced prosperity when their family was at its maximum, depression as their children were trying to get an economic foothold, but they had the prosperous forties in which to build up their savings prior to retirement. Families formed in 1920 experienced depression when needs were approaching the maximum but moved into a prosperity period as their children were seeking jobs or a college education. What will happen to these parents in their later years is unknown. Two conclusions are inescapable: (1) the economic welfare of families cannot be disassociated from the general level of income and employment in the society of which they are a part and (2) the effect upon them of prosperity or a depression, of inflation, deflation, of shrinking or advancing asset values, depends upon the particular period of the family life-span in which it is encountered.

ECONOMIC EXPERIENCE AS A FUNCTION OF SOURCE OF INCOME

The effect of the occupational skills or type of employment of the family head upon the course of his income during the family life-span is evident. There are skills and capacities, innate or acquired, that are relatively scarce and those that are relatively abundant, those that are in steady demand and those in irregular demand, those that are in increasing and those in decreasing demand, those for which the market is to some degree controlled and those for which the market is wide open. The economic experience of the family in which the head is a physician will be different from that in which he is an unskilled worker. Among the unskilled or semiskilled are those who early attach themselves to an industry for the products of which there is steady or increasing demand, and those who must later seek employment elsewhere or work irregularly. These well-known facts are behind the income distribution of married men previously discussed. Those toward the top are the full-time workers in the better-paid employments during the year in question.

The median money incomes of men in the major occupational groups in 1947 were as follows:[24]

Occupation	Median Money Income
Professional workers:	
Self-employed	$5,472
Salaried	3,075
Semiprofessional workers	2,625
Farmers and farm managers	1,456
Nonfarm business proprietors, managers, and officials:	
Self-employed	3,084
Salaried	3,673
Clerical and kindred workers	2,654
Salesmen	2,687
Craftsmen, foremen, and kindred workers	2,746
Operatives and kindred workers	2,373
Service workers	2,096
Farm laborers and foremen	846
Other laborers	1,707
All	2,230

The distribution of employed married men among nonfarm occupations was as follows in April, 1948:[25]

Occupation	Percentage of Nonfarm Married Men
All	100
Professional and semiprofessional	7
Business proprietors, managers, and officials	18
Clerical, sales, and kindred workers	13
Craftsmen, foremen, and kindred workers	24
Operatives and kindred workers	24
Service workers	6
Laborers	7

About an eighth of all employed married men were farm operators, managers, or laborers during the survey week.

It is not only the difference in level of income between various occupa-

24. U.S. Bureau of the Census, *Current Population Reports*, Series P–60, No. 5.

25. Based upon employment during the survey week (see U.S. Bureau of the Census, *Current Population Reports*, Series P-20, No. 23).

tional groups that is important for family welfare. The course of incomes of different character over time is also important. In which occupations, affecting what number of income recipients, do the earnings move upward with age and experience? The general course of the needs of most families through their life-history is clear. What is the course of the incomes of the breadwinners? Do they in the generality of cases take an upward slant with the birth of the first child and reach a peak when the financial burden is greatest? Or do the incomes of most men reach their maximum in early maried life or before marriage and remain approximately on the same level through the working life except for cyclical changes? The working life of the ambitious, industrious man was once pictured as akin to climbing a ladder, proficiency at one economic level leading to advancement to the next, the business of the enterpriser and his income expanding with experience and growth of the market. Various well-known facts compel us to modify this picture greatly. Most small businessmen, if they survive in that role, remain small businessmen. Through subdivision of process the requisite dexterity in many employments can be quickly acquired. Those who can provide a special skill tend to take what the market offers for that skill throughout their working life. Only a few can or do move from "performance" to the better-paid managerial positions. Management itself requires special skills and knowledge for which men are specially chosen.

These and other often-emphasized aspects of the economic world have, it is clear, great significance in view of the life-history of the typical family. As has been indicated, the line that represents the financial needs of the family rises from an amount represented by the needs of two adults to a peak determined by the maximum number and age of the children before they become economically independent, remains there for an interval, and then declines. What course is the income of the husband and father taking during this time? Wherever the lines representing income and expense near each other, there is strain; where the income curve rises above the expense curve, there is relative prosperity; where it falls below, there are relative poverty, privation, and pressure for income from other sources. From the estimates shown earlier the income must rise more than 50 per cent if the family of four is to live at the same level as the family of two. It must rise still more if the cost of the life insurance men with children are supposed to carry is added. If the typical family has two children born two years apart and each begins earning at eighteen, it would have two children to support for sixteen years, and one for twenty. Advance the school-leaving age, increase the number of children, lengthen the interval between births, and the length and weight of the support burden increase correspondingly.

WHAT IS THE USUAL COURSE OF INCOME?

We do not have data showing the usual course of the income earned by men during their life-history. The Census reports show the median money income of all men, classified by age, in 1947. The figures were as follows:

MEDIAN MONEY INCOME OF MEN

AGE GROUP	Urban	Rural Nonfarm	Rural Farm
25–34	$2,585	$2,480	$1,682
35–44	3,045	2,780	1,987
45–54	2,904	2,519	1,820
55–64	2,617	2,054	1,333
65 and over	1,225	818	725

The medians move up about 18 per cent in the urban and farm communities during the period that the support burden usually increases and about 12 per cent in the rural nonfarm areas. The high point for urban men seems to come not far beyond age forty, and then or soon after median incomes move downward (see Chart I). From a study of incomes in Minnesota, 1938–39, differences in the course of earnings in the various occupational groups can be seen (Chart II). It will be noted that, although the earnings of the professional men in private practice begin at a higher level, rise more rapidly, and begin to decline at a later age than those of other ocupational groups, earning begins at a later age due to the relatively long period of training and apprenticeship necessary. The result is that the period of greatest financial pressure in this group is likely to be in the early years of the family. But after these early years the earnings are likely to rise more rapidly than the cost of family maintenance. In the middle years, unlike the wage-earning group, the economic stress is ordinarily lessened. The family when at maximum size can be maintained at a high level, and the school-leaving age can be postponed to the maximum desirable.

It has already been pointed out that the membership of the various family income classes shown in a distribution is not permanent over time. Some families found in a certain position in one year will in the following year be found at a higher and some at a lower level. In addition to these shifts due to changes in individual incomes, there are those due to the nature of the family itself as an earning and consuming group. The number of earners increases and decreases as well as the number to be supported. All who have attempted to compare the incomes of income recipients with the cost of maintaining those recipients and their actual or presumptive dependents at a specified level, and thereby to draw a "poverty" line, have emphasized that far more families have inadequate incomes for a period of time than are in poverty for their lifetime. Some may remain below the

CHART I

MEDIAN MONEY INCOME OF URBAN AND FARM MEN BY AGE, UNITED STATES, 1947

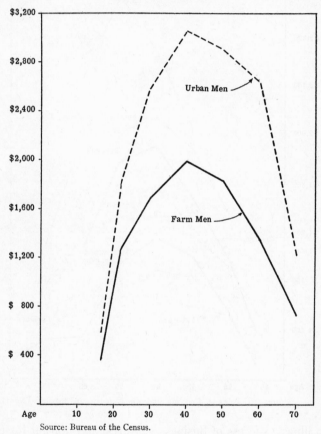

Source: Bureau of the Census.

poverty line through their entire history, but their poverty is deepened and intensified as the burden of support increases and lessened as it wanes. Many others go through a period of relative comfort, then a period of struggle to maintain an adequate standard, enter again a prosperity period when they have amenities and comforts, and possibly move again to a difficult situation if the retirement income is inadequate. Overriding and blurring this picture is the impact of general economic conditions, the general level of employment and income which, as has been emphasized, hits families at various stages and affects some more favorably or more adversely than others. Individual families also have different experiences with

CHART II

MEDIAN ANNUAL EARNINGS OF INDIVIDUALS BY OCCUPATION AND AGE, MINNESOTA, 1938–39

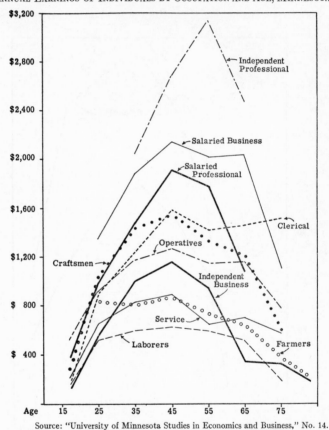

Source: "University of Minnesota Studies in Economics and Business," No. 14.

respect to illness, success of business ventures, and market for the skills of the breadwinner. Some are broken early by death or divorce. But the very nature of the family itself during its normal life-span has inevitable and unavoidable consequences.

CHAPTER VI

IMPROVEMENT OF INCOME POSITION

VIEWED as a social problem, the improvement of the income position of families takes three forms. One is the general and basic problem: Under what conditions and by virtue of what arrangements and stimuli does the general level of income move upward? The second: Under what circumstances or by virtue of what developments does the degree of inequality diminish? The third: What diminishes the proportion of those who are in poverty?

To the individual family the problem likewise may be how to escape from what its members deem poverty, the lack of those things which by their personal standards are essential for their well-being. Or it may be how to secure more of the amenities, comforts, and luxuries desired. To what extent the desire to improve income position in unrelated to a felt lack of essentials or desire for specific goods but is based instead upon the fact that increase in income carries with it increase in prestige and symbolizes success to the family and to others is unknown. In this chapter it is primarily individual efforts to improve economic position that will be under review, the routes that families follow or may be instructed to follow to achieve that end. The limitations upon individual efforts and the social effects of some means adopted to improve income position will also be noted.

PRIMARY VERSUS SECONDARY POVERTY

Until what Rowntree called "primary" poverty is distinguished from "secondary" poverty, the discussion of either the social or the individual problem is likely to be confused.[1] Families in primary poverty are those with incomes insufficient to obtain minimum necessaries as defined either by their own or by a more general standard. To secure them, they must use savings or go into debt. Those in secondary poverty have income sufficient to attain the standard but use their resources in such a way that they lack many things considered necessary. As Rowntree describes it, "Some portion . . . is absorbed by other expenditure either useful or

1. B. Seebohm Rowntree, *Poverty: A Study of Town Life* (London: MacMillan & Co., 1901), pp. 86–87.

111

wasteful."[2] Rowntree reported that secondary exceeded primary poverty in York at the turn of the century. His estimate seems to have been based upon observations of the housing, the health, and the living conditions of the families visited. From the total number showing lack of things deemed essential he then subtracted the number with incomes insufficient to meet the cost of his budget. When he came to make his second survey, however, he concerned himself only with primary poverty. It was impossible, he concluded, to assess the number in secondary poverty reliably.[3]

Attempts to reduce secondary poverty must of course be based upon knowledge of the "useful or wasteful" expenditures that have caused it. Among the "useful" expenditures that may reduce families to poverty are those for expensive and prolonged medical care. Special needs or extraordinary demands upon income may impoverish the family with income otherwise adequate. Drinking and gambling were the "wasteful" expenditures that most frequently reduced Rowntree's families to poverty. "Wasteful expenditure" is but another name for misuse of income, and the reduction of secondary poverty would involve attempts to alter its use. Secondary poverty is not directly, at least, an economic problem. It is a problem of the impulses, drives, and compulsions that lead to a seeking of certain types of satisfactions rather others, a problem of ignorance, opportunities, values, and interests rather than of limited income.

INDIVIDUAL EFFORTS TO REDUCE PRESSURE ON INCOME

There are five possible ways, suggested or practiced, by which families can reduce pressure upon money income and thus their sense that it is not enough. One, the most obvious, is to increase the amount available, either by increasing the income of those presently providing it or by increasing the number of earners. Another is to take steps to make the money income go farther by increased home production or by care and prudence in buying and in use. A third is to reduce "wasteful" expenditure by a better allocation of funds. A fourth is of quite a different character: keep down the birth rate and thus the mouths to be fed. The fifth is more likely to be an admonition to others than a prescription for one's self: "Lower your sights." Do not want so much; thus "felt poverty" will diminish.

Great emphasis has always been placed upon increased home production, less extravagance and waste, greater prudence and intelligence in the use of income, as a means of improving economic well-being. To some it has been, and to some it still is, "the" remedy not only for secondary but for pri-

2. *Ibid.*, p. 87.
3. B. S. Rowntree, *Poverty and Progress* (London: Longmans, Green & Co., 1941), Introduction, p. vi.

mary poverty. When the state of the poor first became a subject for systematic study in the latter part of the eighteenth and first part of the nineteenth century by Eden, Davies, and others, the investigators were wont to prescribe not only changes in public policy, especially with respect to the poor law, but changes in the domestic economy of those in distress. The more favorable position of laborers in the north as compared with those in the south of England was in part ascribed to the former's adoption of that cheap and wholesome food, the potato. The spread of the pernicious habit of tea-drinking was compared unfavorably with the abandonment of the use of wholesome home-brewed ale. Later it was the soup kettle that was found lacking in the kitchens of the poor.

In the avalanche of information, advice, and special pleading directed to the housewife that comes over the air and from the daily press, magazines, pamphlets, and books is that designed to help her effect economies as well as that designed to stimulate new wants and a desire for more expensive goods. But the theory and practice of economical living, generally speaking, are not mysteries to those who feel pressure upon money income. They reduce the list of goods and services purchased and increase the number of goods the family members produce or of services they perform. Wastes are reduced; leftovers used; articles repaired or renovated. Purchases are more carefully considered. Time and effort are spent in finding when and where goods are cheapest; lower-cost substitutes are purchased if possible. The slack that can be taken up by these methods varies with circumstances. There are obvious limits upon home production imposed by location, resources, and time available. Gardening, poultry, and cow-keeping are impossible for the urban family even if notable economies could be effected thereby. Shoes must be purchased and similarly a long list of goods and services. Planning, economical purchasing, and careful use can reduce the money cost of maintaining a given level of living only to a degree. The fact is that only an industrial and domestic revolution and a change in consumption standards in many respects could reduce greatly the command over money required to maintain a designated consumption level. It would be an interesting but difficult exercise to estimate how much the money cost of the level defined in the budgets developed by public welfare and other agencies could be reduced through changes in the knowledge and skill of the homemaker, increase in consumer production, reduction in waste, improved planning of expenditures, and better buying techniques. Many of these are indeed desirable goals, but they are not complete solutions of the problem of poverty or answers to the question of how to get ahead in the world.

In *The New Survey of London Life and Labour* the following comment is made:

Statistical estimates of poverty and comparative indices of material progress are necessarily based on estimates of "real" income, and of its adequacy to furnish a family with the minimum means of subsistence. This is the only practicable method because it is the only one which admits of quantitative measurements. Nevertheless it has its shortcomings when its results are applied to the individual families. . . . In any particular family the degree of actual deprivation depends not only on the deficiency of purchasing power, but also on the use made by the housewife of the purchasing power at her disposal.

Good and bad catering, marketing and cooking are therefore important elements in the ultimate assessment of individual well-being or poverty, though they cannot be brought into account in statistical estimates or comparisons, and moreover there is room for a good deal of difference of opinion as to the precise nature of the relationship between poverty and bad housekeeping. There is a school of thought which regards ignorant and wasteful methods of marketing and cooking on the part of the housewife, and the irrational prejudices and fastidiousness of the family for which she caters, as important factors in the causation of poverty, while an opposing school of thought tends rather to regard defects in working-class household management as the direct result of bad housing and poverty.

This difference of outlook has more than an academic importance, since it leads to deep differences of view as to the possibilities and means of practical improvement.[4]

INDIVIDUAL EFFORTS TO INCREASE MONEY INCOME

Our economy is based upon the assumption that everyone strives to maximize income whether it be in the form of pay or profit. Acting under this motivation, parents seek to equip their children with vocational skills and professional knowledge in high demand, and individuals seek the place, the kind of employment, and the employer offering the best rates of pay or, if in business for themselves, the line of production or service that will yield maximum returns. Thus labor and other productive resources tend to be apportioned as market demand indicates and to be utilized most effectively. In such an economy the consumer is king; his preferences in so far as they can be expressed and detected through dollar votes on the market govern the uses of resources. The account of the deliberate departures from this arrangement by state action, the obstacles to effective expression of consumer preferences and to response by producers, would modify this picture considerably. Here the major questions are, How strong is the motivation to increase income? and What are the chances of success?

Current rates of pay clearly are not the only consideration in choice of

4. Sir Hubert L. Smith, director, *The New Survey of London Life and Labour* (London: P. S. King & Son, 1934), VI, 23–24.

job or place of employment. Workers have their preferences as to kind of work and working conditions. They consider the probable permanence of the employment and opportunities for advancement, but this is but considering income in the long run. Climate, living conditions, schools available for children, and like considerations may outweigh income differences. Attachments to those with whom they work or near whom they live may deter workers from moving from one job to another. Yet in our culture consumption standards continuously move upward and press upon income. Money income per se is a measure of prestige and achievement. One can scarcely escape the conclusion that in the minds of people generally economic welfare is an important although not the sole component of welfare in general. Economic welfare, moreover, is generally measured by money income. Prices are taken as given or as conditions over which the individual has little or no control. Standards of what is necessary are also taken in the main as an unalterable fact. Although, as was said, under economic pressure families attempt to improve buying practice and other skills, exercise greater foresight and economy, and do more things for themselves, it is to increase in money income that they look for improvement in their economic situation.

It is in the expanding, dynamic economy that individual efforts to maximize income are most successful, one in which new opportunities for employment and enterprise are many, widely available, and made known. Many of those represented in the income distribution at a particular time can maximize their money incomes, however, only within relatively narrow limits. They must take what the market offers for the skills and capacities they command. Dependents, limited resources, or age make it impossible or impracticable for them to alter to any great degree their general occupational classification. Few men shift from one profession to another or from one skilled occupation to another. They change employer, industry, or place of employment. Even spatial mobility is likely to be limited with increasing age and family responsibility, and the older workers are unlikely to move unless forced to by unemployment or extreme underemployment. Their fortunes are tied up with the demand for the product or the service they can furnish. They were largely committed in their early maturity to the prevailing wage scale for a particular type of labor or the returns in a particular type of business enterprise. Extended opportunities for education and widened knowledge of the market improve in the main the position of newcomers to the labor market and thus alter the income distribution. Those who have been earning for some time are likely to put their emphasis upon job security, a dismissal wage, seniority rights, tenure, and other efforts to insure that they are the last to be laid off or dismissed. They are likely to emphasize the maintenance of the status quo, to feel that their economic interest lies in the preservation of wage differentials. Less clearly perceived, perhaps, is their stake in the upward movement of the general income level by which means they too move to new levels.

INCREASING FAMILY INCOME BY INCREASING

NUMBER OF EARNERS

Although most individuals already in the labor market can increase their incomes only within narrow limits, if at all, the income of the primary earner may be supplemented by the earnings of one or more of the other family members. The frequency of at least part-time earning by those under eighteen has been noted. The school-leaving age is likely to be near the legal minimum in families with many dependents and low parental incomes. In one of the earliest studies of family incomes and expenditures in this country, made by Carroll D. Wright, then head of the Massachusetts Bureau of Statistics of Labor, it was suggested that earning by the wife or children under fourteen was an indication that the husband's wages were inadequate.[5] Today we might hold that the full-time work of children under eighteen was such an index.

The most frequent source of supplementation of the husband's income today is from the earnings of the wife. It has already been noted that the frequency of earning by married women increases as the husband's income decreases. The gainful employment of the wife may be regarded as both a result and a remedy for inadequacy of income from other sources. It is an unfortunate result which brings with it a new problem when there are children left without needed supervision, or where the family level of living is adversely affected by her inability to perform necessary tasks, or where in the attempt both to earn and to perform her usual tasks the length of her working day or week far exceeds that of other workers. The greater the inadequacy of money income from other sources, the more likely are the children to be inadequately cared for and the more likely is she to attempt to do all the usual work in the home as well as that for which she is paid. The more likely also is she to take any job that offers without regard to wages, hours, and working conditions. Supplementation of husband's earnings by the wife is a satisfactory remedy for inadequacy of those earnings when home conditions facilitate such supplementation.

    5. Massachusetts Bureau of Statistics of Labor, *Sixth Annual Report, 1875*, "Condition of Workingmen's Families," Part IV, pp. 195, 442.

Under these conditions her earnings may be desirable whether his income alone provides an adequate level of living or not. When she does not have to earn, in the sense that essentials would be lacking without it, she is less likely however to take a highly unattractive job.

It is the families without children whose incomes are most likely to be raised by the wife's earning. Where there are children, and especially where these children are below school age, the mother's earning is less frequently the family's solution of the income problem. Unfortunately, it is among these families, especially those with three or more children, some of whom are likely to be quite young, that the highest proportion of fathers have incomes insufficient to provide the desired level of living. It is undoubtedly the young couples and the middle-aged without children who find the joint income a satisfactory method of raising their consumption level. Among the older families the age of the wife is often a deterrent to earning.

COLLECTIVE BARGAINING AS A MEANS OF
IMPROVING ECONOMIC POSITION

In the preceding discussion the ways in which families, and individuals, each acting singly, may attempt to improve their economic position have been emphasized. May wage and salary earners find that by acting collectively through a labor organization their rates of pay will move upward? Will this be to the general social advantage? Increase in wage rates is by no means the sole objective of labor organizations. Their other objectives *in toto* may outweigh wage increases in importance. Agreements arrived at through collective bargaining include such matters as hours of work, vacations, working conditions, procedures for hiring, firing, laying off, and promoting workers as well as sickness, old age, and other benefits. Organization has been extending among American workers. In general, its movement has been from the more highly skilled and better paid to the less skilled and lower paid; from craftsmen to all employed in a mass-production industry; from the highly urbanized to the less urban areas; from the older to the more recently industrialized areas; and from wage-earners to those called salary-earners. About two-fifths of all wage- and salary-earners were members of unions in 1946.

Union membership is not always optional with the worker. There may be no union in his trade, community, or plant. The law may obstruct or facilitate the organization and growth of labor unions, as may the attitudes of the business community and of the workers themselves. Unions cannot operate at all unless there is legal recognition of their right to exist and of workers to join them without penalty. Recognition of the right to strike, to picket, and otherwise to attempt to dissuade others from working for or buying from the offending employer are also important sources of strength. The union is placed in an even more favorable position if by law employers must, if requested, bargain collectively.

Some workers may find that union membership is not optional for them, because, although there is a union, membership, openly or in effect, is denied to them. Only white workers, for example, may be eligible for membership, or the quota set for new entrants, apprentices, or trainees may be full. Entrance fees may be inordinately high with the obvious purpose of limiting membership. If membership is a condition of employment, the trade or occupation is in effect closed to those whom the union excludes.

As has been suggested some workers may find that union membership is mandatory if they are to work in a particular trade or for a particular firm. Membership may be a condition of employment or of retaining employment. Unions with such "closed-shop," or union-shop, agreements are in a strong position. Organizational efforts may be at a minimum. The total group must pay dues to the union treasury and come under union rules.

Whether union membership is optional or mandatory, to what level and under what conditions may the union raise the wages of its members? The individual asks, "How will the standard rate fixed by union agreement compare with what I would otherwise secure both immediately and in the long run?" He will also ask whether the stability of his employment will be greater or less with or without the union. The question for the community as a whole is somewhat different. It is not simply, What can a union do for its members? but, To what level can it increase their wage rates without reducing the number employed and without affecting adversely the wages of other workers?

The essence of unionism as it operates in negotiations concerning wage rates is that a single seller of the service or services in question is substituted for many competing sellers. The situation of the buyer, that is, the employer, when confronted with a single seller is obviously different from what it is when there are many. The monopoly represented by the union may be partial or complete. It is complete not only if it speaks for the total labor supply at the moment, but also if, by control of entrance to the trade or occupation, it is able to limit the supply. Such a union may raise the wages of its members over what they would otherwise be, but "outsiders" will find employment only at levels below what they would otherwise attain. If product prices rise, the real wages of those who use them decline. Clearly also the wages of those in the occupations into which the "excluded" workers go tend to be lower because of the increase in supply.

Less clear are the effects of unionism when the union, although acting as a single seller, has no control and attempts to have no control over supply through limitation of membership. In periods of prosperity for business in general or for a particular industry, when there is high demand for labor, unions that are capably led are able to prevent the lag in wage rates that was common before they existed. Thus they offset the effect of the immobility, ignorance, and inertia of the individual workers. As they may prevent lags in a generally upward movement of wages, they may also by establishment of a standard rate iron out discrepancies in rates between employers and localities.

It may be agreed that unions can prevent lags in the upward movement of wage rates and standardize rates, but can they raise them above what they would have been in the long run? Here is the crux of the problem. They may do so if by virtue of unionism and its effects the productivity of the workers is increased. Does it follow that, if there is no increase in productivity, they can do so only at the expense of unemployment? At this point the situation of the employers, the buyers of labor, becomes of great importance. If the employer is but one of many firms whose products are selling in the same market, it is clear that the wage rate paid can be no higher than that paid by competitors. If collective bargaining is industry-wide but the industry is composed of price-competing firms, a wage rate that cuts down the net revenues will lead to a cutback in production, and the unemployed workers will be reabsorbed in this industry only at a lower wage rate. If they turn to other industries, the increase in supply will likewise depress rates. These effects may be concealed in a dynamic society where improvements in technology are taking place, but it still remains true that the wage can be no higher than it would otherwise have been without the effects noted.

In actual fact unionism operates largely in a world of limited price competition. The buyers of labor, the employing firms themselves, if not partial or complete monopolists, may be few in number. The price at which they sell is not a competitive price in the sense that it is when sellers are many and acting singly. The competition is among products and brands and processes of production. In such a situation without organization many workers as sellers would confront one or few buyers. Not only is it possible under these circumstances that the wage rate may be raised above the preunion level but that it may be raised without decreasing employment, and even possibly increasing it. With a standard wage rate the employer's profits may not be maximized by decreasing output and number employed.[6]

Chamberlain in analyzing this situation says, "American unions have benefited by the relaxation of competitive standards." It still remains true that there is a limit beyond which wage rates cannot go without creating unemployment. But:

> Businesses relieved of inexorable pressure by the market are in a position to make concessions in collective negotiation which otherwise they might not be in a position to make. . . . So important has the relaxation of competitive restraints been to the unions that where businesses have not achieved this for themselves the unions have been forced to provide it for them by organizing small-scale individual employers on an association basis. Every metropolitan area has . . . associations of building trades and contractors, dry-cleaners, laundries, truckers, barbers and so on, supported by the labor unions who realize the damaging effect on wage and working standards of competition from any of the individuals who compose the local industry.[7]

CHILDREN AND POVERTY

In her book *Nation and Family* Mrs. Myrdal says, "The dilemma has to be faced: the chief cause of poverty is children."[8] The relation of the size of the family to the adequacy of the family income to maintain the family members at a given level was discussed in chapter v. The number of persons that a given income must support is a function not only of the number of children who are born and survive but the length of the period they are dependent. Lowering of the school-leaving age would reduce the burden of child support carried by families with children and the estimates of the proportion in poverty at any one time. American families have consistently raised their standards with respect to the education of children. The proportion of young persons eighteen and over in school has been increasing. In April, 1950, a fourth of the civilian noninstitutional population eighteen and nineteen years of age was enrolled in school. The social objective is to increase these proportions. A reduction of the period of child dependency would not generally be regarded as a solution of the problem of poverty.

Overpopulation is clearly a basic cause of poverty in a large part of the world. Along with high birth rates go high death rates and a per capita

---

6. A calculation of profits at various rates of output, product prices, and costs with and without standard wage rates will show that the employer who has no or few competitors may increase output and number employed if a standard wage rate exists.

7. Neil W. Chamberlain, *Collective Bargaining* (New York: McGraw-Hill Book Co., 1951), pp. 351–52.

8. Alva Myrdal, *Nation and Family* (New York: Harper & Bros., 1941), p. 66.

income and level of living beside which "poverty" as judged by American standards is comfort or luxury. These are the countries that pose the problem pondered by Malthus when as a young clergyman in 1798 he wrote his famous *Essay on the Principle of Population.* How can we raise the level of living of all mankind, he asked, if population continues to press upon the means of subsistence? Only if birth rates decrease as well as death rates and the means of subsistence increase at a higher rate than does the population. The overpopulated countries are generally the underdeveloped, that is, the nonindustrialized with productive methods in agriculture and elsewhere that give a low yield per worker. With increase in capital investment and improvement in techniques would the general level of well-being increase? Death rates could be reduced, but, if birth rates are not, population pressure continues.

Population increased rapidly in most of the Western countries following the Industrial Revolution, but the ultimate fall in the birth rate previously noted in the United States caused more apprehension than approval. A high over-all rate of natural increase has not been considered a factor in the problem of poverty in this country. Immigration, it is true, has been restricted to dam the flow from the overpopulated countries. The relation of population to the means of subsistence is shown by the upward movement of per capita income, while at the same time the school-leaving age has moved upward and the age of retirement and length of the work day and week have moved downward.

One other facet of the relation of children to poverty remains to be examined—the differential birth rate. In this country as in others the birth rate is inverse to economic status. The Bureau of the Census reported the following relationship between number of children under five per 1,000 married women fifteen to forty-nine classified by family income in April, 1949:[9]

Family Money Income	Children under Five per 1,000 Married Women Fifteen to Forty-nine (Standardized for Age of Women)
Under $1,000	677
$1,000–$2,000	628
$2,000–$3,000	580
$3,000–$4,000	571
$4,000–$5,000	476
$5,000 and over	407

Ideally the relationship studied would have been between the birth rate and the usual income of the husband rather than the current income of all

9. U.S. Bureau of the Census, *Current Population Reports*, Series P-20, No. 27 (Washington, February, 1950). (Processed.)

family members. Other studies using other tests of economic status, such as rental value of the home, have consistently shown the same relationship, however.[10]

A variety of factors, their relative weight unknown, affect the birth rate in societies like our own, the general standard of living, standards for child care, the whole mode of earning and living, prevailing attitudes toward childbearing and rearing, the family size considered ideal, and knowledge and acceptance of birth-control methods. Income, present and expected, at any one time is variously correlated with these factors, but the over-all result is as shown. Mrs. Myrdal reasons on the basis of observations in Sweden and other societies like the United States that "the most important explanation of the apparently irrational relation between low income and large family is . . . that the very process of rationalization has spread at different speeds among the different groups." In her opinion the data showing "the richer the family, the fewer the children" "relate only to the transition period." There is a "different time order and velocity in the acceptance of birth control" by the different social groups.[11] Thus, although at any one time in the modern industrial countries there may be an inverse relation between income and number of children at each level, over time the difference may be diminishing.

POVERTY AND CONSUMPTION STANDARDS

Families feel poor when their incomes are insufficient or barely sufficient to provide what by their standards is essential. Are there forces at work which force these standards continuously upward? Instead of the struggle for more income, should families seek contentment with what they have, thus allaying the tension, decreasing the striving and the degree of felt poverty? The extent of poverty found in any community is also a function of the consumption level that defines what is necessary by prevailing standards.

It is true that our forefathers did not "need" as much as we do, but it is also true that the more that is generally desired and enjoyed, the more that, in a real sense, is "needed" by everyone. The consumption standards that make us feel poor and by which we measure extent of poverty are not

10. P. K. Whelpton and C. V. Kiser, *Social and Psychological Factors Affecting Fertility* (New York: Milbank Memorial Fund, 1946), I, 18. The inverse relationship between economic status and birth rate does not necessarily mean that in a distribution of families of all types by income the proportion of children at the lower income levels is greater than the proportion of families. The distribution of children under eighteen by family income was approximately the same as the distribution of families in the Census study of family incomes in 1947.

11. Myrdal, *op. cit.*, p. 62; see also *ibid.*, pp. 48–67.

absolutes always and everywhere the same. Rather they are relative—relative to the general level of income and consumption. If the budget priced by Rowntree in York in 1899 to measure the extent of poverty is compared with those recently constructed for similar purposes, great differences appear. The family diet allowed for in the first Rowntree budget included no fresh meat; boiled bacon three times during the week was the only meat. No eggs were included, and the only vegetables besides potatoes were dried peas for pease pudding and vegetables for vegetable broth twice a week. Most of the houses priced contained no bath. All outer garments for men were to be bought in the secondhand market. In recent budgets only the automobile and, of course, the house might have been used by a previous owner. The wife was allowed one pair of shoes and two pairs of stockings per year and one of each article of underclothing.[12]

Similarly one may compare the clothing budget for an American workingwoman given by Carroll D. Wright in the report of his pioneer study of the condition of wage-earning families in Massachusetts in 1875 with another constructed in 1946 by the same state agency. Both budgets purport to show the clothing required, but the "requirements" altered greatly in the seventy years that separate their compilation, a reliable indication that the economic status of Massachusetts workingwomen generally had altered greatly (see p. 124).

There is little to suggest that consumption standards will move downward in the sense that the quantity and variety of goods considered essential will decline. Rather they are likely to move upward as in the past with the general level of income and consumption. One now sees mention of a television set as a "necessary luxury." Soon the word "luxury" will be omitted. The high and ever expanding American standard has long been a matter of national pride, that is, the avidity with which new goods are seized upon and more and more of varied types of goods sought. Whatever may be the possibility and the desirability of simplifying consumption standards—of lessening the interest in food, clothing, swift transportation, visits to faraway places, material possessions—one fact is certain: the minimum standard, the line that marks off "not enough" from the levels above it in the minds of the community as a whole, will not change unless consumption standards in general change. This minimum standard is a culture product; it moves with and reflects prevailing standards. So far as consumption standards are concerned, ours is increasingly a classless soci-

---

12. Rowntree does not give his complete budget as priced. Sufficient information is given about it to warrant these generalizations (see *Poverty: A Study of Town Life*, pp. 99–102, Appendix C).

ety. The process of democratization of consumption began when people began to work for pay or profit and spend their money in the market. One man's dollar was as good as another's, and the great mass of sumptuary laws by which it was sought to preserve class distinctions in dress and even in diet fell into desuetude. Democratization of consumption is fostered by

CLOTHING REQUIRED BY AN AMERICAN WORKINGWOMAN

1946*	1875†
2 coats, to last 3 years	1 shawl, to last 3 years
1 suit, to last 2 years	5 dresses, to last 2 years
1 skirt, to last 2 years	12 yards of print for aprons
3 dresses, to last 2 years	2 hats, to last 2 years
2 dresses, to last 1 year	1 pair gloves
1 blouse, to last 1 year	2 pairs shoes
1 pair slacks, to last 1 year	5 petticoats, to last 2 to 3 years
1 compact and 1 cosmetic bag, to last 1 year	20 yards cotton cloth and trimming for chemises
3 slips, to last 1 year	2 corsets
1 nightgown, to last 2 years	2 sets of underwear
4 pairs panties, to last 1 year	5 pairs of hose
3 vests, to last 1 year	4 handkerchiefs, to last 1 year
2 girdles, to last 1 year	Collars, cuffs, scarfs, ribbons, etc.
3 brassieres, to last 1 year	
18 pairs of hose, to last 1 year	
4 pairs of anklets, to last 1 year	
2 hats, to last 1 year	
2 pairs gloves, to last 1 year	
2 pairs shoes, to last 1 year	
2 pairs playshoes, to last 1 year	
1 pair galoshes, to last 2 years	
1 raincoat, to last 4 years	
1 umbrella, to last 4 years	
1 bathrobe, to last 3 years	
1 housecoat, to last 2 years	
4 handkerchiefs, to last 1 year	
1 handbag, to last 2 years	
1 handbag, to last 1 year	
1 scarf, to last 1 year	

* Massachusetts Department of Labor and Industries, "An Annual and Weekly Minimum Budget for Certain Employed Persons in Massachusetts, September–October, 1946." (Mimeographed.)

† Massachusetts Bureau of Statistics of Labor, *Sixth Annual Report, 1875*, Part IV, "Condition of Workingmen's Families," p. 431. When the time the article was supposed to last is not given, probably one year was assumed.

schools, by national advertising, by new means of observation and communication, by the spirit of the times. We learn what there is to enjoy and what we need by what we see others enjoying or asserting that they need. The solution of the problem of poverty cannot be found in a reduction of felt wants and their intensity or in the restoration of class standards rather than a standard that is the same for all.

No defense of existing consumption standards is implied in the foregoing conclusions. The great need for improvement in the values, interests, and tastes that are reflected in the types and kinds of goods sought is another story and another problem. Even if this improvement should take place, it does not follow that the money cost of attaining the new standard would necessarily be lowered. It might even be increased if some observations made by Knight are correct.

It should be emphasized that the main difference in content between a high standard of living and a low one lies in the field of esthetic and social values. "Decency" and indeed cleanliness, is only a very low level of beauty. One great difference between liberal civilization and religious barbarism roots in the recognition that beauty is a good in human life and that it is frightfully expensive. . . . The great achievement of modern civilization in the scale of living lies in the diffusion of standards of decency, a minimum of beauty, among the masses of the people. . . . The living standards of the potentates, political, religious or economic, have in essentials been far less affected. It is a relatively simple matter for a society to provide the essentials and even a high level of beauty and culture, for a small elite, if the lives of the masses are used as a means to that end through an appropriate system of power or servility relations. . . . The complaint as to the materialism of our civilization reflects the interest of beneficiaries of power relation in our own society; one main root of it is the fact that the "lower classes" have come to demand a fair share in the benefits of the cultured life and to show a degree of independence and self-respect.[13]

POVERTY AND INEQUALITY

It has already been noted that poverty may be described either as a lack of specific goods and services or as position in the income distribution. By the latter test those lowest in the income scale are the poor, no matter what their attainable consumption level may be. Felt poverty is peculiarly a function of relative economic position, especially of changes therein. Greater equality in the distribution of income means that the proportion of the total received by each given percentage of the income recipients becomes more equal. Thus if the lowest tenth of the families is receiving one-twentieth of the total income, inequality diminishes as their share climbs closer to one-tenth of the total, or that of the lowest fourth toward one-fourth. Correspondingly, the share of the tenth or the fourth with highest incomes must diminish.

Economic forces that reduce inequality affect the contract incomes of the individual income recipients, that is, wages, salaries, entrepreneurial profits, rents, interest, and dividends. The first three are largely labor income; the last three, property income. The latter is far more unequally distributed than the former. Those at the top of the money-income distribution may get as much as 90 per cent of all received. At incomes below $3,000 less than a fourth of the urban families studied by the Bureau of Labor Statistics in 1941 reported property income. Half of the families

13. F. H. Knight, *Freedom and Reform* (New York: Harper & Bros., 1946), pp. 170–71.

with incomes of $10,000 or over had such income, however. About a seventh of the incomes reported by this top income group was of this character. If families with incomes $50,000 and over had been isolated, these percentages would undoubtedly be much higher, and still higher if those with incomes of $100,000 and over had been separately studied.[14] A wider ownership of income-yielding property would lessen inequality to some extent.

If the total personal income in the form of rentals, interest, and dividends in 1947 as estimated by the Department of Commerce had been divided evenly among all the money-income recipients twenty years of age and over reported by the Bureau of the Census in that year, each would have had about $300, all families and individuals who were separate economic units about $440. The lower incomes would not have increased by that much, since some in this position already had income of this character, especially rental income from home ownership or otherwise.

The case against a high degree of concentration of ownership does not rest entirely upon the fact that it increases inequality in income. High concentration of ownership means a high concentration of economic power, of control over income-producing wealth and business enterprise. In any society where new fortunes are being made, old ones being kept intact and added to by investment and reinvestment, high concentration of ownership is found. Large income from ownership is both a cause and a result of large incomes. The larger the income from any source, the larger may be the accumulation and investment. Is a high rate of creation of new fortunes in and of itself an index of something right or something wrong with the economy? Obviously that depends upon the conditions which give rise to them. Do they represent venture in new enterprises, a high level of business acumen? Are they symbols and results of a dynamic economy with a high and upward movement of the level of production? Or are they the fortuitous and unfortunate results of a free-enterprise economy and of our inability or failure to limit size of business units and prevent a high degree of monopolistic control? Each large fortune has its own story. Sometimes an invention is responsible, sometimes a new product, sometimes an oil strike, sometimes a timely land purchase, sometimes the kind of management that builds a small business into a large one, sometimes speculation in or manipulation of corporate securities, sometimes business practices recognized too late as undesirable, sometimes il-

14. The Bureau says: "It seems likely . . . that there was a large amount of understatement for these sources of income in the field survey" (*Wartime Spending and Saving in the United States,* Bull. No. 822 [Washington: Government Printing Office, 1945], p. 47).

legal operations. To the degree that new fortunes result from conditions and practices not in the public interest, or represent economic empire-building by means made possible by the corporate form, restraints upon free entry, unfair competitive practices, and the like, there is more than inequality to cause concern.

Not all large fortunes were made by their present holders; some were inherited. Without some rule like primogeniture or strict intermarriage and low birth rate among the rich, old fortunes tend to be broken up as new ones are added. Inheritance as a source of income from ownership is a by-product of the family system, not of economic forces. Those with such income derive it from their family status, their relationship to a person of wealth. Dalton's quotation from Spender on the anomaly thus presented may be noted:

> A logical individualism requires a fair start and an equal opportunity for each individual within the period of his own life whereas the actual unit, the family, is all the time doing its utmost to abolish the boundaries between life and death and to give its members with the aid of the dead hand as well as the living a long lead and a safe retreat.[15]

The defense of inheritance of great accumulations is a weakened version of the defense of the accumulation. It may be argued that it is part of the price we pay for economic enterprise, for top-flight business venturesomeness, business acumen, striving, foresight, insight, new ideas. The imposition of taxes upon the larger inheritances, graded according to the degree of relationship of the heirs to the deceased, represents a decision that such transfers in unlimited amounts are not socially desirable and that diminution of the amounts so acquirable will not interfere with the forms of economic enterprise desired.

Defenses other than the economic have been advanced for the existence in every society of a few with relatively high incomes and large holdings of wealth. From this source, it is said, come the endowments of colleges and universities, hospitals, research and philanthropic agencies. It is true that historically such endowments have come from such sources. In this country many of those who made great fortunes (and their widows) have been great and wise donors. Wealth passed on to children is much less likely to be given away. Without new fortunes or increase in number of small donors, we must look to the state for the support of many enterprises once maintained wholly or largely by private benefactors. The argument is also made that in every society in the past the few with wealth and leisure

15. Hugh Dalton, *Some Aspects of the Inequality of Incomes in Modern Communities* (London: G. Routledge & Sons, Ltd., 1935), pp. 21–22.

have been the patrons of the arts and the innovators and demonstrators of the modes and manners of civilized living. This is an argument for inheritance rather than the creation of new fortunes. The effect of a leisure class upon our consumption standards was thoroughly examined by Veblen as well as what he called "pecuniary emulation."[16] Whether the existence of a group with "outsize" incomes is necessary to prevent us from becoming a society of rude barbarians is rather questionable.

INEQUALITY OF EARNINGS

The degree of inequality in earnings is far less than that in income from ownership. The importance of wages and salaries as a component of personal incomes was emphasized in chapter iii. About seven-tenths of all "contract income" received by individuals in 1950 was of this character, according to the Department of Commerce estimates. "Proprietors' income," about a sixth of the total, is also largely labor income, the income of the self-employed, such as farm operators, retailers, other small enterprisers and persons in the professions in private practice. If wage-earners were distributed by the amount of their earnings in a particular year, at the bottom would be found not only those whose rates of pay are relatively low but also those not fully employed during the year either from choice or involuntarily.[17] Some farm operators at the bottom of the distribution may have had a bad year, while the following one may be a good one. Normal or usual rates of pay or profit may be more equal than current earnings. A certain percentage of the wage-earner families in poverty, as measured by inadequacy of their current income, are there because of unemployment or disability of the breadwinner, the percentage being low in times of business activity and high during depression.

Inequality in earnings is lessened by the shifts of the labor supply from employer to employer and place to place and, most important, from one type of occupation requiring a particular kind of knowledge and skill to another. It is the mobility of the labor force that reduces the differentials in rates of pay between kinds of work, industries, and places. As has been pointed out, it is mainly the entrance of new workers with qualifications for the higher-paid employments into the labor force that lessens the inequality between occupations. Those already in the labor force move in the main from employer to employer and place to place. If they move because of unemployment or underemployment to places and industries offering steadier employment at the same rates, they likewise prevent or re-

16. Thorstein Veblen, *Theory of the Leisure Class* (New York: Macmillan Co., 1899).
17. Some may have farmed or been otherwise self-employed for part of the year.

duce inequality in annual earnings. To the degree that workers lac knowledge of opportunities in other locations or employments, or the financial resources necessary for a change in location, these equalizing movements will be limited. Restrictions upon output resulting from either business or labor monopoly increase inequality in earnings. All restrictions upon freedom of entry into employments move up the earnings of the favored and at the same time move down the earnings of the disqualified.

The essential conditions for equalization of earnings are equalization of freedom, power, and willingness to enter employments and markets. Power to enter is the power to offer the abilities, the skills, and the knowledge each job requires. So far as the requisite capacities are inborn, differentials in earnings will persist. Diversity in gifts, in energy, in the whole compound of physical, mental, and emotional qualities that make for difference in capacity to do a particular job, means diversity in earnings. Differentials in rates of pay also exist because other considerations besides possible earnings affect the choice of a job. Some employments are hazardous; in some, working conditions are generally distasteful; others offer nonfinancial compensations in the way of location, security, prestige, or kind of work involved. If relatively few are willing to enter certain employments, labor can be drawn into them only by relatively high rates of pay.

To the extent that the capacities requisite to qualify for a particular job can be acquired, equalization of earnings evidently depends upon equalization of opportunity to acquire them. These opportunities, it has already been pointed out, must come largely in childhood and youth. Their equalization will, over time, decrease inequality in earnings. Opportunities to acquire vocational skills and knowledge are notoriously unequal in our society, although notably less so than in others past and present. Differentials in rates of pay are greater than the differences in the inborn capacities of the population. Family incomes are unequal, family knowledge is unequal, and families to large degree are responsible for the start in life young people receive. Thus the family system fosters inequality in earnings as it does inequality in wealth. When, however, a high standard for children's education is prevalent and families are striving to prepare them for the higher-paid jobs, earnings are more equal than when no such ambition is found. In some societies sons are expected to follow in the father's footsteps, and there is no aspiration to move into a higher economic position. In others the code that is in the ascendance is quite different.

Although equalization of opportunities to acquire marketable skills and knowledge, and extension of knowledge with respect to wage differentials, job requirements, and related matters would tend to equalize earnings, some differentials are inevitable. There remain unalterable individual differences, and differences that we do not seek to alter. Differences in human personality affect the incentive and drive to take advantage of opportunities among those for whom they are ostensibly equal. Changes in demand alter the market value of acquired skills and knowledge. Employments are deliberately chosen for other than economic reasons.

Freedom to enter employments, given the capacity to assume the responsibilities and perform the tasks involved, means absence of restraints, legal or otherwise. It means no discrimination upon the basis of sex, race, or other considerations irrelevant to the competence of the individual. Standards that all job applicants must meet are one thing; quotas and barriers not related to such standards are another. We have had and still have such barriers, not only to employment but also to schools and other means of acquiring training.

Unreasonable restraints upon freedom of entry are either hidden or masquerade as reasonable restrictions in the public interest. It is not easy in some instances to draw the line between requirements in the public interest and those that are only protective devices which place a favored few in a market sheltered from the competition of those kept out. Sounder decisions would be made if the distinction between the interest of a few and the public interest in general were less frequently confused and if it were remembered that the burden of proof is upon those who seek to impose barriers.

Two observations should be made in regard to the effects of equalizing forces and conditions of the character under discussion. One is that they do not merely alter the income distribution; they also raise the general level of production and income. They make for an improvement in human resources and for their better and more effective use. The second is that, as opportunities are equalized, the relative position of those in the better-paid employments will tend to move down. It should be obvious that wage and salary differentials cannot at one and the same time be lessened and maintained. President Conant of Harvard has pointed out that, as the proportion of those who go to college or enter professional schools increases through federal aid to education or otherwise, the market situation for the graduates will be different from what it was when only a small percentage had such training. The relation between the factory operative's earnings and that of the lawyer may change. Some seem to see these changes in relative position of earners as an evil. Their goal is the preservation of the status quo, that is, the relative advantage of their group. We cannot, however, both have competition and not have it, equalizing forces and, at the same time, no equalization.

CHAPTER VII

PUBLIC POLICY AND THE INCOME PROBLEM

A SURVEY of public policies proposed or in operation with direct or indirect bearing on the income problem would be lengthy indeed. Such policies range from proposals for a planned economy with nationalized industry to those designed to strengthen the free-enterprise system. They include a wide range of regulatory measures and governmental activities as well as subsidies and other aid, direct and indirect, to business enterprises and persons. Certain policies have as their primary objectives the immediate reduction of inequality, others the alleviation of existing poverty, and others the attainment and maintenance of those conditions which over time move the general level of income upward and tend to equalize earnings and ownership. Some are focused upon the economic distress and inequities of the moment; others, upon basic underlying conditions and their long-run effects upon the economic welfare of the population as a whole.

In this chapter certain measures that fall in the former rather than in the latter category will be discussed. In no sense are they substitutes for those policies designed to lessen cyclical fluctuations in production and employment, to prevent unreasonable restrictions upon freedom of entry into employments and markets, or reduce controls of production and in general make for a more efficient use of resources and a generally higher level of consumption. Policies with short-run objectives are necessary supplements to those with effects, however great, showing themselves only over time. The latter do not reduce economic distress of the moment or even possibly of the decade or longer.

Public policies may be classified by their avowed objectives, but their appraisal involves something more than acceptance of these objectives as desirable. Objection to specific policies may come from two sources. On the one hand, they may come from those whose economic position is adversely affected. Policies that immediately or in the long run would operate to the advantage of some groups as income recipients or of all groups as consumers may be disadvantageous to the income position of others. The opposition of the latter is inevitable, especially if the effects will be immediately felt. Division on policy questions therefore takes place on the basis of real or assumed self-interest at the moment or in the long run. Objection to a specific policy may have, however, quite a different basis. Analysis may indicate that what is proposed or in operation would not or does not attain the proposed objective or that another policy would be more effective. Analysis may even indicate that the policy in question operates perversely; that immediately or in the long run it aggravates the situation it was designed to correct or brings in its train other evils that outweigh those it was designed to eliminate. These are the real issues which make sound policy decisions difficult.

THE INCOME TAX AS AN EQUALIZING MEASURE

A personal income tax with rates that move upward with income is a powerful means of altering the distribution of disposable income. Simons presented the case for it as follows:

(1) Reduction of inequality is per se immensely important; (2) progressive taxation is both an effective means and, within the existing framework of institutions, the only effective means to that end; (3) in a world of competitive, invidious consumption, the gains at the bottom of the income scale can be realized without significant loss to persons of large income, so long as their rank in the income scale is unchanged; and (4) drastic reduction of inequality through taxation is attainable without much loss of efficiency in the system and without much impairing the attractiveness of the economic game.[1]

The federal income tax is at present a means by which inequality in income is reduced. Not only are rates higher at the higher income levels but the amount of income not taxed increases with the number dependent upon the recipient's income. In 1947 the amount of personal income exempt from tax was as follows:

Number of Persons Dependent on Income	Tax-Exempt Income Assuming Standard Deductions*
1....................	Under $ 550
2....................	Under $1,125
3....................	Under $1,675
4....................	Under $2,225
5....................	Under $2,775
6....................	Under $3,350
7....................	Under $3,900
8....................	Under $4,450
9....................	Under $5,000

* Use of tax table by persons with incomes under $5,000 is assumed. On incomes of $5,000 and over, 10 per cent is assumed deduction.

1. Henry C. Simons, *Economic Policy for a Free Society* (Chicago: University of Chicago Press, 1948), p. 65.

In the same year taxes for a four-person family with one income recipient varied with income roughly as follows:

Gross Adjusted Income	Approximate Rate of Tax	Approximate Income after Tax
$ 2,000	....	$ 2,000
$ 3,000	4.6	$ 2,863
$ 4,000	7.7	$ 3,692
$ 5,000	9.7	$ 4,516
$ 10,000	15.8	$ 8,423
$ 20,000	24.7	$ 15,066
$ 50,000	41.4	$ 29,280
$ 100,000	54.1	$ 45,907
$ 200,000	65.1	$ 69,381
$ 500,000	72.7	$136,665
$1,000,000	75.2	$247,600

The difference in income before and after payment of the tax is apparent.

Another important levy of the federal government is the special tax on the income of corporations. Few state and local governments use the personal income tax. Many of the taxes imposed by these bodies are regressive, bearing most heavily on those at the lower end of the distribution. Before the federal income-tax rate reached its present dimensions, the tax system as a whole may have operated to increase inequality rather than decrease it when all kinds of levies are considered and the ultimate incidence of all types.

The sources of government revenues in 1947 were as follows:[2]

Sources of Revenue		Millions of Dollars
Federal government receipts before refunds......................		$46,280
Personal taxes and nontaxes before refunds....................		$21,323
Income taxes....................................	$20,446	
Estate and gift taxes............................	830	
Nontaxes.......................................	47	
Refunds...............................	$1,675	
Corporate profits tax accruals...............................		11,907
Indirect tax and nontax accruals before refunds................		7,943
Excise taxes on liquor, tobacco, etc.................	7,297	
Customs duties.................................	436	
Nontaxes.......................................	210	
Refunds...............................	69	
Contributions for social insurance...........................		5,107
Total receipts after refunds...................................		44,538
State and local receipts......................................		$14,813*
Personal taxes and nontaxes...............................		$ 1,864
Income taxes................................	451	
Death and gift taxes.........................	178	
Motor-vehicle licenses...........................	223	
Property taxes................................	171	
Other personal taxes...........................	141	
Nontaxes.....................................	700	
Corporate profits tax accruals.............................		604
Indirect business tax and nontax accruals.....................		$10,805

2. *Survey of Current Business*, July, 1949, p. 12.

Sources of Revenue		Millions of Dollars
Sales tax......................................		$ 3,212
General tax........................... $1,331		
Gasoline tax.......................... 1,180		
Liquor tax........................... 410		
Tobacco tax.......................... 291		
Licenses of motor vehicles........................	$ 326	
Business property tax...........................	5,349	
Other business taxes............................	1,466	
Nontaxes (fees, etc.)...........................	452	
Contributions to social insurance..............................		$ 540
Total receipts, federal, state, and local, after refunds.............		$58,351

* State and local governments received $1,738 millions from the federal treasury as grants-in-aid.

Of the total receipts in this year, 36 per cent, it will be noted, came from personal income taxes. If the employee contributions to social insurance are added, $2,108 millions, the total direct deductions from personal incomes amount to about half the governmental receipts.[3] From corporate profits came 21 per cent. If the 19 per cent from the sales and excise taxes and customs duties are added, about nine-tenths of the whole is accounted for.

Although personal income taxes at progressive rates tend to equalize disposable incomes, they are levied not for this purpose but to produce revenue. When needs for revenue are high relative to the total national income, the amount of tax-exempt income must be lowered and the tax rate increased. The alternative would be to rely to greater extent upon other kinds of taxes, which may be less productive, less equitable, or with more adverse economic effects. Deficiencies in tax revenue may be made up by borrowing and thereby increase in government debt. If the bonds and notes issued are taken by banks, it is likely to lead to an increase in checkbook money and thus to inflation. The latter means that most inequitable of all kinds of taxation—that which comes through rising prices from which no income is exempt.

The progressiveness of income-tax rates operates, as has been said, to decrease inequality, but increase in the amount of the rate and decrease in the size of the tax-exempt income decrease the attainable consumption level and increase the proportion of families that fall below the poverty line. When tax rates at the bottom of the distribution are relatively low, these latter effects are inconsiderable, but, as they rise, they are felt by many. The marked increase in rates during the 1940's and again in the 1950's is due primarily to the cost of past wars, of carrying on a war, and of putting the nation in a state of readiness for another one. Approxi-

3. At this date these deductions were at a flat rate upon wages or salaries of covered employees up to $3,000 per year.

mately 70 per cent of the federal budget represents the costs of past wars and of the present military establishments. Here is but one manifestation of the adverse economic results of the diversion of resources to warmaking activities. If not offset by growth in the national product, the result is a fall in the consumption level attainable due to diversion of income from private consumption and investment to other purposes, "useful or wasteful," to use Rowntree's phrase.

MINIMUM-WAGE LAWS

Among the policies designed to reduce the volume of poverty is the setting by law of a minimum-wage rate. The Federal Fair Labor Standards Act passed in 1938 set a minimum of seventy-five cents per hour for workers in interstate commerce. About half of the states have minimum-wage laws applying, usually, only to women workers. The "floors" are usually established by boards set up for that purpose when the state department of labor finds evidence that actual wages in an industry do not meet the general standards prescribed in the statute.[4]

The effects of the establishment of a legal minimum for wage rates will depend upon circumstances and the level at which the minimum is set. To the extent that some of the workers affected are of lower efficiency than the run of the market, they will be thrown out of work, as will any worker whose addition to product is not worth what the employer must pay him. To the extent that the higher wage increases worker efficiency, results are beneficial all round. If the firms paying below minimum rates were keeping their place in the market by virtue of low labor costs alone, they must eliminate wastes and improve the efficiency of their management or be forced out. If the below-minimum wage was due to the fact that the workers in question were selling their labor to only one or few buyers, that is, there was limited competition among the employing firms in that respect, the new rate if not set at too high a level will not decrease employment. In fact, it may even under those conditions increase the rate of production and number employed, since no matter how few workers such firms employ there is no decrease in the rates they must pay after the minimum is reached. If the below-minimum wage has been due to failure of workers to move to higher-paid employments or areas, the unemployment following the establishment of the higher rate may force them to do so, an equalizing redistribution to be desired. To the extent that the workers affected are

4. Such a state law was first passed in Massachusetts in 1912. Connecticut now has statutory minima for the wages of both men and women, and in New York and Rhode Island, after a board has set up an industry minimum for women, no man may be paid a lower rate.

married women or other persons who for personal reasons cannot or will not move, some will be unemployed. If the legal minimum does not apply to all employments, the wages in the uncovered employments will tend to decline as those not absorbed in the covered industries shift to the uncovered. Analysis of the effects of the establishment of a legal minimum wage follows the same lines as that of the possible effects of the establishment of a standard rate by collective bargaining.

The level at which the legal minimum is set is usually with some reference to the estimated needs of the workers, thus raising the same problems in regard to the standards that were discussed in chapter v. The problem is that of determining the amount the worker must have in order to maintain himself at an acceptable level without help from others. The legal minimum wage cannot vary with the number of actual or presumptive dependents of the worker. A wage rate set upon the basis of an average support burden would more than suffice for the needs of some and be insufficient for others. The problem of poverty as a function both of income and of the number of dependents is clearly left untouched by the establishment of a legal minimum wage.

AGRICULTURAL POLICY AND THE PROBLEM OF POVERTY

It has been noted that a large proportion of the low-income group are farm families. Minimum-wage rates would not touch their income position in so far as their incomes are derived from farm operations. To what extent has the complex federal farm program, especially the cash payments "earned" by reduction, alteration, or destruction of products, the minimum prices supported when necessary by government purchase or commodity loans "without recourse," the marketing agreements, reduced poverty in the farm population?[5]

The economic position of farm families as a group improved greatly in the war and early postwar years. The income per person in the farm population moved up more rapidly after its great decline in the thirties than did that of the nonfarm population.[6] The transfer payments from the public treasury directly in the form of cash payments or indirectly through government purchases as a part of the price-support program, and the other measures by which prices were sustained, undoubtedly contributed to this result. Analysis demonstrates clearly, however, that the program could not and did not reduce but rather increased income inequality among farm

5. The research and education program, the crop-insurance program, the low-cost credit program, fall into a different class of government aids to agriculture.

6. U.S. Bureau of Human Nutrition and Home Economics, *Rural Family Living, Charts: Prepared for Outlook Conference* (Washington, October, 1950). (Processed.)

families and did not meet the problem of the poverty group. The cash payments were markedly regressive, largest for those who without them would have had the largest incomes. The price-support program operates in the same way: "Raising the price of farm products does not improve the distribution of income among farm families. As a rule a higher price is likely to help those with low incomes less than farmers already enjoying large returns."[7] About 90 per cent of the farm products sold by farmers are produced by 50 per cent of the farms.[8] T. W. Schultz describes the largely self-sustaining farm families with low production of cash crops as "our rural slums." "Most of the social problems in agriculture associated with bad health, poor nutrition, inadequate housing and substandard education are concentrated heavily in the farming areas that are most self-contained."[9] Unless these families without prospect of a profitable market for the products of their farms, or of nonfarm employment while they still live on farms, shift from agriculture, their incomes will remain inadequate.

PUBLIC ASSISTANCE TO THE NEEDY

The governmental policies that most directly and immediately meet the problem of poverty are those that provide income in cash or kind (or both) to those who otherwise would be in need. The establishment of floors for wages and farm prices is an attempt to raise contract income. Direct cash payments from the public treasury provide for the recipients what in chapter iii was called "civil rights" income or, as a whole, "transfer income."

Not all the transfer payments derive from the inadequacy of income of the recipients. Some are veterans' benefits based on military service. Others, as old age, widows', and survivors' benefits under the Social Security Act, are based on the past payment of a tax for a minimum period. Other cash payments go, however, only to those in need, either to special categories, as the aged, the blind, dependent children, or to those of any age who are without adequate resources.[10] A large proportion of those at the bottom of the income distribution are such income recipients, the proportion varying with the number of families with needy dependent children, the number of aged persons, and others receiving public assistance. In viewing an income distribution it must be remembered that the policy

7. T. W. Schultz, *Redirecting Farm Policy* (New York: Macmillan Co., 1943), p. 35.

8. T. W. Schultz, *Agriculture in an Unstable Economy* (New York: McGraw-Hill Book Co., 1945), p. 223.

9. *Ibid.*, p. 198.

10. See chap. xiii for a discussion of the Social Security Act providing for federal supplementation of state aid to special categories of the needy population.

of making such cash payments creates a low-income group of individuals and families. This does not mean that these income recipients and their relatives are worse off than they would otherwise have been. Without such income many of the recipients would be dependent members of another's household, reducing the attainable consumption level of its members. One of the objectives of public assistance to the aged and to dependent children through cash payments was to enable these groups to live in their own homes rather than as dependents of kindred or in public institutions.

Historically all forms of public assistance grew out of the general responsibility for the relief of the destitute assumed by the state as feudalism declined and the economic and political institutions of the modern Western world developed. Relief ceased to be the exclusive responsibility of individuals and religious organizations and was increasingly transferred to local and, later, to the state authorities.[11] The general principles of the English poor law were transferred to this country and have been the basis of our law and practice. The principles that should govern the discharge of this responsibility were hotly debated in nineteenth-century Great Britain, where to many only the most rigorous treatment of the destitute seemed compatible with a regime of individual initiative and responsibility. But increased understanding of the causes of poverty, of the economic forces that were creating a "new poor," especially among urban wage-earners divorced from the soil, a heightened sense of responsibility for others, and sensitivity to human misery made for principles of administration designed not to stigmatize or punish but to succor without damage to the self-respect of those aided. Nor should Giffen's comment be overlooked: "A condition of great poverty for the masses of the community (as in Oriental countries) implies a lower state than one in which the poor have become a minority, and the question of legal relief for a portion of the minority arises."[12] In other words: "A community which is able to think about the public maintenance of the destitute, is one in which a considerable part has already emerged from a condition of the direst poverty."[13]

Certain of the issues around which the earlier controversies raged do not concern most people today.[14] One point of view then advanced would find few if any adherents—that poverty is necessary and desirable. In the

11. See William J. Ashley, *Introduction to English Economic History and Theory* (London: Longmans, Green & Co., 1906), Vol. I, Part II.

12. Quoted in T. Mackey, "How Far Is Pauperism a Necessary Element in a Civilized Community?" *Economic Review*, X (July, 1900), 419.

13. *Ibid.*

14. One issue still debated is which governmental unit shall provide the public assistance or how its costs shall be divided among town, county, state, or federal government.

words of the Reverend F. W. O. Ward, a prolific writer on the subject:

What would become of such glorious virtues as philanthropy and benevolence if their occupation were gone and the poor man but a tradition or a metaphor? . . . Is poverty . . . what we can honestly designate an evil? Is it not rather a spiritual occasion of the most spacious kind . . . an architect of character second to none? It is the Spartan virtues that build up a State and fashion it strong and stable.[15]

Today we emphasize the high correlation between poverty, vice, crime, and delinquency. So much was this the case at recent hearings before a Senate subcommittee on "Low-Income Families" that one senator exclaimed, "Is the poor but honest family then a thing of the past?"

Also generally rejected is the older thesis that these welfare measures would bring such pressure of the population upon the means of subsistence as to keep the nation always at a low economic level. Malthus on these grounds advocated the gradual abolition of the poor law, and the logic of his argument was accepted by many economists. Closely associated with or a part of his argument was another that does concern many today, that public assistance may make for "improvidence, indolence and self-indulgence."[16] Upon this ground public assistance other than in almshouses and workhouses for the totally destitute was opposed for orphaned children, the widowed, the aged, and, most of all, for the able-bodied adult. The same argument was advanced against free education and other free services provided at public expense.[17] The fears earlier expressed as to the pernicious effects of too liberal measures of public assistance have, however, by no means entirely disappeared. In 1932 an editorial writer in the *Chicago Tribune* made the following comment:

The facts are ugly but there is no point in disguising them. The recipients of unemployment relief are objects of charity. . . . It was their duty to support themselves and their children. . . . For one reason or another they have failed to make the grade. . . . The assumption that they are entitled to support by right . . . is a false assumption and if it is allowed to go unchallenged it will place a premium on incompetence, laziness and shiftlessness.[18]

It was not public assistance per se that called forth most of the early controversy but the standards for such assistance, the tests of eligibility to receive, and the character of the maintenance provided. It was argued

15. F. W. O. Ward, "Poverty and Population," *Westminster Review*, CLXXII (September, 1909), 334.
16. H. Fawcett, *Pauperism: Its Causes and Remedies* (London: Macmillan & Co., 1871).
17. *Ibid.;* Sir William Chance, *The Better Administration of the Poor Law* (London: Swan, Sonnenschien & Co., 1895).
18. *Chicago Tribune*, November 9, 1932. The writer did, rather inconsistently, compare their plight to the victims of a hurricane and say that the community because it had a heart would prevent physical suffering.

that the manner of living made possible through public assistance should be that which all would abhor and avoid if humanly possible; it should reveal the economic status of the recipients and be unlike that commonly desired. Thus it would serve as a deterrent and operate to reduce the number of applicants both immediately and in the long run. In the short run only those completely without resources would apply or only those without kindred or friends, since, if they had kindred or friends, support from them would be forthcoming in view of the abhorrent alternative. In the long run it would operate to reduce poverty by increasing industry, sobriety, and foresight. Fathers seeing the unhappy state of destitute orphaned children would provide against this contingency as well as for their own old age. Thus ran the argument for breaking up families and providing maintenance only in the almshouse, orphanage, or workhouse with food, clothing, and other items kept to a basic minimum.

The weakness of this argument became apparent as the economic facts of life became apparent and as the springs of human action were better understood. The theory was rejected that it is "improvidence, indolence and self-indulgence" from which almost the entire pauperism of a country either directly or indirectly arises,[19] as was the theory that these faults when they occur are corrected by the punitive measures described. Especially did it become apparent that a society is acting against its own interest when the sick go uncared for and children are stigmatized, inadequately fed, clothed, housed, and educated.

The question of the standard that should determine incomes of the character under discussion still remains, however, as a major policy issue. The maximum monthly amounts are set by law for old age assistance and public aid to dependent children, the budget for each individual to be determined by administrative discretion. With price movements these maxima represent varying consumption levels from time to time. There is an inevitable inflexibility in these incomes, since statutory changes are not quickly or easily made. If the maximum is none too much according to prevailing standards, the recipients in low-rent or other low-cost areas are likely to receive it, thus in effect receiving a relatively higher benefit payment than those in high-cost urban areas. Payments to families in aid of dependent children vary with the number of children. Since parental incomes do not so vary, the total incomes of families with several children receiving such public assistance may exceed that of some self-supporting families in the community even when the standard payment per child is relatively low. The same situation may exist when large families are re-

19. Fawcett, *op. cit.,* p. 27.

ceiving relief because of prolonged unemployment or disability of the breadwinner. The actual standard will therefore be a varying one, its limits set not only by administrative discretion but by the appropriation made for the purpose. There is an inevitable relation between the general economic level of the community and the income level of the mass of self-supporting families and the standards by which these income payments are determined.

FAMILY ALLOWANCES

Public assistance to the needy and measures designed to insure income during unemployment, disability, old age, or to the surviving dependents of those who die prematurely do not meet the problem of those able-bodied and earning who find their incomes inadequate to maintain at an acceptable level those they are duty-bound to support. The magnitude of this problem is unknown for reasons previously discussed. The so-called "family allowance," a cash payment to the family with amount based upon the number and age of the children, is a policy proposed and in many countries in operation to meet this problem.

The relation of the number of children to income inadequacy has been shown in the analysis in chapter v. The proportion of families with three or more children in the "poverty" group exceeds their proportion among all families. It has also been pointed out that more families go through a poverty period than are in poverty at a particular time, a situation associated with the growth and decline in family size and the changing age of the family members during the family life-span. The argument for the family allowance does not rest solely on the inadequacy of the incomes of some families to provide what is needed for their young members. Such a policy may be viewed as an attempt to widen the basis of child support, to distribute more widely, both currently and over time, the costs of maintenance of the child population. It may be viewed as a means of increasing the total investment in human resources, of lessening the difference between children with respect to the start they get in life and increasing children's share of the total income. Relevant here is the fact noted in chapter i—that only in modern cultures have the security and the livelihood of children been so completely a function of what can be provided by two adults or their claims so completely narrowed to the parents alone.

The International Labour Office reports that in 1947 twenty-five nations had made legal provision for broad family-allowance schemes.[20] The twenty-five included practically all countries on the continent of Europe,

20. *International Labour Review*, LVII (1948), 315–33, 456–77.

the United Kingdom, Ireland, Australia, New Zealand, Canada, Chile, Uruguay, and Lebanon. Included in their survey were only those plans providing "recurring cash payments on behalf of children to a large proportion of a nation's families."[21] They do not consider lump-sum grants or loans, special concessions, or privileges extended to large families or voluntary schemes. Governmental units, nonprofit organizations, or business concerns that are quasi-monopolistic may adopt a family-wage scheme if they desire, but these are not here considered.

The family-allowance systems in Australia, Canada, Ireland, New Zealand, Norway, Sweden, and the United Kingdom most nearly approach universality of family coverage. Allowances are not restricted to families of low income or to those with heads in certain employments. Allowances are not usually paid on behalf of children already benefiting substantially from special state funds or being supported by the state. Since income-tax exemptions based on number of dependent children are in themselves a form of family allowance, both family allowance and exemptions may not be given or the full allowance and exemptions to those in the higher-income brackets.

In most of the other countries eligibility to receive the allowance is an incident of the employment status of the family head. In four—France, Belgium, Spain, and Bulgaria—families of most employed workers and some self-employed are eligible and in thirteen others only employed workers.[22] In the majority of those countries where employed workers only or mainly are eligible, the funds are derived entirely from contributions by employers, but in the others employees also contribute. In the countries with substantially universal coverage the funds come either from general revenues or from a special tax earmarked for this purpose. The International Labour Office notes that from 1940 to 1947, as the number of countries with a family-allowance system rose from eight to twenty-seven, there was a tendency to broaden the coverage of families and the sources of revenue. A system of family allowances that applied only to wage-earners would not benefit the families that need it most in this country, those living on farms. Financing of the program by employers' contributions is, moreover, highly questionable social policy. It is in effect a hidden tax with incidence unknown, affecting variously product prices, investment, and employment.

Once eligibility to receive and method of financing are settled, the important issues are the amount of the allowance; whether it shall be a flat

21. *Ibid.*, p. 316.
22. In Brazil all low-income families of specified sizes are eligible

amount per eligible child or graded according to the number in the family; whether the allowance shall be given to families with only one child or begin with the second, the third, or some higher number. All plans, moreover, must set maximum age limits for the termination of the payments and indicate the effect of continuation in school, disability, or other contingency.

The two basic issues that run through the debate over family allowances are, first, the effect on the birth rate and, second, whether there are other, better ways of attaining the objectives. Some oppose family-allowance systems on the ground that it is not "just" or "natural" to place part of the burden of support of children on anyone except their parents. The discussion in the literature usually, however, revolves around the issues mentioned. Some countries adopted the family-allowance system as a part of a population policy with the expectation that it would operate to check the decline in the birth rate. In others no such effect was desired. The policy was entirely an expression of concern with the nurture of children whatever their numbers might be. Opposition to the policy may be based upon the conjectural effect upon the over-all or the differential birth rate. It may be argued that it would so increase the rate of population growth that poverty would deepen or that it would have an adverse effect from the eugenic standpoint. Since the payments would go in largest proportion to those areas, occupations, and classes with the highest birth rates, those who regard unfavorably the culture pattern or eugenic worth of these groups may take a gloomy view of the possible effects. In this country, if it were a federal program, it would mean a transfer payment from the urban to the farm population, from the North to the South. Adverse judgments of the program on eugenic grounds would be difficult to sustain, and the magnitude of the effect upon the birth rate is highly problematic in view of the variety of factors which seem to influence it.

Whether the family allowance is a part of population policy or has other objectives, there is the question whether its objectives could be better attained in some other way. If the concern is child welfare, shall the supplements to family income for the benefit of children be in cash or in kind? Most of the laws providing for cash payments specify that the money shall be spent for the benefit of the children; but, except in the case of families whose low standards for child care would bring them to the attention of the authorities, this mandate can scarcely be enforced. The question may be put in this way: Will this expenditure of public money yield most in benefit to the children if it is distributed to families to be used according to their lights, or will it yield most if the state decides upon and provides those things for which children have greatest need? The state may view the outlay as an investment and ask: Which uses would be the most profitable if the children are regarded as future citizens and workers? Strong arguments could be made for educational and recreational services, medical and dental service, school lunches, midmorning milk, improved housing, rather than cash supplements to the family income.[23]

Cash supplements to family income and free goods and services are not mutually exclusive alternatives. Many of the nations with a family-allowance system make large outlays for free goods and services, although the provision of the latter could be enlarged by a transfer of the funds paid in family allowances. If a society wants to make sure that all children have the opportunity to benefit from certain goods and services, they must be provided and made available at public expense. Services such as the state can provide may lessen the demands upon family income, but there will remain individual and joint needs for which this income must provide. The family allowance and the provision of free goods and services of suitable kinds may be thought of as complementary rather than as alternative solutions of the problem.

23. Subsidized housing for low-income families with rents graded in relation to the number of children may be regarded as a direct substitute for the family allowance.

CHAPTER VIII

FREE GOODS AND SERVICES

IN MODERN communities a wide variety of goods and services is available without cost or at something less than cost. The level of living of individuals and families is thereby augmented in varying degrees depending upon the extent to which they make use of what is offered or enjoy their benefits. These goods and services are provided at public expense or, less frequently, through private philanthropy. Thus they are paid for by taxpayers and voluntary contributors, but contributions and benefits are in no way related.

There are wide variations from community to community in the free goods and services, but over time their volume and variety have been increasing. For some, local governmental units take responsiblity; for others the state; and, for others, the federal government. For some, responsibility is shared. Their number increases markedly with urbanization, and their variety and quality tend to be a function of the general level of income. The provision of some of the free services is universally considered desirable, with differences of opinion concerning only quantity and quality or to whom they should be available. The provision of others is less generally accepted. Still others are in a distinctly marginal position, with provision a matter of debate and controversy.

It would be difficult to make a comprehensive list of the goods and services now commonly available wholly or partly at governmental expense. Such a list would include the public highways and bridges, the lighting, cleaning, and policing of city streets, fire-fighting, garbage and sewage disposal, elementary schools and universities, libraries, art galleries, museums, parks, playgrounds, bathing beaches, golf courses, picnic grounds, hospitals, and clinics. It would include schoolbooks, transportation of school children, "penny" milk and school lunches, concerts, and subsidized housing.

DEVELOPMENT OF THE FREE SERVICES

Many of the free services, or their prototypes, were once provided by families for themselves or were purchased. Each has its own history of degree and occasion of transfer from private to public provision. In rural communities the family is still responsible for its own water supply and garbage disposal. Free public school education is a relatively recent development, resisted initially by many as a serious infringement of the principle of individual responsibility. The child of former days learned what his elders could teach him or was taught by a private tutor or in a private school. The history of some publicly provided services would show that very few enjoyed them prior to their provision by the state. The history of others would be one of transition from family provision to governmental, of others from business enterprise to the state. The history of schools, hospitals, and art museums would show an early development under the auspices of the church and private philanthropy, then the assumption by the state of an increasing responsibility.

Public provision does not in all cases rule out private provision. Use of the public facilities is not compulsory. Some families today send their children to private schools, fee-supported, church-supported, or privately endowed. Many provide private instruction in addition to that offered by the public schools. Householders may supplement the public police force with private watchmen. A group may form an association to provide additional street-cleaning service, golf courses, and recreational facilities. Individuals may patronize public libraries and also buy and rent books.

WHY THE FREE SERVICES?

The public provision of free goods and services is a form of income redistribution. They represent a form of transfer income, the uses of the funds that provide them transferred from those who furnish them to those who benefit from the services. The redistribution aspect is most marked in the case of free services provided only to the needy, either those whose resources in general are inadequate or the "medically needy" or other designated group. Beneficiaries and contributors are by no means always two distinct groups. The kind of redistribution effected depends not only upon who are the users but who contributes the funds. If the taxes by which the free services are supported bear most heavily on the low-income groups, the result may be an increase in inequality, not a decrease.

From another standpoint the provision of the free services may be described as a planned alteration of consumption, that is, in the character of goods and services available and used. A redistribution of money incomes will alter consumption, but the changes in consumption that follow will be quite different from those effected by the provision of services at public expense. The latter may be described in the economist's language as an abridgment of the system of consumer control of the allocation of resources among alternative uses. Instead of an allocation on the basis of what individuals and families are able and willing to purchase (and business concerns able and willing to supply), there is a decision by the appropriate lawmaking body as to how a part of the national income shall be spent. The deflection of resources into the building and operation of libraries, hospitals, and schools is of the same character as that which follows a decision to prepare for or engage in war. The uses of resources are altered from what they would have been if private decisions as to income spending had completely controlled.

Income redistribution per se is clearly not the purpose that is behind the public provision of many, if not most, of the free goods and services but a specific alteration of the consumption picture. Even in communities with a high degree of income or without concern as to poverty, many of the familiar free goods and services would be provided. The emphasis when free provision is an issue is upon the importance of maximizing the use of the goods and services in question, of insuring that the cost is not a deterrent to the enjoyment of their benefits. If this is to be the case, they must be free, provided at government expense. Behind this is clearly the notion that there are some goods everyone must have and that their availability and the use of those available are to be determined by other considerations than private comparisons of income and price. The general objective of maximizing use may be reinforced by the fact of income inequality or the existence of the needy, but a policy of liberal public provision need not rest upon these considerations alone.

When the provision of a free service is urged as a means of meeting the problem of poverty, the question arises: Shall the need be met in cash or in kind? Will the interests of the needy and those of the community be best served if the transfer income is in the form of money payments or in the form of free goods and services? Which is preferable, the family allowance or an extension of free services for children? More adequate provision of public facilities and free services to rural communities where incomes are low, or attempts to supplement money incomes by transfer payments from the public treasury?

Relief of the needy in their own homes was once in the form of the basket of food, the grocery order, fuel, and clothing. Now public assistance is largely in the form of cash payments. Thus freedom of choice as to what is most needed or desired and the usual family situation and type of domestic economy are maintained. The decision that the cash payment is the appropriate form of public assistance does not negate the strong argument for the free goods and services. The latter policy permits the community to determine what is provided and for whom. It represents a social decision as to relative needs, children versus adults, milk versus "soft drinks," medical treatment or education versus other possible uses of income.

DIFFERENTIATION OF GOVERNMENTAL SERVICES

So far the discussion has been in rather general terms, the applicability of which varies greatly from one class of free services to another. The specific policy questions arising in connection with one class of these highly varied goods and services provided at government expense are quite different from those arising in connection with another. The issues with respect to the extension and improvement of the public highways, for example, are quite different from those with respect to the school-lunch program. Before consideration of these issues it is desirable that the governmental activities which directly enhance the family level of living be differentiated from others that are commonly found, a differentiation at some points easy and at others difficult, as one category of services merges into another. It is not easy to classify the services performed by the state. They overlap on the basis of objectives, interests served, and results.

One class of governmental activities is inherent in the nature of the state and the purposes for which it exists, such as the national defense, the preservation of law and order, the administration of justice, the exercise of the regulatory functions, and the protection of personal rights. The local, state, or federal government may also engage in productive enterprise, such enterprises as those represented by the post office or the ownership and operation of a public utility. Here are included all those designed to pay their own way on the basis of the fees and charges for the services rendered. The charges may be adjusted in such a way as to favor certain users or uses, but the enterprise as a whole is designed to be self-supporting. The enterprises chosen for public operation in nonsocialistic societies are those affected with such public interest that the extent, character, and permanence of services offered cannot be left to private enterprise and those which are by nature monopolistic and require either public provision or public regulation. The former may present fewer problems.

Another group of governmental services are those the benefits of which are so remote in time or diffused among the population that they will not be privately provided. Such are most flood-control projects, many forest and soil conservation projects, and public health measures. Included here also are many of the fact-gathering and research activities increasingly undertaken by government agencies.[1] The special characteristic of many

1. Weather forecasting would also fall in this category.

of this group of activities is that no one can be excluded from their benefits whether he pays for them or not. The only feasible way of securing them is through government enterprise, which can ignore the problem of securing voluntary payments.

This last group of activities merges into another that is distinctive in the sense that specific beneficiaries can be identified, although there are also general benefits. Some are directly designed to serve producer interests; others serve both producer and consumer. Here falls the provision of roads, streets, and bridges; radio programs; and the so-called housekeeping activities of towns and cities, the street lighting and cleaning, garbage and sewage disposal, and the like. More specific are the benefits and identifiable the beneficiaries when we come to the types of free services represented by the schools and universities, recreational facilities, libraries, museums, concerts, schoolbooks and lunches, subsidized housing, medical and hospital services. In this last group of services described are those which are distinctly for consumer use and enjoyment. They directly and immediately supplement what is available through the use of money income. To be included also in this category are the benefits and enjoyments derived from the public acquisition and control of places of unusual natural beauty, historic spots, and works of art. If privately owned and exclusively used, the sum of the satisfactions derived from them would be greatly reduced. If enjoyment by the many is to be insured, there must often be public ownership of lakes, streams, forests, and beaches, since nature may have strictly limited the supply.

FREE SERVICES FOR WHOM?

Some of the free public services are available to anyone who cares to use them. Others are available only to the needy, and still others only to children or to other special groups. One of the issues often arising when free public provision of some service is proposed is: For whom shall it be provided? For everyone, or only for those judged unable to pay, or other prescribed group?

There are obviously some public facilities the use of which could not easily be restricted even if it were desired to do so. Such would be the roads, streets, and bridges, most recreational facilities, the parks, the beaches, and playgrounds, street lighting and cleaning, and sewage and garbage disposal. The restrictions, if any, are likely to be upon their use by the less well-to-do through the imposition of tolls, fees, and charges. The principle that schools shall be free for both rich and poor is well established in this country. It would be possible however to maintain free schools only for the poor children or to give only these children free tuition. All communities do not provide schoolbooks for all children, and it has been hotly debated whether a midday lunch at less than cost should be furnished for all or only for those whose parents could not pay the full cost. Hospital care is usually provided only for the needy or the "medically needy," that is, for those who, although able to pay their own way in other respects, cannot meet the expense of hospitalization. Frequent exceptions are the mentally ill, the tubercular, or those with other designated illness. The policy of providing care and treatment at public expense for all who apply has, however, been questioned. Instead it is urged a charge should be imposed upon those patients, or the relatives of those patients, who are able to pay. Concerning public housing there is no question, since tenancy is limited to low-income families.

To determine sound public policy in this respect, the consequences of restriction of public provision to those judged needy must be weighed. Total public outlay may thus be reduced and more income left in private hands for personal and family use, or the saving in this area may permit the expansion or improvement of some other public service or the improvement of the one in question. Upon the other hand one must ask, "What will be the effect of limited free provision upon the adequacy with which the need for the service will be met?" If with restriction a need will not be met as fully and completely as the public welfare requires, the argument is strong for availability to all without reference to ability to pay.

Restrictions on the basis of ability to pay are one thing, on the basis of age or special need for the service another. There undoubtedly are types of illness that because of the nature of the disability or its duration could only in relatively few cases be adequately dealt with by the patient or his family. In some cases, for the protection of the community, early detection and possibly isolation are necessary. One would expect the care and treatment of such patients to be high on the list of medical and hospital services publicly provided. One would also expect the educational and health needs of children to have a high priority rating. The development of free services for children is a way of lessening the concentration of the burden of support which it has been shown is so great at any given time. It represents, moreover, a social investment in human resources which if wisely directed will yield high returns to the community over time. There is a special argument against the requirement that free goods and services be made available only to those children whose parents are unable to supply them. Unless very carefully applied, the resulting stigma may have undesirable psychological effects. The provision of free schoolbooks or a free school lunch, for example, only to those judged unable to pay is questionable policy unless the greatest care is taken. The invidious distinctions created may injure the children as much in one way as they are benefited in another.

A special problem arises in those communities that insist upon segregation of Negroes. If they provide truly equal facilities to both whites and Negroes, the cost of the services provided will inevitably be much greater than if the two groups were not segregated. The result is that neither group enjoys educational and other services they might otherwise have. When they do not provide equal facilities, as they ordinarily do not, it is the Negroes who suffer. Thus there is least public provision for the members of the community least able to provide for themselves, and economic differentials are perpetuated. It is true of course that services provided for the needy will go in disproportionate amount to the Negro population if need is the only criterion used, since Negroes are found in disproportionate numbers in the low-income and needy groups.

WHAT TYPES OF GOODS AND SERVICES SHOULD BE PROVIDED AT PUBLIC EXPENSE?

Goods and services provided free at public expense have in the main certain common characteristics. One is that they represent values about which there is little or no dispute: health, sanitation, education, recreation. The goods and services in question are those generally considered necessaries, either what everyone wants or what everyone ought to want if aware of what makes for a high level of well-being. The free goods and services therefore constitute a community-provided minimum of items essential for a proper level of living. The community is thus assured that no one will go without because of inability to pay or because he prefers to use his income for other purposes. Free provision tends to correct not only defects in consumption due to limited income but those due to ignorance of need and faulty values. Use of certain publicly provided facilities is made compulsory, the public school system, for example, unless equivalent educational provision is otherwise made for those under a specified age. Vaccination or similar medical safeguards may also be made compulsory. But for most goods and services compulsory use is not desirable or feasible. The individual seeks the benefit or enjoyment provided as he pleases. The free provision simply removes economic barriers.

The second pervasive characteristic of the free services is that the community as a whole has a stake in their widespread use. Use of many of these services benefits others as well as the user. It is almost as important to a family that a neighbor's child be vaccinated as his own, or fire on a neighbor's premises be put out, or a neighbor's garbage collected. The community has a stake in the education, health, and physical development of every child, in the opportunities of all members of the community for recreation and aesthetic appreciation and experience. It is not the immediate happiness of the individual as such that lies behind public policy in most instances of free provision but the benefits to the population as a whole if the utility in question is extensively enjoyed.

The first criterion for choice of the free goods and services is then the social importance of their widespread availability and use. Their provision at governmental expense rests upon the assumption that the only or best way of insuring this availability and use is by this public policy. A second criterion for choice of the free goods and services, or what may be regarded as a special application of the first principle, is that those which are of the nature of investments have special grounds for approval; that is, social benefits, economic and otherwise, may be expected to extend and to increase over time. Of such a nature are those that may be described as investments in human resources. The community's interest here is closely akin to its interest in investment in capital resources. The provision of certain free goods and services is not solely to mitigate the effects of current poverty or income inadequacy but may be a part of a policy designed to reduce it and to raise the general income level.

A third criterion for the choice of the free public services is that they should be those in which the chances of wasteful use are at a minimum and, more important, are those which the state can be expected to supply at a satisfactory level of quality and cost. Considerations that come under this heading are especially prominent when alternative modes of provision are possible, but they suggest and merge into the issue of the cost and quality in general of services provided by public agencies.

COST AND QUALITY OF FREE SERVICES

The provision of an extended list of free goods and services raises some of the same questions as the provision of civil rights income in the form of cash benefits or assistance. How far shall such redistribution of income go and by what system shall the necessary revenues be secured? The benefits of the former, however, are more widely diffused throughout the community, especially if the services are free for all who wish to make use of them. There is not the same differentiation between beneficiaries and contributors. The same questions may be raised in both cases concerning the political implications of the state playing Santa Claus, or providing "bread and circuses," and the same questions concerning the weakening of the individual's sense of responsibility and incentive to enterprise, industry, and thrift. To the latter it may be answered that, if the free services have been wisely selected on the basis of the criteria set up, the effect will have been to advance the standard of living; that is, raise the "sights" of the population with respect to what is desirable. Education, new experience, improved health and vigor, are not conducive to sloth and a narrow range of interests but rather the reverse.

There is also the question of the respective role of the federal government, the state, and the local units. What services shall each provide, set the standards for, and finance? Historically there has tended to be a transfer of responsibility for many services from county or township to the state and from the state to the federal government. Concerning many services there is no question as to which unit shall provide. Those that benefit mainly the local community and in which outsiders have relatively little stake are clearly local responsibilities. The relative diseconomy and inefficiency of a central organization for the performance of local functions are obvious. Street lighting and cleaning and garbage collection are as unmistakably local as the building and maintenance of through roads are central. There are strong arguments for local experiment and community decision in regard to community needs. Upon the other hand, there are services which benefit many or all communities which the central government must undertake whether they involve local operation or not. Not only might they not otherwise be undertaken, but they might be less efficiently and economically performed. The list, moreover, of public services in which all rather than a single community have a stake inevitably grows as, with population movements and developments in transportation, communication, production, and distribution, the social, economic, and cultural unit expands and is no longer delimited by city, county, or even state.

The number of public services provided by the central government has probably not grown as fast, however, as the number provided by the local agencies. The concern of the state and the national government in the quality and volume of the public services has shown itself rather in the desire to exercise some degree of control and the willingness to subsidize. Since standards and ability to pay vary greatly from community to community, there may be great differences in the quality and number of the free public services. When the central government has the power to set minimum standards, it often does so. When it does not, as is usually true of the federal government, conformity to the desired standard, as well as provision of new services, is often "purchased" or stimulated by offering a grant-in-aid. Federal gift and federal subsidy have stimulated the development of various state and local services. Notable examples are the land-grant colleges, vocational education, maternal- and child-health measures, and public housing.

Objections to the extension of public services sometimes focus upon the danger of relatively high costs and low quality due to inefficiency, corrupt practices, and the type of control that goes with governmental operations. The feared impairment of quality will arise from one source in the case of an educational project, from another in the case of medical or hospital services, and from another in the case of garbage or sewage disposal or street cleaning. There may be little likelihood of such impairment, or there may be real dangers to guard against. Whatever responsibilities are assumed by a governmental unit, whether provision of schools or of highways, the problem of insuring efficiency and proper standards for operation arises. Knowledge of sound principles of public administration becomes an increasingly important part of the equipment of the electorate and the elected or appointed officers of the state.

Some goods provided by public agencies are purchased from private suppliers as in the case of schoolbooks. Physicians in private practice may provide medical care at government expense on a fee-for-service basis. Most public services, however, are provided by public employees who work for a wage or salary, as teachers, librarians, police, firemen, and scores of others. Public agencies build and manage public housing, construct and maintain schools, highways, and bridges, acquire and maintain forest preserves, parks, and playgrounds. The danger of inefficiency and relatively high costs in these operations has several possible sources. Among them are limited incentive to reduce costs or improve practices, overelaborate administrative machinery, political pressures that adversely affect operations, the "patronage" rather than the merit system of making appointments, tenure systems that prevent the weeding-out of the inefficient, corrupt practices, and favoritism in buying supplies and equipment. One can unfortunately find examples of many of these weaknesses in the history and current management of public enterprises in this country. Some states, cities, and local units have good records; others, poor. The record of the federal government has generally been superior to that of the states and local authorities. Some agencies at all levels have outstanding records of honest and highly efficient operation; others, indifferent or poor.

Many of the weaknesses shown by public enterprise in this country are not inherent in it. They are remediable. They exist because of the ignorance and low standards of the electorate and the officials they select. If a public service is desirable but not undertaken because of the danger of corruption and malpractice, it means that American communities have not learned how to manage their political institutions to their own advantage and must forego policies that would be for the common benefit. In any case, whenever a public service is undertaken, the quality and economy of its performance must become a matter of public concern. The hospitals for the care of the tubercular or the mentally ill may fall far below acceptable standards; so may the highways or the universities. In a town or city the street cleaning, the garbage collection and disposal, the protection given by the police, or some aspect of the public school system may be seriously defective. If the public does not know how to correct these deficiencies or exert itself to this end, the advantages secured from the outlay involved are correspondingly minimized.

OUTLAYS FOR FREE GOODS AND SERVICES

The data that would show the governmental outlay for goods and services of the type here under discussion are not readily available, either the total or the amounts for the various categories. A study by the Bureau of the Census of governmental expenditures in 1942 shows something of the picture. The major governmental outlays in that year were to pay the costs of past and current wars, around three-fifths of those by all governmental units and four-fifths of those by the federal government. Of all other outlays, those for such services as highways, schools, parks, health, hospitals, and sanitation were from two-fifths to one-half of the total.[2] Well over half of the total outlays for the latter purposes came from the treasuries of the local governmental units. From three-fifths to three-fourths of all local outlays were for such purposes, but only from a tenth to an eighth of those of the federal government. Over half of the nonwar expenditures of the federal government, moreover, were in the form of aid to the states or local authorities, and almost as large a proportion of the disbursements of the states were grants-in-aid to local units. The largest expenditure of the character under discussion, mainly by local units, was for schools. The next largest was for highways. The states' outlay for the latter purpose was higher than that of either federal or local governments, a third in the form of aid to local units.

2. U.S. Bureau of the Census, *Governmental Finances in the United States, 1942* (Washington: Government Printing Office, 1945). The data are not given in sufficient detail to permit exact estimation.

FUTURE EXPANSION OF FREE SERVICES

Expansion of the free services may take three forms. One is expansion of existing facilities to take care of the increasing population. Many schools are now overcrowded at the lower levels due to the recent increase in the birth rate. A second form of expansion is the extension of services to localities or groups, as the Negro population, where the level of provision is below the national average or below an acceptable standard. A third form of expansion is the provision of services not previously, or very infrequently, provided. Difference of opinion as to what is wise policy is especially likely to be found on this third issue.

The improvement of the quality of the free services often, although not always, raises financial issues; their expansion inevitably does so. From what sources shall the funds be secured? Entirely from the community that enjoys the services or the governmental unit that provides them? What aid shall the state give the local communities and what aid shall come from the federal treasury? A current issue is federal aid to education, which has been almost entirely the responsibility of the local communities. If there is federal or state aid, what control shall the fund-supplying agency exercise over the services or facilities provided?

One would be fairly safe in predicting an expansion and improvement in certain public facilities, given peace and prosperity. Such would be the highways and recreational facilities both in city and in country. The automobile, the shorter working day and week, the paid vacation, make possible the enjoyment of the out-of-doors, and of sports and recreations both near home and far away, by an increasing proportion of the population. City and regional plans include generous provision of open spaces and facilities for community activities and recreation. Rural communities are thinking in the same terms. There is little doubt also that educational facilities will expand as well the services offered by schools, libraries, and other agencies that offer educational opportunities. The expansion of educational facilities has come and is continuing in two ways; one, an enrichment of the curriculum; the other, the provision of an educational program for both younger and older age groups than previously. It is less and less necessary for parents to supplement by private instruction the services provided as a part of the public school system. As another form of expansion the kindergarten is becoming an accepted part of the public school system, and not only high schools but local junior colleges as well as state universities are provided for those in the higher age groups. The possibilities and need for adult education are increasingly becoming evident. The next decade or so may well show a great expansion in educational opportunities for those no longer in school as interests and needs appear, either vocational or otherwise. Such a development would alter the school program greatly to its advantage, since it would no longer be considered necessary to pack into it a little of everything the young people might need in the future.

The great increase in the high school and college population in recent years suggests that educational facilities at the higher levels will increasingly be provided at public expense. Two new problems that inevitably arise in this connection should be noted. Both arise from the same source: the need for greater specialization in the course of study of the older students at the higher levels. Practically all children of six have the same educational needs. But, as they move to higher and higher levels, this universality of need gives way to diversity. Differences in interest and aptitude show themselves. General education terminates, and specialized begins. Every community cannot, however, support a specialized educational institution. Universities and professional schools must be regional or national. They must be provided by central rather than local government. Students must leave their homes and reside near them. The costs of residence away from home operate, however, as a deterrent to attendance. Even if tuition is free, the burden of support will be prohibitive for lower-income families. It is clear that if all young people are to have equal educational opportunity, and education is not to be a function of family income, the state or private philanthropy must provide not only free tuition but free or partly free books and maintenance.

The second problem that attends the development of free educational facilities at the higher levels comes from the necessity of developing proper requirements for eligibility. Up to a point the question is: Who must attend school? To what age shall attendance be required? Beyond that point the question is: Who may attend, partially or wholly, at public expense? When attendance is compulsory the assumption is that the school provides a curriculum that meets the needs and capacities of the child and that the investment is to the public benefit. If attendance is not compulsory and investment must be selective, how shall eligibility to pursue a particular course of study be determined? Shall there be pretesting or determination by an expensive process of trial and error?

A further problem of different character, in connection not only with the publicly supported educational institutions but those privately endowed which are given tax exemptions, is becoming increasingly apparent. It is a problem that involves the very nature of the educational process and its objectives. By whom and by what standards shall the teachers be selected, the curriculums be determined? Who shall select the books and the teaching material? What shall be the subjects for classroom discussion and investigation and the procedures and methods of inquiry? On the one hand, there is the belief, supported by man's whole intellectual history, that teaching and inquiry must be free and disinterested; that the capacity to discriminate between truth and error is the fundamental objective of education. On the other, there is the desire of a society to insure that nothing subversive to its own institutions be taught and that the values it considers fundamental be those developed and strengthened by the educational process. In the church-supported schools similar issues have appeared, and those privately endowed were once under the suspicion of adjusting their teaching to fit the interests of past or potential donors. With the development of the publicly supported institutions and with legislative control over funds, new issues appeared. What are the responsibilities of the citizens? What control shall they exercise over the schools and colleges they support? Over the selection of teachers and administrators, curriculums, and textbooks? In a state where the dairy interests are powerful shall the teachers of home economics abstain from mentioning that margarine is palatable and nutritious, or in the "corn-and-hog" states that there are other cooking fats besides lard? What freedom shall agricultural economists have in discussing farm policy in states dominated by agricultural interests, or labor economists in discussing union principles and practices in states where organized labor is strong? Who shall determine what is emphasized in American history? Careful consideration of principle and practice is overdue on these and related issues if the public schools at all levels are to serve their purpose. The resolution of these crucial issues will take one form in the authoritarian societies and another in those built on freedom. The society that expands its educational program beyond the three "R's" clearly has some difficult problems to settle. Investigation might even show that some of the past expansion has been education only in form, not in substance.

While the expansion of educational and certain other free services can be predicted with a high degree of certainty, the policy with respect to others, at least in the immediate future, is by no means certain. There are obvious limits to the expansion of the subsidized housing program. The problems of inadequate supply of low-cost rental housing of acceptable standard, of slums and substandard housing, of high housing costs in general, must be solved in the main in some other way. Nor is it likely, unless a deep and prolonged depression should place great numbers of people in the poverty group, that the cost of food will be subsidized, as was once proposed, by the use of a "food-stamp" plan.[3] The argument is sometimes made that broadcasting, as in Great Britain, should be made a public monopoly with the government responsible for the programs. If supported by a special tax upon those with receiving sets, it would not be a free good but a public utility similar to the postal service. Would the educational and recreational level of the programs improve if radio and television were no longer advertising media, supported for that reason by business concerns? Most important, are these agencies of communication analogous to the press, the freedom of which we consider indispensable?

SHOULD THE HEALTH SERVICES BE FREE SERVICES?

One issue upon which opinion is sharply divided is what expansion should be made in the provision of free medical and hospital care. Some expansion is certain, but for whom and on what terms is an issue hotly debated. Public health measures are generally approved, since there is no other method by which the spread of certain diseases can be checked and the physical environment in which people work and live be kept healthful. The health services that involve individual treatment and care are a different matter. The provision of medical and hospital care for those with certain communicable diseases, notably tuberculosis and venereal diseases, and for the mentally ill and those with certain other disorders, is generally approved and will probably expand. Those receiving public assistance receive some free medical and hospital care. More adequate provision is expected for those toward whose assistance the federal government contributes, since under the 1950 amendments to the Social Security Act the states will be partially reimbursed from the federal treasury for payments for these purposes. In many communities free services are provided for the medically needy, that is, those who, although self-supporting, would be unable without difficulty and deprivation to pay the costs of a major illness.[4] A federal act of 1946, amended in 1949, provides for

3. During the depression of the thirties families receiving public assistance received stamps, good for the purchase of certain foods. The list of foods purchasable by this "currency" was altered from time to time, but within the list the stamp-holder selected as he desired. This plan, it was suggested, could be extended to low-income families. Although when utilized as a part of the relief program the foods so made purchasable, as those provided free for school lunches, were the "surplus" foods bought to support farm prices rather than those most important from the nutritive standpoint, the program was an interesting example of a combination of a degree of private choice and a degree of public control over what was consumed at the public expense.

4. Federal, state, and local expenditures for medical and hospital care of civilians amounted to about $1.6 billions in 1948–49 and for the institutional care of the blind, deaf, aged, mentally ill, and other handicapped about $223 millions. About a third of the combined expenditures for these two purposes came from the federal treasury (*Social Security Bulletin*, July, 1950,

federal assistance to the states for surveys and construction of hospitals. Some medical research is publicly supported, and several states have passed laws to facilitate the formation of nonprofit plans by which families meet the expense of medical and hospital care by fixed, periodic prepayments. In some states public funds are used for scholarships and loans to medical students and for the construction and support of new teaching centers in order to expand the supply of medical practitioners. But the desirability of measures that would provide for the payment of the medical and hospital bills of civilians other than the needy or certain categories of patients is questioned.

In many respects medical and hospital care meet the criteria for services to be furnished at public expense. They are generally considered essential for everyone as and when need is indicated. The prevention and treatment of mental and physical disorders are clearly to the social advantage in the long as well as the short run. Field studies have given quantitative evidence of a fact that can be readily observed: medical and hospital care varies with income.[5] Members of high-income families receive more such care than do those with low income, although the incidence of disabling illness is just the reverse. Lower expenditures by low-income families might be interpreted to mean that hospitals' and physicians' fees were adjusted to the income of the patient, but the services they receive are also less frequent and fewer. Diagnosis and treatment are postponed, or even foregone if expensive, when the income is low. Measures that might detect incipient disorders are rare. Only curative treatment is sought.

There is strong opposition, however, by many members of the medical profession to the transfer of medical care from individual purchase to a free service. Some of the opposition may be based, consciously or unconsciously, upon the fear that it would not be to their financial advantage; that the relatively high earnings that many have enjoyed would disappear. Many also have not looked at the total picture of the distribution of medical services among the population or given thought to its social implications. There is a natural resistance to change. But from those who do see the problem there is argument that other solutions than what they call "socialization" are both feasible and preferable. Some have argued that free services by physicians to the medically needy, and a sliding scale

---

p. 16). For an excellent review of public policy with respect to medical care see Franz Goldmann, "Medical Care," *Social Work Year Book, 1951* (New York: American Association of Social Workers, 1951).

5. U.S. National Institute of Health, *The National Health Survey, 1935–1936* (Washington, 1938). (Processed.)

of fees and charges determined by each physician after investigation of each patient's resources, would solve the problem. They may even point to the volume of bills uncollected as evidence that those who cannot pay do not pay. This argument is so vulnerable that it is receding into the background. As a system supposedly in operation it has not solved the problem, nor has it worked equitably among patients or among the physicians themselves. It places upon the latter responsibilities that will be differently interpreted and carried out and that they are not equipped to discharge. The solution of the problem now promoted by the profession is the extension of voluntary prepayment plans to cover the costs of hospital care and the "catastrophic" illness, which alone involve high costs.

The argument of the medical profession against making medical care a free service as it is in Great Britain rests upon the all-important issue of its effect upon the quality of the service offered. To maintain quality of services and standards for training, the administration of schools, hospitals, and clinics must remain in the hands of the profession and be free from political control or control by public administrative agencies. Financial and other rewards of the profession must be the result of competence and skill if incentives for their attainment are to be strong. Patients must be free to choose their physician.

The case of the medical profession is strengthened by all the weaknesses that have appeared in the administration of veterans' hospitals and in other types of publicly administered institutions. Upon the other hand, if the policy as a whole is sound, it is unfortunate that it may not be adopted on the ground that proper standards and procedures may not be developed and maintained. Health services might be provided at public expense without making physicians the salaried employees of the state. They might be remunerated as at present on a fee-for-service basis with total income determined by those fees and the patients who elect their services. Physicians who chose might remain in private practice or might combine private practice with treatment of those whose fees are paid by the state. Care must also be taken that judgments are not based on a comparison of a system of public health services imperfectly administered and a system or private purchase with the defects ignored. The patient's choice of a physician today is often exercised within very narrow limits and based upon imperfect knowledge, and the system of measuring and rewarding competence and skill by no means works perfectly.

Resistance to the establishment of a system of free hospital and medical service comes also from those who ask: How much would it cost? Who would pay the bill? Under the system of payment as and when services are received, the sick pay the fees. Under the prepayment plans the expenses for those upon whom sickness falls are paid by all currently enrolled in such plans, both the sick and the well. The resemblance to the various types of insurance is obvious. If medical and hospital care were a free public service, the cost would be paid by those who contributed to the public revenues. If payment for these services came from the general revenues, contributed on the basis of ability to pay, the higher-income groups would help to pay for the care and treatment of those with lower incomes. Those with small families or none would help to pay for the care of those with larger. Most of the systems proposed would follow the lines of the Social Security Act and make eligibility to receive health services dependent upon the prior payment of a tax at a flat rate upon a specified amount of earnings. If only the taxpayer were eligible to receive the services, a large part of the population would in that case not be covered. If those of a defined relationship to the taxpayers were eligible, the larger families would receive the greater benefits. If the tax were imposed only upon wage-earners, a large segment of the population would also be left uncovered.

The argument for eligibility based upon tax payment is twofold. The system may be called health insurance, a change from a voluntary to a mandatory prepayment plan. Beneficiaries are made aware of their responsibility for meeting the costs of the services and thus would have a direct interest in the prevention of waste and unnecessary service. The latter issue is important. There is no doubt that, if medical services were freely provided, the total outlay for the purpose would exceed total expenditures at present even if some economies were effected through a different organization of medical practice. This would follow from the premise that many in need of such service are not now receiving it. In time, if the service were secured as and when needed and preventive measures were more generally taken, outlays per person might fall. But would unnecessary calls upon physicians increase and the stay in hospitals lengthen unduly if cost were no longer a deterrent? The answer would seem to rest with the medical profession, since eligibility to receive service would always depend upon their certification.

What the public verdict will be in regard to the policy in question is at present unknown. California in 1949 initiated compulsory insurance against the cost of hospitalization. It may be that the expansion of free medical service will follow the direction of the past: to patients with certain disorders and possibly to children. The latter especially would seem wise if dental service is considered. If provided free to adults, the total outlay would probably increase relatively far more than for the medical service. But if provided free at the outset only for children, the service could be extended later to adults without great increase in costs, since presumably most of them would then have good teeth and healthy mouths.

FAMILY USE OF THE FREE SERVICES

Some of the considerations that determine the public provision of certain facilities and services have been suggested, but what determines family policy with respect to their use when choice is possible? The private school, the private golf course, tennis court, or bathing beach, often is preferred to the public. A family may never patronize the public library and may, as was said, supplement public services with those privately supported. There are certain objections from the social standpoint to the patronage of the privately supported service or facility rather than the public. If families so doing are the more powerful and enlightened, the loss of the pressure that they would otherwise exert for the improvement of the public service may be a serious matter. When only the poorer groups or those with the lower standards patronize the public schools, those schools are less likely to come up to an acceptable standard than when the children of all groups attend them. When the more well-to-do citizens supplement the city street-cleaning and similar housekeeping activities with their own paid service, they are less interested than otherwise in the quality of the public service. The poorer sections of the city are notoriously the less well cared for, since they can usually bring less pressure to bear on the responsible officials.

Patronage of private schools that are "exclusive" or that have high fees may have other undesirable results. The best index of a social democracy and the best instrument for the formation of sound social attitudes is a school system to which all children are admitted on equal terms. Anything else puts an emphasis upon advantages and accidents of birth rather than the merit of the individual. It is of course the parents' responsibility to provide the best for their children, especially the best in the way of education. This principle may at a particular time and place operate against the choice of a public school. Possible distortion of the child's social values and narrowing of his contacts must be appraised as well as formal educational advantages in making the choice.

Whatever may be the social objections to a division of the community on a "class" or income basis with respect to the use of public services, there is no question but that families should be free to provide a substitute for or supplement the public service as income, inclination, or special need indicates, so long as proper standards of health, sanitation, and education are not impaired. The public library is never a complete substitute for the private library. A child may be given instruction in religion, in music, in drawing, in languages, in dancing, beyond what the school provides.

One characteristic of many free facilities is that they involve "socialized" consumption; that is, their use must be shared with many. The limitation thereby imposed upon the users' enjoyment varies with the facility in question and their needs and tastes. Things produced and provided for the many may not meet the needs or tastes of some individuals. If possession or exclusive use is highly important, a facility that must be shared with others gives limited satisfaction. To some, possession in itself is a good; others do not wish to mix with a crowd. If privacy is greatly esteemed, one will not enjoy the public beach or park or playground. But some persons are extremely gregarious and enjoy the presence of many others. What socialized consumption entails varies greatly from one class of goods to another. The individual cannot always enjoy in privacy a public art gallery or concert or swimming pool, but books from a public library may be read at home. Upon the whole, however, preference for privacy, for choice of companions, for exclusive use of books, pictures, and possessions, means that the economies of socialized consumption cannot be widely extended.[6]

6. In chap. i it was pointed out that the family as a way of living arose from deep-seated preferences of this sort.

CHAPTER IX

INCOME INSECURITY

NEXT to prolonged inadequacy of current income comes uncertainty as to future income as an economic problem. Some would argue that it ranks first as a cause of economic distress. However that may be, the command over goods represented by current income is but one dimension of total economic welfare. Two others are what it has cost to secure it and the prospects with respect to the future. The costs of securing it are the irksomeness of the labor, which takes a diversity of forms, and the hours that must be devoted to it. It has been alleged that "the happiest man is neither the richest man nor the quietest man. He is the man who does the most interesting work."[1] Which element in economic welfare comes first may be debatable; that security is one of them is not.

There is abundant evidence that assurance of income continuity is highly desired and actively sought. Few enjoy hand-to-mouth living or take no thought for the morrow. It is true that, when faced with future uncertainties about which they believe they can do little or nothing, men wisely ignore them and live only in the present. It is hope and some degree of confidence in the efficacy of the measures taken that stimulate action to relieve the anxiety of the moment and ward off possible privation in the future. The drive for income security shows itself in manifold ways: in private saving; in the acquisition of assets the income from which will continue in spite of disability, old age, or death; in private insurance against these risks; in the attempts of wage- and salary-earners to secure "tenure" and "seniority" and to make rights to disability and old age income a part of their contract with the employer; in the pressure for statutory assurance of an income from public funds or for price support by farmers; in the pressure for protection against circumstances that threaten jobs or markets. Many restrictive practices of labor and business have as their basis the desire for income security. Some ways of enhancing security are generally considered highly desirable; concerning others there is a difference of opinion, and others are clearly to the social disadvantage. Some

1. David McCord Wright, *Democracy and Progress* (New York: Macmillan Co., 1949), p. 23. The man may be happy, but, if his income is inadequate or uncertain, his family is not.

diminish the current income of the individuals affected; others do not. Some are old; others are relatively new. All indicate an unwillingness to rely upon maintenance by next of kin, in the case of the aged by their children, of the orphaned by parents' siblings, of the disabled by those closest in family ties.

Some of the recent manifestations of the drive for enhanced security have led to the assertion that the population now puts security where it once put economic opportunity and freedom, an undesirable change in values. It is also said that many in the population are abandoning the self-sacrificing, self-reliant modes of making financial provision for life's contingencies to seek provision at the expense of others. Again it is argued that some of the new ways of enhancing security adversely affect mobility, efficiency, and the rate of economic progress. Here are interwoven questions of fact and logic, of motivation and values. We start only with the assumption that security is intensely desired and that the desire finds expression in many forms. Only after the types of risks to which the income of the breadwinner is exposed are analyzed is the setting provided for appraising to what extent and by what means the risks may be reduced and the adverse effect of their impact be lessened.

To some extent the problem of income inadequacy discussed in previous chapters is one of income insecurity. Not all the income recipients represented in an income distribution in a particular year are full-time workers for pay or profit. Some in the distribution are not currently earning but are living on income from investments, annuities, pensions, benefits, or public assistance. Others have been involuntarily idle for part of the period from lack of work or inability to work. Some are heads of families in which there is no adult male contributor. Ideally the data would permit the separation of these classes of income recipients. Thus various causes of poverty could be distinguished; that due to low rates of pay or profit, that due to discontinuity of earnings, and that due to other causes of income insufficiency. The proportions of income recipients in the various classes would obviously vary from time to time.

FORMS OF INCOME INSECURITY

Two quite different classes of contingencies may cause the lapse or termination of income. One class includes those things that destroy temporarily or permanently the earning power of the individual; the other those things that destroy the market for his services, his funds, or the products of his business enterprise. Thus there are two kinds of risks, personal and economic. The personal risks to which the breadwinner and his dependents are exposed are his disability or death from sickness, accident, or old age. The chances of disabling sickness during youth and the middle years are diminishing. Some diseases which once made great inroads upon the population have been practically wiped out, and the death rate from many others has been greatly reduced. Steadily increasing knowledge and practice of methods of preventing and curing illness have more than counterbalanced new sources of bodily ills. We have not been so successful in cutting down the rate of occurrence of disabling or fatal accidents, since new hazards tend to appear almost as fast as we reduce the old ones.

The risk of industrial accident has been notably lessened in recent years. The extended use of safety devices and methods has reduced the number of deaths from injuries sustained while at work, not only relatively but absolutely. The frequency of disabling injuries at work has also been declining. Special effort is now being made to reduce injuries and deaths from motor vehicles. Deaths from this source are about twice as frequent as those from occupational accidents.[2] Nonfatal accidents at work exceed those from motor vehicles, however, by about 80 per cent. Fatal accidents in the home exceed even those from motor vehicles. These accidents occur mainly to the older family members. In 1949, 56 per cent of the fatal accidents in the home were those of persons sixty-five and over, although they were only about 10 per cent of the population. Thus the increased proportion of persons of this age in the population brings up the number of home accidents. About half of all nonfatal accidents occur in the home.

Declining rates of injury and death from accident do not mean that all known preventive measures are in operation or that the vigilance of all is that of the reasonable man of whom the jurists speak in discussing cases of negligence. A major line of attack upon the problem of income insecurity from disability and premature death is the attempt to find and secure the use of preventive measures. Successful efforts mean not only an increase in income security but also a reduction in waste of human resources, as well as of suffering and grief.

OLD AGE AS AN ECONOMIC RISK

Our success in reducing morbidity and mortality rates in the early and middle years and thus extending the average life-span has resulted, however, in increasing the proportion of the population that is sixty-five, seventy, seventy-five, and over. The life-expectation at birth of American white males was 65.9 years in 1949; of white females, 71.5. In 1900 it was

2. National Safety Council, *Accident Facts* (Chicago: National Safety Council, 1950).

48.2 and 51.1 years, respectively.[3] We cannot reduce the number of untimely deaths without increasing the number of persons who live beyond the time they can earn their keep. The proportion of the nonproductive old as well as nonproductive young is steadily growing. Old age is becoming an increasing economic hazard for each individual; the chance that he will live beyond the age when he can work for pay or profit. Medical science is now concentrating on the ailments responsible for the incapacities of older people. Thus the age at which senescence begins may be pushed upward. If there is still a long period of weakened or weakening powers, economic and other problems remain.

Economic old age begins when the employability of the person lessens, when a younger person is preferred, when the older person is the last to be hired or first to be fired, or when there is a fixed age for retirement. In part, it is related to physiological old age. The two may not coincide if chronological age is used as the criterion of employability. Mental and physical powers decline at different rates for different persons, and the powers that decline may be important in one occupation and not in another. Transfer to a new employment with requirements the older person can meet has been suggested, but such transfer is not easy and may be inacceptable if pay and prestige are lower. Compulsory retirement at a fixed age has various roots. A fixed rule for everyone makes planning easier and avoids the necessity of invidious comparisons between persons. It sets a limit to the employment of those who would cling to their jobs indefinitely by virtue of tenure rights. It is related also to the "make-work" philosophy that is a part of the fear of unemployment and is an expression of the desire of the younger for power and promotion.

Old age is the one life-hazard that is bound to increase. It shows itself as an increased proportion of the aged in the population and as a lengthening period in the individual life-span. Its special implications in an industrial urban economy must be noted. In an agricultural economy tasks adapted to their capacities and strength may be found for both children and old people. In the city home where space is at a premium, where every bite of food costs money, where one person can take care of all the household tasks, the position of the older man or woman is far different from

3. The data on which these figures are based are not adequate to permit an estimate of the life-expectancy of the nonwhite population in 1900. In 1930 the life-expectation of nonwhite men was 47.6 years; in 1949, 58.6. For nonwhite women the life-expectation was 49.5 years in 1930 and 62.9 in 1949 (U.S. Bureau of the Census, *Statistical Abstract of the United States, 1952* [Washington: Government Printing Office, 1952], p. 79). For earlier figures for the white population see U.S. Bureau of the Census, *Historical Statistics of the United States, 1789–1945* (Washington: Government Printing Office, 1949).

that in the farm home where an extra pair of hands is usually needed in house or garden. The cramped house and yard, if there is a yard, the limited scope for activity in the city home, aggravate the inevitable problems that attend the adjustment of the lives of two different generations brought together under one roof. For happy and healthful old age the norm should be financial independence and independent living as long as possible with deviation a voluntary choice as circumstances make it desirable.

RISK OF UNEMPLOYMENT

The major type of economic risk for most families is unemployment or underemployment. There are the temporary layoffs because of strikes, shortage of supplies, breakdown in machinery, or similar causes; there is intermittent employment because the work itself is casual and irregular; there is the regular seasonal unemployment of some occupations; there is technological unemployment, the displacement of a given skill or technique by another or by a machine; there is the unemployment due to shifts in population and in location of industries; and, finally, there is the unemployment that comes from a widespread slowing-down in business activity, when the number of unemployed persons may run up, as it did in 1933, to almost twelve millions. The number of families affected by unemployment obviously varies from period to period within the year and from year to year. The risk of unemployment is also much greater for some families than others. Industries vary in the stability of their markets, and business depressions bear more heavily upon some groups than upon others.

The distress occasioned by unemployment is to be measured not only by the number unemployed at any one time or the average number during a period but by the average period those persons are out of work. The unemployed in January may be the employed in June, and vice versa. Along with relatively large numbers of unemployed go relatively long periods of unemployment per person. In 1940, when the average number unemployed was over eight million, about 15 per cent of all in the labor market, the median period that wage- or salary-earners were out of work was about thirty weeks.[4] In 1948, when the percentage of unemployed was only 3.4, the average duration was 8.6 weeks.[5]

The composition of the unemployed group must also be closely ex-

4. *Sixteenth Census of the United States, 1940, Population: The Labor Force, Employment and Personal Characteristics* (Washington: Government Printing Office, 1943), p. 15.

5. U.S. Bureau of the Census, *Current Population Reports*, Series P-50, No. 13 (Washington, February, 1949), pp. 4, 29. (Processed.)

amined before conclusions are drawn as to the adverse effects. The rate is higher for those just entering the labor market than for those who already have a job. In 1940 only 11 per cent of the experienced workers in the labor market were unemployed. The rate varies with age and therefore with family relationship. The Bureau of the Census said regarding unemployment in 1940: "Unemployment was comparatively uncommon among household heads, most of whom were bread-winners responsible for supporting a family. . . . Only 11.1 percent of the male heads of households in the labor force were reported as seeking work or on public emergency work."[6] The percentage of the various age groups in the labor market who were unemployed in 1940 and 1948 was as follows:[7]

AGE GROUP	PERCENTAGE OF LABOR FORCE UNEMPLOYED	
	1940	1948
14–19	31.4	7.9
20–24	18.8	5.5
25–34.	11.6	2.8
35–44	11.0	2.2
45–54	12.9	2.3
55–64	14.2	2.8
65 and over	8.8	2.8
All	14.6	3.4

Up to a point it would appear that the more experienced workers are more likely to be hired and less likely to be dismissed. The Bureau of the Census further comments concerning the situation in 1940: "Special consideration for persons with dependents on the part of employers hiring and laying off workers was probably an important part of the difference."[8] Some of the older workers also may have had tenure or seniority rights. It would appear also that persons sixty-five and over who cannot find jobs retire from the labor market and are no longer counted as unemployed, while the young workers keep looking. It is to be remembered also that among the older workers are relatively more who are managing their own business enterprise, and, as long as they continue to do so, they are not unemployed.

The data available do not support the thesis that a large percentage of those not at work on a particular date are voluntarily idle or that the unemployed are a group which did not make the grade. It is true that some of the idle are more zealously seeking employment than others and that

6. *Sixteenth Census of the United States, 1940, Population: The Labor Force, Employment and Personal Characteristics*, p. 10.

7. U.S. Bureau of the Census, *Current Population Reports*, Series P-50, No. 13 (February, 1949), p. 4.

8. *Sixteenth Census of the United States, 1940, Population: The Labor Force, Employment and Personal Characteristics*, p. 10.

some workers absent themselves from work for a day or a week without good reason. But the ups and downs in the rate of employment from time to time and the differences as between industries do not reflect differences in work habits or sense of responsibility. In 1948 the average number of men twenty to sixty-four years of age who were not in the labor market, as revealed by a monthly sample survey, was only 6 per cent of the civilian, noninstitutional population of that age. A certain proportion of those not in the labor force were in school; others were unable to work. The average number with a job who were not at work when the surveys were made was about 5 per cent of all employed. Not far from two-fifths of these absences were accounted for by vacations and three-tenths by illness.[9] In July over three-fourths of the absentees were on vacation, and in February bad weather and illness were the causes given by over 70 per cent.

ECONOMIC RISKS OTHER THAN UNEMPLOYMENT

Income from ownership and from self-employment is also exposed to economic risk. Capital invested may be lost; dividends may cease. Payrolls must be met whether the owners of the business have income or safety of capital. Income from property, however, unlike compensation for services, is unaffected by things that happen to the recipient. Rent, interest, and dividends continue regardless of sickness, accident, old age, or death, all of which bring an end to wages and salaries.

Income from independent business enterprise stands between income from property and wages and salaries with respect to the degree it is affected by personal mishaps. A day's illness, even a week's, may not affect the year's profits. Prolonged absence of the owner-manager, who also may be the main or sole worker, will, however, affect the business to the degree that its prosperity is dependent upon his personal attention and industry. In the case of his death the family members will suffer the decrease in income that comes from the loss of his services. They will have, however, the capital represented by the business assets and good will.

The incomes of men engaged in business for themselves may be an unstable basis for family support for two reasons. One is the incapacity of many for successful management of the business they undertake. Persons with a small amount of capital are constantly embarking in retail trade or some sort of small business enterprise without qualification for the task. Competition forces them to the wall, and they return to the ranks of wage-earners, and others equally unsuited for the management of a business take their place. Variations in market conditions also bring ups and

9. U.S. Bureau of the Census, *Current Population Reports*, Series P-50, No. 13, p. 30.

downs in their income. A major problem of farm families is the instability of their money incomes. Farm income fell 30 per cent from 1929 to 1930 and by 1932 was almost 70 per cent below the 1929 level.

SECURITY OF SALARIED WORKERS

Wages and salaries are fundamentally the same in that both represent the price paid for services. In practice, however, the name "salary" is usually given to the compensation for services bought by the year or month, while the rate paid for work by the piece, hour, or day is called a wage. The weekly or annual earnings of wage-earners are the product of the rate per piece or hour or day multiplied by output or the number of hours or days worked. Their paychecks reflect the time actually spent at work. The wage-earner therefore may be as much concerned about the amount of part time and overtime as he is about rates of pay. The salaried worker, on the other hand, typically has a longer-term contract, even in some cases for as long as a year. In the latter case his family may plan for some time in advance with a fair degree of security. The salaried worker is fired or laid off at the end of the month or year, and in some occupations it is the custom to give long notice of termination of employment. Salaried workers as a group are less likely than wage workers to find their pay cut for minor absences.

Salary-earners have therefore to a higher degree than wage-earners the financial security that is so desirable as a basis for family support. In the length and the terms of their contracts they have advantages that wage-earners as a group are still struggling to secure. It is true that custom dictates to a large extent whether the pay for a given kind of work is called a salary or a wage. Some so-called "salary-earners" are, in respect to security of tenure, the character of their contracts, as well as in the character of the work done, very like the typical wage-earner, and some groups of wage-earners have terms of employment that in security approximate those characteristic of the salaried class.

To sum up, the financial security of families varies not only with the industry of the breadwinner, his health, and his good luck in escaping accident but also with the economic source of his income. It is clear that one of the factors that has made income insecurity a major problem in our society is the relative growth in the number of breadwinners whose sole or principal income is from a wage or salary, since this source of income is subject to both personal and economic risks. In 1948 over four-fifths of all those working for pay or profit were wage- or salary-earners. Most secure among income recipients are the few whose income is derived wholly from ownership, since this is not subject to personal hazards. Income from ownership varies, however, with the degree of risk taken and, when risk is taken, with the character of the management and the demand for the product of the industry from which the income is drawn. Most secure among those who derive their income from the sale of their services are the salary-earners with their greater permanence of tenure, and among wage-earners those whose terms of employment have been most carefully safeguarded in the bargaining process, who receive a dismissal wage, and who are in industries for which the demand for the product is steady, the management good, and employment possible at all seasons of the year.

CONFLICTING AND COINCIDENTAL INDIVIDUAL AND SOCIAL GOALS

From the analysis of the types of risks to which income is exposed, the broad outlines of the individual problem and the social problem posed by the fact of income insecurity are apparent. For the individual the problem is: By what means can he minimize the risks to which he is exposed and maximize the resources available if and when the feared contingency eventuates? For society there are two questions: (1) What social action is desirable and possible to supplement individual action or achieve what each acting independently could not accomplish? (2) How prevent or reduce individual efforts to enhance security which are not to the social advantage and how facilitate and extend those which are? Clearly all attempts to reduce personal hazards and minimize downward movements of employment, production, and income are to both the individual and the social advantage. Similarly the community as well as the individual has a stake in the success of individuals' efforts to make financial provision against the chance of income disappearance or decline from disability, death, or old age. Both have a stake in the prevention of such upward movements of the price level as would make it difficult to plan for the future.

Conflict arises when the risks in question are those necessarily involved in economic change, change in technique, in demand, in location of industries, in industrial organization, in supply of workers competent to perform a particular job. What may be a maximizing of economic opportunity for some may be a threat to the security of others. Measures designed to assure that everyone's particular place in the market, everyone's vested interest in a particular skill or particular market, everyone's relative position in the income distribution, remain unimpaired are clearly inconsistent with economic progress, technical advance, and maximum chance to improve economic position. It is loose thinking to set up as a goal an income security so all-inclusive that it would seem to rule out the economic hazards that are a part of a dynamic economic society.

CHAPTER X

PROVISION FOR THE FUTURE THROUGH SAVING

THOROUGHGOING provision for the possible future financial needs of a family must cover three types of situations. First is the chance that the flow of income will cease or be greatly diminished through the disability, death, or old age of the breadwinner or through economic vicissitudes. Second is the chance that, with little or no forewarning, need for large outlays will arise, such as those involved in a major illness or the death of a family member. Neither of these two situations may arise, nor except for chronological old age can the time of their incidence be predetermined, and in no case can the amount of money that will be required be estimated with exactness.

The third type of situation to be taken into account in family planning is quite different. Even if there is a steady income throughout the family life-span and no untoward event of the sort described, the family in the present must take account of certain future needs or desires. Many types of goods and services require so large an initial outlay that they cannot be acquired by the use of current income. The necessary outlay for a family home, furniture and equipment, an automobile, travel, children's education, and the like may exceed the monthly or even annual income. If the total income goes to meet current, regularly recurring needs, there will be no funds available to provide for the occasional or nonrecurring. There must be set-asides from current income to cover these anticipated future outlays or to pay the debts incurred if the goods in question are acquired by borrowing or on credit.

The three methods by which families meet the three types of situations briefly described are insurance, saving, or going into debt. The basic policy question is: For which type of situation is insurance the appropriate or best means of attaining the objective and for which either saving beforehand or going into debt? Saving beforehand means the accumulation of a fund which will appear upon the family balance sheet either as a money-income earning or a liquid asset. Each addition to the fund increases the net worth of the family, as do the payments on debts if the net worth has been previously diminished by the contraction of such liabilities.

174

DEBT VERSUS SAVING BEFOREHAND

Although cash loans and credit purchases are methods by which homes and other consumer durables are obtained, medical and other large expenses met, and in that sense are alternatives to saving, debt is not provision for the future or a means of enhancing economic security. Rather it may be described as risk-taking, the risk being the course of future income and of demands upon that income. It is saving after the event rather than saving beforehand. The incurrence of debt is by no means, however, to be considered as under all circumstances unsound financial procedure. It would mean in certain cases a going without or a postponement that would be undesirable, as, for example, of medical, surgical, or hospital care. If families waited for home ownership until they could meet the entire cost, few would be owners until late in their life-span. Great efforts have been made to enable those who wish to purchase a home to do so with a small down payment, with long terms of repayment of the credit extended and low rates of interest. Without adequate facilities for credit, home ownership would be extremely limited, and in emergencies requiring a large outlay families without assets, especially liquid assets, would suffer.

The use of cash loans or credit to secure various other types of "consumer durables" presents a different problem. Saving of the required amount before purchase would not long delay acquisition if the amounts regularly saved were as large as those required later. Many families allege that the will to save beforehand is lacking; that they need the stimulus provided by the obligation to creditors and the risk that, if the payments agreed upon are not made, they will lose what has already been paid. This risk is one of the disadvantages of purchase on credit. If future income fails to be forthcoming as estimated or if unexpected demands upon it materialize, the consequences are serious. Furthermore, interest is earned upon sums saved beforehand, but interest must be paid upon sums borrowed, whether in the form of cash or credit extended.

Instalment credit, moreover, operates in some ways to the buyer's disadvantage. It has often been used as a way of weakening sales resistance and has furthered unconsidered buying or insufficient consideration of alternative expenditures or of saving versus spending. The cost of the credit extended, either as a dollar amount or as a rate of interest, is rarely expressly stated. When the latter has been given, it has often been inaccurately stated at a figure far below the actual rate. Thus the buyer cannot separate the cost of the merchandise from the cost of the credit, know how much he is paying for the credit extended, or compare the cost of either merchandise or credit as between merchants or lenders. Additional charges are sometimes included without the buyer's knowledge. There is clearly strong argument for a legal requirement that these items be stated in a clear and uniform manner in all instalment contracts.[1]

INSURANCE VERSUS SAVING

If debt or saving after the event is ruled out as a method of providing for the future, there remains only saving beforehand or insurance as means of providing for the three types of situations noted. Insurance in its essential features is quite different from the accumulation of funds, income-yielding or otherwise. In essence, what it gives the insured is the promise of the insurer, made legally enforceable by the payment of the premium, that, if an event occurs, a certain sum or sums will be paid or services rendered. Receipt of the funds or services promised are therefore contingent upon the occurrence of the event insured against. This occurrence clearly cannot be under the control of the insured. Also, if the insuring agency is to meet its obligations, it must be able to estimate the claims that will be made upon it during each period. Only when the rate of occurrence of a contingency among a group can be so estimated is the use of the insurance principle possible. Only when the group insured against a certain risk is sufficiently large and representative of all subject to that risk can such estimation be accurately made. The rate of occurrence, in other words, must be predictable. Insurance, then, is a device by which individual members of a group subject to certain risks, unforeseeable and uncontrollable by them, may be assured of a principal sum, an income, or services if the event insured against occurs. Although what may happen to a particular member of the group is unpredictable, what will happen to the group as a whole may be known with the requisite certainty, the number of deaths, for example, among men of a certain age.

Saving is clearly the only means, other than borrowing or credit purchase, by which the funds necessary for certain large future anticipated outlays can be obtained, those outlays which are due to foreseeable contingencies over which the individual has control. The practical problem in such accumulation is one of planning and budgeting. The elements of the problem are known, the approximate amount needed, the time when it will be needed. Therefore the problem is: How long will it take to

---

1. For further discussion of this problem see J. S. Bradway, "The Development of Regulation," *Annals of American Academy of Political and Social Science*, CXCVI (March, 1938), 181–88; Albert Haring, *The Installment Credit Contract* (New York: Consumer Credit Institute of America, 1939); Commonwealth of Massachusetts, *Report of the Committee on Consumer Credit* (Boston, 1936).

accumulate a certain amount, or how much must be set aside in each month or year, if a given sum is to be on hand at a given date? Saving, equally clearly, is not the means or a satisfactory means for providing the funds for the unforeseeable contingency when the amount that will be required or the time when it will be required is completely unknown. Insurance, upon the other hand, makes certain that a given amount will be available as soon as the first premium is paid, and this certainty continues as long as the contract is in force. It lends itself to budgeting, since the premium is a fixed, periodic payment. Insurance whenever available is clearly the means for meeting contingencies, the first two types of possible future situations for which individuals and families desire to provide.

The individual cannot insure against one class of risks, the economic. Insurance is possible only against personal risks and the risk of damage, destruction, or theft of property. The risks of unemployment cannot be insured against, although the risk of death and certain other personal hazards can be. The risk of business losses from market changes and competitive disadvantages cannot be insured against, although the risk of loss of assets from fire, theft, tornado, or similar causes can be. Economic risks do not have the predictability or other features that make insurance practicable. Moreover, insurance against the risk of a need for funds to meet medical and hospital expenses, although extending rapidly both in groups to which it is available and services covered, is unavailable to some and leaves many possible costs to be otherwise met. To an even more limited extent is insurance against loss of income from the disability of the breadwinner available on satisfactory terms. Saving, although unsatisfactory and inadequate, is the only means the family can utilize to meet the economic risks to which it is exposed and in large degree the risks incident to illness and other disability.

MOTIVES FOR SAVING

An important motive for saving is, therefore, not only to provide funds for planned future outlays but for unplanned and unforeseeable events, the so-called saving for a rainy day. The eventual use of a fund saved for this purpose will be uncertain, that is, savings made for one purpose may in fact go for another. If the contingencies feared are slow in coming or when they occur make slight inroads upon the saved fund, some of it may go for a home, furniture, equipment, education, travel, and the like. If, however, rainy days are many and come early, the savings will go largely for current living during these periods or for medical expenses, as will funds saved with a view to making a down payment on a home, buying furniture and equipment, educating children. If the emergencies come early in the saving period, the saved funds will rarely be adequate; if they come after the funds in large part have been used for heavy expenditures for consumer durables or similar purposes, funds also may be insufficient. Items not wholly paid for will be lost or, even if wholly paid for, those salable, as the family home, may be sold. Thus the uses to which families put their savings are contingent upon events. If all goes well, they will eventually have something for old age and in the years between something for the consumer durables and other things so necessary for the generally desired level of living. If not, they go for the uninsurable or uninsured-against contingencies.

Provision for old age always involves saving, either the accumulation of a fund that will purchase a life income from an insurance company when retirement age is reached, or a fund that will provide an income from investment which alone or supplemented by the fund itself will provide a livelihood after that date. Saving is literally a postponement of consumption. Periods of saving are followed by periods of dissaving, the final dissaving period being that during old age. The whole purpose of the saving might be described as maintenance throughout the total life-span of a uniform level of living in spite of the uneven course of income or of demands upon that income. At any moment of time some families would be accumulating, some spending savings previously made.

There are other motives for saving besides those mentioned. Their relative importance is difficult to estimate. Some saving takes place with a view primarily to the income that may be derived from the investment of the saved fund. There are two distinct classes of such saving. One is the saving by those in business for themselves, or by those who propose to make such a venture. The saving is to increase the investment or to provide the initial capital. The other is saving made with a view to investment in corporate securities or similar money-earning assets. Saving to start a business or that represented by turning back earnings into an on-going business venture is an attempt to maximize income rather than to insure its continuance. It is a part of the current income-getting process rather than provision for the future, although the increased capital investment enhances family security. The income is exposed to whatever hazards are peculiar to the enterprise in question.

Investment of savings in securities or in other ways where ownership is divorced from management provides not only a supplement to income from the usual and primary source but a possible substitute for it. Thus income security is enhanced not only by diversification of the sources of income but from the fact that income from ownership is not exposed to personal risks. A saved fund must be relatively large, however, before the income from it is an important source of security. In most cases it is the saved fund with whatever additions the income from it supplies that must be used if special needs arise.

How do bequests to grown sons and daughters rank as a motive for saving? It might be argued that such saving should take place only after other goals, including education for children, adequate medical care, and economically independent old age are fully realized and then not at the expense of an adequate level of living. Large bequests enhance inequality and are of questionable benefit to the inheritors. The small bequests coming from those at the lower ranges of the income distribution are in part planned and in part the inevitable result of premature death or uncertainty as to how much will be required to provide for needs during old age. What is left when the parents die goes as they dictate or, if they die intestate, to next of kin in an order prescribed by law.

The motives for saving probably vary with the source and amount of the family income. At the lower levels the savings are probably primarily for the rainy day, for emergencies, and to secure funds sufficient to cover large, occasional outlays. The more irregular the income, month by month or year by year, the more its recipients might be expected to spread its use out over time. Thus the large saver of one period is the dissaver of the next. The business enterpriser saves to expand his business operations. At the higher levels saving for investment, to acquire a competence that will permit early retirement, to leave bequests to children, to provide trips abroad or similar luxuries, might be expected.

It is probable that some saving has no definite purpose in the sense of a projected use of the funds which could be described as the motive for saving. Saving per se may give satisfaction as the act of a prudent and thrifty man. In our culture it has long been considered a virtue. Satisfactions of various kinds come from large holdings of wealth; from a prosperous business; from ownership of fields, barns, and herds, from corporate control; even from the size of a saving account or the bundle of securities in the strongbox. It is probable also that some saving just happens. Expenditures for consumption, insurance, and planned savings do not absorb the whole income. Those at the top of the income distribution may have incomes that exceed what they could spend and conform to the standards of the community or that exceed the cost of their preferred manner of living. Another such situation arises when families move up beyond their accustomed income position. The consumption level is likely to lag behind the advance in income with a resultant effect upon savings. A third type of situation which fosters saving in general rather than saving for a purpose is that which arises in wartime when some goods are rationed or disappear from the market. Long hours of work and transportation difficulties also limit certain types of expenditures and discourage spending. As liquid assets accumulate from upward movement of incomes or the special conditions of wartime, uses of the funds are planned, however, and in that respect the savings are indistinguishable from those that might be called purposeful.

DETERMINANTS OF AMOUNT SAVED

Analysis of the motives for saving suggests some of the factors that determine amount of saving, who are likely to be the relatively large and who the relatively small savers, and when savings are likely to be relatively large or small. The amount saved will depend, on the one hand, upon the amount of the income, the strength of the motives for saving, knowledge of opportunities to dispose of saved funds profitably and, on the other, upon the need and desire to spend for consumption goods to be used currently and opportunities to do so. A society or a group within a society may develop attitudes favorable to saving or to spending. Emphasis on the virtues of thrift, foresight, and prudence will have its effect upon individual and family behavior as will the manifold forces that create and strengthen desires for consumption goods. Those who save with an eye to investment will be affected by prospective rates of return. In wartime organized effort is put forth to induce savings in the form of purchase of government bonds. Such purchase is made attractive and easy for small as well as large savers by the types of securities offered and the methods and places of purchase.

As has been emphasized, many of the savers of one year will be the dissavers of the next, and vice versa, or the high savers of one year may be the low of the next. Debts incurred to meet an income decline or to make large outlays in one period will be paid in the next. The aged couple may be using accumulations of previous years to supplement income from other sources. The young couple may be furnishing a home. The older and the larger families may have heavy expenses for illness. Some families have currently an income position that is lower than that of the preceding period. Such families are likely to save less than those in the same income class whose income is about the same as usual. The consumption standards of the former tend to be higher than those of the latter, and they may have fixed obligations established when they were upon a higher income level. Similarly among the relatively high savers at each level are those whose current income is higher than that to which they have been accustomed. Both these groups will probably adjust their budget to income received if income continues at the present level. Income expectations also undoubtedly affect rate of saving, expectations with respect both to future amount and to its security. Favorable expectations in either respect would be expected to reduce savings.

The question is sometimes asked: How much should a family save? Or, in another form: Is a given amount or rate too much or too little? The answer would be one thing if the fiscal needs of the nation were extraordinarily great and inflation must be avoided, and another if only the family interest were in question. In the latter case it is as difficult to say what the family's rate of saving should be as to say what its choices should be among consumption alternatives. In general, it is a matter of values, the relative importance to the family of the possession of a fund for future uses as compared with present uses of income. There is no virtue in saving just to save. Saving is for something or because further consumption outlays would serve no good purpose. A given rate may be too little to meet in due time a particular future need, or it may be too much in that it prevents the adequate meeting of a current consumption need. The most difficult budgeting problem arises when the saving is for contingencies. There is no way of determining how adequately a given rate of saving will provide for such events. Saving for future outlays of known amount and date falls in a different category.

DISPOSITION OF SAVED FUNDS

Savers who are accumulating a fund rather than liquidating a debt have the problem of its proper disposition. Liquidity, income, and safety are the three considerations in making this decision. Complete liquidity would mean that the realizable dollar value of the fund is definitely known, and all or a part may be spent at any time. There are clearly degrees of liquidity from cash or checking account, postal savings, savings-bank deposits, Series E government bonds, to securities or other paper with a ready market but uncertain cash value. Equities, claims, and assets for which buyers must be sought or waited for may be liquidated but can scarcely be called liquid assets. There are also degrees of safety, that is, chances of loss of all or part of the saved fund, and closely related are the rates of return, expected or realized.

Two common modes of disposing of savings are special cases involving special problems. They are investment in a family-operated business and in a family home. Investment in a farm or other self-operated business is a special case in that the saver is already such an operator or is contemplating such an occupation. The choice in the latter case is of an occupation; in the former it is whether all or part of the accumulation shall be kept in the business from which it was derived. Ignorance of alternative modes of disposition may be one of the reasons for such turning-back of earnings, but another motive is the one previously discussed, desire to maximize or maintain income from its present source. It is obvious that this disposition of savings provides no diversification of investment or sources of income independent of that which is currently the main source. Furthermore, if the only family asset is the business enterprise, funds for emergencies or large consumption outlays can be obtained only by the sale or mortgage of the business or by extensive withdrawals of funds. If the operator is disabled or dies, the income continues only if another family member takes over the management. If such management is impossible or undesirable, whatever is realized from the sale when the disaster occurs represents the degree of family protection provided. The protection provided for old age will be similarly determined if the family business is the only asset. The owned family home has some of the limitations of an owned family business as a basis for family security. It will provide emergency funds only if the home is sold or mortgaged. The amount that may be realized by either method is uncertain. It provides no money income unless the family lives elsewhere. It does provide an important service income as long as the roof tree stands and taxes and payments on the mortgage, if any, are met.

Most families derive their income not from self-employment but from wages or salaries. What should guide the disposition of their savings? What additional assets should the home owner and the business operator have in order to enhance liquidity, safety, or diversification of income sources? Writers on family and personal finance quite generally agree on the importance of some highly liquid assets. If the accumulation is small or early expenditure contemplated, all savings might well take this form. Whatever the size of the saved fund, if the assets are liquid, there will be no need for sale at a loss, or borrowing, if emergencies occur.

Two considerations limit the holding of highly liquid assets, easily and immediately available. One, emphasized by some savers, is that, the more liquid the savings, the more likely are they to melt away from "borrowings" or the urge to spend for current purposes. The less easily the funds can be tapped, the better, it is argued, if the object is to insure that the sum saved increase and be intact at some future date. The other drawback is that, in general, the more liquid the assets, the lower the income derived from them.

Income is possible only if saved funds are either loaned to government or individuals for consumption purposes or are so disposed of that they enhance the capital resources of business enterprises. There are two ways by which saved funds become, in either sense, invested funds. One is direct investment by the saver. He goes into business for himself, lends to another enterpriser or individual, or buys government bonds or the stock or bonds of business corporations. His status is that of a creditor if he lends money or buys bonds, of a proprietor if he goes into business for himself, of a shareholder if he acquires stock in a corporation. As a shareholder he has the income rights of a part owner without responsibility for (and little control over) management. The other way by which savings become investments is indirect and is made possible by the existence of special financial institutions, such as the savings bank, savings and loan, and investment companies. These institutions become the direct investors. They use the funds deposited or paid for their stock in bond or stock purchase or in loans to individuals as authorized by law or their charter. Insurance companies are also investment agencies. The saver who turns over his funds to a financial institution of the type described avoids the responsibility of appraising investment opportunities, devising an investment program, and diversifying his holdings.

There remains the responsibility of choosing among banks, among savings and loan companies, and among investment companies. Certain legal safeguards to be described later have minimized the risk of a poor choice among banks and savings and loan corporations. The investment companies, which have been increasing rapidly in number, present a greater problem. As their name signifies, they invest the funds of their shareholders in the securities of other corporations. Some buy only corporate stock; some distribute their holdings between bonds and stock; some follow a defined program of investment and disinvestment. Some are "open-end" companies, offering stock or buying it at any time at a price per share equal to the *pro rata* current market value of their holdings, plus usually a charge to cover the costs of distribution. The stock of others can be bought or sold only on the market. The would-be investor in the investment company has clearly a problem of choice and might well diversify holdings in investment-company shares themselves.

The income that may be derived from these various dispositions of saved funds obviously varies greatly. The interest on bank deposits is a fixed amount set by the depository. It will be and must be substantially lower than the earnings from the investments made by the bank, since from these earnings must come its costs and return to its shareholders. The holder of shares in a savings and loan company will participate in net earnings, if any, as and when dividends are declared. The holders of stock in the investment company will similarly participate in net earnings and capital gains if any; as all shareholders they are promised nothing, since theirs is a proprietorship status.

The income from successful direct investment will be greater than from indirect. The direct investor has nothing deducted from his income for the costs of a financial intermediary. The character of his claim will depend upon whether he is a bond (or mortgage) holder or a stockholder. In the first case he has a promised income of fixed amount that has priority over dividend payments. Its payment, if promised by a business concern, will depend upon earnings and solvency. If promised by government—federal, state, or local—it will depend upon tax revenues, which in turn will depend upon ability and willingness to tax. The stockholder's income will depend upon net earnings, a function of many variables, and upon dividends declared.

The liquidity of these various modes of disposition will also vary greatly. With the low interest on savings deposits, and partly responsible for it, goes high liquidity. Holders of savings accounts, including those in savings and loan companies, usually may draw on them at any time, although prior notice may be required. Some investment companies, as was said, will redeem their stock at any time at a price determined by the market value of securities held. The liquidity of other claims and equities comes from their salability to others (except the nonnegotiable Series E bonds). For some there is a ready market within narrow price limits; for others the reverse is true.

Those who place their savings in banks or who use insurance companies in the indicated ways do not do so primarily to avoid the responsibility of deciding upon and diversifying their investments. The bank deposit is chosen because it is known, because it is easy, and because small amounts as well as large can be deposited and similarly withdrawn, usually without notice. There is no broker or brokerage charges. Small savers become direct investors primarily when special measures are taken to reach them and purchase and payment are made easy. Numerous devices have been used to broaden the market and increase the purchase of government bonds: issues in small denominations with a high degree of liquidity, payment by payroll deductions, the use of mass-advertising media, direct mail selling, and subscription counters in banks, post offices, and other public places. Many of these methods of encouraging purchase could not be used by private companies. A few have facilitated purchase of their own stock by their employees by payroll deductions, but "easy payments" for and mass merchandising of corporate securities generally would require a special market organization. The costs of such retail distribution would be high and would leave unsolved some of the most serious problems of the small investor.

The experience of small savers in general as investors in corporate securities has not been, historically considered, a happy one. The heavy and extensive losses in the slump of the thirties are sometimes cited as an example. The losses at that time, however, were sustained by large as well as small investors, and the losses by those holding securities were paralleled by those of home- and farm-owners, holders of other real estate, and even bank depositors. The question is not so much whether many met disaster at this time of generally collapsing values as whether they generally have been or can be wise and informed buyers. Even with fraud and deception ruled out, the fact remains that special knowledge is required to estimate prospective earnings of a business enterprise and the soundness of its financial organization and management. Nor is the small investor in a position to diversify his holdings.

What many purchasers of securities and real estate are seeking is not a steady income from an investment but the appreciation of the market value of their holdings and thus an increase in the saved fund itself. Such use of savings means speculation or risk-taking. To regard funds accumulated for the purposes previously described as venture capital is to defeat the ostensible purposes of saving. Only after the livelihood of the family through its life-span is adequately safeguarded through insurance and relatively safe investment should funds be ventured with a view to the realization of speculative gains or the larger income yields that attend greater risk. The information needed to appraise the chances correctly is available only to a few, and even those few cannot have complete foreknowledge of the course of events. Although the exact dividing line between investment and speculation is difficult to draw, since practically every investment has some speculative features, those "who truly invest seek to conserve what they have, whereas people who speculate endeavor to increase the amount of their wealth."[2]

The primary concern of most savers is not the liquidity of their funds or the income or possible capital gains therefrom but their security. If the

2. D. F. Jordan and E. F. Willett, *Managing Personal Finances* (New York: Prentice-Hall, Inc., 1945), p. 273.

dollars realized when the time comes to draw upon the saved fund are fewer than those accumulated, the purpose of the saving is to that extent defeated. If the dollar amount is the same but the purchasing power of each dollar has shrunk, the result is the same. Obviously there are only degrees of security, but those degrees may be wide. Cash holdings are subject to loss whether kept by the owner or intrusted for safekeeping to others. The repayment of loans depends upon the ability of the borrowers to keep their promises. Investments in business enterprises expose the investors to the economic risks to which those businesses are exposed.

The safety of the funds accumulated by individuals and families is enhanced by developments along three lines. One is extended knowledge of alternative modes of disposition and better judgment in selecting among them on the part of savers themselves. A second is the development of special types of business institutions through which the flow of personal savings can be more safely channeled into business investment than the owners could themselves accomplish it. Third, there is governmental action designed wholly or in part to enhance the safety of the funds of small savers.

Governmental action to enhance the safety of savers' accumulations has taken several forms, since the funds themselves are variously disposed of. The several states authorizing banks to receive savings deposits have long regulated with varying wisdom and rigor the investments in which these funds can be placed. The aim was of course to rule out those most speculative and unsafe. Similarly state laws have regulated the investments of life-insurance companies, since their reserves also are the accumulations of thousands of small savers. Following the spectacular losses in the thirties of saving and checking deposits, the federal government made insurance with the Federal Deposit Insurance Corporation of all checking and savings accounts mandatory, first up to $5,000, now up to $10,000, for all members of the Federal Reserve System and optional for the non-member banks which qualify. Most of the nonmember banks have qualified. Heavy losses were also sustained in the thirties by stockholders and depositors in the savings and loan companies providing funds for home-ownership and improvement. To reduce future losses and encourage a flow of capital to these institutions, Congress authorized the establishment of the Federal Savings and Loan Insurance Corporation. Insurance of all share accounts up to $10,000 is now mandatory for all federally incorporated savings and loan institutions, and optional for the state-chartered which qualify. Shareholders do not receive cash, however, in case of insolvency but either a new account in a solvent company or 10 per cent in cash and the balance in debentures to be paid off within a specified period.

The regulatory laws referred to have been directed primarily to the protection of the small saver and have been designed to insure that banks and insurance companies could keep their promises to him. Other legislation is designed to protect the investor in corporate securities and is necessarily of other character. The general purpose of the regulatory provisions of the latter legislation is to prevent fraud and deception and to insure that the would-be purchaser has information in regard to the real financial situation of the business.

State legislation with this general objective began in 1911, and most states now have some type of regulation, not always effective, however, or sufficiently comprehensive. The great financial losses of the investing public after 1929 led to the passage in 1933 of the Federal Securities Act. This act, with its later revisions, is essentially a disclosure statute. It seeks to insure that full and accurate information is furnished concerning securities publicly offered or sold through the mails. Sales between individuals are not affected. Every issue of new securities must be registered with the Securities Exchange Commission, and, if the registration statement and the prospectus are not satisfactory, sale may not proceed. All issues sold upon the stock exchange must be registered. In 1940 Congress passed an act regulating investment advisers and investment companies. Both counselors and companies must be registered, and certain practices responsible for investors' losses in the thirties are prohibited.

No governmental action in the interest of the small saver or investor could approximate in value policies that would reduce instability in business activity and prevent inflationary price movements. The business losses of a depression period affect the large as well as the small investor but are far more serious to the latter. A fall in the purchasing power of the dollar has the same effect upon savings as the loss of an appreciable fraction of the funds accumulated. A savings program designed to provide college education for children may actually provide a half or a third of the requisite amount because of changing fees and other costs. The fund expected to provide a modest livelihood for dependents in case of death of the breadwinner or for old age actually may provide a meager subsistence. No prudence, foresight, or thrift on the part of the individual can ward off the contingency that the purchasing power of the dollar may fall. Its occurrence in fact tends to penalize and thus reduce these virtues.

ASSETS, LIABILITIES, AND NET WORTH OF AMERICAN FAMILIES

Information concerning the kinds and value of assets owned and debts outstanding of American families has been increasing in recent years largely through the annual "Survey of Consumer Finances" made for the

Board of Governors of the Federal Reserve System. As would be expected, the form in which savings are held vary with income. Marked differences appear between the upper- and lower-income groups in the frequency of ownership of a business and of corporate stock. According to the survey made in early 1949, not until the income passed $5,000 did a tenth of the spending units, including both families and economically independent individuals, report ownership of corporate stock. When the saved fund is small, it goes most frequently into savings accounts and toward home purchase. Even at the $2,000–$3,000 income level over two-fifths had savings accounts, over two-fifths United States government bonds, and over a third owned their home.[3]

In the 1950 survey the attempt was made to discover not only the kinds of assets held by individuals and families but the value of a more comprehensive list of items than had hitherto been ascertained. Since the survey covered not only assets but debts outstanding, the result was to give for the first time an estimate of the net worth of the spending units in the population at the date of the study. Estimates were secured of the value of holdings of liquid assets, of corporate stock open to investment by the general public, interests in private business ventures, of automobiles, homes and other real estate, as well as the amount of all types of debts except charge accounts.[4] An inspection of this list indicates that certain widely held assets were omitted. The owners' estimates of the value of such items as clothing, furniture, and jewelry would have been very unreliable, and few would have known the cash-surrender value of their insurance policies. Experience has shown that large holdings of currency are not usually disclosed. In fact, the value of the liquid assets included in the survey is understated.[5] Coverage of debt outstanding, upon the other hand, was relatively complete, and understatement was believed to be relatively slight. Thus the survey estimates of assets and of net worth are probably minimum figures.

The findings of this survey are of interest in spite of the limitations noted. Less than half of the spending units reported assets worth $5,000 or more. Less than a tenth (only 6 per cent of the nonfarm) reported asset holdings of $25,000 or more. Asset value varies not only with income but with the age of the head of the spending unit. Fifteen per cent of the units with heads sixty-five and over reported assets worth $25,000 or more, but

3. Board of Governors of the Federal Reserve System, *1949 Survey of Consumer Finances* (Washington, 1949), pp. 44, 73.

4. *1950 Survey of Consumer Finances*, Part V, p. 1. Reprinted from *Federal Reserve Bulletin*, December, 1950.

5. *Ibid.*, p. 2.

only 2 per cent of those with heads twenty-five to thirty-four. About 70 per cent of the spending units of all kinds reported liquid assets, that is, a savings account, checking account, United States bonds, or all three. About half of the nonfarm families owned their homes, and slightly over half of the owners were mortgage-free. About a fourth of the nonfarm owners estimated that their homes were worth less than $5,000. About one in twenty owned a home valued at $20,000 or over. The median estimated value of the owned nonfarm homes was $7,500–$8,000 and the median equity (value less mortgage) about $6,000.

About half of these spending units reported that they had no debts. Debt on nonfarm homes was the principal form of consumer indebtedness. Nonfarm home owners were about three-fourths of all spending units with debt, an even greater proportion of those with debts over $3,000. Debt was most frequent among spending units with heads twenty-five to forty-four years of age. These are the spending units buying homes, furnishing and equipping them. These too are the units with young children. Only a third of the married heads with children under eighteen were free of debt.

The net worth (assets minus debts) of the families with a married couple at the head was greater than that of other spending units. The net worth of married couples was closely associated with the length of time they had been married, owing not only to the longer time they had been able to accumulate but to the fact that in the early years of the marriage savings are used to acquire household furnishing and equipment. Debts thus incurred were taken into account in this study, but the goods acquired were not counted among the assets. Three-fifths of those who had been married twenty years or more had a net worth of $5,000 or more; about an eighth, $25,000 or more. These figures correspond closely to the reported net worth of spending units with heads sixty-five or over. Only about a fifth of those married less than three years had a net worth, as estimated, of $5,000 or more.

CHAPTER XI

PROVISION FOR THE FUTURE THROUGH INSURANCE

IN THE preceding chapter it was emphasized that saving, or the accumulation of a fund, is an inadequate means of meeting the situations that give individuals and families major concern for the future, that is, the contingencies that reduce income or bring unexpected need for large outlays. To provide for events which may or may not occur, and, if they do, may come at any time and pose a financial problem of unknown duration and burden, the use of the insurance principle is indicated. The essence of this principle is that, if all or many of those subject to a given risk contribute a small amount each year, those to whom the event actually occurs during that period may receive a much larger amount.

The use of the insurance principle is generally possible and practicable to meet two of the major contingencies that families face—the death of the breadwinner and his survival beyond his earning years. There is a wide range of choice among insurance carriers and among forms of insurance against these financial risks. In the choice among carriers the main considerations are the financial stability of the company and the price (usually called "premium") charged for the insurance contract. The latter is easy to determine by a little shopping around, the former more difficult for the inexperienced unless it be by size and age of the company. The legal safeguards upon the operation of insurance companies are more strict also in some states than in others. The mistakes made by families in planning their insurance program are not in the main, however, in the choice of a company but in choice of type of policy, a mistake that comes in part from failure to assess their needs properly and in part from ignorance of what is available and the relative advantages and costs of one type of contract as compared with another.

Four general rules may be formulated: (1) each family should determine which risks in its special circumstances present the most serious hazard; (2) if insurance against these risks is possible, give insurance first place in its program of provision for the future, a high priority over any extensive program of saving; (3) give insurance against the risk or risks that would be financially most disastrous first place in the insurance program; and (4) compare types of policies with a view to securing the maximum protection for a given outlay.

ASSESSMENT OF INSURANCE NEEDS

If the needs of families are realistically appraised, two facts of importance emerge. One is that insurance needs vary at different stages of the family life-span, and another that the financial consequences of the death of one family member are quite different from those that would result from the death of another. When the family in question is newly formed, for example, the risk of dependent old age is not imminent if the age of the husband and wife is that which is usual at the time of the first marriage, nor will either husband or wife be seriously disadvantaged financially by the death of the other. The earnings of the husband if he is the survivor will continue as before, and the young widow's earning power will not have been greatly lessened by the fact of her marriage even if she left the labor force at that time. The insurance needs of the young couple without children are in other words substantially as they were before marriage. They will still be subject to the risk of illness with its consequent outlays and, if the disabled person is the earner, the risk of loss of income. If insurance is available through the developing voluntary plans covering hospital and medical costs up to a certain maximum, it might well be carried. If either has true dependents, that is, those for whose support they are morally or legally liable, life insurance should be carried. Such dependents are most likely to be aged parents, wholly or partially supported. During the period before marriage when young men and women are earning, and after marriage before children are born, emphasis may well be placed upon saving in order that a fund will be available to meet the necessary expenses of setting up housekeeping and to provide for emergency outlays. After marriage, expenses incident to childbirth must be planned for. Life insurance in this period may be dispensed with or kept at the minimum sufficient for last illness and burial expense.

With the birth or expected birth of a child the situation alters entirely. The parents now face the responsibility for the support of that child until it is of acceptable earning age. If the husband dies, the wife may find it difficult if not impossible to earn, and in any case the child will be deprived of the economic advantage afforded by two parents. The death of the father or his total and permanent disability becomes the greatest hazard faced by the family. Insurance against this risk should take first place in financial planning for the future. Is the risk of death of the mother a financial hazard equally as great as the risk of death of the father? The first fact to be noted is that her death is not as likely to occur. Here is a general consideration that must be emphasized in all planning of an insurance program. In setting up priorities, in determining the amount of insurance, on which members insurance should be carried and the types of policies to be secured, the family can consider only the probabilities. What in retrospect would have been best is one thing; what on the basis of probabilities is likely to be best is another. Dublin and Lotka have estimated that

on the basis of mortality among white persons, 1930–1939, the chances of paternal orphanhood are 74 per 1000 when the husband is 25 years old at the birth of the child, and 184 per 1000 if the father is 40 years old. The corresponding chances of maternal orphanhood are much less, being 59 per 1000 if the mother is 25 years of age and 133 per 1000 if her age is 40.[1]

Not only is the death of the mother less likely than that of the father, but insurance upon his life provides in part at least what is lost by his death: a fund or an income in money. The father is usually the principal if not the sole earner. The death of the mother means the loss of her services, a loss that only to a very limited degree can be compensated by money. The mother's death is more likely to disrupt the family than the death of the father. The widow with small money income is more likely to be able to maintain a home for herself and her children than is the widower, even if his income is supplemented by insurance benefits.

Should life insurance be carried upon children? The answer seems unequivocally "No" in view of the present low child-mortality rate and the fact that there is no financial loss involved. The family does not lose income but a dependent. Such insurance is sometimes justified as provision for the costs of burial. The family with a saved fund equivalent to these costs would have no need for this safeguard. The premiums for insurance of children would usually be more wisely devoted to insurance against the death of the breadwinner and should never be substituted for insurance against the risk that a family member may need expensive hospital or medical care.

Scrutiny of the data given below on insured family members in families with children in early 1947 indicates that practice varies considerably from the principles that have been laid down.[2] About 8 per cent of all life insurance in force on individual contracts with insurance companies in 1949 was on children under fifteen, and the proportion is increasing. About

1. Louis I. Dublin and Alfred J. Lotka, *The Money Value of a Man* (New York: Ronald Press Co., 1946), p. 40.

2. *Life Insurance Ownership among U.S. Families: Special Tabulations for the Institute of Life Insurance by the Survey Research Center, University of Michigan* (March, 1948), p. 9.

16 per cent of all life insurance of this character purchased in 1949 was on children of this age.[3]

Family Member upon Whom Insurance Is Carried	Percentage Distribution of Insurance-carrying Families with Minor Children
Any member..........................	100
No family member.......................	15
Husband only...........................	17
Both husband and wife...................	15
Husband, wife, and one or more children.....	46
Husband and one or more children..........	4
Wife only...............................	1
Wife and one or more children.............	1
One or more children only.................	1

This divergence of practice from the principles suggested raises several questions. Are the principles sound? Would most of these families be able to bury their children without undue sacrifice of current assets or current level of living? Were they improperly advised by insurance sellers? Have they failed to analyze properly their insurance needs or to understand the nature and purpose of insurance? Is the practice a lag from the time when child mortality was high or when children were looked upon as potential assets, their survival the parents' insurance against the poorhouse in old age? Whatever the decision as to the family members upon whom life insurance should be carried, the primary need, it is certain, is for insurance against the risk of death of the breadwinner. This need is especially great if his income is a wage or salary. The amount of insurance needed will increase with the number of children and lessen as they reach economic independence.

What of the life insurance need after the children are married, earning, or able to earn their own living, when the family has become again one of two adults? At this stage in the family life-span the argument for insurance upon the life of the wife becomes weak indeed. But what of the need for insurance against the death of the husband? There are no longer dependent children whose future must be safeguarded, but the economic position of the wife who is forty-five or over is usually far different from that of the young wife. Many of these women will have been only sporadic members of the labor force, and some will never have earned since their marriage. If they are not to be disadvantaged by this withdrawal from earning

3. Calculated from data in *Life Insurance Fact Book, 1950* (New York: Institute of Life Insurance, 1950). Except when otherwise indicated, all data on insurance holdings and insurance practices in this chapter come from this source.

or their status as casual or supplementary earners when working, they will need the financial assistance given by insurance in the event of the death of the husband. At this period in the family history, moreover, a new risk becomes imminent, not of the death of the breadwinner but of his economic old age. Provision against dependency of either spouse in this period now must become a major consideration.

TYPES OF POLICIES

As the foregoing analysis indicates, the insurance needs of the family vary with the stage of the life-span. The insurance program therefore would be expected to vary from time to time as these needs change. The practical problem, after determining which need in a given period should be given priority, is to determine from among the market offerings what type of policy will provide the most of the needed protection for a given premium outlay. As with all spending problems wise choice is most important at the lower-income levels, since at best the attainment of adequate insurance protection, an adequate saved fund, and an adequate level of living will be difficult. The amount of insurance needed against the death of the breadwinner, moreover, moves upward with the size of the family as does the cost of maintenance of a given level of living. Thus there is increased pressure upon income from two sources at the same time. The importance of a sound analysis of insurance needs and selection of the best type of policy is thereby enhanced. There can be luxury insurance protection in terms of amount carried and character of the policies as well as luxury outlays for current consumption.

Life insurance has long been widely sold in this country. Its sales as well as the liquid and nonliquid assets of individuals and families increased greatly in the war years and the subsequent high-income period. Not all insurance in force today was written by companies organized solely for that purpose. In addition, there is the life insurance made available at low cost to servicemen by the federal government and that which is sold by fraternal societies, by so-called assessment associations, and by savings banks. Over four-fifths of that in force in 1949, however, arose from contracts with regular life-insurance companies, over 95 per cent of the amount if government insurance is excluded. The face value of the policies issued by these different types of insurers that were in force in the United States in 1949 was as follows:[4]

4. *Life Insurance Fact Book, 1950,* and *Insurance Year Book, 1950* (New York: Spectator Co., 1950).

Insurer	Face Value of Insurance in Force (Millions)
All	$261,400
"Legal reserve" companies	$214,400
United States government	38,000
Fraternal societies	8,100
Assessment associations	400
Savings banks	500

The relative importance of insurance sold by fraternal societies is decreasing; even the amount in force is lower than it was in the twenties. Sale of insurance by savings banks is authorized in only three states, before 1938 in only one. The holders of the $38 billions of government life insurance are servicemen and servicewomen of World War I and II. Thirty-six of the 38 billions were held by the latter. The insurance held by World War I veterans is called "United States Government Life Insurance," and that held by World War II veterans, "National Service Life Insurance." If all eligible for such insurance were carrying it, the total in force would have been far greater. Almost 16 million National Service policies with a value of over $121 billions were in force in 1944 compared with 5.6 million in 1949 with a value of $36 billion. The total number of persons with any type of life insurance in 1949 was probably at least 100 million, with an average of over two policies per insured person.

The three main classes of life-insurance policies are "ordinary," "industrial," and "group." The relative importance of the three types held in the United States which were issued by regular life-insurance companies was as follows in 1949:[5]

Type	Life Insurance in Force (Billions)	Number of Policies or Certificates Held (Millions)
All	$214.4	193
Ordinary	140.5	63
Industrial	31.8	106
Group	42.1	24
Group borrowers	2.0	6
Employed persons	40.1	18

The first two are contracts which cover specific individuals as such, and the third, as the name suggests, are contracts, usually with an employer, which cover a group.[6] Industrial insurance is sold, usually without

5. Government insurance and that issued by fraternal societies, assessment associations, and savings banks are not included.

6. The insured members of the group receive an insurance certificate.

selection of the insured by medical examination, in small amounts, and paid for by weekly or monthly collections at the home of the insured. All individual insurance that is not of this type is called "ordinary."

If government life insurance and that issued by agencies other than regular insurance companies had been taken into account, ordinary insurance would have amounted to about three-fourths of all insurance in force, and over four-fifths of the insured would have held a policy or certificate of this type.

FACTORS AFFECTING COST OF INSURANCE

A great variety of life-insurance policies is available, both of the industrial and of the ordinary type. Some policies are packages that provide protection against several contingencies. Others provide only against one. What is offered varies somewhat from one company to another. New types of policies appear from time to time, and those formerly offered may be withdrawn. What is promised the insurer may be a principal sum or an income. The mode of settlement may be chosen by the beneficiary or may be determined beforehand by the insurer.

The essential differences between different types of policies and the terms upon which they are offered can best be understood through an analysis of the factors determining the premium that must be paid for the promise of a specified principal sum or an income for a specified period. The premiums, or the amounts paid in by those insured against a particular risk, must cover in the first place the expenses of the insurer. These include the costs of management and investment as well as the costs of selling the insurance, premium collection, and account-keeping. Insurance is usually sold by the expensive means of person-to-person solicitation. Second, the amounts taken in from the insured person must cover all claims to benefits. If claims are underestimated and premiums are insufficient to cover them, the insurance carrier will not be able to keep the promise which is the basis of the insured person's protection. The third factor determining the cost of insurance is the rate of return earned upon the investments made of the funds paid in by the insured over and above expenses. It follows that any conditions which increase costs or claims, or decrease rates of return, will decrease the amount of insurance that can be obtained by a given outlay. Declining rates of return in recent years have operated to offset the declining mortality rates which otherwise might reduce the premium cost.

The payment of what are rather misleadingly called "dividends" to certain policyholders may now be explained. The so-called dividends are not income but the return of excess premium payments. Since premiums are paid in advance of the period during which the insurance is in effect, the costs during the period, the claims, and the rate of return must be estimated and conservatively estimated. At the end of the period the facts in these respects are known. In the mutual companies, which carried 70 per cent of the life insurance in the United States in 1949, the difference between receipts and the necessary deductions is returned to the policyholders, who are in effect the owners. In certain stock companies called "participating," a part of the excess premium is also returned.[7] If "dividends" are paid, the net premium or cost of the insurance differs from the gross amount that the policyholder is pledged to pay. Dividends may be used to reduce the premium payable or left with the insurance company, as with a savings bank, to earn interest at a specified rate. Various options are given as to their ultimate disposal.

The reasons for the relatively high cost of what is called "industrial" insurance are apparent from the foregoing analysis. Costs must be relatively high if death claims are not reduced by medical examination of the applicants, and if premiums are collected in small amounts by frequent visits of a company representative to the home of the insured. Premiums for ordinary insurance are paid by check or money order, annually, semiannually, or quarterly upon notice by mail of amount due. Two-fifths of the industrial life insurance sold in 1949 was on children. The over-all distribution of industrial insurance in force in 1949 as among men, women, and children under fifteen compared with that of ordinary insurance issued by regular companies was as follows:

	PERCENTAGE DISTRIBUTION OF LIFE INSURANCE IN FORCE	
INSURED PERSONS	Industrial	Ordinary
All	100	100
Men	33	81
Women	46	14
Children	21	5

The proportion of industrial policies that lapse every year is relatively high. In 1949, when the ratio of ordinary policies lapsed or surrendered for

7. If group insurance is excluded and only individual contracts considered, the percentage of life-insurance policies promising return of excess premiums becomes higher. The premiums of the nonparticipating stock companies are substantially lower than those of the mutual and the participating companies, since they are calculated on a net-cost basis. The net premiums of the mutual companies may be higher than those of the stock companies that issue participating policies, since there are many factors that determine the price at which a company can offer insurance.

cash to the mean number in force was only 3.4 per hundred, that of industrial was 12.4.

Net costs of ordinary and industrial insurance were compared in the *Study of Legal Reserve Life Insurance Companies* made for the Temporary National Economic Committee, a special investigating committee set up by the Seventy-fifth Congress. The average net premiums payable over a ten-year period on an ordinary life policy were 38 per cent less than those on industrial insurance in six companies offering both types of insurance. If the policies were surrendered at the end of the ten years, the ordinary would have been 53 per cent cheaper than the industrial, due to differences in the cash-surrender value.[8] Yet it will be observed that over three-fifths of the individual contracts in force in 1949 were of this high-cost type.

It is characteristically the low-income families that carry this highest-cost insurance. For the money paid out each year an insurance program could be devised that would provide much more adequately against the major hazards to which they are exposed. The argument is made that without industrial insurance low-income families would have no insurance at all. The small payment required at each collection date can be met from current income, but, it is argued, the pressure of current needs is so great that low-income families would not set aside the amounts necessary to pay the quarterly, semiannual, or annual premium on ordinary life or, if they did, that they would not leave the accumulation intact. The argument is similar to that for instalment buying. Achievement of the objective is easier and more certain when no accumulation over a period is necessary. Ordinary insurance, moreover, cannot be bought in as small amounts as industrial. The average industrial policy was only $300 in 1949, and the minimum amount of ordinary insurance issued by many companies is $1,000. There are families, however, carrying industrial insurance whose incomes are large enough and whose total insurance on all members is large enough to enable them to buy an ordinary policy of $1,000 or more upon the husband's life. Ignorance and high-pressure salesmanship are undoubtedly in part responsible for the extensive use of industrial insurance as well as for the faulty distribution of that which is carried among the family members. All individuals and families should be informed of the relatively high cost of insurance of this type. Many now carrying it are undoubtedly ignorant of the fact that a greater amount of insurance protection could be obtained for the same outlay if quarterly, semiannual, or annual payments were made.

8. Calculated from data in Temporary National Economic Committee, Monograph No. 28 (Washington: Government Printing Office, 1941), p. 286.

The reasons for the relatively low cost of savings-bank insurance are also apparent. Three states, Massachusetts, New York, and Connecticut, now authorize sales of insurance by savings banks under the same supervision and safeguards as exist for specialized insurance carriers. The long experience in Massachusetts with savings-bank life insurance indicates that such insurance can be made available at a cost about 40 per cent lower than weekly-premium industrial insurance and about 20 per cent less than ordinary life sold by insurance companies.[9] All savings-bank insurance is sold over the counter, thus avoiding the cost of person-to-person selling. The insurance business of the bank can be handled with very little increase in the administrative or clerical staff. Funds paid in by the insured go into investments similar in type to those suitable and permissible for savings deposits. Most banks offering insurance will arrange for premium payments periodically in small amounts by the insured in person or by deductions from his savings account, thus making it as easy to pay for as industrial insurance.

The premiums on National Service Life Insurance policies of any type are decidedly lower than those that could be charged by private agencies. All the expenses of administration, including anything that could be called selling cost, are borne by the government and not by the insured. The government also bears the excess mortality cost traceable to the extra hazards of military or naval service. The costs covered by the premium are only the death claims due to the hazards of civilian life.

TERM, WHOLE-LIFE, AND LIMITED-PAYMENT INSURANCE

Whether the insurance contract is with the government or a private agency, whether with a company organized for that purpose, mutual or stock, participating or nonparticipating, whether with a fraternal society or an authorized bank, whether the insurance is ordinary or industrial, the outlay necessary to obtain a given insurance estate will vary with the terms of the policy. Distinction should first be made between insurance issued for a specified period and that which, if the premiums are paid, is in effect indefinitely. Insurance might be issued for as short a period as one year; actually five years is the shortest period for which most companies

9. Assuming policies issued in 1930 to men age thirty-five, and using actual dividend histories during the following ten years, the U.S. Bureau of Labor Statistics compared average net costs of the policies of fifteen Massachusetts savings banks with those of ten insurance companies. Over the ten-year period the average net payments (premiums minus dividends) to the savings banks were less than those to the insurance companies by as much as 12 per cent for endowment policies and 21 per cent for ordinary life (see U.S. Bureau of Labor Statistics, *Operation of Savings Bank Life Insurance in Massachusetts and New York* [Bull. No. 688 (Washington: Government Printing Office, 1941)], pp. 51–54, 118–19).

offer it. The shorter the period for which insurance is issued, the lower the premium. If for one year only, the calculation of death claims to be met during the year would be on the basis of the actuarial probability of death of persons of the age of the insured. Thus men of twenty-five would pay one rate and men of forty-five another. If the insurance is for a period of five or more years, the practice is to make the premium a level amount for each year, on the basis of death claims expected to be met during the period. Thus if the insurance is for a five-year term taken at age twenty-five, the claims to be met arise from the death of insured men twenty-five to twenty-nine years of age; if taken at forty-five, from the death of men forty-five to forty-nine. When the insurance issued is whole-life, that is, in effect indefinitely, the premium again is a level one with death benefits calculated on the basis of the life-expectation of persons of the age of the insured. The premium again would be lower for persons insuring at twenty-five years of age than for those insuring at forty-five but in neither case as low as if the insurance were for a five-year term, since the whole-life policy must cover possible death benefits paid to beneficiaries of men from twenty-five to ninety-five years of age, if none is assumed to survive beyond that age, or forty-five to ninety-five, and the five-year term must cover only, as was said, claims of beneficiaries of men twenty-five to twenty-nine years of age or forty-five to forty-nine.

Term insurance may be "renewable" or "nonrenewable." Some companies offer only the latter. "Renewable" means simply that the contract may be renewed at the end of the first period for a period of the same duration without medical examination and therefore the chance of rejection. Upon renewal, however, the man of thirty must pay the rate indicated by his age, and correspondingly the man of fifty. Thus the premium for five-year term insurance would rise by a series of steps for as long as the insurer carried it. If the term had been one year, the rate would rise each year, very little in the early years and sharply upward in the latter. Chart III shows the relation between the annual premium per thousand dollars for whole-life level premium and renewable one-year term insurance beginning in each case at age twenty-five. The cost of the latter is much lower than the whole-life to age fifty-one, and then becomes much higher. If the insurance had been taken out at age thirty-five, the term would have been lower than the whole-life until about age fifty-five. The term insurance available is less likely to be renewable than it is convertible, that is, convertible at the option of the insured into whole-life insurance. Twenty-year term is unlikely to be renewable.

Life-insurance companies usually discourage the purchase of term insurance except for special purposes, and what is offered varies from company to company and time to time. One form of "special purpose" term that is available at low rates is the so-called "mortgage term" to run ten, fifteen, or twenty years, the period that a home may be mortgaged. Thus, if the breadwinner dies, the money is available to clear off the mortgage. The amount of this insurance usually decreases annually, hence the low

CHART III

ANNUAL PREMIUM FOR $1,000 OF (*A*) ONE-YEAR RENEWABLE, CONVERTIBLE
TERM, AND (*B*) ORDINARY LIFE INSURANCE BEGINNING AT AGE 25,
BOTH NONPARTICIPATING

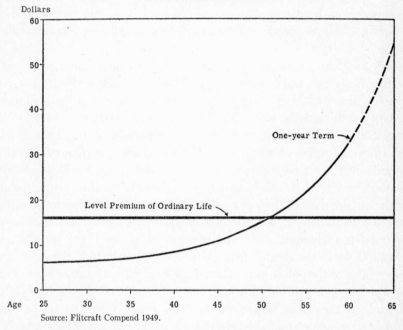

Source: Flitcraft Compend 1949.

rates. Certain groups in the population, Negroes, for example, may not be able to obtain term insurance. A high minimum is usually set for the amount of term insurance that will be issued, $2,500 or $5,000.[10] The argument given by the salesmen to those seeking a term policy is that it is only temporary protection while whole life is permanent. A twenty-year term policy, however, will cover the entire or the major period of a child's dependency. If the father dies during this period, a given life insurance estate will become available at lower annual outlay than if whole-life had been carried.

10. About 7 per cent of the life insurance in force taken out on an individual basis in United States companies in 1946 was term (*Insurance Yearbook, 1948*, p. 183A).

Whole-life policies after a period, usually three years, have a stated cash-surrender and loan value. The leveling of the premium is the source of this value. The insured in their earlier years pay more than enough to cover the claims of beneficiaries of persons of their age in order that in their later years they may pay less. This prepayment is the essence of the level premium. By law the insurance carriers must treat these prepayments as a reserve which the insured may claim if they relinquish their insurance. They may also borrow from it without relinquishing their insurance. Thus, after a period during which certain costs, mainly the salesman's commission, are written off, each policy has a specified cash or loan value, rising each year the insurance is in force. Thus the person taking out whole-life level-premium insurance is said to combine insurance and saving.

Cash and loan values of life-insurance policies have some of the attributes of savings, but in other respects they differ markedly from bank deposits, securities, and other assets. They represent readily realizable funds of a definite dollar value, but they may be secured only by surrender of the insurance contract or in the form of an interest-bearing loan. If the cash-surrender value of a policy is $500 and there is need for $300, the less amount cannot be secured except as a loan. Several policies should therefore be carried if cash in amount less than the total surrender value is to be obtained other than as a loan. If the fund in question were in the form of a bank deposit, any amount could be withdrawn, the insurance program left unchanged, and it would not be necessary to pay interest for its use. At death the estate of the insured does not include the cash-surrender value of the policy as it would if the fund were a bank deposit. The life-insurance estate is only the face value of the policy. Beyond question the family of the person who saved the difference between the cost of a renewable term policy and the level-premium whole-life would be in a better financial position during life and at his death than the one whose "savings" were in the form of the cash-surrender or loan value of a whole-life policy. But again we are faced with the question: How many would regularly save the difference between the annual cost of the two, keep it safely, and forbear spending it except under the same circumstances that would bring surrender of the policy or a loan? The insurance companies allege that few can be expected to act in this manner. Possibly so, yet it is also true that few have been informed as to the alternatives and have chosen their course of action in the light of the clearly understood facts of the case. The saving that comes from the payment of a level premium on a whole-life policy is enforced saving; the insured must save as well as pay for insurance protection. There are times, however, when spending for current consumption is better than saving or when increased insurance protection is better than saving. The argument for the level premium is that it prevents the outlay for insurance from rising in the later period of the insured person's life. The outlay might also be reduced by decreasing the amount of insurance carried since his need for it at that time is usually less.

It would be hypothetically possible to pay for any type of insurance in a lump sum rather than by payments at stated intervals. Thus a person could be insured during his whole life by making a single payment. Few would consider such action wise, since, if the insured died soon after making such payment, his insurance estate would be no larger than if he had paid for but one year or fraction thereof. Whole-life insurance to be paid for in a limited number of payments is frequently purchased, however. So-called "twenty-payment" life policies are common. At the end of twenty years the insured has his insurance paid up for the balance of his life. The annual payments for such policies must obviously be larger than for the whole-life with an indefinite number of payments, and their cash-surrender and loan values are larger. The argument for the twenty-payment life is that the payments are concentrated during the period when the earnings of the insured are likely to be largest, from ages twenty-five to forty-five, for example. The argument against it is that during that period his insurance needs and burden of support are also likely to be largest, while later they are smaller. If he dies within the twenty years his insurance estate is no larger than if he had chosen a type of policy requiring smaller annual outlays.

The twenty-year (or other period) endowment policy is a special combination of saving and insurance. It provides insurance for the specified period and at the end a cash payment of the same amount but no further insurance. It is term, not "permanent," insurance. The annual premiums on this type of policy are larger than for any type mentioned, since the insurance for the term must be paid for and a sum put into the hands of the insurance company which accumulated at a specified rate of interest will amount to the sum promised at the end of the term.[11] The cash surrender or loan value of this type of policy is therefore higher than for any other. What is returned if the policy is surrendered is not prepaid insurance but the saved sum to date with interest. If the policy-holder dies

11. The proportion of the premium that is insurance diminishes from the beginning at of the end of the period, since each year the accumulation available to pay death benefit increases until at the end accumulation and death benefit are the same.

during the period, his saving does not enrich his estate beyond what it would have been if he had carried term insurance only.

The annual outlay required for $1,000 of ordinary insurance on a man twenty-five years of age for different types of policies, calculated so far as possible on the basis of the rates and dividends of one of the largest companies in 1949, was as follows:[12]

	AVERAGE NET PREMIUM PER $1,000		
	First Five	First Ten	First Twenty
TYPE OF POLICY	Years	Years	Years
Five-year renewable term............	$ 5.43	$ 5.17	$ 5.85
Ten-year renewable term............	5.56	4.97	5.59
Twenty-year nonrenewable term*.....	7.86	6.76	5.50
Term to age 65*....................	11.50	10.97	10.34
Whole-life (paid up at 85)...........	18.86	18.12	16.85
Twenty-payment whole-life..........	30.45	29.54	28.05
Twenty-year endowment.............	48.14	47.10	45.53

* Since the company chosen did not offer policies of this type, rates and dividends of another large company were taken. Thus differences in market cost of these policies as compared with others may be partly due to the necessary shift in company.

The cash-surrender value of these policies if in force ten or twenty years later would be as follows:

	CASH-SURRENDER VALUE PER $1,000 AT END OF	
	Ten	Twenty
TYPE OF POLICY	Years	Years
Five and ten-year term........	......	
Twenty-year term...........	$ 4	......
Term to age 65..............	57	$ 119*
Whole-life (paid up at 85).....	125	290
Twenty-payment whole-life...	238	559
Twenty-year endowment......	424	1,000

* The cash value of these policies declines in the later years and will ultimately become zero.

Again it must be emphasized that the savings above are realizable if the insured surrenders the insurance, as he might well do if the need for it is reduced or ceases. Those with five-year term have had more money for current consumption; or if they saved the difference between the cost of the whole-life and the term as well as a possible $2\frac{1}{2}$ per cent interest on it compounded annually, they would have approximately $150 for each $1,000 of insurance at the end of ten years, with correspondingly larger amounts if the saving were the difference between the outlays for term and that for the limited-payment of the endowment policy.[13]

12. Rates and dividends as given in *Flitcraft Compend* (New York: Flitcraft, Inc., 1949). Earlier and subsequent rates and dividends might differ.

13. After a whole-life policy is surrendered, the net cost of the insurance protection during the period the policy is carried is sometimes calculated by subtracting the dividends and surrender value from the total gross premium payments. This is misleading. The insured has gained by virtue of his enforced saving and the interest received on his saving. If he had volun-

What types of policies do families buy? In 1949 the policies on the lives of persons fifteen years of age and over purchased from regular insurance companies were distributed as follows:

Type of Policy	Percentage of All Policies Purchased Represented by Each Type
Limited payment	26
Endowment	24
Straight life	23
Term and modified whole-life	12
Retirement income*	6

* These policies are similar to endowment except that they carry the option of taking the proceeds at maturity in the form of a life income instead of cash.

Over half of the insurance purchased in 1949 on the lives of children under fifteen was limited payment, a third was endowment, and the remaining tenth, straight life. The aim of the buyers of the limited-payment insurance was presumably to provide the children upon maturity with a certain amount of paid-up insurance for life or with the amount of cash represented by the surrender value. If the aim had been merely to insure that the parents would have money to pay the burial expenses in case of the child's death, straight life would have been chosen. Whether such a gift to the child at maturity is more desirable than enhancing his protection during infancy and childhood against the loss of the father is highly questionable. The endowment policy makes possible a larger cash gift to the child at maturity than does straight life or limited payment. If one takes the position that the parents owe the children, not gifts after they are grown, but security while they are young, these purchases seem especially unsound. In this connection Jordan and Willett say: "It should be unnecessary to stress the fact that a policy to provide funds for education should be carried on the life of the person paying for the education, not on that of the person to be educated."[14] Insurance on the father and saving by the father are the methods of insuring funds for children's education.

GROUP INSURANCE

As was previously shown, about 18 million employed persons held group-life-insurance certificates in 1949. The master-policy is issued to the employer. Only those employing at least fifty are eligible for such a policy,

---

tarily saved, he would be in approximately the same position. The holder of the whole-life contract seems to have reduced the cost of his insurance because he has deducted from it the interest on his savings.

14. D. F. Jordan and E. T. Willett, *Managing Personal Finances* (New York: Prentice-Hall, Inc., 1945), p. 199.

and the major portion of the employees must elect to be covered, since the group insured must include both the younger and the older employees, both the good and the poor physical risks. Group insurance is low-cost insurance, especially for the older employees. It provides insurance for some who otherwise could not secure it. The reasons for its low cost are evident. There is no expense for medical examinations. The selling expense per person insured is very low. The employer usually collects the premiums by payroll deduction. It is usually one-year term insurance, renewed each year. In some cases the employer pays the entire cost, but costs are shared in two out of three group-life plans. A common practice is for the employer to pay such share as will keep the cost of the insurance the same for each employee over the years.

Group insurance clearly should not be the sole reliance of persons with dependents, since it terminates with employment or with employment by an insured firm or institution. Usually in such event he may purchase another type of policy without medical examination, but in the case of an older person the rate would be relatively high. The amount of insurance available under the group plan usually varies with the wage or salary and sometimes with age or with experience.

PROVISION FOR OLD AGE

The use of the insurance principle to provide against the chance of survival beyond one's earning years requires the purchase of an annuity, the promise of an insurer to provide a given income for as long as the annuitant survives. Especially appropriate for a married couple is a joint-and-survivor annuity which provides not only an income while both are living but one for the survivor of the same or a lesser amount. Complete use of the insurance principle to provide for old age means a life-annuity, an income as long as the insured lives but nothing for his heirs even if only one payment has been made. The refund type, in which the unused principal becomes a part of the estate if death occurs while there is still such a sum, will not give the annuitant as large an income during his lifetime.

The cost of an annuity contract varies as does the life-policy with the selling and other costs of the insurance company, the rate of return on its investment, and with life-expectations. The cost of annuities goes up with increased life-expectation for older persons. For this reason women must pay more than men for the promise of a life-income of given amount. Annuities may be paid for in a single lump sum or by fixed payments over a period. Single-payment annuities are usually immediate, that is, go into effect at once, although they need not do so. Those otherwise paid for cannot go into effect until the accumulation with interest reaches a certain amount, at which time the purchaser will have reached a specified age. He may then elect to defer receipt of the income. The later in life the annuity contract goes into effect, the larger the income that will be guaranteed for the remainder of the life of the annuitant. At any time before an annuity goes into effect the contract may be relinquished and the accumulation as of that date, after allowance for interest at the agreed upon rate and for the insurer's expenses, may be withdrawn. If an annuitant dies before the annuity goes into effect the accumulated amount, similarly computed, is a part of his estate.

What are the advantages and disadvantages of the contract made early and paid for by fixed payments during a period of twenty, thirty, or more years? There is the advantage that the savings plan is definite, lends itself to budgeting, is more likely to be carried through and savings left intact, than if another plan of providing an annuity for old age were used. The income certain at a specified date is also known and the saved fund is relatively secure against loss. An alternative procedure is to plan upon using the cash value of life-insurance policies at age sixty-five or later for annuity purchase. Others might prefer to keep their saved funds in their own hands with a view to direct investment at a higher rate of return than insurance companies could guarantee. An annuity contract obtained in one's early or middle years may or may not be more favorable to the annuitant than one obtained at age sixty-five or older. If rates of interest have fallen or life-expectancy after sixty-five has risen, the earlier contract would be the more favorable, otherwise the reverse.

Is the purchase of an annuity preferable to reliance on the income from invested savings, or the use of the saved fund itself and the income on the declining amount, as the basis for support in old age? The annuity provides the more certain income, since assets may be lost or dwindle in dollar value and income. Assuming that neither of the latter contingencies need be feared, the annual income realizable from $10,000 by various uses of the saved fund is as follows:[15]

Source of Income	Amount per Year
Single life annuity at age 65:	
Men	$755
Women	641
Joint and survivor annuity—$\frac{2}{3}$ to survivor (husband and wife both 65 when annuity begins)	643
Investment, interest at 4 per cent, principal remaining intact	400
Investment, interest at 4 per cent, using up principal in:	
Fifteen years	880
Twenty years	720

15 Calculated using costs of annuity contracts as given in *Flitcraft Compend* (1949).

When the saved fund is used for current living, a chance is taken upon the length of time that income will be needed. At sixty-five the chance that either husband or wife will survive for twenty-five years may be slight. The chance that one or both will survive for twenty years is greater, and for fifteen years still greater except for those with a physical disability likely to shorten life. The decision as to the wiser policy must be made by each individual in the light of all the circumstances. It will be noted that to secure an annuity of $100 per month while both husband and wife are living, and of two-thirds that amount for the survivor, would require an accumulation of almost $20,000.

A major problem faced both by those providing for old age and by those providing for dependents is the possibility of a marked change in the price level between the time insurance contracts are made and when they are kept. A life-income of $100 a month supplemented by home ownership might at one price level provide decent maintenance for an aged couple but at another be entirely inadequate. The only way the individual as such can meet this problem is to make no or few contracts for a fixed dollar income but instead invest directly in stock or other assets the dollar value of which may be expected to rise as much as the price level. The income and value of such holdings will fall also with a contrary movement. As has already been pointed out, such investment as a hedge against inflation or for any purpose is a hazardous process except for a few. Adequate protection against inflation will come only through understanding of its causes and adoption of the public policies that prevent it.

Not all annuities sold by insurance companies are individual contracts. Of all in force in 1949, the largest number came from group contracts. The number of annuities represented by group certificates increased almost 150 per cent from 1941 to 1949, while the number of individual contracts increased about 30 per cent. The average annual income value of the individual contracts is higher, about $500 in 1941 and $475 in 1949. That of the group annuities rose from about $210 in 1941 to about $260 in 1949. The great increase in group annuities came in part from the successful efforts of trade-unions to make such provision a part of the collective agreement with the employer. It was a result also of high war and postwar corporate earnings and tax rates combined with a general increase in interest in pension plans for employees.

Some employers do not turn over their pension programs to insurance companies through the purchase of group annuities but pay the retirement income agreed upon from current income or from reserves established for the purpose. The certainty of the payment under these plans will depend upon the willingness and the ability of the employer to carry out the program as time goes on. The claim of the holder of a group-annuity certificate, however, is upon the insurance company, not the employer. In most modern pension plans the employee pays at least part of the cost through regular payroll deductions. Under the contributory system the employee is entitled to a refund of his payments with or without interest if he changes his employment or employer. Under most group-annuity contracts he is given credit for all payments made to his account. He may usually withdraw this fund, or he may keep the contract in effect by continued payments of the former or a smaller amount, or he may settle for whatever annuity the amount due him would yield at a specified age if he ceases to be a member of the insured group. In case of his death before the annuity goes into effect, his heirs will receive the accumulated amount.

PROBLEMS IN PLANNING AN INSURANCE PROGRAM

The problems that arise in planning an insurance program can best be seen by attempting to devise one. Such a procedure involves analysis of the specific family situation, estimation of its probable change in the course of time, examination of the kinds of insurance policies offered on the market, exactly what each one would provide under given circumstances, and their relative cost. The amount of insurance needed is, of course, directly related to the number dependent upon the income that may be lost by death or retirement. Income from other sources must be taken into account and such assets as an owned family home. Social Security benefits or those that might come through group insurance are also highly relevant. The stage in the family life-span in which either or both might augment individual insurance, and the conditions under which either would be forthcoming, should be noted. A widow, for example, is entitled to no Social Security benefits unless she is sixty-five or over or is the mother of a child under eighteen. Since the number of dependents in families with children first increases, then decreases, the amount of life insurance might rise and fall correspondingly. At a minimum standard the period of child dependency would run from the birth of the first child to the date when the last would reach the legal school-leaving age. A higher standard would allow for school attendance beyond that age.

After the children leave school provision for old age should take ascendancy in the insurance program. If there are two children born two years apart when the father is in his mid-twenties, and both children leave school at eighteen, before the father reaches sixty-five, there will be a short period when the family has only one child to support and a much longer one when there are none. If the father's earning power does not decline, this period may be one of relatively high saving. The wife may re-sume earning, full or part time, and thus enhance the prospects of accumu-lating sizable assets. The larger the number of children and the later the school-leaving age, the shorter will be the period of augmented saving. If a married couple can save about $65 per month for twenty years, when the husband is sixty-five they can have, at present rates, an annuity of about $100 per month for as long as both live, with the survivor assured of an income of two-thirds of that amount until his or her death.[16]

HOW ADEQUATE IS INSURANCE PROTECTION?

From an analysis of data on life-insurance ownership in 1950 it appears that in that year the median annual premium payment in families with a married head and children under eighteen was approximately $125. The face value of the policy or policies held by half of the families was under $5,000.[17] By no means all of this insurance was on the life of the father. The amounts indicated were for life insurance on all family members. It is obvious that few families carry enough insurance upon the life of the husband to permit the wife to abstain from earning during the period of the children's dependency unless she has other sources of income. It would also be necessary for many older persons, immediately or soon after re-tirement, to derive their support wholly or partially from their children if no income were available other than from their own investments or an-nuity contracts.

It is not difficult to see what forces and conditions would operate to make families' provision for the future more adequate. A generally higher level of real income and a heightened sense of the importance of such pro-vision would work to that end. Operating against more adequate provision is the upward movement of standards for consumption as the number and cost of things urgently desired and generally accepted as necessary in-crease. But without change in incomes or standards it is clear that insur-ance programs of families could be more adequate than they are. With low-cost forms of insurance more widely available, with greater knowledge and use of them, insurance protection would become more adequate. A sounder assessment of insurance needs, and a change in the family mem-bers upon whom insurance is carried, would make it more adequate. More

16. The accumulation represented is about $20,000, assuming interest at 2½ per cent com-pounded annually.

17. *Life Insurance Ownership among American Families 1950: Special Tabulations for the Institute of Life Insurance by the Survey Research Center, University of Michigan* (Ann Arbor).

disinterested counseling and less aggressive selling would help to make it more adequate.

One further important consideration must be noted. The success of a saving or insurance program in providing against the risk of death of the breadwinner or his survival beyond his earning years depends in part upon the steadiness of the family income and its freedom from heavy expense from illness or other disability. Prolonged periods of unemployment or disability of the earner or the necessity for large outlays for hospital, medical, or surgical expense will disrupt the most wisely planned program.

INSURANCE AGAINST RISK OF ILLNESS OR ACCIDENT

An ideal insurance program would include insurance against all personal risks: death of the breadwinner, old age, and disability, both of the breadwinner and of other family members. The accident and sickness program would include insurance against loss of the breadwinner's income, especially its loss for an extended period from a long-term disability. Generous provision of sick leave lessens the need for such insurance during temporary disability. The effect of the latter upon the family finances, even without this provision, is not so disastrous as the long continuing disability. The ideal program would also include insurance that would meet hospital, medical, and surgical expenses incurred on behalf of any family member.

The fact is, however, that relatively few families are able to approximate this ideal program. Some are able to put part of it into effect because of their eligibility for participation in group plans. Workers in certain industries or those employed by certain companies may participate in group insurance that provides a weekly cash income in case of disability from accident or sickness. Some of these plans were initiated by the company and others through collective bargaining. The benefits are usually limited to a certain number of weeks in one year or for any one continuous disability. Some trade-union members or members of fraternal or mutual benefit societies are also eligible for varying types of disability insurance.

Far more extensive in coverage than group plans providing cash benefits to offset loss of income are those that for a fixed periodic payment provide service benefits to the breadwinner or the members of his family: hospital services of specified kind for a certain period, surgical and/or medical services of specified character to hospital patients. First to develop and largest in coverage are the hospital service plans. Most of these plans involve a contract between the insured and a group of hospitals. The plans approved by the American Hospital Association carry the Blue Cross insignia. The groups insured under these plans are usually the employees of a particular firm. In that case the payments may be made by payroll deduction. Membership on an individual basis, with direct billing and payment, is more costly but is the only type possible for a person not a member of an insured group. At an appropriate increase in cost hospital insurance policies may be drawn up to cover the whole family. Such coverage is important, since outlays for the hospital care of women and children exceed considerably those for adult males. Group plans, distinguished as Blue Shield, are being developed in conjunction with the Blue Cross plans. Persons participating in the latter plan are eligible to participate in the former. Under the Blue Shield plan the insured individual and, if so desired, the wife or husband and children under nineteen, if hospitalized, are guaranteed specified surgical and medical care, or cash offsets on the bill for such services. The contract in the case of the Blue Shield insurance is with a group of physicians and surgeons, usually the local medical society. Commercial companies also offer insurance in the form of guaranteed cash indemnities to offset the cost of hospital or medical care. The various group plans providing services are usually cheaper and more convenient and are generally recommended in preference to such insurance.

It should be noted that neither the group plans nor other types of accident and illness insurance will cover the full cost of extensive medical, surgical, or hospital care. If the stay in the hospital is prolonged, the Blue Cross insurance will not cover the cost. Various services and supplies often required are not included. Nor will the medical and surgical services provided under the Blue Shield be adequate for many serious and prolonged illnesses. Furthermore, the group plans cover only medical care received by a hospitalized patient, not office calls or home visits. Some experiments are being made with arrangements by which medical services are paid for not on a fee-for-service basis but by fixed, periodic payments to a group of physicians which entitle the individual or family to whatever services are necessary, both preventive and curative. These payments may be allowed for in the budget as is the outlay for food or rent. Such arrangements would require a reorganization of medical practice as well as of the family's procedures. It would mean payments when there is no or little need for the services as well as when they are needed. If widely adopted, it would spread the sickness bill during a period over the whole population rather than entirely upon those who are sick. Its wide adoption would also widen the patient's choice of a physician, since choice is now limited to those who co-operate in the program.

The major gap in insurance against the financial hazards of accident or illness, so far as most families are concerned, is in provision against the loss of income occasioned thereby. Few breadwinners are members of groups for which such insurance on a group basis is possible, and the number for whom protection against extended disability is thus provided is negligible. As with group life insurance, protection is lost if membership in the group ceases. Nor can this gap be adequately bridged by individual contract with an insurance company.

A number of life-insurance companies, although not as many as formerly, offer for an extra premium a monthly income until a specified age to holders of life-insurance contracts who suffer extended and total disability. The age to which such payments are made is usually fifty-five, and the income is a certain percentage of the face value of the policy but may not exceed a certain maximum. The disability must usually be such as to keep the insured from engaging in any employment, and payments do not begin until the disability has continued for six months. Practically all life-insurance companies, a few without extra premium, waive premium payments on life insurance in case such disability occurs. Insurance against "total and permanent" disability is usually tied with life insurance, and the amount of the disability payment with the life-insurance coverage. It is practically impossible to secure insurance against extended disability on a renewable basis except as a rider to a life-insurance contract.[18] The more restricted are the types of disabilities covered, the period during which payments will be made or the aggregate amounts that will be paid, or the longer the period after disability begins before payments start, the less adequate the insurance. If the only disability covered is that which confines the person to his home and prevents him from engaging in any employment of any kind, the less adequately it meets the need. It should be remembered, however, that insurance adequate in these respects would be difficult if not impossible to provide other than at a prohibitive cost.

Policies which cover short-term disability are relatively numerous.[19] The offerings of this general character are far from standardized, and those of each company vary from time to time. The protection offered suffers in the main from the limitation that most policies are cancelable at the option of the insurer. If it is feared that a disability may recur, or if for other reasons the individual is considered a bad risk, he will not be able to con-

18. Philip Gordis, *How To Buy Insurance* (New York: W. W. Norton & Co., 1947), p. 273. Gordis found but one company offering such a policy.

19. To cover temporary disabilities, there must be no "waiting period" before payments begin, or it must be short.

tinue his insurance. He has protection of course as long as the policy is in effect.

To understand this market situation, one must review the conditions that make insurance against a risk possible. There must be large and unselected coverage. This means that the rates must be those that many people can pay. Those who are not prone to accident or illness, as well as those who are, must be covered. In addition, eligibility to receive the promised benefits must be easy to determine. Proof of death or attainment of a given age is relatively simple; proof of disability, especially the period that disability continues, is far less so. In periods of economic depression claims under disability insurance increase greatly. Persons without jobs do not recover quickly from sickness or accident. It is for this reason that women, especially married women, are usually ineligible for disability insurance.

It is clear that a modest provision against the risks of death, disability, and old age, even with the use of low-cost insurance on an individual or group basis, would cost far more than most families devote to this purpose. Most difficult to guard against are the risks of disability and of dependent old age, the former because of the lack of adequate types of insurance as well as their cost, the latter because of the accumulation required. Protection of the wife in her later years if she has withdrawn from the labor force presents a special problem. Protection of children during the period of dependency is the least difficult problem, but the income that could be provided by most families in case of the breadwinner's death will be insufficient to enable the mother to abstain from earning.

CHAPTER XII

SOCIAL SECURITY

IN THE preceding chapters the methods by which individuals upon their own initiative may make financial provision for the future have been discussed and the adequacy of that provision appraised. It has been pointed out that individuals can insure against personal, but not against economic, risks and that saving is an inadequate method of providing for events of unknown incidence and time of occurrence. It has also been noted that many of the families currently unable to maintain adequate standards of food, clothing, or housing are in this position because of the death, disability, or advanced age of the breadwinner or the need for large outlays for medical and hospital care. The general policy question to be discussed in this chapter is: To what extent should society as a whole through governmental action assure individuals and families that a minimum of money income will be forthcoming if one or more of the contingencies noted occurs? Such income has been loosely called "civil rights" income to distinguish it from that based on private contractual claims. Such income has also been described as "transfer income," since it comes from the public treasury, is transferred there from private sources by the power of the state, and is transferred to the beneficiaries by the same authority. Specifically the issues are: To whom, on what terms, and by what governmental agency shall money income be assured in case of unemployment, widowhood, orphanhood, disability, or old age? How shall the amount paid be determined, and what shall be the source of the funds?

POSSIBLE SCOPE AND CHARACTER OF PUBLIC POLICY

The provision of income from the public treasury is not the only approach to the problem of income insecurity. Other governmental policies directly related to this problem have already been discussed. They are those designed to reduce the incidence of the contingencies that cause lapse of income as well as those designed to protect individual savings and improve saving and insurance programs. Wise governmental action may increase stability of incomes, improve health, lessen accidents, and stimulate individual thrift. Still in every community there will be some currently unemployed or disabled, as well as those widowed, orphaned, or aged.

In the broadest possible terms either of two policies may be emphasized or adopted. One, the state may, as it has long done in some fashion, take responsibility only for the needy among these groups. Its policy with respect to these needy persons and their dependents could also be developed along either of two lines. One would put the maximum possible responsibility upon the next of kin of the needy, extending it to remote degrees of relationship. Public assistance would be provided only after all resources of the individual were exhausted and then on such terms as might be held to have a deterrent effect on readiness to accept and be of minimum cost to the community. Or the policy may be that which is increasingly found in our society and others like it: a minimizing of responsibility of relatives, a liberalizing of the definition of need, and provision of support on terms increasingly free from stigma, in the preferred form of cash payments, sufficient to enable the recipient to live in health and decency, according to prevailing standards.[1] In either case need may be the only criterion of eligibility for public assistance, or special provision may be made for each category of needy persons, the unemployed, the disabled, the widowed, the children, the aged.[2]

An alternative policy that is relatively new is to establish a right to income from public funds in the event of specified contingencies without regard to the need of the individual or family, that is, without consideration of the resources of those affected or their relatives. The statutory right to income may be contingent, for example, upon the attainment of a specified age, as in Canada, where everyone at age seventy is entitled to an income of $40 per month; or, as in this country, where the right to receive is contingent upon attainment of a specific age or unemployed status if a specified tax has been paid for a specified period. In either case the right to receive is not determined by need.

The actual system in operation at a particular time may be based upon a combination of these principles either for an interim period or as permanent policy. The American social security system obviously is such a combination. Mrs. Burns says: "Several social security systems are in simultaneous operation, social insurance, special and general public assistance, and status provisions for veterans. All play an important part

1. What is described here is the general trend. There are marked ups and downs from time to time as well as variations from community to community at the same time in liberality of provision for the needy.

2. A vexed question in all public assistance programs is: What governmental unit has responsibility? To settle this, residence requirements are established. Some needy may not be eligible for assistance in any jurisdiction.

in the total combination."[3] "Assistance" is a money payment made to individuals or families upon evidence of need, while what is here called "social insurance" entitles those with insured status under the law to cash benefits without reference to their financial resources. The moot question is: Which principle should be emphasized in modifications of the system? Should need be increasingly emphasized in determining eligibility for receipt of income or amount received, or should status without reference to need be paramount?

As Mrs. Burns further says, "No one law codifies the whole American social security system."[4] To know its details, one would need to know not only federal laws but those of the states, the territories, and the District of Columbia. In addition, one would need to know the regulations and practices of the administrative agencies charged in each jurisdiction with the interpretation of the statutory principles. It is proposed to deal here with the Social Security program in its broad outlines only and as it relates to the causes of income insecurity previously discussed: death of the breadwinner, his disability or that of other family member, unemployment, and old age. The provisions of the Social Security Act passed by Congress in 1935 and amended notably in 1939 and 1950 will inevitably form a large part of the picture.

AID TO DEPENDENT CHILDREN

The first group for whom special assistance in the form of cash payments was provided in the United States was needy children, that is, those deprived of parental support or care because of the death of one or both parents or for other reasons. By a cash payment to the mother or other relative with whom the child was living, maintenance of these children was made possible in their own homes rather than in foster-homes or institutions. These payments were first called mother's aid or widow's pensions, now "aid to dependent children." The first statutory provision for such assistance was made in Illinois in 1911, and by 1936, when the Social Security Act went into effect, it was found in all the states (except Georgia and South Carolina) as well as in the District of Columbia, Alaska, Puerto Rico, and Hawaii. The majority of the state laws, however, merely authorized towns or counties to make such cash payments from their own funds, with the result that in many localities the system was never adopted or the allowances were very inadequate.

3. E. M. Burns, *The American Social Security System* (Boston: Houghton Mifflin Co., 1949), p. 45.
4. *Ibid.*, p. 44.

Among the grants-in-aid to the several states authorized by the Social Security Act is one designed to extend and increase aid to dependent children in the form indicated.[5] In all states with an approved plan for such aid the federal government will share the cost by reimbursing the state for a certain portion of its outlay. No plan is approved that is not operative throughout the state. The federal portion of the average monthly payment made by the state varies with the amount of the payment. The reimbursement authorized for the two-year period beginning October, 1952, is four-fifths of the average monthly payment when the latter is $15 or less for the responsible relative with whom the child is living and for each dependent child.[6] As the average monthly payment goes above $15 per person, the proportion of the total paid by the federal government decreases, although up to a point it shares the increases in monthly payment equally with the state. That is, if a state's average monthly payment to mothers with one child rose from $30 to $60, the federal government's reimbursement would increase from $24 to $39, but its share in the average payment would fall from 80 to 65 per cent of the total. If the average monthly payment in the state goes above $30 for the responsible relative, $30 for the first child, and $21 each for all others, the federal government does not share the added cost. The federal government will pay no more than $39 per month toward the support of a mother and one child, $54 if there are two children, $69 if there are three; that is, $15 for each additional child. The entire amount above these maximums must come from the state treasury.

Included since 1950 in state payments for calculation of federal reimbursement are not only the monthly cash payments for maintenance but outlays for the medical care of the children or the mother or other relative with whom they are living. The average monthly payment under this program was $71 per family in December, 1950, and about $20 per person wholly or partially maintained.[7] About 3 per cent of all children under eighteen are aided. The proportion of all children living with but one parent who benefit would of course be much higher. There is great variation from state to state. In New Jersey in December, 1949, only about 1 per cent of the children were aided by this program, but in Louisiana

5. Authorized for Alaska, Hawaii, the District of Columbia, and also on less favorable terms for Puerto Rico and the Virgin Islands.

6. The federal government does not participate in grants to children sixteen to eighteen who are not in school or to those who live with relatives other than those of a specified degree or in payments on behalf of those who require institutional care.

7. *Social Security Bulletin*, September, 1951. The average for all states and territories and the District of Columbia excluding payments for medical care.

about 8 per cent.[8] An investigation of low-income families with children would show many who were receiving this type of public assistance.

The Social Security Act authorizes federal participation in payments on behalf of children who are deprived of parental support or care because of the death, continued absence from home, or physical or mental incapacity of either parent. A special study by the United States Bureau of Public Assistance showed that in June, 1948, death of the father was the reason for the children's dependency in less than a fourth of the families receiving this type of assistance.[9] About a fifth of the fathers were living and in the home but incapacitated. Thus the father was living but not in the home in over half of the families. A few of the absent fathers were in hospitals, a few in penal institutions, but six-sevenths of the absentees had either deserted their families, were divorced, were legally separated from the mother, or had never been married to her. Thus the major causes for the dependency of these children were the father's failure to meet his responsibility and the failure or inability of the state to compel him to do so. In about a fifth of the families both parents were in the home, in about two-thirds the mother only, and in about two in every hundred the father only. In about a tenth of the families the children were not living with either parent. Only 6 per cent of the mothers, if living, were not in the home.

The federal government has left the definition of a "needy" child to the states and requires only that in its determination the income and resources of the child must be taken into account. The state laws all define need in much the same manner. Need is said to exist when the income of the child or of the responsible relative with whom he is living is insufficient to supply an adequate level of living. The standards used to determine when such income is insufficient vary greatly from state to state. The number of needy in relation to the funds available inevitably has its effect, as does the level of living that most families in the community are able to attain.

The purpose of the program of assistance to needy children, as usually described, is "to prevent disruption of families on the ground of poverty alone and to enable the mother to stay at home and devote herself to housekeeping and the care of her children."[10] But the question arises:

8. *Social Work Year Book, 1951* (New York: American Association of Social Workers, 1951), p. 371.
9. U.S. Bureau of Public Assistance, Federal Security Agency, *Characteristics of Families Receiving Aid to Dependent Children* (Public Assistance Report No. 17 [Washington, 1950]). (Processed.)
10. U.S. Federal Security Board, *Social Security in America* (Publication No. 20 [Washington: Government Printing Office, 1937]), p. 233.

Under what circumstances should mothers be encouraged to earn if they are able-bodied rather than accept public assistance? In some jurisdictions the policy is to do so if the children can be adequately cared for and if there are opportunities for earning as much or more than the grant. It is in large part the number of children to be supported that makes it necessary for mothers without other resources to seek aid. The average for such mothers in June, 1948, was 2.49 as compared with 1.87 for all families in which only the mother was present.[11] Not only would it be more difficult for the mothers with the larger families both to earn and to care for their children, but their earnings are less likely to be adequate for their support.

The large proportion of aided children whose father is living and able-bodied led to the provision in the 1950 revision of the Social Security Act that prompt notice should be given to law-enforcement officials of the furnishing of aid on behalf of a child "deserted or abandoned by a parent." The effectiveness of this procedure in altering the situation may be doubted. Involved here is the general problem of enforcing the father's responsibility for the support of children born out of wedlock and of those whose parents are separated or divorced.

OLD AGE ASSISTANCE

A second group to be given special treatment under the public assistance laws were those who were approaching the end of their life-span. During the 1920's the economic plight of the aged was the subject of investigation in several of the more populous, highly urbanized states, and by the end of 1928 six states and one territory had old age assistance laws. All were of the optional type; that is, local units were authorized to provide for the aged needy by regular cash payments. The depression gave the movement great impetus, and by 1935, when the Social Security Act was passed, twenty-eight states and two territories had such laws, usually making the provision of cash aid mandatory throughout the state. The stimulus provided by the offer of federal participation in the cost has meant the establishment of old age assistance programs in every state and territory. Thus the needy aged, who formerly were dependent upon their children or lived in the county poorhouse, can maintain themselves in their own homes or pay their way if they live with a son, daughter, or other relative.

To secure a federal grant-in-aid, the program must be operative in all counties and towns of the state. The age requirement for eligibility may

11. U.S. Bureau of Public Assistance, Public Assistance Report No. 17, p. 16.

not be over sixty-five nor the residence requirement greater than five of the nine years immediately preceding application, with one year immediately preceding; nor may any citizen of the United States be excluded. The federal government reimburses the state for a specified portion of its monthly payment for the maintenance and medical, hospital, and nursing care of the aged.[12] The share assumed by the federal government for a two-year period beginning October, 1952, is four-fifths of all payments of $25 per person or less, and one-half of payments above $25 up to a maximum of $55 per month per person. Thus the share of the federal government cannot, as the law now stands, exceed $35 per month.

The principle of old age assistance in the form of cash income is now well established in all jurisdictions. In December, 1950, 2,786,000 persons were receiving such aid, approximately a fourth of all sixty-five and over.[13] In Louisiana more than four-fifths of the population sixty-five and over were receiving, but in Delaware and New Jersey only about a sixteenth.[14] The proportion of the aged population receiving public assistance will vary with many factors: the opportunities for employment, the proportion with income or savings adequate for self-support, the degree of stigma attached to public assistance, the criteria used to determine need. The average monthly payment to aged persons in December, 1950, was $43, ranging from above $77 in Colorado to $19 in Mississippi. Married couples and individuals whose incomes were mainly or wholly old age assistance are clearly a large part of the lower-income groups. Without this income most of them would probably appear as no-income members of the households of their children or other relatives, or their incomes, if any, would be merged with the incomes of others. Experience has shown that relatively few, mainly those without children, would be in the poorhouse.

Only the needy aged are eligible for old age assistance. The statutory definition of need in most of the states is in general terms. The New York law says: "unable to support self in whole or in part or without other means or sources of income by which he can be maintained." Alabama phrased it as follows: "insufficient income to provide a reasonable subsistence in proportion to his accustomed standard of living." Some states

12. There is no federal participation in the cost of maintenance or care of the aged who are mentally ill or tubercular either in public or in private institutions or for those living in a public institution such as the county home.

13. *Social Security Bulletin*, September, 1951. Average for all states and territories and the District of Columbia. Included in this total are those sixty to sixty-four, who in Colorado are aided entirely from state funds.

14. *Social Work Year Book, 1951*, p. 370.

leave the screening of applicants wholly to the agency set up to administer the act, but most of them do not and indicate in the law the amount of income, liquid assets, or other property that would disqualify the applicant.[15] The amount of the monthly payment to those qualifying as "needy" is also left by a number of states to be determined by the administrative agency, but a larger number have established a statutory maximum.[16] A few states have also established a minimum. The maximum in Illinois is to be adjusted by the use of a cost-of-living index.

A major issue, both in determining the eligibility of those who apply and in determining the amount of the grant to those who qualify as "needy," is the responsibility of relatives, especially children, for the support or contributions to the support of the aged person. In calculating income or resources, should the actual contributions that are being made by relatives be considered? Should potential contributions be considered as well? Potential contributions are those for which relatives would be liable if action were taken under those provisions of the poor law which define the legal responsibilities of relatives of the needy.

Practically all of the early old age assistance laws stated that no applicant could qualify who had relatives legally liable and able to support him. Even without this express statement if, under the poor law, relatives are responsible and this responsibility not waived in the old age assistance law, the state administrative agency must rule as to the extent to which potential contributions are to be considered in determining need for assistance and what if any pressures applied to convert them into actual cash payments. The federal law prohibits reimbursement if the state in determining need does not take into consideration "any other income or resources" of a claimant. The federal administrator's ruling is that actual contributions from relatives must be taken into account. The federal agency urges, but cannot require, that the states take into account only the actual, not potential, aid from relatives.

A number of states now have laws under which the applicant's or recipient's need is determined without reference to the economic position of his relatives. At least two by changes in the poor law have eliminated the legal liability of relatives. Others expressly require that only actual contributions from relatives shall be considered in determining need. In two others the law even forbids the investigation of the children's ability

15. Assignment or transfer of property without reasonable consideration or for the purpose of qualifying is, however, always forbidden. The state laws also indicate the character of the state's claims upon property remaining at death.

16. The administrative agency may itself set a maximum.

and willingness to contribute in order to insure that the contributions made are completely voluntary. The states vary probably more in administrative practice than they do in their statutes in the pressure brought to bear upon relatives and in what is counted as a resource in estimating need. Each state also varies from time to time in law or in practice or both. The situation reflects the prevailing uncertainty as to principle, with confusion also as to the exact effect of a change in law or practice.

The argument that, if relatives are able to contribute to the support of the aged person, the amount of this possible contribution should be taken into account in assessing need for assistance finds support in the generally accepted principle that kinship carries with it economic rights and responsibilities. The specific question is, however: In the community as a whole how is this principle interpreted? What is the prevailing concept as to the proper economic relation between parents and their grown children? What does each willingly give to and receive from the other? The accepted unit of economic responsibility is the nuclear family. Must not the law reflect this concept? If parents generally do not consider it the duty of their children to support them, and such support is generally considered an unfair burden, can the concept of legal responsibility be maintained? The approved social family includes only a husband and wife and their unmarried children. Only when it is the free choice of all concerned is the presence of other relatives approved. Such a standard implies that contributions to support of parents must usually take the expensive form of cash contributions to permit the parents to live independently. The standards we have developed as to who should live together may be sound or unsound, but they do not facilitate support of aged parents by their children.

There are those who assume that, if potential contributions from relatives were taken into account, the number of aged receiving public assistance would decline greatly. The decline in numbers would depend in the first instance upon the number of aged having legally responsible relatives. In general, the legal responsibility falls upon sons and earning daughters. Second, it would depend upon the standard used in determining the ability of the responsible relatives to contribute. A son's ability is not measured entirely by his income. The aged parent is only a "second-mortgage" claimant. His wife and children have first claim. Our standards for children and for family living in general are relatively high. It should also be noted that, if potential contributions are not transformed into actual contributions, the economic distress of the aged is not in fact relieved. This transformation will usually not come about through legal action. Aged persons will rarely bring action to compel their children to support them. Even if the state agency administering the old age assistance law is given the responsibility for bringing the court action, as is done in Massachusetts, the aged person is likely to prefer economic distress to legally enforced assistance. The need of the parent to whom public aid has been refused, or whose allowance is small, will, of course, induce their children to aid them, as was the case before old age assistance began.

The administration of the old age assistance law poses in all states in which children are legally liable the difficult problem of determining their ability to contribute to the support of the aged parent. In effect this means a comparison of the income of the son or daughter with the estimated cost of his or her own support and, if the son is married, the support of his wife and children. One state, Massachusetts, has been unwilling to leave the matter entirely to administrative discretion and has written into the law the dollar incomes below which no child shall be judged able to contribute, the amounts varying with the domicile status of the unmarried and the number of dependents of the married.

The income exemptions fixed in the 1944 law were as follows:[17]

Family and Marital Status	Living Apart from Parent	Living with Parent
Unmarried..............	$1,750	$1,500
Married:		
No children............	2,750	Same as when
One child..............	3,300	living apart
Two or more children...	3,300 plus $500 for each child after the first one	

The law further specifies that one-third of the excess above the incomes indicated should be the contribution to the parent's support if required.

In most states the amount of the cash payment is determined on a budget-deficiency basis. That is, a budget covering food, clothing, and other items to be purchased is developed, and, after pricing, its cost is compared with the money income from all sources. The state's payment makes up the difference or covers the whole amount if there is no other income. In a few states, as in California and Washington, the dollar cost of the basic requirements for the aged person is stated in the law. Therefore the state payment is the difference between this amount plus any addition for special needs and the income from other sources in cash or in kind.

17. See Alton A. Linford, *Old Age Assistance in Massachusetts* (Chicago: University of Chicago Press, 1949), chap. iv.

The question has been raised whether the highly individualized system of administration that has been described is the proper and efficient method of treating the large numbers of persons who are certified as eligible for old age assistance. Mrs. Burns argues that a more formalized system would reduce administrative supervision and expense as well as be more acceptable to the recipients. She suggests a system on the order of that found in New Zealand and other countries where the law itself defines exactly the eligibility requirements: what types and kinds of income are to be considered, the maximum that the applicant may possess to be certified as "needy," and the money payments which eligible applicants may receive. Responsibility for reporting changes in economic situation is placed upon the recipient, as are income-tax returns, with the kind of checking to which these returns are subjected to discover errors and false statements.[18]

ASSISTANCE TO THE BLIND AND DISABLED

The third class of needy persons receiving special assistance are the blind and the permanently and totally disabled. When the Social Security Act was passed, twenty-seven states had already provided for cash payments to the blind, nineteen of the laws being operative throughout the state. In one state only those sixty and over were eligible, and in one only those over forty, but the other states all set lower age limits—sixteen, eighteen, or twenty-one years and over. The Social Security Act provided from the beginning for federal participation in the cash payments made by the states to the needy blind. In 1950 all jurisdictions except Alaska were giving assistance to this group. The federal law, as amended in 1950, requires that in determining need the first $50 per month of earned income shall be disregarded if federal reimbursement of part of the cost is desired.

Special assistance to other disabled in the form of cash payment did not begin until 1945, when Wisconsin made such provision for the totally and permanently disabled. In 1950 federal participation in aid to needy members of this group, eighteen years of age or over, was authorized to the amount and on substantially the same terms as in the case of the blind. The federal government will pay a share of the outlays for remedial, medical, and hospital care except those made on behalf of tubercular patients or those suffering from mental disorders. The definition of permanent and total disability and the modes of determining "perma-

18. E. M. Burns, "Income Security for the Aged," *Social Service Review*, XXII (1948), 286–97.

nency" and "totality" have been left to each state. The federal administrator suggests that such disability be defined as a significant, permanent physical or mental impairment, disease, or loss that substantially precludes the individual from engaging in useful occupations within his or her competence, either holding a job or homemaking.

Some of the special problems arising in connection with each of the special-assistance programs have been noted. A basic issue is: Why single out categories of the needy for special treatment? Why not provide for all needy under a general-assistance program? The groups singled out for special treatment are those for whom public sentiment will support relatively generous aid, and the standards that control the assistance to each can be established by statute. The disadvantage of special assistance is that some groups may exert political pressure to obtain for themselves more and more favorable treatment. The vote of persons sixty-five and over, for example, may affect the program for old age assistance, while the program for aid to needy children can enlist no such support.

SOCIAL INSURANCE PROGRAMS

We turn now from public assistance programs to measures of different character but similar objectives: assurance of money income to children deprived of parental support, to those suffering from certain disabilities, and to those with limited or no earning power because of age. These measures are part of what is commonly called a "social insurance" program. The distinctive characteristic of this program is that need is not one of the criteria that determine eligibility to receive cash payments and does not determine the amount. Under the statutory formula the destitute and the well-to-do may receive the same benefit. In this respect the arrangement is like private insurance.

COMPULSORY INSURANCE AGAINST RISK OF INDUSTRIAL
ACCIDENT AND OCCUPATIONAL DISEASE

State laws designed to insure compensation for the worker or his dependents in case he is killed or injured on his job were the first part of a social insurance program in the United States. There are a number of reasons why those contingencies first received public attention. Not only did it become apparent that occupational accidents and diseases were incidents of the techniques employed in production, that a large proportion of those occurring were not due to lack of care by the injured, and that wages were, if anything, inverse to the risk assumed by workers, but also that without express statutory action the injured worker was in a weak position in pressing a claim for damages. Not only was it necessary that he, as any other injured person, take on the novel and expensive role of litigant but under the common law he was also required to prove that he did not assume the risk of the accident in question when he took on the job, that his lack of care did not contribute to the cause of the accident, and even that a fellow-employee was not guilty of negligence. These requirements in many cases debarred him from compensation.

By the eighties various states were enacting employers' liability laws removing these common-law defenses of the employer, thus enhancing the chance of successful suit and stimulating employers to instal safety devices and to insure against financial losses from this source. It became apparent, however, that most workers and their dependents with limited financial resources, unversed in matters of law, gained little from their improved position as litigants. Furthermore, "these laws could not reach an underlying weakness . . . the unsound assumption that a personal blame could be fixed for every industrial accident."[19] Beginning about 1910 the states began to substitute workmen's compensation laws for employers' liability, and by 1948 such laws were in effect in all states as well as in the District of Columbia, Hawaii, Alaska, and Puerto Rico. Most of the laws cover at least one occupational disease, and about a third cover all, thus recognizing that no proper distinction can be drawn between the hazards of occupational accident and disease. The essence of these laws is that they substitute hospital, surgical, and medical benefits and cash payments on a fixed scale for the chance of cash awards by a jury in a suit for damages. Administrative agencies take the responsibility for the establishment of claims.

It is impossible to describe in brief compass American policy with respect to those disabled by virtue of their employment, since there are great variations from state to state. In about half of the states employers in the occupations affected come under the law automatically, but in others, in most or all of the employments included, they may elect to do so. In most of the states with an elective system specific notice of nonelection of the act must be given, or the provisions apply. In all with elective laws employers who remain outside the statutory system have none of the common-law defenses previously enumerated in case of suit by an injured worker or his dependents. The extent to which workers in any state are covered depends upon the employments that come under the law. In some states only those occupations specifically listed as hazardous are covered. Farm and domestic workers are usually excluded, as are those

19. Frank Lang, *Workmen's Compensation Insurance* (Chicago: R. D. Irwin, 1947), p. 5.

employed in small establishments. The excluded employers in many states may elect insurance and thus limit their risk to the benefits established by law. In most states the employers must insure with an approved carrier or under specified conditions may self-insure. In a few states they must insure with a state fund, and in others they may do so. The rates paid vary with the estimated risk of the industry or work in question. Large firms may secure a special premium based on their experience rating. Thus there is financial inducement for industries and firms to reduce their disability and death rate. The insurance companies also actively promote "safety-first" campaigns and the adoption of safety devices. No tax is imposed to provide funds to pay benefits to injured workers or their dependents, and the workers typically make no contribution. Instead the financial risk involved is considered that of the employer, against which he must provide adequate insurance.

The adequacy of the protection given to workers who are covered by a state law depends in the first place upon the injuries and diseases which, if incurred, give them a claim. Greatest is the protection in those states which give general coverage for all occupational diseases and for all injuries arising out of or in the course of employment. The medical benefits are most adequate when unlimited in time and amount. In most states this is not the case. The cash benefits to the disabled workers are most adequate when the waiting period before they begin is short or, if the disability continues beyond a fixed period, the benefit is retroactive. In most laws the amount of the benefit of the totally disabled worker is a certain proportion of his wages, usually from three-fifths to two-thirds. In a few states the rate varies with marital status and number of dependents. Most states, however, set a dollar maximum for weekly cash benefits, and some set a minimum. "Under the maximums in effect October 1, 1949 a single worker in receipt of the average 1948 wage would have been paid, under more than half of the laws, a benefit amounting to less than 50 percent of his wage."[20] The average dollar wage has risen more rapidly than the dollar maximums under the law. In most states also there is a limit upon the number of weeks during which compensation may be paid or the total dollar amount that may be paid or both.[21] Every state except one in 1946 provided for lump-sum payments in case of death to cover burial expenses and for either lump-sum payments or weekly

20. *Social Security Bulletin*, July, 1950, p. 10.

21. Benefits for permanent partial disability present the most difficult administrative problem, since the effect of a given degree of disability upon earnings will be the product of many variables. Death benefits present the least problem in determining eligibility to receive. Permanent and temporary total disability are determined by medical certification.

cash benefits to dependents. The period of time during which the latter will be paid and method of determining the amount are prescribed in the several laws.

FEDERAL OLD AGE INSURANCE

The passage of the Federal Social Security Act in 1935 altered the picture greatly with respect to social provision against the hazards that make for income insecurity. The grants-in-aid established by that act with a view to expanding and to some extent standardizing certain public assistance programs of the states have already been mentioned. Federal grants-in-aid to the states were already well established policy. The new and distinctive parts of the act were those designed to insure an income for the aged, the widowed, the orphaned, and the unemployed, not as relief or upon establishment of need, but without respect to their resources. To accomplish these objectives, the Congress used two of its expressly stated constitutional powers—the power to tax and the power to appropriate money for the general welfare.

The Federal Act of 1935 established a federal old age insurance system. By amendment in 1939 "survivors' " insurance was added. In 1950, in addition to increasing the benefits, setting up a new formula for their computation, and making certain other changes, the coverage of the act was greatly extended. In 1952 Congress again increased benefits. In an average week in 1951 about forty-five million persons were paying the required tax and thus establishing eligibility to receive benefits for themselves or their dependents. More than a fourth of the labor force are still not included in the program. More than a third of those, however, are covered by the federal, state, or local retirement plans for their civilian employees or by the Railroad Retirement system. Others excluded are all farm operators; physicians, lawyers, and other professional workers in private practice; unpaid family workers; irregularly employed domestic workers or those who work each day for a different employer; and the nonfarm self-employed whose net earnings are less than $400 for the year. Coverage of employees of nonprofit organizations is optional. Such an organization must certify that it desires the coverage with the concurrence of two-thirds of its employees.

Under the law the wages of all employed persons and the net earnings of all self-employed not specifically excluded are subject to a specified tax. The tax due from employees is deducted from their wages and is paid by the employer to the Bureau of Internal Revenue along with an excise tax of the same amount levied upon his payroll. The tax upon the self-employed is three-fourths of the combined rate on employers and employees and is paid when they pay their income tax.[22] Neither the self-employed nor those employed by others pay on net earnings or wages over $3,600 in any one year.

Old age benefits are paid only to those sixty-five years of age and over. Those sixty-five and under seventy-five who are earning more than $75 per month in a covered employment are ineligible for benefits, but those seventy-five and over may earn any amount and still receive benefits. Any recipient may have income of any amount from annuities, investments, and the like. Aside from these prerequisites, eligibility to receive old age benefits is determined by the number of calendar quarters that the individual has paid a tax upon at least $50 in wages or $100 in self-employment income. The general rule as established in 1950 is that to become "fully insured," that is, entitled to old age benefits, the tax must have been paid for at least one-half the number of quarters elapsing after 1950, or after the quarter in which the person became twenty-one, whichever is later, and the quarter he retires, but never less than six or more than forty. Quarters of coverage before 1951 may be counted toward the requirement. As a result of the application of this rule the minimum requirement for those forty-five years of age or younger on January 1, 1951, is forty quarters of tax payment on at least $50 of wages or $100 in earnings from a self-employment. The minimum requirement for persons over forty-five at that date is less, declining with age to six quarters for those sixty-two and over on January 1, 1951. This rule was adopted in order to enable the older persons at that date to receive benefits at sixty-five if they desired. If the minimum requirement for those who were sixty had been forty quarters, they could not have become eligible until they were at least seventy. An objective of the law was to reduce the proportion receiving old age assistance by increasing the proportion eligible for benefits. The law as it stood before 1950, although the older person was there also favored, had not been successful in doing so. In December, 1950, the number of recipients of old age assistance was still greater than the number of persons sixty-five and over receiving benefits. It should be noted that the discrepancy in quarters of tax payment required for eligibility decreases as time elapses. Unless the law is changed and a new start established, the minimum requirement will ultimately be the same for all.

Prior to the 1950 revision of the act the monthly cash benefit to which

22. Currently the tax rate on the net earnings of the self-employed is $2\frac{1}{4}$ per cent, that on employees and on employers $1\frac{1}{2}$ per cent each.

the "fully insured" person of sixty-five was entitled was related to the period of time he had been paying taxes, as well as to the average monthly income upon which he had paid. Now for persons whose quarters of coverage are all secured after 1950 the period of coverage does not alter the benefit. Their primary benefit is 55 per cent of the first $100 of their average monthly taxed income and 15 per cent of the next $200. Thus if the average monthly income taxed is the maximum, $300, the primary benefit is $85. The minimum benefit payable is $25.

The starting point for computing the average monthly income may be either December 31, 1950, or, if later, the day preceding the quarter in which the person reached twenty-two, whichever date gives the higher average monthly wage when calculated from the starting point to the date of retirement. Persons with some quarters of coverage prior to 1951 and who *have secured at least six quarters after 1950* may choose a benefit computed according to the foregoing formula, or they may choose December 31, 1936, as their starting point (or, if later, the day preceding the first quarter they reached twenty-two) and receive the benefit computed by the pre-1950 formula, which is then raised by a conversion table to the higher level established in 1950 for all current beneficiaries.[23] If benefits are computed under the old formula, 1 per cent is added for each year income of $200 or more was taxed. Those who do not acquire six quarters of coverage after December 31, 1950, have no option but receive the benefit to which they would be entitled by the earlier formula converted to the new, higher dollar amount.

If a man entitled to an old age benefit is married, his wife at sixty-five, or at any age if she has in her care an unmarried child under eighteen, is entitled to a benefit equal to one-half that of her husband unless by virtue of her own employment she is entitled to a benefit of the same or larger amount. Each child is also entitled to a benefit that is one-half that of the father. In no case, however, may the total family benefit exceed approximately $169 or 85 per cent of the average monthly wage, whichever is lesser. The husband of a woman entitled to old age benefits is also entitled to a benefit equal to one-half that of his wife under certain additional conditions. She must have been not only fully insured, that is, meet the eligibility requirements for old age benefits, but currently insured as well. An individual is "currently insured" if he had at least six quarters of coverage during the thirteen quarters *immediately preceding* the one in

23. The 1950 law increased the benefits of those currently receiving them by about 77.5 per cent on the average. In 1952 they were again increased by $5.00 per month or 12½ per cent, whichever is greater.

which he became entitled to old age benefits or in which he died. Further, the husband must have been receiving at least one-half of his support from the wife when she became entitled to old age benefits if he is to receive a husband's benefit. Women of sixty-five are not likely to have children under eighteen except those who have been adopted. If there are such children and they were receiving their support from her and she is currently insured, they are entitled to a child's benefit.[24]

SURVIVORS' BENEFITS

The widow of a fully insured man (or the widower of a fully and currently insured woman if he was receiving at least one-half of his support from her at the time of her death) is entitled at sixty-five to a benefit that is three-fourths of the deceased husband's primary benefit unless by virtue of her own employment she is entitled to an old age benefit of the same or larger amount.[25] An important provision of the law is that which authorizes benefits to the child or children of those men who die either fully or currently insured and to the mothers of those children, whether widowed or divorced, so long as they do not remarry and have such a child or children in their care. Only unmarried children under eighteen are thus provided for, and the divorced wife only if she was receiving at least one-half of her support from her former husband at the time of his death. Thus orphaned children and the mother who is caring for them receive the benefit of this monthly payment in addition to whatever provision was made through private insurance or other means. The benefit of an only child is three-fourths of the old age benefit to which the father would have been entitled. If there is more than one child, each receives one-half of such benefit plus one-fourth divided by the number of children. The mother's benefit is three-fourths of the primary benefit to which the husband was entitled. The limitations upon the total amount of a family's benefits have already been noted. The child or children of a fully or currently insured woman either married or unmarried at the time of her death are also entitled to benefits if they were dependent upon her at that time.[26] No benefit is paid to any individual under seventy-five, the month

24. The terms "wife," "husband," "child," "widow," and designations of all others entitled to benefits by virtue of relationship to an insured person are defined in the act.

25. Lump-sum benefits equal to three times the primary benefit are payable to the widow or widower of a deceased individual.

26. A surviving parent of an unmarried, fully insured individual without dependent children is also entitled to a benefit equal to three-fourths of the primary benefit of the deceased son or daughter if he was receiving at least one-half of his support from this person at the time of the latter's death.

that he or she earns from covered employment or self-employment more than $75.

In December, 1950, 3,477,243 individuals were receiving old age or survivors' benefits. Their status and average monthly payment were as follows:[27]

Status	Number	Average Monthly Payment
Old age beneficiaries	1,770,984	$44
Wives, 65 and over	507,553	24
Husbands, 65 and over	797	20
Widows, 65 and over	314,126	37
Widowers, 65 and over	63	37
Children:		
Of retired workers	46,241	17
Of deceased workers	653,462	28
Mothers of children under 18	169,438	34
Parents, 65 and over	14,579	37

Analysis of the Old Age and Survivors' program shows that in many ways it is unlike insurance as described in the preceding chapter. It is like insurance in that it assures a money income in the event of the occurrence of certain contingencies. The assurance is, however, in the form of a statutory right to receive benefits if the prescribed conditions for eligibility are met. These rights could be abrogated or the eligibility conditions changed by the Congress. They have been changed, as has the scale of benefits and the method of computing them, whereas the dollar benefits promised in a contract with an insurance company are fixed and remain the same whether the price level moves up or down. The tax system associated with the program may be changed; the rates increased or decreased; the tax on employers and employees, or either, altered or removed. Only in a very limited sense can the Social Security tax deductions from wages be described as savings, or the special income tax paid by the self-employed. The sums paid become part of the general revenues of the government and are used to meet current needs. There could be no investment in income-earning assets as in the case of a private insurance carrier.[28] The so-called "insurance" is mandatory. The risks covered, how the benefits are paid, and to whom they go are determined by law.

The benefits provided under the OASI program, it should also be noted,

27. *Social Security Bulletin*, September, 1951.

28. The tax receipts not required for current withdrawals are "invested" in United States securities which may be purchased on the market or newly issued exclusively for the purpose. Accruing interest is credited to the Fund. This means that the excess receipts over withdrawals, large in the early years, may be spent and that, as withdrawals later become greater than receipts, funds for payment will be obtained by placing the bonds on the market. An alternative would be to reduce taxes in the early years and increase them in the later, the so-called "pay-as-you-go" system.

are not closely related to the tax contribution made. Once the necessary quarters of coverage are secured, years of coverage and tax payment do not alter the benefit. The old age benefit after ten and after thirty years of coverage varies only with average monthly wage. As has been pointed out, the rule determining the number of quarters of coverage required to entitle one to a benefit at sixty-five favors those over forty-five when the act went into effect. A person aged sixty-three and a half in January, 1951, would be eligible for a benefit of $85 per month at sixty-five if his average monthly income for six quarters had been $300. If he was married to a wife also sixty-five, their joint monthly benefit as long as both live would be $127.50, but the total tax paid only $81. Others for the same benefit might pay tax for forty years or more. Survivors' benefits, moreover, are paid not because special contributions have been made but because of the existence of persons of a specified relationship to the "fully or currently insured" person.

The OASI program obviously in many respects is a program designed to meet need. Not only are those above forty-five when the act went into effect favored but those with relatively low incomes. Otherwise the benefits of the older persons and of those with low incomes would have been extremely small, insufficient by any standard to meet need. The setting of a minimum and a maximum payment as well as the formula for computing benefits reflect considerations that have to do with need. The provision of a benefit for the wife, the dependent husband, the widowed mother, the orphaned children, the aged widow, the dependent parents, is a program designed to make incomes vary with family need.

A program shaped in large degree by considerations that have to do with need invites comparison with the public assistance programs. The old age and survivors' benefits are designed to constitute a basic minimum which other resources supplement. If the other resources are lacking or limited, beneficiaries with monthly payments near the minimum will need assistance also. In some states the average monthly payment to the aged needy is more than the old age benefit for those whose average monthly wage was $100 or less.

Proposals for change in the OASI program range from those that are but changes in details to those that are broad and sweeping. There are those who would merge the assistance and so-called "insurance" programs and provide from the public treasury only for those who are in need.[29] At the other end of the pole are those who would merge the old age assistance

29. See especially Lewis Meriam, *Relief and Social Security* (Washington: Brookings Institution, 1946).

and old age benefit programs but, ignoring need, would guarantee a flat amount to all above a certain age.

Among the pertinent issues is the effect upon individual saving of alternative policies. The rate of saving prior to the passage of the Social Security Act was clearly insufficient to insure economic independence for the majority of the aged or those widowed and orphaned. With higher income levels would the rate be more adequate, and with wise handling of savings and proper use of insurance would adequate individual provision be approximately attained? One enemy of the attainment of this ideal is the felt needs of the present and their constant acceleration. Modern communities are subjected to conflicting pressures. On the one hand, we preach thrift and hold up the thrifty family as a model of economic virtue. We emphasize the importance of penalties for not taking thought of the morrow. Upon the other, to an even greater extent, we promote spending. Invitations to buy on "easy terms" surround us. The movies, radio, and television, the press, the schools, stimulate new interests and new desires. The spirit of the times induces the belief that what one needs or enjoys others also need or should enjoy. Are the public assistance programs and the old age and survivors' program also deterrents to thrift? If widows, orphans, and aged are assured a minimum income, will efforts be made to supplement it from other sources? With American standards of living as high and as dynamic as they are, there would still be strong incentive to do so.

If the benefit system is retained, shall the tax system at present associated with it be retained? There is strong argument for the retention of the special tax paid by wage-earners and the self-employed. Tax payment may thus be a condition of eligibility to receive benefits which increases willingness to pay and gives the beneficiaries the knowledge that they helped to pay for what they receive. It may also reduce unconsidered insistence that the benefits be increased. The excise tax upon employers, in effect an increase in labor costs, is a different matter. Ability to pay is not measured by the size of the payroll, and the incidence of the tax will vary with the particular enterprise. Who is affected by the tax, to what degree and in what manner, will be generally unknown. An alternative would be to provide part of the support of the program from the general revenues, largely the proceeds of the general income tax.

It has already been noted that under the present system benefits are not in proportion to tax contributions. It should also be noted that some who are taxed do not receive benefits by virtue of that payment. When coverage is not universal, movement to a noncovered occupation before the necessary quarters of coverage are attained will mean payment without entitlement to benefits, as will any circumstance that prevents acquisition of fully or currently insured status. Practically all women will pay tax for a period, or during several periods. Many, however, will not secure the forty quarters of coverage that makes them fully insured, and many others will not be currently insured when they die. Possibly a larger number even if fully insured will not have in their own right a primary benefit larger than one-half of their husbands. That is, the wife's benefit and the widow's benefit will be determined by the husband's monthly average wage and be the same for those who worked for a short period and paid little tax as for those who worked for a much longer period and made a much larger total contribution. Discontinuity in working, so characteristic of women's employment, reduces the average monthly wage upon which benefits are calculated. In general, women as workers are disadvantaged under the law, while as mothers, wives, and widows they are favored.

UNEMPLOYMENT COMPENSATION

As has been pointed out, unemployment is a risk against which private insurance is impossible. The wage-earner can make financial provision against it only by saving or by seeking the most secure employments and striving for a favored position on the list of those to be laid off or fired. This latter position may be secured in a variety of ways, from superior efficiency to seniority rights and other rules governing the order in which job severance is made.

Legal rights to unemployment compensation were established in the main in the years immediately following the passage of the Social Security Act. It was accomplished by the imposition in that act of a federal tax upon the payrolls of all but a specified list of employers of eight or more persons. The most important exclusions were public agencies, nonprofit institutions, railroads, and those employing domestic and agricultural labor. In states with an approved unemployment compensation law, however, 90 per cent of the payments under that law might be used as an offset to the federal tax. Thus the states had the strongest of incentives to pass such a law. Without a state unemployment-compensation law the tax payments would be part of the general revenues of the federal government. With such a law nine-tenths of the amount would go into an Unemployment Trust Fund administered by the Secretary of the Treasury for the payment of compensation claims of covered employees within the state, and from the other tenth the costs of administering the state law would be paid. Under these circumstances the states rapidly passed laws that would permit the tax offset. Although the state laws must comply with certain federally imposed conditions, wide latitude remains for state action. Thus there is no uniform system of unemployment compensation throughout the country. Employments not subject to the federal tax may be covered by the state law. Some impose the unemployment compensation tax on employers of only one person. The exclusions are still such that in an average week in 1947 only about 54 per cent of all employed workers were in covered employments.[30]

The typical state law imposes a payroll tax upon the employers up to $300 of each worker's monthly earnings. The theory is that thus unemployment compensation becomes part of the labor costs of production, but the actual economic effects upon firms and industries, their workers, consumers of their products, and other workers and consumers are complex and variable. It is argued that, if workers contributed directly through a payroll deduction, they would be less likely to press unduly for an increase in benefits and would be more interested in the administration of the system, since benefits cannot be paid after the reserve fund is exhausted. Correspondingly, employers would be less inclined to press for reduction of benefits and unduly rigorous standards for eligibility to receive benefits. In some countries part of the costs are paid from the general revenues as a more equitable way of distributing the costs.

As the state laws have developed, the principle of so-called "experience rating" has been introduced. That is, the tax is not uniform but varies with the employment record. Those employers with the lowest record of compensable claims pay the lowest tax. Those paying less than the standard rate receive offsets against the federal tax as if they were paying the standard rate. The desirability of such an arrangement has been disputed and is one of the issues currently under intensive consideration. The major purpose of a tax adjusted to experience rating is to give employers an incentive to stabilize production and provide steady employment. The theory is that the firms and industries responsible for unemployment would bear the greater part of the cost.

The principle of experience rating is based to a large extent upon the assumption of a parallelism between unemployment rates and rates of industrial accidents. The state laws providing compensation for workers disabled in the course of their employment were so drawn that the employers' costs of insurance were related to their safety records, and an increase in the use of safety devices and methods resulted. But the power of employers, especially those in the seasonal industries, to provide steady

30. Burns, *The American Social Security System*, p. 130.

employment is decidedly limited, and, even with the utmost effort and intelligence put forth in that direction, unemployment rates are altered relatively little. Over against the stabilizing effect of experience rating, moreover, must be placed certain disadvantages of the system. One of the satisfactory features of unemployment compensation, especially with uniform tax rates, is its anticyclical effect. In good times unemployment reserves increase in proportion to the increase in payrolls, and benefit payments are relatively small. With decline in business activity benefit payments increase and counteract somewhat the decline in aggregate personal income and hence in demand. This anticyclical effect is reduced by experience rating, and the latter even has a perverse effect. In good times all employers tend to have good employment records—rates go down, and the movement from income stream to reserves is not so great as it would otherwise be.[31] With decline in business activity, tax rates increase, withdrawing from the income stream more than payrolls decline, thus counteracting the effect of increase in benefit payments. The higher tax rates also increase labor costs at a time when sales and profits are already declining and thus actually operate to reduce the level of employment. There are other repercussions of experience rating upon the unemployment-compensation system itself that will be noted later.

The eligibility of workers to receive unemployment compensation cannot be based, as is eligibility to receive old age benefits, upon work at any time in a covered employment. In general, eligible workers must have worked for a specified period or earned a certain minimum sum in the base period which precedes their benefit "year," that is, the period in which, if otherwise entitled, they may draw benefits. The general objective of the requirement is to allow benefits only to those who are normally attached to the labor market. One noticeable effect is to disqualify irregular workers. New entrants to the labor market also find it difficult to acquire eligibility. They are the first to be laid off, especially if employers do not wish to have compensable claims marring their employment record. The major unemployment problem today is that of these two groups of workers.

Even if the conditions mentioned are satisfied, not all who apply will receive compensation. They may be disqualified for other reasons. The question will be: Is the worker "unemployed" within the meaning of the law? That is, in general terms, is he able and willing to work, but for

31. Burns points out that the experience rating of an employer might be determined against a norm for a period and in the industry as a whole (*ibid.*, p. 163).

reasons beyond his control without full-time employment?[32] The answer depends in the first place upon the reasons for his severance from the job in which he has been employed. If he gave it up voluntarily without good cause, he is not unemployed or compensable. There are great variations from state to state in the law and administrative rulings as to what does not constitute a good reason for quitting a job as there are concerning other disqualifying conditions. The search for sound principles continues, and in the course of time a generally approved code will be worked out. A person may quit his job for personal reasons or for reasons connected with the work. Should only the latter be recognized, and, if so, what is a good reason? If a married woman leaves for family reasons, should she be disqualified? Then there are the workers who are discharged. If discharged for misconduct, are they compensable, and, if not, how shall misconduct be defined? Under the experience-rating plan, employers have a clear interest in these definitions and the strictness of the investigation of each case. Too rigorous a definition of what is a compensable case may defeat the purpose of the law, but too broad a definition may do so also.[33]

The second question concerning the otherwise qualified worker is: Can he find a new job? To test this, there must be a state employment agency where job-seekers and employers needing workers may register. Such an agency is desirable for the proper functioning of the labor market even if there is no system of unemployment compensation; but, if there is such a system, it is indispensable. The unemployed person to receive benefits must be registered for work; he must apply for jobs to which he is referred; he must be actively seeking work and appear at specified intervals to report on the progress of such job-seeking.[34]

Possibly the most difficult question in determining the right to draw benefits concerns the type of work the worker may refuse or not apply for and still draw benefits. The law may say it must be "suitable," the rate of pay that prevailing for its type, and not with a firm where a strike is in progress. The worker may prefer to wait and draw compensation until he can be employed in his usual line at his usual rate of pay. How long shall he be permitted to do so? For the full benefit period or for a shorter time?

32. Benefits are usually provided according to a prescribed formula for both partial and full-time unemployment.

33. Many difficult questions arise. For example, what of the worker who absents himself from his job and returns to find another hired in his place. Did he voluntarily leave or was he discharged?

34. A special question is whether a person otherwise eligible who left his job without good cause might later after a specified time qualify for benefits if he registers for employment actively seeks work, and fails to find it.

Again, where may he be sent or expected to apply for work? How far from where he now lives? In another locality which would necessitate moving?

The maximum period for which benefits may be drawn is established by law. In 1948 in no state did the period exceed twenty-six weeks. The system is one of compensation for relatively short periods of unemployment. Setting a limit reduces the risk of subsidizing unnecessary unemployment if tests of compensability are not rigorous or administrative checks upon ability to find work are not thorough. A waiting period, usually one week, between filing claim and drawing benefits is usually imposed. The agency thus has opportunity to determine eligibility. Some will find work, and no great hardship is experienced.

The amount of the weekly benefit is related to past earnings, with usually also a dollar maximum and, less commonly, a minimum. The principle is to fix the benefit not so high as to reduce incentive to look for work or take what is offered, or so low as to necessitate assistance. In early 1949 the typical benefit was about 36 per cent of average weekly wages. There are wide variations from state to state. In a few jurisdictions dependents' benefits are added to the base benefit. Thus need as a function of family size may alter the relation between past earnings and benefit.

Should we substitute a federal system of unemployment compensation for the present state or federal-state plan? There would then be uniformity throughout the country, and interstate agreements by which workers qualified in one state may file claims and draw benefits in another would be unnecessary. Reserve funds would be merged, and the problem that now arises, since the geographical incidence of unemployment is uneven, that the reserve of one state is exhausted while others are high would disappear. The ownership of the industries in one state may be geographically widespread as are the customers. There would, however, be no opportunity for experimentation with varying devices for solving the problems hitherto suggested and for state decision and control of a matter of great concern to its citizens.

SICKNESS AND DISABILITY BENEFITS

Although the establishment of a legal right to cash income for a specified period in case of occupational accident was the first part of a social security system to develop in the United States, a similar right in the case of other disability was the last and is still very limited. Only three states in the early part of 1949, beginning with Rhode Island in 1942, had provided for such cash payments.[35]

35. The others were California in 1946 and New Jersey in 1948. Five states provided for continued payment of unemployment insurance during a period of sickness.

In most respects the state systems for disability benefits parallel or are developments of their unemployment compensation rather than their workmen's compensation laws. The same workers tend to be covered; the same agency administers; the scale of benefits and period of payment are the same. All this may be quite different as other states develop a program. In one feature the California law resembles the typical workmen's compensation system. Employers are permitted to self-insure or to insure through an approved company. Unlike both unemployment and workmen's compensation in most jurisdictions, the laws impose a tax upon the covered workers to be paid by payroll deductions into the fund from which benefits are paid. Unlike workmen's compensation, no medical benefits are provided for, only cash benefits to compensate in part for loss of earnings. As has been pointed out earlier, the problem of the cost of medical, surgical, dental, and hospital care is a larger and different problem, and the separation is sound in principle. The combination of cash and medical benefits under workmen's compensation has a special justification, since the disabilities arise from very special causes, and represents an attempt to place the costs on the responsible industries.

Certain special problems arise in devising a sound system of cash benefits for disabled workers. Since the objective is to make up for income they would have received if illness had not interrupted their employment, eligibility must be determined by their previous position in the labor market, that is, their earnings in some closely preceding period. Disability must be defined in the same terms, as inability for physical or mental causes to perform the regular or customary work. The existence of such disability and of its duration must be certified. A special question of importance arises in this connection. Shall the physician chosen for treatment be the one to make this certification? There are strong arguments that he should not but that others chosen by the administrative agency have this responsibility. A question may also arise concerning those who refuse treatment, not so serious in connection with the short-period disability here being considered, as when benefits during extended or "permanent" disability are provided. A special question concerning employed women is whether the interruption in earnings occasioned by pregnancy shall be among those for which cash benefits may be drawn. A good case can be made for relating the benefit for any certified disability to earnings, partly because contributions are so related and partly because the objective is to prevent the individual or family from falling too far below the usual level of living. A waiting period before benefits begin conserves the funds for the benefit of those whose disability would cause the more serious hardship. The worker with many relatively short illnesses, even from the same cause, would not, however, then receive the same benefit as one with the same period of illness who was continuously disabled. There must be a limit upon the maximum benefit period both to encourage recovery and to differentiate the problem from that of "permanent" disability.

A broader policy question is whether the provision of cash benefits to the disabled worker shall be left to the states or whether there should be a federally administered program. The arguments for state systems of unemployment compensation apply in this case. Both federal and state programs would require highly decentralized administration. With state programs only, great gaps will appear in the system viewed from the standpoint of the nation as a whole and wide variations in important features from one jurisdiction to another.

CHAPTER XIII

CONSUMER PRODUCTION

THE transition to a money economy has concentrated the attention of more and more families upon the amount of their money income as the basis of their economic well-being. The intricate problems having to do with production for the market and the sharing of the product have absorbed the attention of economists and others interested in economic arrangements. Historical accounts have emphasized the home industries transferred to the factory and those that are upon their way or likely to go.

Production, not for pay or profit, but for the use of the producer or his family, still, however, increases by an appreciable proportion the total income of most families and of the nation as a whole. As has been pointed out, a money value cannot be placed upon most of the commodities and services so produced; nor is it possible to give a measurement by count or weight that would show the relative importance of this type of production. The number of persons whose productive effort is of this character is known, however. If it is taken as an index of the volume of the product, consumer production cannot be dismissed as of negligible economic significance. A census survey of the employment status of the civilian noninstitutional population in April, 1950, showed thirty-three million persons devoting their time to housework in their own homes. Twenty-eight million were eighteen to sixty-five years of age, 32 per cent of all of that age who were able to work.[1] Their activities are not the whole of consumer production, since others in school or gainfully employed may perform services or make goods for their own or their families' benefit and use. The fact of major significance, however, is that the whole economic contribution of so large a proportion of the adult population is of this character.

How effective is this use of labor power? How do the "wages, hours, and working conditions" of this group of workers compare with those of other groups? Are the changes that have occurred in the activities of the home properly understood or the forces making for and resisting change? To what extent if at all is consumer production tied up with the continuation

1. U.S. Bureau of the Census, *Current Population Reports*, Series P-57, No. 94 (Washington, May, 1950). (Processed.)

of the family and with other aspects of our way of living? Difficult questions having to do with the present and the future economic position of women are also involved in this analysis.

DIFFERENTIATION OF CONSUMER PRODUCTION FROM OTHER ACTIVITIES

There is danger both of viewing consumer production in a too limited and too all-inclusive way. Those who conceive of production in too limited a way are likely to ignore many activities that are truly productive, although not performed for pay or profit, and thereby minimize the volume of consumer production. Such statements as the following abound: "The home has ceased to be the glowing center of production from which radiate all desirable goods, and has become but a pool toward which products made in other places flow—a place of consumption not of production."[2] The home is not the center of production, but many productive activities still go on there if "productive" is judged by the same criteria that are applied to gainful activities. If production, on the other hand, is too broadly defined, insufficient distinction will be made between those activities of the consumer that are productive in the economic sense and those that are not properly so designated. Neither of these difficulties is so likely to arise when pay or profit results from the outlay of time and effort. We are more ready to classify the gainful worker as productive without examining the character of his product. We find it easier also to determine when his "work" or his "production" ends and his "leisure" or "consumption" begins.

Production, whether paid for or unpaid, is the creation of utilities either in the form of services or embodied in some material economic good. The position of the early economists that those performing personal services—the musician, lawyer, actor, teacher, and physician—produced nothing because their efforts effected no change in volume or value of the stock of material wealth has long been abandoned. Some who emphasize the absence of productive activity in the modern household are obviously using the older definition of production or even limiting it to such processes as those typified by agriculture and manufacturing. So limited a concept would rule out of the ranks of productive workers a large part of those gainfully, as well as of those nongainfully, employed.

It should be pointed out also that in the case of unpaid as well as paid workers the criterion of their productivity is not the "usefulness" of their

2. Ellen H. Richards, *The Cost of Living* (3d ed.; New York: John Wiley & Sons, 1905), p. 25.

labor judged by the degree to which it meets needs. Both paid and unpaid labor may be utilized in undesirable ways from the welfare standpoint. The products may be trivial, ugly, or positively harmful. The fact that in one case they have a monetary value and in the other that they do not does not alter the situation. The test is the want-satisfying power of the product, whether sold on the market or used by the producer or his family.

When the test of salability is removed, however, a difficult problem remains. How differentiate between those activities properly classified as production, providing the means to satisfy wants, and those which should be classified as consumption, using the means provided?[3] In many cases the border line will be vague and ill defined. The home is a center for family life. There the members of the family receive the companionship, sympathy, affection, and counsel which are the desired by-products of their association. But how can they distinguish between those activities which make home life in the material sense possible and comfortable and those which result in the other group of values? The fact is that in the family the economic are so intertwined with other relationships, the problems and responsibilities of the members as unpaid productive agents so intertwined with their problems and responsibilities as individuals, as husband or wife, as parent or child, that it is difficult to separate them. Yet without this differentiation great confusion results in discussions of household production and of the life of homekeeping women. Some distinction is necessary that will, roughly at least, separate labor from leisure, production from consumption, economic from other problems, and contribution to the family through productive activity from the contribution arising from a peculiar status or emotional relation.

A definition of production so phrased as to make the differentiation desired is that of Black, who says: "Production activity is always intended either to satisfy somebody else's wants or to build up potential want-satisfying power in something or somebody."[4] Any leisure-time activity which one carries on for one's own amusement or enjoyment is quite properly excluded, whether it be playing bridge, tennis, or the piano. As Cassel says:

> The act of satisfying need is not itself to be regarded as an economic activity. The satisfaction of a need as such generally means a certain more or less active preoccupation on the part of the person who satisfies his needs. The man who wishes to satisfy

3. Production is a process of using scarce means to achieve certain ends. But, if all use of such means were called "production," the distinction between production and consumption would disappear or be made arbitrary. Eating food would be production as well as growing, processing, and preparing it.

4. John D. Black, *Production Economics* (New York: Henry Holt & Co., 1926), p. 25.

his hunger must eat; the man who seeks the recreation of a walk must use his legs; the man who desires to provide his own music must play or sing. Activities of this kind do not come within the economic sphere.[5]

Taking tennis lessons or bridge lessons, however, or reading in order to secure tool knowledge would be productive activity according to Black's definition. One is building up potential want-satisfying power in somebody, that is, in one's self.

It is evident that Black's definition will cover a wide range of activities. It includes all production of material goods for one's self as well as for others, all personal services performed for others, and those performed for one's self when the results to be secured are postponed. No one, not even the most heavily burdened gainful worker, can fail to carry on a great deal of production so defined aside from that directly associated with his job. Most of us dress ourselves and do some fetching and carrying for ourselves and ordering of our possessions. We labor to acquire new skills and new knowledge as well as to teach others and to render services for them in many ways. Some productive activities are the source of great enjoyment; others are uninteresting and monotonous, and their burden is great. Some forms of purely individual production have no great economic significance; other forms of production for one's self and for others raise important economic questions.

Margaret Reid has suggested that for practical purposes it is advisable to limit household or consumer production to those activities carried on by and for the members of the family that may be delegated to someone outside or replaced by goods bought on the market if income, market conditions, and personal inclination permit.[6] This limitation is suggested in order to rule out the creation of those utilities due to the association of husband and wife or parent and child. It is obvious that these utilities, although not costless in time and energy, are not economic in character or origin. The associations that result from family life are valued products, but the mother's joy in the child does not make the child a producer or give rise to an economic problem, nor do the companionship, counsel, sympathy, and pleasure that any member of the family may receive from another make of that other a productive worker.

A clear and definite concept of what is involved in "household" or consumer production is necessary, not only for an intelligent discussion of its character and problems, but also as a basis for the discussion of the economic position of homekeeping women. Today practically all the full-

---

5. Gustav Cassel, *Theory of Social Economy* (New York: Harcourt Brace & Co., 1924), p. 5.
6. *Economics of Household Production* (New York: John Wiley & Sons, 1934), p. 11.

time workers in such production are women. From the circumstances in which they live and work these women and others as well find it difficult to disentangle their activities and responsibilities as productive agents from those as wives, mothers, or even as citizens. Judgments in regard to their economic contribution to their families and to society become accordingly hopelessly confused. How, for example, would such activities as those Veblen calls "conspicuous consumption" or "conspicuous leisure" be classified? He contends that these are the main responsibilities of the upper-class wife. They satisfy a want; they require time, energy, and a special equipment and technique. The same question arises about other activities of the wife as hostess or lady of the house.

If we accept Reid's qualification upon household production, that it shall include only the activities that can be delegated to those outside the family circle, such activities as the above would in the main be excluded. That is, if the above activities could be performed only by the wife and mother, if they are the products of that status and that status alone, they are not to be classified as production in the economic sense. This, it is believed, is the only way of looking at it if we do not wish to live in a topsy-turvy world, where consumption in some mysterious way becomes production and leisure becomes labor.

CHANGES IN THE CHARACTER OF CONSUMER PRODUCTION

The historic changes in the character of the tasks performed by members of the family for themselves or for other members of the family have often been noted. Basically, this shift from consumer to commercial production is the result of the great productive efficiency of specialization, mass production, and the use of power machinery. Consumer production is unspecialized production; it is small scale and decentralized. Only recently have certain types of power machinery been made in units suitable for household use. Accordingly, as the growth of the market has made specialized, large-scale production and the use of power-driven machinery possible, the making of one article after another has left the home.

The forces that were ultimately to break up almost completely the mold in which household activities had been cast for centuries were first set in operation in the free towns of western Europe. Here the economic principle of specialized production for sale by skilled craftsmen came into operation. The economic order came to be one of production by specialists and market exchange. Since that time the situation has never reversed itself but has gone steadily forward, first slowly, then by leaps and bounds as the commercial revolution of the sixteenth and seventeenth centuries was followed by the industrial of the eighteenth and nineteenth.

At first one may imagine that the character of the household activities of the majority of medieval town families was little affected by the development of skilled crafts. The fine products of the craftsmen and the wares brought in by foreign merchants were out of reach of the great mass of families. Only the more well-to-do burghers and the nobility could command them. The bulk of the population wore homemade clothes and used homemade furniture and utensils. Gradually, however, as more and more heads of families made goods for sale, or, as more and more families worked for wages, as shops became more numerous, as the market place grew larger and the goods offered there became cheaper, as access to the great fairs where domestic goods could be exchanged for those of other districts became easier, more and more would the home production of certain articles be abandoned. Materials would be taken to the craftsman's shop to be made to order. Clothing and other articles for everyday and common use might continue to be the product of the housewife's skill, but for feast days and holidays at least the superior goods bought on the market would come into use.

Town life meant quite early an abandonment of the major agricultural pursuits. For basic foodstuffs and raw materials the town households became in the modern fashion dependent upon the surrounding countryside. This in turn affected the economy of the rural families that it touched. The sale of their produce gave them the means to buy from the occasional peddler or chapman who came to their doors and, as opportunity permitted, to experiment with the goods offered in the shops by merchants.

Although one must be aware of the forces operating in these early centuries to remove from the hands of the family activities that had been there from time immemorial, there must be adequate realization of the fact that rapid and extensive change did not and could not take place until after the technological changes in manufacturing processes and in transportation that began at the end of the eighteenth century. Before that time towns were few and small by modern standards. The craftsman in his shop and the mother and daughter in their home used the same tools and the same methods. Consumer production and production for the market could take place side by side, the same worker going from one to the other as under the same conditions this still happens today. Markets were limited, and the volume of trade and commerce small. The great bulk of the population was rural, with no outlet for its products. The preparation of food and the making of clothing and many other goods were in large degree in the hands of the household.

At any one time, especially in a new country like the United States, families would vary in the degree to which they had given up their old arts and crafts. The variations would correspond to the stage of the industrial development of the various districts, to the degree of urbanization, to the extent to which they had been tapped by transportation lines and their power resources developed—in short, to the extent to which the homes in question had been caught up and woven into the new economic pattern. Whatever variations a cross-section might reveal, the trend of events from decade to decade was unmistakable, a steady abandonment of many ancient and honorable activities. Fewer and fewer families raised and stored their own vegetables; took their wheat and corn to the miller and brought back flour and meal; kept their own cows and made their own butter; provided their own beef, pork, and mutton; cut and carded the wool from the backs of their own sheep. Spinning and weaving disappeared along with shoemaking, candlemaking, and soapmaking, except in out-of-the-way corners. The volume of canning and preserving, baking, and sewing lessened. The burden of fetching and carrying lightened.

The removal of the production of foodstuffs and raw materials from the hands of those who were to use them was an inevitable result of the growth of towns and cities and the preoccupation of those living on farms with production for the market. At the same time came the movement from the family of the primary manufacturing processes. Still later, with the invention of new processes and new machines and with the extension of industrialization and urbanization, more and more of the secondary processes of manufacture departed. Finally, even the end processes began to go with the production of ready-to-serve foods and ready-to-wear clothing outside the home.

Another series of changes that have greatly altered the character of housework is that illustrated by the piping of water into the house, modern methods for the disposal of garbage and sewage, the provision of such fuels as gas and electricity for heating and lighting, and arrangements for central heating. Certain of the "housework" may also be given over to commercial agencies. Washing, ironing, dry-cleaning, dyeing, repairing, and renovating are losing their place as the foreordained tasks of the members of the family or their hired servants. Still another group of transfers is made up of personal services. Many personal services once wholly or mainly family-provided are now largely the job of the outside specialist. They range from the care of the sick and the education of children to manicuring, hair-cutting, shampooing, and dressing.

The delegation of any or all of the tasks above mentioned to persons who were not family members was by no means unknown in the past. In fact, whenever and wherever it was possible, this was done. The others to whom they were turned over, however, were servants who served this one family alone. What is new is turning them over to outside agencies which serve many families and the adoption of the practice by an ever increasing number of families.

The change in the character of household production is only partially told by an enumeration of the old activities that are no longer performed or are performed with less frequency by members of the family. There are certain new tasks and new responsibilities peculiar to the modern household. One necessarily present is buying. Goods and services not produced by the household must be sought in the market and made available in the time, place, and combinations desired. Along with this go certain financial responsibilities which require planning, calculation, and record-keeping. In spite, too, of the withdrawal of many arts and crafts and many kinds of service production from the home, there is still a residuum. There are still many end processes of production, especially in connection with food preparation and serving. There is the periodic requirement of "housework," the ordering and care of the house, its equipment, and the personal belongings of the members. Furthermore, standards for housework are decidedly higher, and the equipment to be looked after is greater. There is also the care of small children and the supervision and training of older ones. The care of children, once rather incidental and casual, a response to their more obvious physical needs, is more and more coming to be regarded as a weighty responsibility requiring intelligence and unremitting attention.

SOME CHARACTERISTICS OF MODERN HOUSEHOLD ACTIVITIES

Certain aspects of the changes in the activities carried on by and for the members of the family group should be noted in order to understand more clearly the character of consumer production today. As compared with earlier days, consumer production is more a process of creating time, place, and possession utilities and less one of creating form utilities than heretofore. The tasks that remain in the home can less and less be described as making goods; they may be better described as making goods available at the time and in the place and combinations desired. Housekeeping women can no longer be classed occupationally with farmers and manufacturers; instead, their activities are analogous to those of middlemen and those who render services. The increase in the relative importance of activities such as these is an outstanding feature of our society. One consequence of this change is that the results of consumer production have become much less tangible. The housewife of earlier days could point with pride to the garments she had constructed, snowy linen she had laundered, jars of jam and jelly she had made, bread, cakes, and pies she had baked. Today much of her work does not show. It becomes more difficult to measure the results of her labor. It cannot be done by an inventory of the goods in pantries and closets; nor can she show a money income as could a wage-earner or a business concern with an equally intangible product. It is not strange that superficial observers say there is no product and that the workers find it difficult to appraise the results of their efforts.

Another result of the relative decrease in the arts and crafts is a decrease in the physical burden of household labor. There is less heavy lifting, less backache, and less strenuous physical activity in household production than heretofore. At the same time, however, the enjoyment that the majority of women get out of their work may have decreased. With the passing of the old arts and crafts that required manipulative skills, that gave tangible products that could be measured and displayed, a special source of satisfaction and pleasure has disappeared. Where now can Veblen's "instinct of workmanship" or the "creative impulse" find expression? Teachers of home economics have made heroic efforts to interest women in keeping household accounts, but the results are almost negligible. There are various reasons for this, but among them is the uninteresting character of this work in and of itself. Most women would far rather try out a new recipe or a new pattern. The suppressed desire for the manipulative arts shows itself in the enthusiasm with which thousands of women go in for "fancywork" and the pseudo-arts and crafts of the day.

A third change in the character of the activities that constitute household production is that they are now less of a primary character, less essential for physical existence, than they once were. The great labors involved in feeding and clothing the race are not household activities. The family has only the end processes of manufacture, if any at all. The activities of the household enable us to live as we desire rather than enable us to live. That is what is in the mind of those who say, "The homemaker is a luxury." She has more to do with providing the amenities and comforts of existence than with providing the basic necessaries. It is the member of the family who works outside who "makes the living." We can live without the peculiar utilities that the homemaker provides, although we cannot live in the way that we desire.

THE CHOICE BETWEEN MAKING AND BUYING

The shift from consumer to commercial production, as other economic changes, is the result of a choice made by individuals and families between alternative modes of obtaining a livelihood in the situation in which they find themselves. The abandonment of consumer production is the correlative of a turning to earning or production for sale in order to obtain a money income with its wider range of choice and other advantages. Thus the choice between making and buying is first of all a choice as to the use of the labor resources of the family, a decision as to which or how many of the family members shall earn or produce for the market. A subsequent decision is: What shall be purchased and what consumer-provided?

Actually with the standards and under the conditions that now prevail in modern communities it is necessary that families have a money income —there is no choice about it—and, because of compulsions and circumstances to be analyzed later, the pattern of husband earning, wife usually not earning, and children earning only after a certain age is followed. Conscious choice enters only when the advisability of deviating from that pattern is being considered. Similarly families may have no choice as to whether they shall make or buy many of the commodities and services desired. If certain goods are to be enjoyed, they must be purchased or provided by the community. The family cannot make or provide them. The length of the list of goods and services available only by purchase is imposing. Many of the articles on the must-be-purchased list are new goods never consumer-produced. The new goods may be substitutes for those once home-provided, or they may serve an entirely new purpose.

There are, however, some goods with respect to which a choice is possible between purchase and home provision. Families with a plot of land may grow fruits and vegetables. In a rural community they may keep a cow, pig, and chickens. Even urban families have a wide range of choice between home production and purchase. Garments may be made at home; food processing may begin at the initial stages rather than at the last before eating.

Whether there is a group of goods that must be furnished by the family members—that cannot be purchased—admits of some debate. If the income is large enough, there is scarcely any economic good that cannot be purchased; in other words, someone stands ready to supply it. Only when the market to which the family has access for some reason does not supply a desired good or service is the only recourse home production. Actually for most families income is insufficient to enable them to hire a cook, a housekeeper, or child's nurse. For this sort of service in a private household they must rely upon a family member.

The family's choice between buying and "making" is therefore limited by many factors outside its control—by its place of residence whether city or farm; by its power to command the materials, techniques, and tools necessary for production; and by its money income. Within the realm where choice is possible the most important determinant is probably the amount of the money income. In the household with relatively large income few tasks will be performed by the family members. Even in families with moderate income home production may cease when there is still a slight financial advantage in its favor. The saving is so small that, if there is little pressure on income, the article or service will be purchased.

As has been suggested the choice made between making and buying often depends upon the estimation of the relative importance of more leisure and more goods. The outcome will depend in part upon the relative supply of each. If the money income is sufficient to provide what the family considers essential, leisure for the wife or other family members will increase and their productive activities decrease. If there is pressure upon money income and it is insufficient to provide all the essentials, consumer production will increase. The valuation placed upon leisure is not, however, purely a matter of taste. It is partly a matter of the possibilities for the use of free time which are functions of the social setting as well as the age, habits, and education of the individual. Highly important also is the standard of the group with respect to the wife's occupations, the group whose opinion governs the behavior of the family in question. If "housework" and multifarious productive activities are her proper and approved role she is likely to busy herself accordingly; if "leisure" and "ladyhood" are her proper role, every effort will be made to make it possible.

There is, finally, however, the choice between making and buying that is a choice neither between earning and consumer production nor between leisure and labor. It is the choice of what is to be made or provided. In other words, it is a decision as to the allocation of time analogous to the decision as to uses of money. Just as the uses of the money income will vary with the size, composition, and other need-determining character-istics of the family, so will the uses of the time of the wife or other family member. The large family with children under school age will show one pattern for consumer production; the family with two adults, a different one.

The uses of time will also depend upon such obvious factors as the opportunities for gardening, cow-keeping, and similar agricultural pursuits. Labor-saving equipment also stimulates home production by making the tasks less burdensome, disagreeable, and time-consuming or the product more satisfactory. The skills of the homemaker will also determine what tasks she undertakes. The situation when new goods come on the market should be noted. There is no tradition of home production or knowledge of the process. The result may be that articles that could easily be made at home without expensive equipment are purchased without question. The abandonment of home production for a generation will fix the habit of purchase and make its restitution difficult. Other considerations are the relative quality and money cost of the commercially made and the home-made articles. A lag often occurs between the time when commercial production begins and its complete occupation of the field. The consumers may have to be reassured as to the healthfulness of the commercial methods, prejudices may have to be broken down, and the quality of the article or service reach a certain standard before those who might buy the commercial product will do so.

As in the choice of who shall earn and whether the wife shall be a lady of leisure or a working housekeeper, the actual tasks undertaken by the wife or other family member are in part a matter of social code and social approval. There are the approved and traditional tasks, those performed by every "good" wife. There are those that spell poverty. "Homemade" is a desirable quality of some articles and an invidious term when applied to others.

The amount and kind of consumer production carried on are therefore much the same from family to family of the same time, place, and class. There are variations in the skill with which given tasks are performed, in the standards of performance, and in the time spent on each. But upon the whole the tasks follow a similar pattern. The activities vary primarily with the degree of urbanization of the place of residence, the amount of the money income, and the size and composition of the family.

EFFICIENCY IN CONSUMER PRODUCTION

There are two reasons for attempting to analyze the factors making for efficiency or the reverse in consumer production. Only by a correct judgment of its relative efficiency as compared with commercial production can we know what it costs us to enjoy the way of living that seems to carry with it this manner of production. The second reason is to discover how if at all the efficiency of this type of production may be increased. "Efficiency" is a term often used very loosely. In exact terms it means either a reduction in the time, energy, and resources expended in securing a given result or, what is equivalent, securing a better or greater product for the same expenditure. The more efficient worker is one who does her work more quickly or achieves her result with less expenditure than others. From another standpoint she is one who can turn out a better product than others without increasing the costs in time, energy, or money. Outlay of time, energy, and resources may be reduced by changing one's standard for performance or product. There are hundreds of examples: dusting twice a week instead of every day, using paper napkins instead of linen, serving meals in the kitchen. Such reductions in time or money costs do not come from changes in efficiency. In the measurement of efficiency the ends sought, the scale of values, must be taken for granted and only economy in the use of means be considered.

Broadly speaking, there are two possible forms of inefficiency in consumer as in commercial production. One is the inefficiency of an inadequately utilized or idle plant, equipment, or worker. The other form of inefficiency is the unskilful, unintelligent use of the working period, the ineffectiveness of workers while on the job.

EFFICIENCY AS A PROBLEM OF REDUCING OVERHEAD COSTS

In so far as inefficiency takes the form of inadequately utilized plant, equipment, or workers, it may be regarded as a problem of high overhead costs per unit of output or person served. The "waste" and diseconomy of consumer production from this point of view arise from the maintenance of over forty million households as centers of such production with their equivalent number of cookstoves, kitchens, dining-rooms, refrigerators, vacuum cleaners, and other equipment to serve often only two or three persons. In three-fourths of these households, moreover, an able-bodied woman devotes her entire working time to the productive activities arising from the needs and desires of such households. The emphasis here is upon the small scale of the operations of these producing units, since each serves only one consuming unit, a family of limited size.

Clark in his *Economics of Overhead Costs* discusses briefly overhead costs in the household, those that vary little with the size of the family or with the volume and variety of things produced:

The fixed investment in a dwelling-house is a constant and more or less specialized outlay. It can shelter a larger family without corresponding increase in cost: and it is hard to adapt to changed conditions in the character of the demand—witness many residence districts full of misfits and anachronisms. The growth of apartments testifies to the economies of size, and central heating plants contain possible savings of combination. The work of the household—buying, cooking, planning meals, etc., is largely an overhead cost. Here the economy of a large family is very real, though it is so narrowly limited and so bound up with other and more important qualitative values that a serious economic discussion of it might seem to argue lack of a sense of humor. It is of substantial importance, however, in the present-day attempts to produce a scientific measure of the minimum needs of families of different sizes. More complex are the possibilities of combination and co-operation.[7]

The overhead costs in the household are, in part, money costs and, in part, time costs. The time of the homemaker who withdraws from other productive activities in order to carry on the household enterprise may be considered *in toto* an overhead cost. Clark calls it a "sort of human overhead outlay." Her investment of time is like the investment of capital necessary to carry on a business. It is true that the homemaker allocates definite hours of her time to specific tasks—baking, canning, sewing, marketing, and so on. The period of time spent on each task may be considered the direct time costs of various products. Comparisons of these direct costs are valuable in deciding between alternative uses of time. But it is nonetheless true that, if all her potential working time is reserved for household production, it is a kind of overhead cost. Decreasing production may decrease her actual working time, but some of her potential productive capacity goes unutilized. The effective use of the homemaker's time presents the same sort of problem as does the utilization of any other sort of fixed investment.

There are peculiar obstacles in the way of spreading the overhead costs of the household whether they are in time or money. How can the money overhead costs be spread over a greater volume of output? The money paid for house rent is an overhead cost. If a house is used only for sleeping and the family dines out, the whole rental value of the house must be allocated to the cost of a place to sleep. On the other hand, if the house is used for many and varied purposes, the overhead cost for any one of them is greatly reduced. In the same way, if the kitchen range is used only for breakfast, its whole cost per month or year must be charged against breakfast. The same principle applies to the use of the sewing or washing machine. The more frequently they are used, the less the cost per unit of service. Furthermore, if the house and its equipment serve but two persons, the cost per person is greater than if it served three or four. Unit costs are also reduced when a given expenditure, as for fuel, is spread over a maximum product. The more potatoes the housewife bakes at one time, the less the fuel cost per potato, or, if she bakes the potatoes while the beef is roasting, the less the fuel cost of each operation.

7. J. M. Clark, *Economics of Overhead Costs* (Chicago: University of Chicago Press, 1926), p. 354.

The household manager is familiar with all these methods of reducing costs, but they are of limited applicability. The practical situation in which she operates is quite different from that of the business manager. She cannot increase the size of the family in order to spread the overhead over more persons. The economy of a large family may be great in one sense, but the fact that income earners do not increase in proportion changes the situation greatly. The only practical way of spreading the overhead over more persons is by taking boarders and lodgers, but this is not done unless the need for reducing costs is great.

The family may find it possible to reduce some money overhead costs by sharing the burden with other families. It may move to an apartment house where many of the costs of the dwelling, equipment, and fuel are spread over several households. It may patronize the commercial laundry and the taxi and thus share overhead costs with other families. In fact, the movement from consumer to commercial production could be described in large part as a movement to share overhead costs. Wherever expensive facilities are required which one family cannot use to full capacity, there is a strong push toward communal use through co-operative or commercial arrangements in order to spread the cost burden. In Middletown the Lynds make this comment on the advent of the electric washing machine.

This is an example of the way in which a useful new invention vigorously pushed on the market by effective advertising may serve to slow up a secular trend. The heavy investment by the individual family in an electric washing-machine costing from $60 to $200 tends to perpetuate a questionable institutional set-up whereby many isolated homes repeat common tasks day after day in isolated units by forcing back into the individual home a process that was following belatedly the trend in industry toward centralized operation.[8]

The "human overhead outlays" involved in consumer production are at their maximum when the workers have no other employment. As in the case of the money-overhead costs of the household, there are obvious limits to the extent to which the "human overhead" can be spread over a larger output. Probably a homemaker could plan meals, keep books, and buy food for a dozen in the same time required for two. The care and supervision of three children do not require triple the time required for one. Yet the only way her output can be thus maximized is by some arrangement that amounts to an exchange of services between households, that is, an adoption of the principle that underlies the whole exchange economy.

8. Robert S. and Helen M. Lynd, *Middletown* (New York: Harcourt, Brace & Co., 1929), pp. 174–75.

One peculiar result of the phenomenon of overhead costs, whether in the home or in the factory, must be noted. After the overhead costs have been incurred, once they are inevitable, they will be ignored in figuring costs of activities or services which are considered exceptional, additional, or sporadic. For example, if a relative comes to live with a family in the house previously occupied, his or her shelter will be said to cost nothing. Or if the cost of home production of some article is being compared with the market cost, only the direct costs of home production will be considered. The cost of raw materials or prepared food does not represent the total cost of feeding a family an orderly sequence of meals in the conventional fashion day after day. To it should be added the expense of providing a place, equipment, and supplies for preparing and storing the food, serving the meals, and restoring order afterward.

One of the most interesting manifestations of the household manager's attitude toward overhead or fixed costs, however, is when she is considering not money but time costs. Certain tasks require her daily presence in the home. Furthermore, certain of the major demands upon her time are not consecutive but periodic. They are spaced at intervals throughout the day. A plotting of her work curve would show an uneven distribution of tasks. She must be on hand, however, to meet the peak of the load whenever it comes, though she is idle in the meantime. As a result any task that she puts in between these periodic demands she is likely to regard as without time cost. It was performed in her "free" time when she sacrificed nothing to its performance. This calculation has a sound basis. It is true economy to utilize time to full capacity and thus secure larger returns for the investment of time or money. It leads, however, to the use of time on tasks which do not net a high return per labor hour. The saving in money, for example, may be very little as compared with the return in certain other activities. The homemaker cannot specialize in the activities yielding a high return, in making party dresses or slipcovers, for example. But if there was no more profitable alternative use of the time spent on the low-return activity, it was an economy so to use it.

EFFICIENCY AS A PROBLEM OF INCREASING SCIENTIFIC MANAGEMENT

We come now to the other aspect of efficiency in production, the effectiveness of the workers while on the job. For adequate appraisal of the relative efficiency of consumer production in this sense it must be noted that all the activities involved may, as in commercial production, be divided into two broad categories: management and performance. The efficiency of a worker on the job is a function, first, of the intelligence of management and, second, of the skill of performance. Management is the decision-making or planning aspect of production—decision or plan as to what to do, when, where, by whom, and how. Performance is the "doing," the carrying-out of the plan.

It is difficult if not impossible to differentiate management from performance in consumer production. The manager and the worker are usually the same person and not differentiated, as is the case in large-scale business concerns. The decisions and the plans in regard to specific activities are therefore closely associated with their performance. When the manager and the worker are different persons, the manager schedules the tasks and frequently standardizes the process to the degree that its performance is pure routine. Such "scientific" management means that to a large extent thought, skill, and intelligence have been transferred from the worker to management.

Management, however, whether found in close connection with performance or entirely separate, means decision in regard to the best good for the purpose, the best use of money, the best use of time, the best way to perform a given task—best, of course, in view of the end to be attained. It is management that answers the questions what, where, when, by whom, and how. Of these, "what" and "how" are most difficult. What to feed the two-year-old child? What to do for a temper tantrum? What to buy for the family dinner or for living-room curtains? How to take rust from table linen, to make biscuits, or to serve a dinner?

The division of consumer production into management activities and performance activities may seem to some far-fetched and misleading. There is no other way, however, except by this logical separation to show clearly the difference in the character of the activities, the skills, and information they require. In any discussion of the efficiency of consumer production it is important to note that the causes of inefficiency in management are quite different from the causes of inefficiency in performance. The most serious doubts concerning the relative efficiency of consumer production arise on the first score. By and large it is probable that unpaid workers are as efficient in performance pure and simple as are the gainfully employed. It is true that their lack of specialization and of certain types of incentives militate against the acquisition of skill. Upon the other hand, the prerequisite to skill in performance is repetition of the process, and most household workers have long experience on the job. There is little labor turnover compared with business concerns. The major issue is the efficiency of the performance of the management function. There are greater obstacles to the adoption of "scientific management" in the household than in the business enterprise. The limitations upon its extension are such that there is bound to be a marked lag between science and practice, a lag greater than that found in commercial production.

Management, it has been said, is of three kinds; conventional, systematic, and scientific.[9] "Conventional" management is management by rule of thumb, by trial and error, by following the conventional pattern as to what to do and how to do it. "Systematic" management involves record-keeping, scheduling, and budgeting. It means deliberation and careful consideration of issues. "Scientific" management, however, means decisions as to what and how on the basis of scientific or at least quasi-scientific knowledge. It means in the most literal sense planning on the basis of the results of experiments made under controlled conditions or, more liberally interpreted, decision on the basis of the judgment of the most informed and thoughtful as to what to do and how to do it.

There are those who associate scientific management wholly with time-and-motion studies or studies of tools, equipment, and layout of work units. The purpose of scientific management thus conceived is to reduce the expenditure of time and energy. But scientific management in the household is not limited to the adoption and use of the one best way for such tasks as making beds, washing dishes, or cleaning a room. It means also seeking and using the one best way to feed and train a child, to cook vegetables, and to make a cake. Those who seek and use the one best way in the latter cases are not so much interested in saving time as in securing uniformly superior results. There was a time when all these problems of management were in the realm of guesswork. The last few decades have seen great changes, however.

The extension of scientific management does not require that household managers themselves find the one best way for performing household tasks, the best foods for various ages, and so on. Household managers must necessarily rely mainly upon outside sources for finding the one best way as well as the one best article for a particular purpose. The responsibility of management is to adopt the standard practice, adapting it if necessary, and to secure and use the one best article for a given purpose. The growth and dissemination of scientific knowledge provide her increasingly with answers to these questions. Knowledge of the "one best way" is becoming available on how to feed a child, make muffins, clean carrots, combine colors, make a bed, wash dishes, take out stains, arrange a kitch-

9. C. B. Thompson, *Scientific Management* (Cambridge: Harvard University Press 1914), pp. 50–51.

en. In classroom and over the radio, in books, periodicals, and newspapers, formulas, rules, and recipes are passed on to her. Manuals and charts for ready reference become part of her working equipment. In fact, one might say that there tends to be a transfer of thought and intelligence from the manager to her files and catalogues. Increasingly also her tools, equipment, and materials make procedure easy and performance foolproof. Prepared cake flours, for example, and automatic ovens require little knowledge on the part of the one who is to manipulate them. Finally, it is to be observed that the modern manager of the private household takes an increasing number of her problems to the outside consultant—the physician, the child psychologist, the interior decorator. Her responsibility becomes that of seeking expert guidance and following the rules laid down. The rise of the expert and the development of automatic machinery, standardized materials, and manuals giving exact formulas and rules of action operate to simplify the task of management.

Yet it is sometimes said that, although performance has become easier, management has become more difficult. Various circumstances do tend to make it more difficult or, at any rate, to seem so. The decisions of the household manager, as those in every other department of life, were once made on the basis of experience or custom. Furthermore, the range of choice was small; there were experience and precedent to guide in most household problems. Today with the wide range of choice, with the emphasis upon the importance of the choices, and with the growth of scientific knowledge which the intelligent manager feels should whenever possible be made the basis of her decisions, the situation is quite different. New problems arise unknown to parents or grandparents, those, for example, that arise in connection with the rearing of children under modern city conditions or those that appear when the family changes its economic status. Neither experience nor custom is then an adequate guide. The very growth of knowledge seems at times to make management more difficult. The consciousness of ignorance makes the homemaker unwilling to follow custom, folklore, or the advice of the elders. Problems which once were simple, such as meal planning and child management, become difficult and complicated. Knowledge that there is a "right way" makes one fear to go wrong.

OBSTACLES TO IMPROVEMENT IN MANAGEMENT

The number of persons who must be kept informed as to the best way of performing their tasks is in itself an obstacle in the way of making home management as efficient as other management. A further obstacle is the nongainful, nonspecialized, and small-scale character of their operations. These workers are Jills-of-all-trades as compared with those in the management role in business or the professions. The homemaker cannot be given the training equivalent to that of a specialist in all lines of her activity, nor can she keep herself as well informed of the progress of scientific knowledge, market conditions, and technical methods in all lines of her work as can the more specialized worker. The variety of tasks undertaken means that she must remain to a large extent an amateur in many. When tens of millions of persons must be stimulated to seek, find, and use the best way, a decided lag between science and practice may be anticipated. A similar lag is inevitable in all occupations—teaching, manufacturing, farming, the practice of medicine—but the smaller numbers to be reached in these occupations make the problem far less formidable than in the case of household production.

In a business enterprise a slight saving in unit cost may mean the difference between profit and loss. In the small-scale household small savings may be of little significance, although if disregarded in millions of households the total loss is very great. In buying materials needed by her household how much time and energy will a sensible housewife give to searching for the lowest price on the market? If by spending an hour she could find sugar at nine cents a pound instead of ten, she would reduce the cost by 10 per cent, but she will save ten cents only if she buys ten pounds. She will have twenty-five cents for her expenditure of an hour's time only if she buys twenty-five. Again, the housewife, by adopting a certain technique for cleaning carrots, may be able to reduce her time cost one-fifth and save 180 seconds on every dozen cleaned. But, to save six minutes a week and five hours a year, she must serve twelve carrots regularly twice a week.

A further difficulty arises from the fact that, in household production, management and performance are carried on by the same person. Slichter says: "When methods of production are determined by the persons who use them, industrial technique has a tendency to become fixed. Men dislike to change their ways of working because things usually go more smoothly when the habitual routine is faithfully followed."[10] Although a new method may save time or give better results, it does so only after it is learned. During the learning period the hand slips, the knife falters. The experienced worker who tries out a new process becomes again a learner and experiences all the discomforts of an awkward and inexpert beginner. The learning period is one of fatigue, constant attention, mis-

10. S. H. Slichter, *Modern Economic Society* (New York: Henry Holt & Co., 1931), p. 98.

takes. It is not strange that many cannot believe the new process superior to the old and that many after a trial or two slip back into the old "easy" method in which performance is almost automatic.

What incentives to improve efficiency have those who work only for themselves and their families? The pecuniary motives upon which we rely and think we must rely as an incentive for other workers are largely lacking. It is true that alertness, zeal, and intelligence in the performance of some activities save money. Especially is this true in the case of buying, but in other cases the gain is only in time saved or in enhancement of health, comfort, beauty, prestige, or similar values. By and large these workers operate outside the usual system of financial rewards and penalties. Homemakers are not drawn into their jobs by a wage offer or profit lure. They are not discharged if they prove inefficient. Their share in this world's goods has only a limited relation to the skill or intelligence with which they carry on their productive efforts.

Occasionally one comes across the statement that running a household is like running a business and that they should be run on the same principles. Literally, of course, this would be quite impossible. What is meant presumably is that the housewife should buy in the cheapest market, budget, keep accounts, adopt time-saving methods, and so on. But no home can be run like a business and no business like a home. The man who tried the latter would soon have no business to run, and the homemaker who tried the former would soon find herself at an impasse. Fundamentally the business enterprise and the household enterprise are completely unlike.

Those who emphasize the similarity between household management and business management have probably wished to stress the fact that both have the problem of policy-making and of planning and of making limited resources yield the greatest possible results. To some extent also they may have been misled by the superficial similarity due to the fact that both are vitally concerned with a money income and a money outgo. The economic history of the two may to a certain extent be written in dollars and cents, but the relation between income and outgo is quite different in the two cases. In the business outgo comes first and the income second. The aim of the business is income, the expenditure is to secure it; in the household the end is expenditure, the income is to make it possible. Household management, like business management, may strive to lower costs, but the aim of the one is thereby to maximize income and of the other to maximize satisfactions.

Financial rewards and penalties are not, however, the only incentives that spur people on or deter them from action. They may be necessary in the nature of the case for paid workers but not for unpaid workers who are vitally interested in the results of their efforts in terms of their own or their family's satisfaction and well-being. Affection and a feeling of responsibility for those for whom the work is done would certainly for many women be an even stronger incentive for seeking and using "the best way" than any hope of a financial reward. Certainly this is the case when the health or obvious well-being of the members of the family depends on the quality of the work. Few would agree that the pecuniary motive would lead to greater zeal in seeking knowledge of child care and training, or greater assiduity in following directions, than does the present motivation.

Family affection is not the only force that makes for zeal and efficiency in household management and performance. Of unknown but decided weight is the fact that these qualities are expected of those who assume the responsibility. A stigma attaches to the neglectful mother, the lazy housewife. The good opinion of neighbors, friends, and relatives is a motive for efficiency very strong in some women—more potent in inducing efficiency in some lines and under certain conditions than others. Craft pride also enters in, a pride that may be deliberately stimulated by medals and prizes. To a large extent it might be said that the efficiency of household production rests upon the code that society develops for workers in this field, what it expects, and to what qualities it gives recognition.

So far as incentive alone is concerned, it is doubtful whether consumer or commercial production could put up the better case. The system of pecuniary incentives as it actually operates is by no means perfect as a stimulus to efficiency on the part of the great mass of wage-earners. The profit motive leads at times to modes of production that are wasteful and to the impairment of the quality of the product. In consumer production there is no gain in scamping or adulterating. It has the qualities of production for use as distinctly as it lacks the qualities of production for sale.

The motivation in consumer production is weakest perhaps when it comes to saving of time. There are some workers whose emotional set toward their job expresses itself in a keen desire to do it in the most efficient way, that is, with the least expenditure of time, energy, and resources. Just as they wish the product to be up to a certain standard, so they take pride in their dexterity and their knowledge of the best way.

There are also those women at the peak of their housekeeping burden, when their families are largest, their children requiring the most attention, and perhaps at the same time the family income the smallest, who see that only the most efficient methods will enable them to perform each day or week all the activities that they wish to carry on. There is also the over-lapping group of women who wish to reduce time and energy spent on a given job, not that they may take on more jobs, but that they may have more rest, more leisure, or activities of another kind. But there are other groups that feel little incentive to reduce their working time.

Other advantages may be claimed for consumer production. It is production at or near the place of consumption by the consumers them-selves. Transportation, selling, and other distributing costs are therefore at a minimum. Further, it is not subject to certain of the wastes of gainful production. It is not subject, for example, to cyclical change. There is no periodic unemployment of workers and lessened use of equipment. To some extent this offsets the daily and weekly failure of the small-scale households to utilize fully their workers and their tools.

THE FUTURE OF CONSUMER PRODUCTION

What is to be the future of consumer production? Will the movement of productive activities from the home and the hands of consumers to outside agencies, commercial or communal, continue at the same pace as in the recent past? Will the home in a few decades become a place for consumption and for leisure-time activities only? Will this be the solution of the problem of increasing household efficiency and the problem of the education of women? The question that troubles some, "What in that case will happen to the family?" is not ours to debate. Those who adopt the old Hindu concept of the family as those who cook together may well tremble for the permanence of family ties. Those, however, who find other bonds of union foresee a longer continuance of family life.

Perhaps the majority of those who have seriously considered the future of consumer production have considered its decline inevitable. By projecting what they consider the trend line of the past into the future, they have predicted its ultimate shrinkage to the negligible proportions of purely individual production. Most of this group have not only predicted but hoped for this decline.[11] They have believed that the disappearance of household production was not only inevitable but highly desirable. They have regretted the inertia, the sentiment, the alleged lack of perception of the line of true advantage, that obstructed and delayed the movement.

11. Gilman, Black, Parsons, and Pruette are among the spokesmen for this group.

They have been eager to promote acceptable substitutes either commercial or co-operative for the lingering household activities—child care, cooking, laundering, cleaning, and so on.

The arguments of those who would accelerate the decline of consumer production are based to a large extent upon the inefficiencies of such production previously noted. Household production, they allege, is a belated industry; the family cookstove is an anachronism. The organization on a new basis of the production now carried on in the home is essential, they argue, for still another reason. It alone will release homekeeping women from their present economic position, solve the problem of their education, utilize their powers effectively, and place the economic relations of husband and wife on an acceptable basis.

Spokesmen for the contrary point of view can be found.[12] Mr. and Mrs. Ralph Borsodi have argued that factory production has increased altogether too much. It has resulted in an ugly civilization, and, although it has through mass production reduced certain costs, it has brought with it new costs and new problems. What is needed, they say, is a new economy made up of households that are far more nearly self-sufficing than at present. They would retain factory production for those goods that can best be produced in that way, but they maintain that the list of such goods is far shorter than is generally supposed. Consumer production has in many lines marked advantages over specialized commercial production. They would have a domestic revolution in the twentieth century to counteract the industrial revolution of the nineteenth. They would have consumer production assume such proportions that it would absorb not only the energies of women and children but a part of the working time of men. They believe that the productive possibilities of domestic machinery have barely been tapped; that with modern technology and a rehabilitated domestic economy families could enjoy for the same effort a decidedly higher standard of living than at present. Through this increase in household production they would solve the problem of "careers for women," furnish to children naturally the education that city children must now get artificially and expensively at school, solve the economic problem of old age, and increase the security of the family. Families, they argued, have failed to see the line of true advantage. They should cling to what is left of the household arts and crafts and resume others as new tools and devices make it feasible. The social attitudes of the time have been unfavorable to consumer production. The convention in the main has been against the homemade and for the ready-made. Advertising

12. Ralph Borsodi, *This Ugly Civilization* (New York: Simon & Schuster, 1929).

and sales promotion, they think, are largely responsible for this, although the makers of electrical appliances put up a strong countercampaign.

Although some families have demonstrated the feasibility and advantages of increasing consumer production beyond its usual volume under certain conditions, there are obvious limitations upon its wholesale adoption. A basic one is the difficulty of providing all families with a homestead and an acreage of adequate size and location. A second difficulty related to the first is that of combining the requisite amount of earning with the requisite domestic production. Can all families, in other words, be part of both a rural and an urban economy? Can centralized factory production of certain products be combined with the decentralized domestic production of others? Few would agree that as many goods of satisfactory quality could be made at home as the Borsodis allege. The Borsodis' analysis is valuable, however, if for no other reason than that it compels the critics of consumer production to re-examine their assumptions. It is probable that many, both of those who desire and those who regret its decline, have rather unthinkingly labeled all movements toward mass and commercial production "progress" and the reverse "inertia and backwardness."

There are certain pervasive, underlying forces that in the future as in the past will, in so far as they come into operation, tend to substitute production outside the home for production within. It is the productive efficiency of specialized machinery and labor utilized to full capacity under centralized management, and the power of associative effort functioning through exchange, which have drawn task after task from the unspecialized household worker's hands.

There are several circumstances, however, that set up limits to extra-household production and block the transfer of certain productive activities from the household. One is the necessary relation between the time of production and the time of consumption of some goods. If the two are practically simultaneous, as they are in the case of service production, or if little time can elapse without affecting the quality of the article, production and consumption must occur in the same place.[13] The end processes of food preparation, the broiling of the steak, the mixing of the salad, are of this nature. Most of the "housework," too, must be carried on in the house itself. If activities of this sort were to be taken over by paid workers, either they would have to come to the home, the place for

13. If the means of transportation available are sufficiently swift and the means of handling perishable goods in transit are adequate, the place of production may be separated from the place of consumption.

consumption, or else the consumers would have to go to the place of production. The first procedure would effect no economy. A transfer of tasks to a full-time paid worker does not alter the small-scale, unspecialized character of the activities, nor does it solve the problem of overhead costs. Specialized workers who go from house to house can be economically used only for certain tasks. The first procedure, then, is not generally feasible; the second, the coming-together of many consumers at the place of production, is only within limits found satisfactory.

The care and training of children are outstanding examples of a group of personal services that resist complete transfer to paid workers inside or outside the home. Unless we are willing to alter greatly the degree of association between parents and children, someone in each family must take the responsibility for care if children are young, and supervision of their activities if they are older. Even when they are absent from home almost every day and for the larger part of each day, the responsibility continues. Only in the higher-income groups can it be turned over to a paid person. Unless we turn over to community and commercial agencies all care of children from infancy on, in most families with children a family member must assume this responsibility.

Another condition that blocks the transfer of certain productive activities from the home is the limits imposed by the standards of living upon socialized consumption. As long as people want to live in independent households, as long as they desire privacy and places of retreat from all except a small family group, as long as they wish to eat at home in small family groups, as long as they wish some books, music, pictures, and games for use in these private households, so long must consumers' goods be made available there in the form, time, and combinations desired. Certain productive activities are therefore likely to be carried on very near the time and place of consumption.

The essential point is that production takes place not only in order that we may live but that we may live as we desire. One of our preferences is life in family groups in independent households, with the possibility of privacy, close association between parents and children, and with many activities limited to that family group. This way of living may be more costly than others that could be devised. The nation that is hard pressed as in a war economy, or as in Russia in the days when her productive capacity was low, may resort to communal meals and communal living and use its womanpower in factories and similar ways. The private household consisting of the small family group may be one of the luxuries that only a surplus economy can support. But the same thing is true of many other of our desires. Production in this respect, as in others, is organized to give us what we want most. If our desires were other than they are, production could be organized on a different and, from one standpoint, a more efficient basis. Those who attack household production should really attack the standard of living that at present makes some degree of it essential.

CHAPTER XIV

THE ECONOMIC POSITION OF HOMEKEEPING WOMEN

CONSIDERATION of the social aspects of consumer production leads directly to the question of what it entails as now carried on for those workers whose whole or major economic contribution is of this character. These workers with insignificant exceptions are women, mainly married women. Practically all men whether married or single seek work for pay or profit. Single women are also likely to be found in the labor force, the percentage so found increasing decade by decade as opportunities for such employment increase, as barriers of various kinds are broken down, and as the need for their services at home to supplement those of the house-mother decreases. Gainful employment does not preclude the performance of some services for one's self and for the common benefit. The degree to which this happens varies with inclination, habit, training, and opportunity. Gainfully employed women are more likely than men to perform personal services, to help with or even carry on single-handed the customary housework. All members, both young and old, of families with a farmstead or homestead are likely to be doing a good deal of work for their own use and benefit.

In most homes, however, most of the "production for use" is carried on by one person whose principal job it is. Husbands and sons on the whole take relatively little part in housework; unmarried daughters work outside the home, and fewer maiden aunts and grandmothers than formerly share the homes of their kindred. In a study of 513 Oregon homes the average amount of assistance given the homemaker by other members of the family was only about nine hours per week. Husbands gave the most time in families where the children were all under six years of age, an average of 3.6 hours per week. In families where the children were older most of the help came from them, the amount increasing with their number and age.

The facts to be faced then are that about thirty million women in the prime of life, a good-sized fraction of our potential labor power, make their economic contribution through work for themselves and their families and assume whatever are the special benefits or disadvantages of this peculiar economic status. The questions previously raised concerning

270

this situation had to do primarily with their productivity: Is their economic contribution as great as if they were employed in specialized occupations as a part of larger-scale enterprises subject to pecuniary competition? The question here has to do with these women as workers. What of their "wages, hours, and working conditions"? How do they fare as compared with other workers and how, if at all, does their peculiar economic status affect the status of women as such, their education, their personal development and welfare?

DIVISION OF LABOR BETWEEN MEN AND WOMEN

Division of labor between men and women is a very ancient arrangement. Specialization according to sex is the first form of specialization of which there is record. So marked and so persistent has been that division that many attempts have been made to find the basis of the distribution of tasks. One great difficulty in arriving at an explanation is that the work allotted to women varies from group to group and has varied even more greatly from time to time. Sumner and Keller say, "Within any limited group the occupations of men and women are seldom the same."[1] But between different groups it is difficult to generalize as to women's work and men's work. We may say with Rivers, "The general rule throughout the world is that certain occupations are regarded as proper to men, others as proper to women, while others, again, may be followed by both sexes,"[2] but there seems to be no way of forecasting definitely unless all the circumstances are known which at a given time in a given group will be considered proper for women and which for men.

All authorities agree in the main as to the way tasks were divided among peoples on the lowest cultural level. "Upon the woman devolves, as a rule, the procuring and preparing of the vegetable foods and for the most part also the building of the hut, while hunting and working-up of the products of the chase fall to the man," says Bücher.[3] Similar is Müller-Lyer's generalization:

> On the lowest stage of culture known to us among the hunter folk, there is only one kind of division of labor, viz., that between the sexes. The man is a hunter . . . , he procures all the animal food, he prepares for himself the weapons and tools which he needs for that purpose, and trains his boys when they have reached a certain age. . . . All other labors devolve on the woman. As a complement to the man who procures the animal food, the woman is expected to gather the vegetable food, berries, roots, bulbs,

1. W. G. Sumner and A. G. Keller, *The Science of Society* (New Haven: Yale University Press, 1927), I, 138.
2. W. H. R. Rivers, *Social Organization* (New York: A. A. Knopf, Inc., 1924), p. 147.
3. Karl Bücher, *Industrial Evolution* (New York: Henry Holt & Co., 1901), p. 31.

etc., from the forests, carry home water and wood, keep up the fire, erect and pull down the huts, prepare the skins and make the clothes. When travelling she is laden with all the goods as well as with the smaller children.[4]

It is this situation which Mason described in detail in his *Woman's Share in Primitive Culture*.[5] The productive arts initiated and first developed by women range from tilling the soil to basketry, spinning, weaving, cooking, and pottery-making. Among some primitive peoples on the higher cultural levels certain of the industrial arts belong to men. Sewing and weaving, for example, Sumner and Keller found frequently in the hands of men, less often the making of pottery, basketry, and other arts.

As groups pass from the primitive to the civilized or semicivilized level, changes take place in the distribution of tasks between men and women. Here again the authorities agree. When a group turns from hunting or collection of foods in their natural state to cattle-raising or other pastoral pursuit, the men become herdsmen and the women continue to procure the vegetable food. If, on the other hand, systematic agriculture develops as the main source of food and raw materials, the women turn over the cultivation of the soil to the men. They work in the fields only in the heavy seasons. In their hands are the housework, the cooking, the brewing, the baking, the spinning, the weaving, and so on—the multiplicity of household arts found in all the early records. The majority of the industrial arts remain in their hands until specialization, exchange, and, finally, power machinery take them away and deliver them into the hands of men.

In the search for a guiding principle with reference to the age-long division of labor between men and women, one fact seems to stand out. That is, whatever at the time is the major occupation of the group, its main reliance for subsistence is the occupation of the men, assisted perhaps at certain points by the women. In the hunting and fishing stage, so called not because there were no industrial arts, no domesticated animals, no use of vegetable foods, but because the life of the group was organized around these two major forms of food production, the women are the collectors of grain and berries; they carry on the crude agriculture, and they have in charge most of the industrial arts. When cattle-tending or its equivalent assumes the place of hunting, the men take it over, and, as permanent settlements are made and systematic agriculture begins, men take over the tilling of the soil. Women to a large extent retain the in-

4. F. C. Müller-Lyer, *The History of Social Development* (London: G. Allen & Unwin Ltd., 1920), pp. 205–6.

5. O. T. Mason, *Woman's Share in Primitive Culture* (New York: D. Appleton & Co., 1910).

dustrial arts until with the development of trade and commerce and new technological methods they too become important sources of wealth and are taken over by men for systematic and large-scale development.

Here is one reason for the age-long feeling that, whatever the work of women may be, it is insignificant and minor compared with the work of men. Actually in every age and every group the activities rated as most important have been mainly in the hands of men. In the hunting and fishing stage women are agriculturalists; in the agricultural stage they carry on the industrial arts; in the industrial age they cease to manufacture. Nor is it more true today than heretofore that women's work is highly rated.

Another reason frequently given for the persistent and marked difference in social attitude toward women's work and men's work is that outlined by Veblen in his *Theory of the Leisure Class*. The distinction "of an invidious character" between the occupations of men and of women is, he argued, the natural outcome of the "barbarian culture" of the "predatory stage" that followed the state of "peaceful savagery." In such societies, he said, there are two classes of activities—exploit and drudgery. Exploit covers all those predatory activities by which the group asserts its mastery over other groups and by which it enlarges its possessions and gathers spoils and trophies. It covers all those activities which stimulate the pride of the group and give a sense of achievement and power. Exploit becomes those things that are worthy, honorable, and most important. Drudgery covers all those things which in this group at this time one wins no acclaim for doing. Men's work is the exploit, women's the drudgery. Down through the ages men's work has been the honorific, women's the nonhonorific. It has been considered a disgrace for a man to do a woman's work and an exceptional honor for a woman to be permitted to do men's work.

Why have the major activities always been in the hands of men, why in the division of tasks were women assigned a secondary role? Why to men the exploit, to women the drudgery? Why should arts carried on by women for generations, perhaps even initiated by them, be developed and become important sources of livelihood only when they are taken over by men? Thomas, in his essay on *Sex and Primitive Industry*, attempted to explain the early distribution of tasks. "Among primitive races," he said, "men are engaged in activities requiring strength, violence, speed, . . . and the slow, unspasmodic, routine, stationary occupations are the part of woman."[6] This habit, he said, was based on a physiological difference

6. In W. I. Thomas, *Sex and Society* (Chicago: University of Chicago Press, 1907), p. 123.

between the sexes. "Man is fitted for feats of strength and bursts of energy; woman has more stability and endurance."[7] Veblen developed the same idea. "The sexes differ, not only in stature and muscular force, but perhaps even more decisively in temperament, and this must early have given rise to a corresponding division of labour." Exploit requires, he says, the stouter, more massive males, more capable of a sudden, violent strain, more assertive and aggressive. The women will do the other work there is to do.[8] Whatever is the explanation of the early or the late division of tasks between men and women, once the differentiation is made, custom, tradition, and superstition operate to maintain it.

Is it this alleged psychophysical difference alone that explains the early division of labor between the sexes? And to what degree does it explain the present distribution of tasks? There is certainly one other circumstance of considerable potency in determining both the primitive and the modern allotment of tasks between men and women. It must be noted that there is one task that is always delegated to women, the care of children. Even without the prolongation of infancy that has marked the progress of the human race, there is a long period during which the human young must be cared for by adults. Very early in human history man came into possession of fire and learned many of its uses. A habitation, a hearth, a fire, cooking, three meals a day, were joined to the cradle as a center around which many activities would inevitably revolve. Might it not be that by a sort of natural economy this aggregation of tasks would be taken over by the mothers of the children, their first protectors and source of their food supply? The same person could most conveniently care for the children, kindle fires, carry wood, cook, make the drink, do the housework. To this aggregation of tasks others that might be picked up or laid aside, that would fit in, would be added. Women could not undertake an enterprise that would keep them too long from the home center or to which they could not carry their children. They could carry on stationary activities. They could devise ways and means of improving their foods, clothing, and shelter, new ways of cooking, new cooking utensils, new means of food preservation and storage. They could develop basketry and pottery, spin, weave, make garments. Thomas says:

> Woman developed the constructive or industrial activities as a simple consequence of her more stationary condition of life. The formation of habit is largely a matter of attention and the attention of women being limited by her bodily habit and the presence of children to objects lying close at hand, her energies found expression in connection with these objects.[9]

7. *Ibid.*, p. 51.
8. Thorstein Veblen, *Theory of the Leisure Class* (New York: Macmillan Co., 1899), p. 13.
9. *Op. cit.*, p. 134.

Women, it will be noted, are always Jills-of-all-trades. They do, as Veblen said, "all the other work there is to do." They cannot concentrate upon some one line of production and subordinate all others to it. Instead, all others are subordinated to the children and the three meals a day. Around these as a nucleus they gather whatever activities they can. Is not this a partial explanation of the fact that they are the eternal amateurs; that the systematic development of not a single art has come while it remains in their hands? While it is in their hands it is subject to the exigencies of their preoccupation with children and housework. In the hands of those who are freed from these preoccupations a more intensive and vigorous cultivation is possible.

PECULIARITIES OF ECONOMIC STATUS OF WOMEN

The division of labor between men and women today takes the form of a concentration of the former upon gainful employment and of the latter upon nongainful. The result is an economic status for the latter that in many ways is in marked contrast to that of other workers. Here is a group producing for use and not for profit, whose incentive to efficiency and effort is not financial reward, and whose returns are largely the health and happiness of others. In a world engaged in creating exchange values these workers are creating use values. From this flows the fact previously noted that no financial value can be placed upon their services. As a consequence also the wife may be considered a dependent of the husband without a claim to money income independent of his discretion. The propriety of such a status may well be questioned. It is obviously out of harmony with our accepted ideas in regard to the appropriate relation between adults.

In other respects the economic position of homekeeping women is unique in the modern economic world. Their jobs and status are the by-product of marriage. With marriage comes responsibility for certain tasks without reference to differences in inclination, aptitudes, training, or experience. These tasks vary with the financial position of the husband and the place of abode rather than with the capacities and interests of the wife. A trained nurse who marries has the same allotment of jobs as the stenographer or cook or lawyer who marries. It is conjugal status, not competition, that places workers in this field. As these workers are not hired, neither are they fired for inefficiency or incapacity. There is no promotion. The wife who is inefficient as a household worker and manager may find herself elevated to a state of affluence through the earning power of her husband, and the efficient household manager may find herself in a state of poverty through the financial incapacity or misfortune of her husband. It is the money-making power of the men these workers marry that determines whether they have the place and privileges of the rich or the limitations of the poor, not the competence with which they meet their responsibilities.

THE VOCATIONAL DIVIDE IN THE LIFE OF WOMEN

One of the most serious results of the economic role allotted to women is that it creates what has been termed a "vocational divide" in their working lives. From youth to old age men expect to follow a gainful pursuit, marriage only intensifying its importance. There are risks and difficulties in choosing the employment for which to acquire training or experience, but there is no uncertainty as to the character of the responsibility that will be theirs: they must provide the money income necessary for their own support and, when they marry, for that of wife and children.

The usual course of the economic life-history of women is different. The pattern is ordinarily as follows: gainful employment from the time of leaving school until marriage; thereafter, sole or major responsibility for the performance of those services for self and family that the time, place, husband's income and occupation make necessary. For a few, gainful employment continues after marriage with only the interruptions that might happen to the gainfully employed man; a larger group is employed sporadically as necessity or opportunity determines; but many others do not resume gainful employment while the marriage endures. Women who do not marry, and most of those widowed or divorced while still of working age, ordinarily look toward gainful employment as their proper and necessary economic role.

The unpredictability of the duration of the gainful employment of women and, whether or when, having abandoned it, they will wish to resume it, has many consequences. How much is it wise to invest, for example, in the training of women for a professional or other gainful pursuit? The returns upon the investment will ordinarily not be so great as if the same amount were expended upon the training of men. Further, in some jobs their usefulness is lessened by the probable brevity or discontinuity of their stay in the labor market. To deny women the same educational and employment opportunities as men would, however, conflict with our standards of what is fair and desirable. Restrictions on such opportunities mean that, when women enter the labor market, they enter at a disadvantage. They are forced to crowd into the less-skilled and less-well-paid pursuits. Their capacities are not utilized to the best advantage, and, as individuals, they are penalized because of the special role they assume in the family economy.

The problem of the education of women is not solved by insuring that they have the same opportunities as men. With marriage they usually assume the management of a household and with motherhood the care of children. Some of the information and skills required to meet these responsibilities efficiently will have been acquired in family living; others may best be acquired on the job. If a substantial body of knowledge remains that will be acquired by only a few without opportunity for systematic study, a further educational problem remains. If women must fit themselves for both gainful employment and homemaking, they, inevitably, are unequally placed as compared with men, who can concentrate upon preparation for earning. There are those who argue that the homemaking skills and knowledge can be used in work for pay or profit and that a dual-purpose program can be developed. Education for homemaking, properly conceived, differs, however, in basic respects from education for earning. The former is general and extensive; the latter, specialized and intensive. The former would be substantially the same for all girls and women, varying only with educational level. Ideally it would reach all conditions and classes, the many rather than the few. The latter is diversified. Its character varies as greatly as the employments for which it prepares. Ideally the number preparing for each employment would vary with aptitude, inclination, and market demand. If girls and women were prepared only for the vocations closely related to homemaking, they would enter a crowded market unless their numbers were few and their working lives short.

CHARACTER OF WORK AND WORKING CONDITIONS

The dissimilarities between the economic status of homekeeping women and that of other workers are more clear cut and pronounced than the dissimilarities in the nature of their work and working conditions. It has already been pointed out that the work of one homemaker is very similar to that of another. They are unspecialized, in other words, while other workers are just the reverse. It is therefore difficult to compare the ease and the irksomeness, the pleasures and pains, of the tasks the two groups perform. The gainful employments with which the homemaker's activities might be compared vary from heavy toil to the sedentary occupations, from the creative and varied to the repetitive and monotonous, from those ranked as menial to those of great prestige and honor. Homemaker's activities also cover a wide range in all these respects; some require judgment and information equal to the demands of a profession, and others are of a routine, manual character; but one person is likely to perform all of them

If thirty million homemakers were to be transferred to specialized, gainful employment, all could not be placed in pleasant, easy jobs.

If a general comparison were to be made between the nature of the work and the working conditions of the majority of homemakers and the majority of the gainfully employed, the results would be in many respects unfavorable to the latter. Relatively speaking, the homemaker's job is more varied both during each day and from day to day than is that of most of the gainfully employed. The variety of the tasks should relieve not only the monotony but also the fatigue and strain. The homemaker, furthermore, since she is both manager and worker, is able to plan her own tasks and is free to lay them aside or to take them up in the order she chooses. She has no boss except the exigencies of the work itself; she need punch no time clock; she can arrange her own rest periods and vacations. There would be, it would seem, a sense of freedom in work of this character not found in many forms of paid work. Furthermore, the housewife works in her own home with working conditions in the way of light, air, cleanliness, and layout of workroom under her own control. She need spend no time going to and returning from her work. The fact too that the work is for herself and her family should augment its interest and relieve its tedium. It is true that household production does not permit the exercise of the manipulative arts as it once did, that there is no longer the same volume of tangible goods to bear witness to the craftsman's skill as heretofore, but it still probably compares favorably in this respect with most jobs. There are still opportunities for working over materials, for assembling, arranging, and combining. The order, harmony, cleanliness, beauty, healthfulness, and restfulness that she achieves are the product of her labors and hers alone. They are not lost in the contributions of scores of others.

Upon the other hand, those engaged in household production work largely in isolation. Those who have the habit of working with others in factory, store, or office, or who are of an especially gregarious disposition, may find this objectionable. The household worker must find her social life outside her work. This may create a real problem when the husband seeks solitude and rest in his evening or holiday hours and his wife wishes to mingle with others. The household worker may also complain that she can never escape from her job. It is indeed true that she punches no time clock, since hers is a twenty-four-hour day, a seven-day week. Her work and her life are inextricably joined together; she cannot put her work behind her every evening as can many other workers.

If a representative sample of homemakers were to record their preference as between the work for money carried on before marriage and their occupation thereafter, certain relationships would undoubtedly appear. Those women who before their marriage were engaged in some form of creative work with interesting contacts and varied experience, or whose gainful employment gave opportunity for the expression of special aptitudes or utilization of professional training, are clearly more likely to regret its abandonment for housework than those whose work was not of this character. Others who prefer gainful employment will be those who are untrained and unskilled in household activities. A poll of the sort suggested might, however, be misleading. Homemakers, for example, would be better able to state which household tasks they found most fatiguing or disagreeable than to express a general preference. More important, for all workers circumstances other than the character of the job per se and the working conditions affect greatly their attitude toward it and their fatigue and boredom. Gainful workers are subject to competitive stresses and strains that the nongainful are not: getting and keeping a job, producing up to an acceptable standard, being dealt with on a "business" basis.

The fact that home management and housework are a concomitant of marriage makes an objective view of them as "a job" a difficult matter. Knowledge that one is performing the proper role of a wife and mother makes the tasks involved less onerous if that role is highly esteemed. What a job as a whole or a particular task symbolizes to the worker affects profoundly not only her willingness to undertake it but the irksomeness of its accomplishment. Here is the clue to the dissatisfaction felt by a few homekeeping women; they are obliged to perform tasks they consider "menial," those that should properly be performed by a domestic servant and not by the wife or other family member.

WOMEN AND LEISURE

The whole situation of homekeeping women cannot be understood without analysis of what society expects from them and what in their minds is their ideal economic role. Here we are confronted with a rather complex situation—complex because it involves attitudes of which we are largely unconscious and of which perhaps we prefer to remain unconscious because they are in disharmony with others which seem to us right. Our attitudes toward the proper economic role of homekeeping women have implicit in them a double standard, that is, one that is different for women from what it is for men; and also a class standard, that is, the assumption that what is right for one group of women is not for another. Our code with respect to the economic responsibilities of women still embodies to some extent what has been called the "ideal of lady-hood." This is a survival, as so many other parts of our standard of living, of the attitudes and values of older regimes of status based on birth and inherited privilege. The "lady" from the economic standpoint is a woman of leisure; that is, she has time for pursuits that people who work cannot engage in or can engage in to a more limited extent.[10] She toils not; she is the ornament of the home. She displays in her person, her clothing, her accomplishments, her activities, her exemption from the heavy, the irksome, the menial tasks of life. She may retain the management of her household, but the detailed carrying-out of her orders, the physical care of her children, the hourly watching over them, are delegated to others. She dispenses hospitality but she does not perform the tasks involved. The maintenance of this standard is possible only for those with relatively high income or with the right otherwise secured to draw upon the labor of others. Its correlative, assuming a standard of living in other respects like that currently accepted, is an adequate supply of domestic workers. The lower their earnings relative to those of others, the lower the income upon which an idle wife may be maintained.

The standard described, as has been said, is a class standard, evidence of belonging to the financially successful or other favored class. For the masses such a standard is remote and unattainable; it is not even in one sense their standard. The economic life of the wife is assumed to be one of labor, not of leisure. There is no thought that some household tasks are menial or not suitable for family members. Only for some in the middle or upper-middle class is there struggle to maintain this standard, dissatisfaction and a fear of loss of prestige and place at the failure to do so. Yet in another sense this is everyone's standard; it is the standard of everyone who feels that it is right and fitting for the wives of men who can afford it to become ladies of leisure, who would themselves adopt this standard if able to do so, or who take pride in its achievement by their daughters or other kin.

The lady of leisure has been found in the upper levels of every society characterized by wide differences in economic power. In such societies there is usually an abundant supply of domestic servants at relatively low rates or even a "servant class." In any society there is such a supply if the power of some groups to enter other employments is highly restricted, as has been the case of the Negroes in many American com-

---

10. Leisure, of course, is not synonymous with inactivity. The worker as well as the non-worker may be very busy in her leisure time.

munities. In others the supply was in a sense imported, that is, the available workers were those newly come from other countries, handicapped by unfamiliarity with the language or ignorance of employment opportunities, and not averse to domestic employment as native-born workers are likely to be.

Many women besides those freed from labor by the size of the family income find themselves with a shorter working day and week than gainful workers enjoy. Their leisure is created not by turning over the care of children and other household tasks to hired workers but by the decrease in the number of children per family, by the transfer of tasks to commercial agencies, and by the lightening of those that remain by new equipment and materials. These women, it is said, constitute a new leisure class. How many of these women are there? Do they constitute an increasing proportion of all able-bodied women? But before going to these questions we should make certain that the implications of the existence of a leisure class, no matter who compose it, do not escape us.

The position, all too often encountered, that it makes no difference how much leisure women have provided they use it well does not stand up if critically analyzed. Leisure, of course, is like money in that its value to the individual, its enrichment of his life or the life of others, depend upon the uses made of it, and wise use is greatly to be desired. But, if leisure is good, then it is something that as many as possible should enjoy. If leisure is an opportunity for the free play of interests that cannot be expressed in one's work, all groups should share in this opportunity. Inequality in the distribution of leisure is as greatly to be deplored as inequality in income. A society divided into a leisure class and a working class on the basis of sex would deviate widely from the type of culture that we ostensibly esteem. To argue that women could with social benefit take over all religious, political, and social activities, all patronage of the arts, could "represent" the family in every role except earning, is to argue for the patently impossible. One person cannot assume another's social responsibilities or vicariously acquire for him personal values and experiences.

WHAT ARE THE FACTS?

What are the facts in regard to the length of the working day and week of homekeeping women? How many women are ladies of leisure by virtue of their own or their husband's income? How many others have an inordinate amount of leisure because of the small size of their family, their household conveniences, the limited number of their tasks? How much time the women who report their employment as housekeeping spend on their jobs we do not know. The number of able-bodied women whose housework and child care are completely or partly turned over to paid helpers is unknown. For our purpose we would wish to subtract from that number those who were themselves in the labor force full or part time. The data on family expenditures indicate that the families with paid household help are very few and that they are concentrated at the higher-income levels. At no income level shown in the 1941 study did as many as half of the farm families report an expenditure for this purpose, and the average outlay for those in the highest income group having such help was so low as to indicate that it was available only occasionally.[11] Fifty-five per cent of the urban families with money incomes ranging from $5,000 to $10,000 reported such expenditures, but the average expenditure for those having such help was only about $4.00 per week. All the urban families with incomes of $10,000 and over had some expenditures for this purpose, on the average slightly under $10.00 per week.[12] The outlays included here were for household help of all kinds, from the full-time cook or child's nurse to the laundress or window-washer. Only the seamstress and sicknurse are excluded.

Most of the women who are reported as keeping house are devoting at least part of the day to this job. But how many hours do they actually work? We have more opinions than facts on the hours of work of home-keeping women. Such statements as the following are frequently found: "The occupation of home-making and housekeeping is not a full-time job for the woman of average health and energy. Especially in our urban communities, housekeeping has been reduced to a matter of, at most, half-time work."[13] Supporting evidence is lacking, however. Some women undoubtedly exaggerate their working time by including activities belonging to their personal, family, or social life such as everyone engages in but which the gainfully employed do not confuse with their work. When this is allowed for, how many hours are left?

The only data available on the actual working time of homemakers, its distribution among various tasks, and its variation with degree of urbanization of place of residence, economic status, and other factors come from studies made between 1925 and 1929. Records were kept by the women

11. U.S. Department of Agriculture, Misc. Pub. No. 520 (Washington: Government Printing Office, 1943), p. 50.
12. U.S. Bureau of Labor Statistics, Bull. No. 822 (Washington: Government Printing Office, 1945), p. 126.
13. E. J. Hutchinson, "The Economics of Marriage," *World Tomorrow*, X (1927), 271.

themselves for a two-week period; the classification of the activities reported was made by the investigators. Some of the results are shown in Table 4. These figures do not suggest that, by and large, the housewives reporting had an excessive amount of leisure. Even in the city homes of

TABLE 4*

LENGTH OF HOMEMAKERS' WORKING WEEK
(Hours per Week)

ACTIVITY	REPRESENTATIVE RURAL HOMES		CITY HOMES OF THE BUSINESS AND PROFESSIONAL CLASS	
	550 Farm Homemakers	249 Other Rural Homemakers	178 Homemakers in Cities of 50,000–250,000 Population	222 Homemakers in Cities of 250,000 Population or More
Purchasing and management..	2.2	2.7	4.2	5.3
Care of family.............	3.9	4.7	9.8	9.3
Meals.....................	22.8	20.7	14.6	11.7
Care of house.............	9.6	9.4	7.4	7.2
Laundering................	5.3	5.2	3.2	2.5
Mending and sewing........	5.5	6.2	4.1	4.1
Other homemaking..........	2.3	2.6	4.3	4.8
Total homemaking.......	51.6	51.5	47.6	44.9
Farm and other work........	9.6	4.5	2.0	2.4
Help received in homemaking..	9.3	9.6	30.5	36.6
Average size of household.....	4.3	4.0	4.0	3.9

* Source: President's Conference on Home Building and Home Ownership, Committee on Household Management, Vol. IX: *Household Management and Kitchens* (Washington: President's Conference on Home Building and Home Ownership, 1932), pp. 27–28.

the business and professional class the forty-eight-hour week came close to being the mean. In the rural homes fifty-two hours a week was the average. It is important to know, however, not only the mean but how many work more than forty-four or forty-eight hours a week and how many work less. The Bureau of Home Economics, in the report of a study covering primarily farm and village women and a small sample of the lower-income groups in cities, said: "Five-sixths of these home-makers spent over 42 hours a week in their homemaking, more than half spent over 48 hours, and one-third spent over 56 hours."[14] Only 10 per cent of the women in large cities reported spending less than thirty-five hours a week.

14. Hildegarde Kneeland, "Is the Modern Housewife a Lady of Leisure?" *Survey*, LXII 1929), 301.

In comparing the length of the working week of housewives with that of other workers, certain considerations should be kept in mind. One is that the homemakers need spend no time going to or returning from their work. Another is that these figures include the total time spent on all productive labor for themselves or their families. To make the working week of gainfully employed men and women strictly comparable, any time the latter give to housework, caring for children, caring for fires and lawns, making household repairs, mending, and so on, should be added. Over against this should be set the fact that the housewife's average working time is the sum of her working periods during the day or week. Her daily average does not represent continuous work broken only by lunch and one or two short rest periods. Rather it represents blocks of time varying in length, spread possibly from 6:00 A.M. to 7:00 P.M., or even later if she is caring for an infant under one year. One clear disadvantage of the discontinuity of her working time is the resulting discontinuity of her leisure time. The uses of a half-hour or even an hour of leisure are limited. Furthermore, her work is spread through seven days of the week. She seldom has a twenty-four-hour period completely free.

The conclusions that one may draw from the evidence available seem to be as follows. For the majority of women today homemaking is not a part-time job measured by the hours actually spent. If all worked with maximum efficiency and zeal, that is, if all possessed superior equipment, had knowledge of the "one best way," and a strong incentive to reduce working time, it might be only a part-time job. But it is not on this basis that the hours of other workers are measured. It is also true that changes in standards of living might greatly reduce the time spent in housework. There is no doubt that time in the home and money on the market are both used for purposes that might be deemed unnecessary and undesirable. Davenport, writing on "The New Domestic System," spoke of "the two hours' labor that should suffice for all rational daily needs."[15] Perhaps so, but if "rational" and "needs" were strictly defined and there were no production except to supply them, the hours of all workers could be reduced far below the present length of the day or week.

WHAT FORCES ARE INCREASING AND WHAT
DECREASING THE WORKING WEEK?

Those aware of the continuous process of transfer of tasks from the hands of family members to paid workers may be puzzled by the results of

15. Published in W. H. Hamilton, *Current Economic Problems* (Chicago: University of Chicago Press, 1925), pp. 148–51.

the time studies. How is it that the working week still remains so long? Is not the trend inevitably toward a decrease in hours and therefore toward an increase in the number of housewives with but a part-time job? Why does the total time spent in housework increase with urbanization and income? In the city homes of the business and professional class about eighty hours was spent each week in such activities by all persons both paid and unpaid and in rural homes about sixty, yet the former undoubtedly had more labor-saving devices and purchased more goods ready to use. To answer these questions, it is necessary to review the forces that operate to increase the working week as well as those that operate to decrease it.

It has already been pointed out that the relative number of persons engaged in consumer production has been declining. As the work concentrates in the hands of one worker, her hours tend to remain long. As transfers from the home to commercial agencies continue, however, they should operate to reduce her working time. It has also been pointed out that new tasks have resulted from the change in place and personnel of production. Buying, with all it involves in shopping, ordering, assembling, account-keeping, is a notable example. It is perhaps not so clear that a new demand for the co-ordinating and supervisory function of management arises whenever tasks are shifted to others. Hiring helpers reduces the time cost of securing the utilities desired, but it does not eliminate it entirely unless all responsibility and all choice are also shifted. Concretely, the ready-made clothing industry, the nursery school, and the domestic servant reduce the time spent by the homemaker in clothing the family, caring for children, and keeping the house in order, but they do not take the entire responsibility from her so long as she remains the manager. There still remain planning, co-ordinating, assembling, supervising—tasks that grow with the number of helpers, agencies used, and wider variety of things to be bought. This situation is not peculiar to the household; it appears in all business enterprises and in all forms of associated effort. If the occupations of those who work for pay are examined, an increase in the proportion in the service industries, the distributive trades, and in management is apparent. Correspondingly the proportion of the time spent by women in analogous activities has increased, and the proportion in growing and making has dwindled.

Another force that has operated to increase the time spent in household production is the elaboration or elevation of the standards of performance, the increasing time cost of the maintenance of the current standard of living. Some have seen this as a result of the decline of the old arts and crafts and of really important activities. The housewife finding time hanging heavy on her hands, in the lack of anything better to do, begins to elaborate her meal preparation and service, makes a fetish of order and cleanliness, lengthens the time spent on her wardrobe, and becomes over-solicitous concerning her children. In consumer production, as elsewhere, there is a tendency to use the time freed by labor-saving machinery not for more leisure but for more goods or services of the same general character. The invention of the sewing machine meant more garments, for a time garments on which there was an enormous amount of sewing—tucks, ruffles, and so on. The invention of the washing machine has meant more washing, of the vacuum cleaner more cleaning, of new fuels and cooking equipment more courses and more elaborately prepared food. This, however, is only a partial interpretation of what has happened. The changes in standards of child care, of meal preparation and service, of housekeeping generally, are part of changes that have taken place in the whole standard of living, partly desirable and partly undesirable no doubt, but changes that affect greatly the money as well as time cost of family maintenance. The standards once attainable only by the few are now the standards of the many.

It is difficult for us to picture accurately the housekeeping conditions in times when the paraphernalia and standards of living were other than they now are. Houses are larger; wardrobes are larger; there is more furniture and gear of all kinds to be looked after.[16] Mumford says: "All the separate courses on a restaurant menu were a few hundred years ago cooked in the same pot. So the different sub-divisions of the modern house were originally combined into a single room."[17] Miss Breckinridge, discussing the new housekeeping conditions faced by European peasants in America, sounded the same note:

> The duties of the housewife may not be as many but the work they involve may be more. This is true, for example, . . . in feeding the family. In Lithuania soup was the fare three times daily, and there were only a few variations in kinds. Here the family soon demands meat, coffee, and other things. . . . In spite of all that has been taken out of the home the duties of the housewife remain manifold and various.[18]

The same circumstances that explain why it is that the homemaker's week remains so long in spite of labor-saving devices and the transfer of tasks to outside agencies explain also why the city homemaker's work week is almost as long as that of the farm woman and that of the woman

16. The houses and perhaps the wardrobes of the well-to-do are tending to grow smaller, but not those of the masses if we go back in time.

17. Lewis Mumford, *Sticks and Stones* (New York: Boni & Liveright, 1924), pp. 25–26.

18. S. P. Breckinridge, *New Homes for Old* (New York: Harper & Bros., 1921), pp. 44–45.

in the higher-income group not far from the length of those in the lower. One can easily explain why the homemaker with children and low income, especially if she lives on a farm, must work long hours. She can hire little or no assistance; she must make rather than buy so long as a money saving is effected thereby; she can buy little of the more expensive equipment. Her house is likely to be poorly planned. If she lives in the city, it is likely to be in the more grimy districts. What happens if the family income increases materially? The family moves to a cleaner district, into a house more conveniently and efficiently planned; labor-saving utensils and equipment are acquired; hired workers employed; goods and services previously supplied at home are purchased, but the house is larger, its furnishings more abundant and elaborate; in time, if not immediately, standards rise; time released at one point, as in cooking and cleaning, goes into care of children, buying, and management, and the homemaker's week may not be far below that under the living conditions of the earlier years. The time cost of the standard of living of urban, higher-income groups with their many things to care for, their variety in foods, their elaboration of meal service, their need for constant supervision of children, may exceed the working powers of one person and necessitate the employment of domestic help.

Yet, if one were to predict the future course of events, it would be that the average working week for homemakers will decline and that the group with a short working week will grow relatively larger. The trend has been in that direction. The forces working for decline are stronger than those that counteract it. The decrease in the frequency of large families, the introduction of time-saving methods and equipment into the home, and the extension of the use of paid agencies for tasks now carried on by unpaid household labor push steadily toward a reduction in hours. The forces that make for a declining burden of household production are so manifold as to defy enumeration. One must think of new cleansing agents, new finishes and polishes, new textiles that require no ironing, of stainless steel, of aluminum, and linoleum as well as of bathtubs, vacuum cleaners, gas stoves, and furnaces. The change in standards has also at some points decreased time costs. A meal may be served without polished damask; certain dust-gathering draperies and folderol have become less popular.

THE UNEVEN DISTRIBUTION OF THE BURDEN OF HOUSEWORK

It is the uneven distribution of the burden of housework that is the real problem, not the heavy burden per worker. The length of the working day and week varies, as has been pointed out, with income, size of family, place of residence, size of establishment, and standard of living. The fact that it varies with the size of the family means that it varies during the working life of any one woman as her family increases and then decreases in size; as her children pass from infancy to adolescence and maturity. Thus homemakers fall into two groups with respect to their working time; one group has hours that are too long as compared with other workers; another by the same standard has too short a working day and week. Each homemaker, moreover, passes from one group to another as the burden of housework changes through the successive stages of the family life-span. At one period of her working life she may have heavy tasks and long hours; at another few tasks and short hours.

The effect of the presence of young children upon the mother's working time is suggested by Table 5. In the homes of the business and professional class studied by the Bureau of Home Economics the mothers of children under one year reported a work week of fifty-eight hours in spite of the fact that paid workers and members of the family gave forty hours of assistance in various tasks.[19] In this connection the data showing the frequency of households of various sizes may be reviewed. In nonfarm communities about a third of the families have only two members. Only a fifth have five or more. Over two-fifths have no children under eighteen, seven-tenths none under six. Yet at some time in most families there will be one or more children to care for. If there are only two, the period of responsibility for children under six would run from seven to twelve years, the period lengthening with number of children and space between them. The period that there are no children in the home lengthens with life-expectation and as children leave home at an earlier age.

In the main, then, the cause of long hours is an untoward combination of circumstances such as the following. The children are young, and the family is at its maximum size. This peak of the housekeeping load may coincide with the peak of the financial load. If the income is small, it accordingly becomes difficult if not impossible to buy labor-saving machinery, employ commercial agencies, or hire domestic assistance. If at the same time standards for child care, housework, meal service, and so on are relatively high— the working period of the homemaker tends to lengthen unduly. Or if she lives on a farm and must carry water, build fires, gather vegetables, and perhaps cook for farm labor, she is again threatened by overwork. It is these women who are most eager for labor-saving methods but who find it most difficult to secure those that are costly.

19. President's Conference on Home Building and Home Ownership, *Household Management and Kitchens*, Vol. IX, p. 30.

The group of women whose hours of labor are relatively short is the converse of the first. They are to a large extent those who have no young children, a small household, and relatively little pressure on income. These are the women who find it possible to hire assistance and to buy labor-saving equipment. Does the group with the short working week in-

TABLE 5*

EFFECT OF CHILDREN IN HOUSEHOLD UPON LENGTH OF HOMEMAKERS' WORKING WEEK AND AMOUNT OF HELP RECEIVED

CHILDREN IN HOUSEHOLD	NUMBER OF HOME-MAKERS	AVERAGE SIZE OF HOUSE-HOLD	HOURS PER WEEK			
			Homemakers Only		Help Received in Home-making	Total Time Spent in Home-making
			All Work	All Home-making		
Farm Homemakers						
No children................	89	2.7	60.5	44.9	4.3	49.2
No children under 6...........	105	4.6	62.3	51.0	12.6	63.7
Youngest child between 1 and 6..	78	5.0	66.5	56.0	10.7	66.8
Youngest child under 1.........	16	5.7	77.3	69.4	11.9	81.3
Total................	288	4.2	63.9	51.6	9.5	61.1
Town Homemakers						
No children................	23	2.6	49.5	44.2	5.6	49.9
No children under 6...........	53	4.5	52.5	47.9	11.0	59.0
Youngest child between 1 and 6..	69	4.7	56.8	54.9	12.9	67.8
Youngest child under 1.........	9	5.3	67.3	65.5	28.2	94.2
Total................	154	4.4	54.8	51.5	12.1	63.6

* Source: Maud Wilson, *Use of Time by Oregon Farm Homemakers* (Agricultural Experiment Station, Oregon State Agricultural College, Station Bull. 256 [Corvallis, 1929]), p. 29.

clude also the more efficient workers and those who have simplified or lowered their standards so that the time cost is less? Undoubtedly representatives of these groups could be found. But here are found many also whose hours, relatively short as they are, are needlessly long. That is, pressure upon their time is so slight that they feel no incentive to seek and learn labor-saving methods. Some may even deliberately work slowly and elaborate their standards.

THE PROBLEM OF OVERWORK

The difficulty in meeting the problem of overwork, with its possible impairment of health, nervous strain, and limited leisure, arises from the fact previously noted. Overwork comes most frequently in conjunction with a situation that prevents the adoption of certain obvious ways of reducing working time. In so far as it is true that low income, young children, and long hours fall together, one cannot lightly recommend labor-saving devices, modernized kitchens, and domestic service as means of meeting the problem.

The development of standards for housing and furnishing that reduce the time cost of maintenance and the more efficient arrangement of work areas are directly related to this problem. Another step is taken toward its solution whenever the price of labor-saving equipment falls through mass production, cheapening of materials, technological improvements, or expiration of patent rights. Even more effective is the development in the community of satisfactory substitutes for household production at low cost, such as bakeries, laundries, and nurseries or the cheapening of any good or service that the homemaker is now providing. As more and more households have access to electric power at low rates, the burden of housework is materially lessened. The elimination of the smoke nuisance in cities would save time as well as money. The work of mothers with young children is greatly reduced if safe places for the children to play are readily accessible.

An educational program would also help this group of homemakers. They may not be so easy to reach as the women with more leisure, but they have greater incentive to adopt time-saving methods. It is these women who need information in regard to inexpensive tools and supplies. Their money should not go for poor knives or the wrong kind of brooms and brushes. They are the group too who should scrutinize their standards with especial care. Undoubtedly the overwork of many women would cease if they could discriminate between the essentials and the nonessentials. They should make their own valuations of the uses of their time rather than blindly following a conventional pattern. This practice would be desirable for other reasons than shortening hours. Nor should the possibility of meeting the problem of overwork by an increased participation of husband and children in household tasks be overlooked. Sometimes a re-education is necessary to accomplish this. But a situation where the husband has an eight-hour day while his wife has a ten-hour day is as undesirable as the reverse.

No one knows to what extent hours could be shortened by using the "one best way" for every task. There are at least three lines of attack upon the problem from this standpoint. One is to budget time and dovetail tasks in such a way as to make working time as continuous as possible through the day or week. As a result the free time of the workers becomes more consecutive and can be utilized more effectively. Reference has already been made to the fact that certain of the major tasks in household production, preparing meals, for example, are periodic. The time when the first meal must be prepared comes before other workers begin their work, and part of the work attendant upon the last one comes after other workers have ceased. This lack of continuity, this ascent and descent of the work curve during the day, cannot be entirely remedied. But to the extent that the work curve can be smoothed out household workers can have effective leisure rather than time for the use of which there are few alternatives.

A second line of attack upon the problem of excessive hours is to work out ways and means of utilizing each unit of working time to full capacity. This may mean either of two things. It may mean adopting such performance policies as buying the largest supply that is feasible at each trip to the market, making each trip upstairs, to the basement, the dining-room, or kitchen yield its maximum in fetching and carrying. Or it may mean doing as many different things at the same time as possible. Many instances of this policy could be enumerated, worked out by the common-sense experience of thousands of housewives as well as by the systematic taking thought of students.

The third line of attack is the one most frequently cited when efficiency methods in the home are under discussion, that is, the reduction of the time and energy used in each specific activity—washing dishes, shelling peas, cleaning carrots, mixing muffins, ironing sheets, and so on. To carry out this line of attack as far as it could be carried would mean a careful analysis of each operation, time-and-motion studies, discovery of fatigue factors, experimentation with different kinds of tools, materials, equipment, and procedures—undertaking, in short, the engineering problem that is involved in finding the "one best way" of doing a particular job. There is no doubt that many steps could be saved, output of energy diminished, and strain reduced by the substitution of scientific management for haphazard, rule-of-thumb management.

THE PROBLEM OF UNDERWORK

Underwork presents a more difficult problem than overwork because the individuals affected may be quite satisfied with their state. What to society is a waste may be to the individual a good state of affairs. The woman with a short working day or week is ordinarily not concerned about it. Nor is her husband or other members of her family. They would, if income permitted, free her entirely from economic responsibilities. Yet, clearly, if the number of such women increases, as the evidence indicates is happening, the community of which they are a part is losing a large part of its potential labor power.

There are only two ways of lessening the social waste resulting from excessive leisure of homekeeping women; one, an increase in consumer production; the other, some form of gainful production. Few families, however, are likely to adopt either policy unless the goods thus provided are estimated more highly than the leisure of the wife. If the homemaker's inclination and that of her family is against paid employment, only a strong push from economic necessity or the sharp pull of an attractive job opening will bring it about. If, however, employment is sought, shall it be full or part time? There are those who urge that whenever possible arrangements should be made that would permit married women to take on full-time gainful employment. This suggestion is indorsed most strongly by those who believe that the economic dependence of women has very undesirable effects upon both men and women and by that group of women who find themselves forced to sacrifice inclination, aptitude, and training in order to take up the tasks that marriage brings. There is no doubt that any arrangements that will utilize time of adult women not completely utilized, and that will prevent the loss that occurs when trained and perhaps gifted women are obliged to abandon the work for which they are most fitted, are to be furthered and approved.

The great problem of these who seek part-time employment is, of course, to find a job where a part-time worker is wanted. It is not always easy for the full-time workers to find and keep a wage-earning job, and those who can offer only part time have obviously a more limited market. The part-time worker must find an employer who wants the particular hours of the day or week that she is free. In an industry or business operating on a full-time basis additional shifts mean additional costs of handling personnel. On the other hand, some employers have noted that the output of the part-time worker tends to be relatively greater than that of the full-time. There is less slackening-off toward the end of the working period, fewer breaks or periods for which workers are paid but not working. In certain businesses there is a demand for part-time workers to meet the daily peak of the load, and there is some demand from employers who need supplementary aid and from those who employ only one person and have not a full day's work. In the main, however, business and industry are geared for full-time employment. Women who write or who work on a commission basis, women who work for themselves and not for an employer, as lawyers and doctors with a private practice, may perhaps most successfully solve the problem of combining housework with work for pay. Obviously, however, in a world where a larger and larger proportion of persons must enter the employed class, this solution is of only limited application.

As candidates either for full- or for part-time employment married women as a group suffer from certain economic disabilities. A hostile attitude toward their employment is often encountered from both employers and fellow-employees. This has sometimes been strong enough to write itself into law when the state was the employer. Married women have been barred from teaching in the public schools in some states. To the extent that this attitude exists, married women will find themselves the last to be hired and the first to be fired and will discover the market for their services is more limited than the market for the unmarried. Furthermore, those married women who are carrying household responsibilities may find that it is difficult to hold their own with workers who do not have this demand upon time, energy, and attention. Unless married women are as free from such preoccupations as other workers, they are handicapped in the competitive struggle.

Unfavorable attitudes toward the employment of married women stem from two sources: one, the assumption that employment means neglect of family responsibilities and leads to disharmony between husband and wife; the other, that the employment of a married woman takes a job away from a man or reduces rates of pay. In times of business depression and widespread unemployment, objections to the employment of married women rise to a peak. What in effect is then urged is that workers be chosen on the basis of their family status and need, a policy that in all fairness should be extended to all applicants for job, all female as well as all male. Attempts to maintain or increase wage rates by restricting the number eligible for employment are by no means uncommon, and the demand that married women be placed upon the ineligible list is often but a special instance of such attempts. Such abridgments of freedom on the basis of personal characteristics, whether they are sex, marital status, national origin, race, or religion, are indefensible unless a clear case can be made that the abridgment is in the public interest. Married women barred from employment still exist as consumers. They share with their husbands a responsibility for dependents. Shall they decide or shall others decide what their place in the economy shall be?

Married women, it is also argued, undercut the wages of men, since they are supplementary workers and are willing to work for less. This is not possible immediately if a standard rate is established by collective bargaining or otherwise. Are married women willing to work for less? Those who work from strict economic necessity presumably would not refuse any wage offer. Those who do not work unless the wage offered is relatively high would, on the other hand, be expected to give up the job if the rate falls too much. Married women, however, lack the ability to move freely from place to place. This relative immobility would be expected to show itself in the wage rates.

The disability of the married woman, which most markedly limits the market for her services, is the fact that, if she wishes to live with her husband, she must find a job in the same community that he finds his. The women who suffer most from this limitation of their market are those with the most highly specialized training and experience. The demand for their services in the locality where their husbands find the best market may be limited or nonexistent. If they earn, they must enter some line for which they are not prepared and which may not be highly remunerative. If both husband and wife seek gainful employment the question, therefore, often arises whether their home shall be in the best market for the wife's services or for the husband's. Rarely will a given market be best for both of them. In the choice of the domicile, it is ordinarily the husband's economic interest that is considered, for a reason that must now be taken into account, since it constitutes one of the main economic disabilities of the married women.

Most married women will also be mothers. This means inevitably that for certain periods of time they must abandon gainful employment and that complete financial responsibility must be assumed by their husbands. The economic interests of the husband must therefore be safeguarded even if the wife's are sacrificed. Motherhood may also mean a discontinuity in gainful employment that is inevitably a handicap. The period of time that women must give up gainful employment for childbearing and rearing will vary with circumstances. The minimum time that is necessary for physical reasons will depend, of course, upon the nature of the employment and the working conditions. If, in addition to this minimum period, it should seem wise to remain out of gainful employment until all the children are in school, the average period would be more than five years. If mothers waited until all the children were older, the period would be even longer. Whatever the period, whether short or long, it introduces a discontinuity into the gainful employment of married women that must inevitably be a handicap. If it is a long period, the effect upon opportunities for employment and earning would be very great.

Another practical problem arises when the wife obtains full-time employment. How will her former tasks be performed? In some cases they can be satisfactorily cared for after working hours, but in others they cannot. If the husband assumed the same responsibility for housework and child care as the wife, the problem would be solved in some cases. Working against this solution are old traditions and attitudes concerning men's work and women's work. Working against it also is the feeling, perhaps well grounded, that the husband's economic interests are paramount and must on no account be sacrificed. If there is any danger that his money-earning power may suffer from this dual responsibility, the arrangement will not be tolerated. Can the household tasks be satisfactorily cared for by paid workers inside or outside the home? Two difficulties arise when the attempt is made to use part-time workers and commercial or community agencies. One is that their use requires planning and supervision. There must be someone to check and to take care of emergencies when their services fail. A more important drawback is their expense. There is a certain economy in concentrating in the hands of one worker that miscellany of tasks that must be done at or near the time and place of consumption. If the wife's earnings are relatively large, a competent full-time worker or workers may be employed, and the family as well as the wife gains considerably by the arrangement. But this is clearly a solution only for special cases. The wife's earnings would in many cases not exceed the wage of those who replaced her in the home, nor would there be any economy in a wholesale transfer of some workers from their homes to industry and of others from industry to homes. There is, it would seem, no easy solution to the problem of transferring married women and mothers from nongainful to gainful production either full time or part time.

There is, of course, one alternative that would in large degree solve the problem, that is, the abandonment of family life in independent households. It is to be remembered that our whole analysis of consumer production and its *raison d'être* was based on the assumption that we desire to live in small family groups. If this should cease to be the case, the whole situation would be changed. Large-scale, centralized, specialized production would take the place of small-scale, decentralized, nonspecialized household production. The vocational divide would be eliminated. Other economic and social results cannot here be speculated upon. The point is that the present position of homekeeping women is tied up with our desire to live in a particular way. Müller-Lyer says: "The future of female differentiation [specialized work by all women] will thus in all probability depend on the development of a new form of organization . . . which we might call the Cooperative joint household."[20] Such a development is obviously far in the future if it comes at all.

20. *Op. cit.*, p. 230; see also *ibid.*, pp. 218–34.

CHAPTER XV

INCOME AND PROPERTY RIGHTS OF HUSBAND
AND WIFE UNDER THE LAW

ARE LEGAL RIGHTS OF IMPORTANCE?

WHAT is the effect of marriage upon the ownership of property held at the time of marriage or acquired later by either husband or wife? What legal claim has either spouse upon the income of the other? In specific terms, what under the law is his, what hers, and what, if anything, is theirs? If the husband has a separate estate, is it as completely and unreservedly his as if he were unmarried? May he use it as he pleases during the marriage and direct its disposal after death? Do the same rules apply to the separate estate of the wife? If the marriage is broken by divorce, under what conditions has either partner claims upon the separate estate or the future income of the other? If there is property that is legally "theirs," how did it become so? By the fact of marriage or by specific action on the part of one spouse or the other? A discussion of the property rights of husband and wife clearly must fall into three parts: (1) the situation while the marriage endures; (2) when it is broken by the death of either; and (3) when it is terminated by divorce.

Rules of law are necessary to prevent or settle disputes concerning claims to property and income. Creditors must know who is responsible for debts contracted and upon what assets they may levy if debts are not paid. But between husband and wife does it matter whether the income or property is legally his, hers, or theirs? Are not the resources of the family shared among the family members without reference to legal ownership? To achieve equity, must we not rely upon sense of duty, generosity, and affection? If these fail, can the law provide a remedy? Legal rights matter least while the marriage proceeds in amity. Family living requires a sharing of resources and some more or less systematic and mutually agreed-upon method of sharing the contents of the family purse. When a marriage is terminated by death or divorce, interest in the law quickens. Few would argue that the legal rights of the surviving spouse do not matter or that the law governing the disposition of assets in case of divorce is of no importance. Even during the period that the marriage

297

continues the position that the law does not matter is dubious. The law may be in accord with prevailing standards as to the proper economic relation between husband and wife or the reverse. It may promote sound practice in the control of family resources or the reverse.

It is not possible to describe in brief compass the property rights of husband and wife in the United States. What is his or hers during the marriage or what either may claim when the marriage is terminated "is a question that cannot be answered except as with 50 tongues speaking at once. What is the law in Illinois may not be the law in Massachusetts or in California."[1] There is no one law governing marriage or divorce in this country. Who may marry, what constitutes a legal marriage, the conditions under which divorce is granted, as well as the property rights of husband and wife, are matters which each state determines. Furthermore, although the statutes in two states may be similar, the courts in their application may have followed a somewhat different line. To know the law that governs in each case, one must know which state has jurisdiction, the law, and the court decisions in that state.

Three systems of family law must be examined to understand what principles govern the rights and responsibilities of husband and wife in the United States. One is that known as the common-law system, another is that which exists where the common-law disabilities of married women have been removed by statute, and the third is that which embodies the community-property principle. What is his, hers, or theirs by virtue of marriage differs under these three systems. In no jurisdiction in the United States are the property rights of husband and wife as they were under the common law. Yet for several reasons that system should be examined. Common-law principles governed in most American states and territories until well after the middle of the nineteenth century. The system that now prevails in most jurisdictions is but a modification, although a most important modification, of that system. Points of law not covered by statute are still ruled by common-law principles.

The common law of the various states "consists of the principles of the English common law, developed and modified by American custom and

1. John H. Wigmore, *Treatise on Evidence* (2d ed.; Boston: Little, Brown & Co., 1923), I, Preface, xv, quoted in U.S. Women's Bureau, *The Legal Status of Women in the United States of America, January 1, 1948* (Bull. No. 157 [Washington: Government Printing Office, 1941]), p. 3. This bulletin gives a summary of family law in the United States especially as it affects married women.

judicial precedent."[2] Its special characteristics as it applied to the property rights of husband and wife arose from the adoption of the fiction that the *feme covert* had no existence. By marriage a woman lost her legal personality and had no identity in the eyes of the law. Only one marriage partner was recognized, and that one the husband. Legal matters having to do with the income and property of married persons were thereby simplified. The results of the fact that marriage made of the wife a legal nonentity are commonly described as the common-law disabilities of married women. They were legally incapacitated from actions possible to men and unmarried women. The married woman could make no legal contract; could not sue or be sued. She could not be guardian of her own children. Not only was the father sole guardian during his life, but he could appoint a guardian by will. Even when a divorce had been granted to the wife, the control usually continued to rest with the father. It follows that the control and administration of property would be impossible for the married woman. Under the principles of the common law she had no separate estate. Nothing was hers during marriage that she could manage, control, and dispose of as could other competent adults.

> The Common Law deprived the wife of the control of her real property and she lost even the title to all personal property in her possession even though it had been acquired before marriage. . . . The wife's real estate did not become the husband's while the wife lived, although there were so few restrictions on his control over it that it was his in fact until his death if there were children or until his wife's death if there were none. . . . A second class of property was that in the immediate possession of the wife at the time of marriage—such as clothing, jewelry, and house furnishings. These became the husband's absolutely and could be sold, taken for the husband's debts or destroyed by him without the wife's consent. The wife's clothing and jewelry, designated as her "paraphernalia," could not, however, be willed away from her, and she secured possession of them at the death of the husband provided he had not sold or given them away while he was alive or his creditors did not take them for his debts if he became insolvent. . . . Another kind of property was usually designated as *choses in action*. This consisted of notes, bank stock or other chattels not in the immediate possession of the owner. The husband was entitled to the absolute ownership of these by Common Law, if he reduced them to possession during the marriage.[3]

The common law in effect transferred to the husband the property owned by the wife at the time of marriage or acquired afterward by gift or inheritance, most of the personal property completely, and the real property for the duration of the marriage or until his death if there had

2. W. W. Willoughby, *The Constitutional Law of the United States* (2d ed.; New York: Baker, Voorhis & Co., 1929), p. 1306.

3. Ruth A. Gallaher, *Legal and Political Status of Women in Iowa* (Iowa City: State Historical Association of Iowa, 1918), pp. 5–7.

been a living child. The husband, however, had certain responsibilities. He was liable for the wife's debts incurred before her marriage. This was the due result of the transfer to him at marriage of any property she might then possess. He also was responsible for her support and in return had a right to her company and services. He might therefore sue for damages for injuries to the wife, a right that she did not possess. He could collect her earnings if she were an earner, as he could those of minor children.

THE WIFE'S RIGHT TO SUPPORT

The substance of the wife's right to support lies in her means of enforcing it. Under the common law she had no direct means of doing so. To obtain food, clothing, and medicine which the husband failed to provide, she must find a tradesman willing to supply her on credit. The husband was held liable on the ground that this transaction was "agency of necessity." For success in his suit against the husband in case of non-payment, the tradesman who supplied the wife was obliged to prove that the husband failed to provide and that the goods supplied were necessaries. The courts took the position that what was necessary for the wife's health and comfort was relative to the rank and fortune of the husband; silver buckles and a carriage and pair in one case, but only what would ward off hunger and cold in another. Money was not, in itself, considered a necessary, and consequently the husband was not liable for money lent to his wife.

The inadequacy of "agency of necessity" as a means of enforcing the wife's right to support has been recognized and statutory provision made for a more effective remedy in case of separation or failure to provide. An Illinois act in relation to married women passed in 1877 provided that married persons who

without their fault, now live or hereafter may live separate and apart from their wives or husbands, may have their remedy in equity, in their own names, respectively, against their said wives or husbands in the circuit court of the county where the wife or the husband resides, for a reasonable support and maintenance while they so live or have so lived separate and apart; and in determining the amount to be allowed, the court shall have reference to the condition in life of the parties at the place of residence of the wife or husband, and the circumstances of the respective cases. . . .

A later act provided:

Every person who shall, without any reasonable cause, neglect or refuse to provide for the support or maintenance of his wife, said wife being in destitute or in necessitous circumstances, or any person who shall, without lawful excuse, desert or neglect or refuse to provide for the support or maintenance of his or her child or children under the age of eighteen years, in destitute or necessitous circumstances, shall be deemed guilty of a misdemeanor.

Instead of imposing the penalty provided, or in addition thereto the court in its discretion, having regard to the circumstances, and to the financial ability or earning capacity of the defendant, shall have the power to make an order . . . directing the defendant to pay a certain sum periodically . . . to the wife or to the guardian or custodian of the said minor child or children.[4]

Thus the wife's right to support if the husband fails to provide may be evidenced by a court order that he pay her a set sum in money weekly or monthly rather than by his liability to pay tradesmen who have supplied her with necessaries.

AGENCY OF FACT

To be differentiated from "agency of necessity" is "agency of fact." The latter is the situation when husband and wife live together, and she buys the household supplies, clothing, and other goods for herself and other family members. Even under the common law it was held that in such transactions she acted as agent for her husband and that he as principal was bound by her acts. Without such an arrangement it would not have been possible for her to take over the family buying unless in all instances cash were paid. The goods that she buys need not be necessaries. Whatever they are, the husband's credit is pledged unless he has expressly indicated that he will not be responsible for her debts.[5] When husband and wife are living together, the tradesman's presumption in the absence of notice to the contrary is that she is acting as the husband's agent. If the husband has been paying the bills without demur, only by due notice can he avoid liability for future debts. The husband, however, has the right to decide from whom the goods shall be purchased. He may rebut the presumption that his wife was acting as his agent by showing that she was properly supplied and that she was without authority to deal with this tradesman. Madden says:

> If he is regularly supporting her, and has not given her authority to pledge his credit, if she needs a dress she must ask him to provide it, rather than go and buy it and charge it to him. He may have opinions as to what kind of a dress it should be, from what store it should be purchased, the wisdom of going into debt, etc., which he has a right to insist upon.[6]

4. If there are no living children, separate maintenance is not paid for more than two years (see *Illinois Revised Statutes, 1951*, chap. 68, sec. 22).

5. Newspaper notices are considered adequate for large firms.

6. J. W. Madden, *The Law of Persons and Domestic Relations* (St. Paul: West Publishing Co., 1931), p. 187.

It will be observed that the rule is that when husband and wife are living together he determines the standard of living.

A husband must support his wife according to his station in life but a wide latitude of discretion must be allowed him as to how much of his income it is advisable to spend, and how much should be retained for the purpose of establishing a competence for the future, and he is entitled to a large extent to dictate the manner in which the money shall be spent. If the husband abandons the wife, or gives her cause for living apart, he loses much of this discretion, and the standard becomes more objective.[7]

SURVIVOR'S RIGHTS

Termination of a marriage by divorce was rare when common-law principles governed the property rights of husband and wife, nor did common-law courts deal with such matters. In England legal separation might be allowed by ecclesiastical courts and absolute divorce by special act of Parliament. In this country until general rules were established by statute each divorce required a special act of the state legislature. Definite common-law rules covered, however, the disposition of property when a marriage was terminated by death. Here a basic distinction existed as between real and personal property. If the husband died without a will, the widow was entitled to one-third of his personalty after payment of debts if there were children, one-half if there were none. If he died testate, the terms of the will would determine her share, although it might include personalty she owned before marriage, or thereafter acquired by gift, inheritance, or earning. Only those items not merged into this separate estate would be hers to bequeath if she predeceased him.

The rules governing real property were different. Although the husband had a freehold interest in such property owned by her at the time of marriage or acquired afterward by gift or inheritance, that is, he controlled it and collected all rents and profits, at his death if she survived him it came back into her possession. Nor could he will away from her all interest in his real property. She had a right called "dower" to a life-estate of one-third of all real property inheritable by his heirs "of which he was seized during coverture." To bar her dower right, it was necessary that she join him in conveyance. The wife could not will her real property to her husband as he could his to her, since she was presumed to be under his coercion. The surviving husband, however, had a life-interest called "tenancy by curtesy" in the whole of her lands if a living child had been born of the marriage. He had a similar life-interest in any property held for her by a trustee.

7. *Ibid.*, p. 195.

EQUITABLE SEPARATE ESTATES

Although under the common law women lost upon marriage practically all power to call any property their own, by the creation of "equitable separate estates," incomes could be provided for their sole and exclusive use. By setting up a fund under the management of a trustee, a father could insure that his daughter would have the benefit of property he might set aside for her and be protected against the selfish or incompetent husband. Marriage settlements creating an equitable separate estate for the sole benefit of the wife might be made by the husband himself. It should be noted that this method of softening the rigors of the common law was purely discretionary. Only those women benefited whose husbands or fathers were persons of wealth, willing to make the arrangement described. It did not give the married woman control over property, but it made her the beneficiary of a trust.

One further protection to the married woman was found in the proceedings of courts of equity. When the husband sought their aid in reducing to possession the wife's *choses in action*, the court might compel him to make a suitable settlement upon her. The principle was that he who seeks equity must do equity. The device of "estates in entirety" should also be noted.

Conveyance or devise of property to husband and wife by deed or other instrument creates an estate by the entirety. This estate exists only between husband and wife. . . . The spouses take the property as one person and have but one title, each owning the whole. Neither acting alone can convey the property to bind the other, but the joint act of both owners is required to mortgage or convey the title to the whole property. During the marriage the husband has possession and control of the property and is entitled to its income. When one spouse dies, the estate continues in the survivor, and is not subject to laws of inheritance.[8]

STATUTORY REMOVAL OF COMMON-LAW DISABILITIES
OF MARRIED WOMEN

Whatever the virtues or the defects of the common-law system, by the middle of the nineteenth century a movement was developing to alter it in those jurisdictions where it was operative. Whether Blackstone's oft-quoted comment on the status of women under the common law is acceptable, "so great a favourite is the female sex of the laws of England," or that of a jurist speaking a century or more later, "of every human status devised by civilization that of the *feme covert* was the most ignominious,"[9] Great Britain by a series of Married Women's Property Acts

8. U.S. Women's Bureau, Bull. 157, p. 42.
9. Robert Grant, *Law and the Family* (New York: Charles Scribner's Sons, 1919), p. 6.

(1870–1907) and the American states one after another removed all or most of the common-law disabilities of married women. The older system seemed clearly incompatible with new concepts of individual rights and the proper relation between husband and wife and ill adapted to a society where family income was largely in money, wives frequent contributors, and personal property of increasing importance.

Within the United States today two systems of law govern the property rights of married persons. One prevails in those jurisdictions, the great majority, where by statute all or most of the common-law disabilities of married women have been removed; the other, in those few jurisdictions where the law has always been, or is now based, on the community-property principle. As a result of statutory changes in the common-law states, the rights of married women to be guardians of their children, to sue and be sued, to contract in their own right, to collect their own earnings, and to a separate estate in property held at the time of marriage or acquired by gift or inheritance afterward have been generally established. "Though the several states have not been uniform in the extent of their modifications of common-law rules, in none of them today is a married woman under the legal 'blackout' created for her by the ancient feudal system."[10] The various statutory changes place her partially or completely in the same legal position as men or unmarried women.

As has been emphasized, in the jurisdictions with a common-law background the common law governs on matters not covered by statute. The statutes do not change the general status or relation of husband and wife but leave the duties and responsibilities of each to the other, in matters not relating to the wife's separate property, as they were at common law.[11] It is also true that the courts may construe the statutes strictly or that they may take the view that their purpose was to extend generally the legal powers of married women.

Although each state by statutory enactment has built up its own arrangement with reference to the right of husband or wife to control, administer, and dispose of property and earnings, the direction and purpose of the changes made in the common-law states are unmistakable—an increase in the power of the wife. The principle upon which the law is now based in the jurisdictions in question has been described as equality between the two sexes. Both spouses may have a separate estate. The legal identity of neither is destroyed by marriage. Within those jurisdictions

10. U.S. Women's Bureau, Bull. No. 157, p. 9.
11. James Schouler, *A Treatise on the Law of Marriage, Divorce, Separation and Domestic Relations* (6th ed.; Albany: M. Bender & Co., 1921), I, 801–2.

studies would show families in which both husband and wife had property and income. The number in which the wife had no property would, however, undoubtedly exceed the number in which the husband had none, and the size of her separate estate would on the average be far smaller than his. The reason for this situation is evident. The relatively small earnings of most married women preclude any extensive accumulation of property. Savings and investments would come in most cases from the husband's income. The wife's estate is most likely to exceed that of her husband if she has previously been married and inherited a sizable sum when widowed. The chances of inheritance from parents are probably about equal for the two spouses, since sons and daughters are likely to be treated equally in making bequests. The fact is, then, that although husband and wife are equal under the law in their power to earn, inherit, and accumulate assets, their property holdings in the course of the marriage are likely to be quite unequal unless special action is taken to equalize them.

In the states with a common-law background no property or income becomes joint by virtue of marriage alone. Even if the wife has assisted the husband in his business or profession, the income therefrom is the husband's and the chattels and valuables he buys with it.[12] Without express action the family home, the car, the farm, the securities, the bank deposit, are either his or hers, not theirs. In many states gifts or agreed-upon transfers of property from one to the other may equalize or alter their holdings.[13] Some states require that both spouses must join in a conveyance of the family home to a third party, and, if either has dower rights, buyers would require that these rights be waived to give them a clear title.

Two forms of joint ownership are possible as between husband and wife as they are among others, related or unrelated. They are joint tenancy and tenancy in common. Under the latter each has a half-interest in the property so held with right to dispose of the half and to claim it upon the death of the other. Under joint tenancy, indicated by the fact that title is in the name of husband or wife as opposed to husband and wife, they have joint control, use, and benefit during marriage. Either has right of sale and claims to the whole upon the death of the other. By these discretionary arrangements in the common-law states property may exist which is "theirs" in the legal sense.

12. If a definite agreement on distribution of earnings can be proved, a small number of states will allow her claim.

13. Such transfers may not be made to defeat the claims of creditors, and in some cases the transfers or conveyances must be by written instrument in legal form placed on record.

Since the principle of equality is supposed to govern in those states which have removed all or the major common-law disabilities of married women, the question arises: Should not the wife be equally responsible with the husband for support of the family members? It is generally true that the married woman may if she wishes pledge her own credit when she purchases goods for her own or family use. A number of states make the wife and her property liable for family necessaries whether she has specifically contracted to pay for them or not. The Illinois law, for example, provides that the expenses of the family and of the education of children are chargeable, upon the property of both husband and wife or of either of them, in favor of creditors thereof, and in relation thereto they may be sued jointly or separately.[14] Neither the pledge of the wife's credit nor the statutory imposition of the liability described relieves the husband, however, of primary responsibility for family support.[15] The husband of course has no longer, as under the common law, responsibility for the wife's debts contracted before marriage, nor has he responsibility for debts she contracts when she engages in an independent business employing her own funds, nor is her separate property or earnings liable for his debts. A variety of measures have been adopted to insure that this freeing of her separate property from the claim of the husband's creditors is not used to defeat their just claims, such as restrictions upon direct conveyance of real property between spouses, exclusion of gifts from the husband from her separate estate, requirement that an inventory of her personal property be placed on public record.

TESTAMENTARY AND SURVIVOR'S RIGHTS IN
THE COMMON-LAW STATES

Marriage restricts greatly the right of disposal of property by will. In the states with a common-law background each spouse has what might be described as an inalienable right to a defined share in the estate of the other.

Under the statutes of a majority of the States, neither husband nor wife can disinherit the other by will. The living spouse may renounce the will and take instead the common-law dower or curtesy, or the statutory share of the estate . . . for the spouse of a person dying without a will. The nature of these statutory provisions varies to such an extent that summarization of them is not practicable.[16]

14. *Illinois Revised Statutes, 1951,* chap. 68, sec. 22.
15. U.S. Women's Bureau, Bull. No. 157, p. 41. In ten states if the husband is unable to support himself and has no separate estate, or in a community-property state if there is no community property, the wife is required to support him from her separate estate.
16. U.S. Women's Bureau, Bull. No. 157, p. 56.

In many states the dower rights of the husband are the same as those of the wife: a third part of all lands owned by the decedent at any time during the marriage that have not been relinquished in legal form. In some states, as in Illinois, the surviving spouse may elect, instead of the provisions specified in the will, the rights given under the dower act and, in addition, one-third of the personal estate after claims of creditors against it have been met if there are children surviving, one-half if there are none; or, as a substitute for dower, one-third absolutely of the net real and personal estate if children survive, one-half if there are none. A few states protect the rights of the widow in the estate of the husband but make no corresponding provision for a surviving husband. The latter may seem to be a departure from the principle of equal treatment, but, in fact, the position of a disinherited or inadequately provided for widow would usually be far more serious than that of a widower.

Inheritance laws in all states determine the claims of a surviving spouse as well as of other relatives of the person who dies without leaving a will. In most jurisdictions husband and wife inherit under similar provisions. When either is favored, it is usually the wife. In many states the surviving spouse receives the whole personal estate if there are no descendants. In fewer does he or she receive the entire estate in lands.

THE COMMUNITY-PROPERTY SYSTEM

There remains to be examined the law in those states where some form of the community-property principle obtains. In those jurisdictions there is or may be property which is his, that which is hers, and that which is theirs. What is theirs is determined not by a decision on the part of either spouse to place it in that category but by the law with respect to property acquired by a married person. In general, property acquired during marriage (by either spouse) "through gainful pursuits or through the expenditure of skill or industry" is community property. Put in a negative way, property owned by either spouse at the time of marriage or received afterward by gift, devise, or inheritance is his or her separate estate. All other is community. The husband, however, is the curator of community property. Its control and administration are in his hands. Thus he controls the wife's earnings and the income from her separate estate unless she is expressly given control. It is his duty under the law to administer the community for the benefit of the wife and family, but usually as long as he is capable of management the wife has no control. The wife's consent in some jurisdictions is required to certain transactions, such as mortgaging or sale of real estate or gift of community property.

The community-property system is older than the common law. It is said to be Teutonic in origin and was the governing system among Germanic people into modern times. It was carried by the Visigoths into Spain and had developed in France with the exception of Normandy prior to the end of the thirteenth century. Thus the community-property system governed the property rights of husband and wife on the continent of western Europe as did the common law in England. In those areas within the United States settled by French or Spanish people and that were once under the flags of France or Spain—Louisiana, California, and the Southwest—the community-property system was therefore indigenous. It was in force in certain states when they were admitted to the Union and has continued with statutory modifications.

The law in eight states is based upon the community-property principle: Louisiana, Arizona, New Mexico, Texas, California, Nevada, Washington, and Idaho. During the 1940's community-property laws in some form were passed in five other states. One of these laws, that of Pennsylvania, was held to violate the state constitution, three were repealed, and one, that of Nebraska, so amended that community property exists only upon proof that the assets in question are not part of the separate estate of husband or wife. These temporary additions to the list of community-property states were due in most if not all cases not to a desire to improve the law governing marital property but to secure for the married members of their population an income-tax advantage possessed by those residing in community-property states. The Supreme Court had held that community income, though it be all the earnings of one spouse, could be split for income-tax purposes. Thus the total tax payable by a married couple in a community-property state was generally lower than that of one with the same income in a noncommunity-property state. Since the federal income-tax law now permits an equivalent splitting, this advantage no longer holds.

Each community-property state (and the courts therein) has made its own special modification or application of the community-property principle. In most states income from separate property is separate, and in Idaho, and under certain conditions in Nevada and New Mexico, the wife, dying before her husband, has no power to dispose of any part of the community property by will, although, if she survives the husband, he cannot deprive her of her half by will. Varying rules govern the disposition of the community property of the person who dies intestate. In some states all goes to the surviving spouse; in others, it goes to the spouse only in the absence of children or other related persons.

The difference in the legal position of either husband or wife in the community-property and other jurisdictions depends upon the precise statutory arrangements and judicial decisions in each state. In one important respect the two systems are similar. The husband is head of the family. He chooses the domicile and has the responsibility of family support. The majority of the community-property states impose mutual obligations of support upon both husband and wife, but his is the primary responsibility. As in the common-law states the marriage partners may exercise their discretion as to property ownership. By prenuptial or post-nuptial agreements they may make separate property out of what would otherwise be community. In some states the common-law devices of joint tenancy and tenancy in common are possible. The difference between the two systems is greatest where the strict community principle prevails. In that case personal earnings and income from the separate estate of each spouse become a part of the community. Upon the dissolution of the marriage each comes into unrestricted possession of his or her half of the community, and each has unrestricted power to testamentary disposition of each half. If either spouse has rights of the nature of dower, the difference between the two systems is lessened. The difference between the two systems would be especially marked if the spouses jointly controlled the community: that is, if the wife as well as the husband could bind the community as principal. In fact, in no jurisdiction having the community-property system is there a true partnership in the legal sense any more than there is in any other. As Justice Holmes noted, "The community is a partnership that begins when it ends."[17]

SPECIAL PROBLEMS OF THE COMMUNITY-PROPERTY SYSTEM

The community-property system presents three special problems. One is that presented by the intermingling of assets that is likely to occur during a marriage so that what is the husband's separate estate, the wife's separate estate, or the community may be difficult to establish. Antenuptial inventories reduce the problem, as do broad and inclusive definitions of community. A second problem is not inherent in the system but arises from the fact that many states operate under a different system, and a conflict in laws with respect to ownership may arise. In general, domicile governs the ownership of movable property and situs that of immovables. If the domicile is changed from a noncommunity to a community-property state, as often occurs, the status of the movable property that has already been acquired does not change.

17. *Arnett* v. *Reade*, 220 U.S. 319 (1910).

Thus, property which is separate property under the law of the noncommunity state under which it was acquired remains separate—likewise community property according to the law of the community property state in which it was acquired will be recognized as the property of both spouses in a noncommunity state to which they thereafter remove. The foregoing is true even though the form of the property is changed after it is brought to the new domicile.[18]

"If community funds are invested in a non-community state, the rights of the spouses are protected by creating something in the nature of a trust in the investment. Separate funds invested in a community state retain their separate character."[19]

What is his, what hers, and what theirs is important not only to the two spouses but to creditors looking for funds against which to levy their claims. Their question is: What property is liable for a particular debt? The principle that the separate property of one spouse is not liable for the antenuptial debts of the other is one uniformly established, but there is little accord regarding the liability of community property. Some states make the entire community liable for the husband's but not the wife's antenuptial debts, and some make it liable for either. In some states the liability of the community may be enforced only after dissolution of the marriage and the division of community assets.

The general principle is that all debts contracted on behalf of and for the benefit of the community are claims against the community. Such would be all obligations incurred to secure family necessaries and other goods for family use. If the community funds are insufficient, to what other assets may the creditors lay claim? For food, clothing, and similar items the husband's separate estate would be obligated, since he has primary responsibility for support. The wife may of course pledge her separate estate, or by statutory provision, as in Washington, the living expenses of the family and the education of children may be charges upon the property of either spouse, and they may be sued jointly or severally. If the community debts are incurred in business transactions and community funds are insufficient, the claim would lie against the separate estate of the contracting parties, usually the husband. A second question is the reverse of the foregoing: What property is liable for the separate debts of husband or wife? In some states it is held that only the separate property of either is liable for debts contracted for one spouse's individual

18. W. H. de Funiak, *Principles of Community Property* (Chicago: Callaghan & Co., 1943), I, 252–53. See De Funiak also for property removed to or acquired in a state other than the state of domicile.

19. W. L. Nossaman, "The Origin and Incidents of the Community Property System," *New Jersey Law Journal*, LXXI (February 12, 1948), 51.

or separate benefit. In a larger number the community property is also responsible for the husband's debts even when incurred for his separate interest.

DISSOLUTION OF MARRIAGE BY DIVORCE

The dissolution of marriage by divorce presents so many grave problems especially if there are children that the economic results for the persons affected have received comparatively little attention. What rules govern or should govern the distribution of assets between the spouses, and what claims should either have upon the future income of the other? An award of property or order for payment of specified weekly or monthly sums is called "alimony." The former might be regarded either as a settlement of the property rights of the parties or as serving the same purpose as the allowance. Alimony may include both a property award and a future income. The right to income may be conditional, and the amount subject to review and alteration. Only the wife may have a right to alimony or either husband or wife.

Divorce of parents does not affect their moral and legal duty to care for and support their children. The custody of the children usually goes to the mother. That arrangement is usually less disruptive to the lives of the children, and she can continue to provide care. The father in that case theoretically would continue his usual role of providing financial support. If he also supports the mother while she is caring for the children, the economic situation might seem to be little affected by the divorce.

Who actually supports the children of divorced parents is a matter about which little or nothing is known. There is evidence that in many cases the father does not support; in others, that his support is partial; and, in others, that his contribution continues for only a short period. When he does not support or his contribution is inadequate, there are several possibilities. One is that the mother supports entirely or partially. The high percentage of divorced mothers who were earning was noted in chapter iv. These mothers may be providing singly what two parents normally are supposed to provide. Another possibility is that other relatives come to the children's assistance either by money contribution or by sharing their home with the mother and children. Many divorced mothers remarry. In that case the stepfather may assume their support. One fact is known about the economic situation of the children of divorced parents. Many are supported by the state through the federally supplemented aid to dependent children.

In most cases the ability, and often the inclination, of the father to contribute to the support of the children of the broken marriage declines.

Since he lives separately, the total burden upon his income is greater than when a joint household is maintained. The divorced father is more likely to remarry than the divorced mother. His income must in that case cover the expense of two households. Since he is no longer in close touch with his children and aware of their needs, his inclination to provide for them generously will often decline. The requirements of his new household, which may also include children, are likely to take first place both in his mind and in that of the second wife. The proportion of men with income adequate to meet the expenses of two households is certainly not large.

The conclusion is that the children of divorced parents are usually economically disadvantaged by the divorce. Both parents are adversely affected if both meet their responsibilities. If the mother has the responsibility not only for care but for all or a large part of the financial support, she is particularly disadvantaged. She is likely also to find that her earning power is relatively low if she left the labor market at the time of her marriage or earned only occasionally thereafter.

RIGHTS AND RESPONSIBILITIES OF DIVORCING SPOUSES

Quite aside from their responsibilities as parents, what are the financial rights and responsibilities of the divorcing spouses as such? In the community-property states what are their respective claims to such property and in those states as well as in the common-law states may either establish a claim upon the separate estate of the other? Does the husband's duty to support continue after the dissolution of the marriage, and, if so, is it conditional or unconditional? If property is to be divided or support provided, on what basis is the division made or the amount to be paid for support determined? As with respect to the custody of children, the court granting the divorce, more and more frequently in the larger cities a special court with jurisdiction over problems involving domestic relations, is authorized to make these decisions. Even when no alimony is asked for and the division of assets and other financial arrangements are a matter of mutual agreement, they must have the approval of the court.

The court in exercising its discretion takes into account the circumstances of each particular case. Among these circumstances is one that has nothing to do with the needs or the financial condition of either spouse or his or her contribution to the estate. It is rather what might be called the morality of the husband or wife or their relative responsibility for the failure of the marriage. In only two of the community-property states must this property be divided equally between the spouses whatever the grounds of divorce. In theory no marriage is dissolved unless one partner is at fault or incapable of meeting the responsibilities of marriage. The divorce is granted to the innocent partner. The other is guilty of the fault which is the ground for divorce. Divorce, theoretically, is not granted merely because one or both wish it. Actually, as is well known, the legal concept of divorce is quite different from the way it is commonly regarded. The divorce proceedings conform to the legal technicalities but do not always disclose what has actually led to the suit for dissolution. The wife usually files suit, but it may be because of the husband's chivalry, or because she alone has grounds for or wishes a divorce, or it may be because he has asked her to "give" him a divorce, or because neither wishes to continue the marriage.

The theory that marital misconduct or fault should affect the amount of the alimony award has one or both of two implications. One is that alimony is a compensation for the right of support lost by the dissolution of the marriage, with the right disappearing if the one claiming it is at fault and has not met marital obligations. The other is that the alimony award is a punishment of the guilty partner. It is a penalty for misconduct and at the same time a reward of the innocent partner for fulfilment of the obligations of marriage. Even if the divorce proceedings disclosed the true reasons for the divorce, it is questionable whether judgments in terms of relative guilt or blame can be made and, if so, whether monetary fines or rewards are appropriate.

WHAT SHOULD THE LAW BE?

What changes, if any, should be made in the law pertaining to marital property in all or in certain jurisdictions? Are the rights and obligations of each spouse what they should be during the marriage? What should be the rights of the surviving spouse when the marriage is broken by death? On what basis should the property be divided in the case of divorce, and what responsibility should either spouse have for the future support of the other? Is the community-property principle to be preferred to that which prevails in other jurisdictions? For discussion of these issues one must go largely to the law journals and commentaries. Outside of legal circles little attention has been given to the system of familial property.

Many if not most of the facts that would be useful in assessing the law as it stands are lacking. The actual practices of married couples with respect to the control of income and assets have not been the subject of investigation in this country. Who actually controls the disposition of income from various sources, the relation between law and practice, in whose name existing property stands and who administers it, extent of knowledge of legal rights and responsibilities, satisfaction of husband and wife with their respective roles in the handling of money—all are unknown. Very little is known concerning the property adjustments and alimony awards at the time of divorce, although these are a matter of record. The Johns Hopkins Institute of Law made a beginning at furnishing such information in a study of the data available in the office of the clerk of court in Maryland and Ohio.[20] This study made clear that "the entire problem is substantial; that it reaches many social and economic classes; that, in addition to a comparatively few cases where the accusation of an [alimony] 'racket' may be made, there are many in which the funds provide only a meagre basis for support of wife and children."[21]

In the opinion of many who have made this matter the subject of special study, review and appraisal of the law concerning marital property are long overdue. A committee of the Columbia Law School in a report on *The Family and Familial Property* in 1927 said: "It is therefore the conclusion of your committee that the approach to familial law is at least two or three decades behind the present state of wisdom as to business law."[22] Harriet S. Daggett, professor of law at Louisiana State University, has written: "Nowhere has the law lagged so perceptibly and so distressingly as in the field of family relations."[23]

The first question that arises in any attempt to appraise the law as it stands in any jurisdiction, or any proposed change, is: What criteria should be used? One finds in the law journals various attempts to formulate the principles upon which the law should be based. One writer starts with the proposition that the law governing marital property embodies a concept concerning women. They may be regarded, he says, "as the weaker sex, best served by benevolent domination or as individuals with rights."[24] If the former, their status is that of the recipients of gifts; if the latter, that of those whose claims are independent of another's discretion and generosity. The law which expresses this latter concept must, this writer believes, place the marriage partners in a position of "complete equality." He adds to his argument the thesis that the sharing which is a

---

20. See L. C. Marshall and Geoffrey May, *The Divorce Court*, Vol. I: *Maryland* (Baltimore: Johns Hopkins Press, 1932); Vol. II: *Ohio* (Baltimore: Johns Hopkins Press, 1933).

21. J. S. Bradway, "Alimony: Foreword," *Law and Contemporary Problems*, VI (spring, 1939), 184.

22. Quoted in report on *A Research in Family Law* under the direction of A. C. Jacobs and R. C. Angell (1930), p. 3.

23. H. S. Daggett, "Division of Property upon Dissolution of Marriage," *Law and Contemporary Problems*, VI (spring, 1939), 225.

24. R. R. B. Powell, "Community Property: A Critique of Its Regulation of Intra-family Relations," *Washington Law Review*, XI (1936), 12.

part of marriage is on the best basis when the partners are independent entities before the law. The degree of equality in the treatment of the marriage partners is not, however, his only criterion of a satisfactory system of family law. It must meet two other standards. It must provide adequate protection to the parties with whom the family deals, that is, those from whom it buys and those to whom it sells; and it must be simple, otherwise uncertainty and frequent litigation ensue. Another statement of the criteria to be used in evaluating a system of marital law is as follows. The law should be such, says this writer, again in a law journal, as to promote family solidarity, make for a sound development of individual personality, and provide for a satisfactory adjustment of rights among the family members and with respect to third persons.[25] The "third persons" would again be outsiders having claims against or business transactions with the marriage partners. Still another guiding principle is that suggested by Jacobs in his discussion of "Marital Property" in the *Social Science Encyclopedia*. Family law, he says, is par excellence customary law. It succeeds when it best gives expression to customary modes of living.

It seems fairly clear that all those quoted have in substance the same standards. The position of the married woman under the law must harmonize with her status in other respects and with the prevailing philosophy in regard to personal rights and obligations. The law must reflect practice, since prevailing practice reflects the prevailing concepts of individual rights and proper human relations. The law is to be judged by the family relations it supports or promotes. It is to be judged by its effect upon the family members as individuals. It must also be judged by its effect upon those with whom the family deals in the process of earning and spending and thus upon the economic life of the community. The crucial problem is the reconciliation of these standards, once it is decided what type of law achieves each objective.

The common-law system was long extolled by commentators as reflecting those relations between husband and wife that conformed both to the Scriptures and to natural law. It ultimately came to exemplify those relations that were disappearing, disapproved as inequitable, and the source of friction and unhappiness. It expressed a concept of women once approved, later generally rejected. The possible effect of the legal position of married women upon personality and behavior traits should be especially examined. Could it be that many of those attributes and modes of

25. Charles Horowitz, "Conflict of Law Problems in Community Property," *Washington Law Review*, XI (1936), 121.

behaving that came to be considered characteristic of wives and thus of the female sex in general arose primarily from their position as recipients of gifts rather than as those with financial rights and reponsibilities? From the fact that their control over money was a function of another's discretion who might be cajoled to be generous or otherwise led into parting with funds? Would we not expect that the personality development of the recipient of gifts would be different from that of one with rights? And that the personality of the giver, the one with discretion, with power to be generous, would also be shaped somewhat by this role? The common-law system, however, made the creditor's position easy. There was in substance but one person and one set of funds to which he need look to meet his claims.

How shall the system in the common-law states where the disabilities of married women have been removed, and husband and wife are equal in rights and obligations, be assessed? They are equal in legal right to earn, to spend what they earn, and to hold and manage property. In fact, they are not equal in power to earn or to accumulate. Many wives are wholly or largely dependent upon the husband's income. They have the right to support but with the husband legally in the position to determine how and where he will support as well as the expenditures and provision for the children. Except as he has acted to make ownership of property joint or to transfer title, assets acquired during the marriage are likely to be a part of his separate estate. In case of divorce unless awarded property as alimony or by his consent, she would have none no matter how long the marriage had lasted or how great her part in accumulation. The position of the widowed woman in these states has been safeguarded by limitations upon the husband's power of bequest. Her share if she elects to exercise her rights may be at no one's discretion. Nor is her share related to the duration of the marriage. It derives purely from status and rights based upon it. The widow, unlike the divorced woman, moreover, feels no sense of guilt in taking her share as often does the divorced woman in asking for a property award, nor is there any disapproval of her taking it.

The community-property system is often described as that which best meets present-day standards with respect to family relations and as giving the husband and wife their proper position as individuals. Jacobs says that, even where no legal system of community property is recognized, the practice of the middle classes approximates it.[26] Mrs. Daggett maintains that "the theory of community property presents the soundest and most equitable base of all systems. . . . When the earnings, income, and

26. "Marital Property" (art.), *Social Science Encyclopedia.*

assets of the two individuals vest jointly during coverture a real economic, as well as conjugal partnership, results."²⁷ The theory of community property is only imperfectly realized, Mrs. Daggett has argued, in the so-called community-property states either because the law has been encumbered with what she calls "common law legislative trimmings" or because the legislatures or the courts have not brought it into accord with modern conditions. The system in Louisiana seems to her "most basically sound, most equitable—possibly because it is true parent stock and has been least weakened by the influence of the Common Law idea of marital rights."²⁸ Especially is this true in its treatment of the married persons when the marriage is broken by death or divorce. Upon dissolution by death one-half vests of right in the surviving spouse. Both husband and wife may make testamentary disposition of one-half of the community as well as of his or her separate estate. Thus the inalienable right of the surviving spouse is confined to one-half of those assets which were accumulated during the marriage. However, "if one spouse dies, leaving the other 'relatively poor,' the latter may demand . . . a forced share of separate property, common property, or both, so that his or her financial station may not too abruptly descend."²⁹ The position of the two spouses in case of divorce is closely analogous to that when death breaks the marriage bond. "No matter what the marital wrong may have been . . . the property of the community belongs, half and half, to the spouses, guilty or innocent."³⁰ The contrast with the common-law states should be noted. If assets have been accumulated during the marriage, other than as gifts or bequests, one-half goes as a matter of right to each spouse, not as a property award by the court or by agreement by the spouses. Nor, as in many so-called community-property states, is the ownership touched by the marital "faults" that led to the dissolution of the marriage. The right to ask for alimony still remains either in the form of an award of a gross sum from common or separate property or periodic payments from future income.

Should the right to apply for and to be granted alimony continue, and, if so, what should determine the amount? Alimony might be considered as analogous to the property rights of a surviving spouse when the marriage is broken by death, designed to avoid hardship from an abrupt descent in

27. *Op. cit.*, p. 230.

28. H. S. Daggett, *The Community Property System of Louisiana* (Baton Rouge: State University Press, 1945), p. 5.

29. *Ibid.*, p. 315; see also *ibid.*, chap. xvi.

30. *Ibid.*, p. 327.

financial status or the greater hardship that might come from the lack of adequate funds for maintenance. Neither concept carries with it the implication that the divorced spouse has indefinitely a claim to support. If the earning power of the wife has been adversely affected by the marriage, alimony might be considered a social protection against undue hardship from this cause. Should the award or its amount be affected by the guilt of the divorced spouse? Or should the idea of punishment or reward enter into the court's reasoning? Strong argument is now being made that the entire law of divorce should be recast on a new basis. An Interprofessional Committee set up by the Bar Association has suggested that for "guilt" of one partner as a criterion for dissolution of the marriage should be substituted "what is best for the family." With such recasting the matter of alimony would be placed in a new setting and the award lose its punitive character.

There remains the question: Does the wife have greater equality under the community-property system while the marriage endures than in the common-law states? If husband and wife are treated alike, the earnings and income of each from all sources fall into the community. If the husband then controls and administers, what of the wife's position and her sense of financial independence and responsibility? In some of the community-property laws passed in recent years to reduce the federal income tax of the more well-to-do citizens the wife was given control of that portion of the community the title to which stood in her name or which consisted of her earnings or income from her separate property. Various other devices to improve the wife's position are found. Her income may be excluded from the community, while the husband's is not, or her consent may be required to certain transactions. But the exclusion of her income from the community, giving her control over it if it remains therein, or of community property in her name, does not help the wife who is not earning, without separate property, or has no community property in her name.

The issue of single or dual control of community property cannot be resolved without taking into account other criteria for a satisfactory law, besides equity as between the marriage partners. The law must also be simple and operate equitably with respect to third parties. Jacobs has said, "In a sense we have an institutional conflict, the rights of creditors versus the rights of the wife."[31] The interests of third parties may demand that one spouse represent the family. It may also be argued that the system in the common-law states presents less practical difficulties in the

31. *A Research in Family Law*, pp. 649–50.

family's business transactions than does the community system and thus is to be preferred.

Proposals for change in the existing system of marital property laws present a different problem from that of drawing up an ideal system *de novo*. Against change from one system to another, even if that worked greater equity, is the argument that it would carry with it the cost of a period of uncertainty and increased litigation until claims to specific assets complicated by the transition were adjusted. Yet, if research into relevant facts and consideration of principles involved so indicate, changes in the law must be made.

CHAPTER XVI

PLANNING EXPENDITURE OF INCOME

WHEN claims upon the social product are in the form of money income, the recipient's real income may take whatever form he desires. The dollars represented may be converted (in the absence of rationing) into whatever goods and services are available in the market up to the limits set by prices and total dollar cost. Money income expands vastly not only the recipient's range of choice among consumption possibilities, that is, the form in which he takes his real income, but also when he shall take it. Dollars are not perishable. Consumption or acquisition of goods and services may be postponed. The money-income recipient may save or spend now. Fear of an upward price movement or expectation of a down-ward movement may affect this decision. With stable prices other considerations only would prevail.

The alternative uses of time and energy in direct production of goods and services are relatively limited. They are limited by the resources and the technical competence of the worker in question. Hours or days of time, moreover, cannot be hoarded. They must be used as they pass. The goods provided, if not perishable, may be for future use, but their form and amount cannot be altered when the time for consumption arrives. Dollars saved, however, can be used for the purposes deemed most urgent when tomorrow arrives.

INCOME RECEIPTS VERSUS OUTLAYS THROUGH TIME

Receipts and outlays of money income are not and cannot be completely synchronized over time. If the income were the same day after day, received daily and expected to remain at the same level, we would not spend as we go for many reasons. Such "hand-to-mouth" buying is wasteful of the time of the buyer and increases the costs of the seller. Some needs arise only weekly or monthly or once a year. Some things used daily are paid for weekly, monthly, or quarterly. Furthermore, the cost of some items exceeds the day's earnings, and we must therefore set aside from the current income sufficient to acquire them at a future date.

Money income, in fact, is not usually received as earned or accrued but weekly, biweekly, monthly, or quarterly. The longer the interval between payments, the more necessary is the "husbanding" of funds to make them last through the period if feast is not to be followed by famine. There must be some taking thought for the morrow. Complicating the problem and necessitating further forethought and planning is the fact that the income payments are sometimes at irregular intervals and often in different amounts. Periods of high income may be followed by periods of low or no income. Such irregularity in receipts may be the usual course of events or a possibility that must be taken into account.

ARE EXPENDITURES PLANNED?

To what degree and to what extent are expenditures planned? The answer to that question depends in the first place upon what is meant by "planning." Does it mean a systematic weighing of alternative uses of the total income expected over a period of time, followed by a similar consideration before each purchase in the light of the over-all plan? All expenditures *pro forma* represent a choice among alternatives, since choices open to the spender are not made. Are they, however, acts based upon deliberation or upon impulse or habit?

Objection may be made to the concept of spending as a considered choice among alternatives on the ground that for many outlays there is in a practical sense no alternative. There are no pros and cons to weigh. There are, for example, at any moment of time the commitments one has already made. One may be honor bound or legally bound to meet them. They represent, however, decisions previously made from which one cannot escape without sacrifice of money, good will, or self-respect. The present decision is not to make this sacrifice. Also there are those things that are necessaries. By definition they are what one must have. They admit of no alternative. If the income will encompass only their purchase, in what sense are there alternatives? There are alternatives in the sense that there are degrees of necessity, and, if a less necessary item is purchased, it follows that one more necessary is foregone. It is those in the economic situation described who might be expected to weigh alternatives most carefully. When the margin between the cost of essentials and income is narrow, special concern lest the whole coat could not be cut from the cloth would be expected and special care to see that no one category of expense took dollars that preferably would have gone for another. We may say that as to the purchase of food we have no choice, and similarly with clothing. But there is choice as to the specific kinds and amounts, and the total outlay may be kept within limits.

Exception may also be taken to the statement that money income offers the possibility of choice among a wide range of goods and services. In fact, most consumers' knowledge of what is available is limited in spite of various devices that sellers employ to bring information to them. No one could know all the alternatives that are theoretically or actually existent, nor could anyone when actually buying usually go far afield or consider all the possible alternatives.

Observation of one's own and others' behavior will, however, lead to the conclusion that extensive weighing and balancing of one possible expenditure against another constantly goes on. Scarcity of resources makes it necessary to sacrifice some things desired in order to obtain those for which the desire is greater. The exactness and divisibility of money income, the postponability of its use, these attributes previously discussed, all tend to enforce a consciousness that spending is an either-or process. In a real sense there is a great deal of planning and replanning of expenditures. This is not to say that the expenditure of all funds expected to come in over a long period is completely planned or that, if assumptions made as to future income, prices, and needs prove inaccurate, there is immediate review and revision. Rather there is what one might call partial planning of the expenditure of part of the income, possibly over a short period only, or possibly in a rough fashion over a relatively long one.

BUDGETING

A considered plan for the expenditure of the whole income over a long period is probably relatively infrequent. Such a plan could rarely be made or kept in one's head but must be on paper. In that form it constitutes what is usually called a budget, and the planning becomes budgeting. Strong arguments can be made for such a procedure. The argument for it rests not on the advantages of a plan versus no plan but on the advantages of complete versus partial planning. Although few families or individuals may report that they budget their incomes, many would say at the same time that they plan their expenditures. They plan to paint their house, to buy a new car, to wear an old coat for another season, to increase life insurance, and so on. They reduce food expenditures to release funds for other purposes. The argument for the complete plan is that it permits a review of the whole pattern all at one time. All parts of the spending plan are tied inescapably together, and they can be reviewed in relation to one another. Scrimping at one time with relatively lavish outlay at another can be more readily avoided if the plan is adhered to. What is involved in the accumulation of funds to meet large occasional outlays or to meet debt payments may be more readily seen, to what extent such subtractions will reduce other outlays, and what outlays might be foregone for these purposes. Budgeting is a process of allocating income among various uses. Thus limits are set for the major categories of expense. Partial planning continues within the limits set: the planning of the weekly food outlays, the clothing outlays, and so on. The budget is the master-plan, not a detailed plan for day-to-day expenditures.

WHEN IS BUDGETING MOST IMPORTANT?

Budget-making is more important under some circumstances than others. The new family without experience to guide its expenditure clearly needs to plan far more than the family that has a well-established expenditure pattern. The latter knows approximately what its food, clothing, shelter, and so on will cost if established habits are maintained. The family that moves to a new place needs to obtain some advance information concerning prices and re-examine its budget if it is to avoid mistakes in expenditure.

Families when questioned concerning financial policy frequently report that they used to make a budget but do so no longer. This statement does not necessarily imply that they found no value in budgeting. Rather it may mean that these families no longer have need for the formal budget. Their manner of living and habits of expenditure may have become so standardized that they follow a similar plan year after year without deliberate revaluation and revision. A change in income or in size of the family might again make formal budgeting necessary. The family that has incurred debts or made commitments to pay definite sums in the future is also likely to be particularly interested in budgeting. An upward movement in prices or a downward movement in the income level always brings a flare-up of interest in budgeting.

The importance of budgeting to the low-income family is evident. The smaller the income, the more important is it that a "less essential" or "nonessential" does not take the place of a "more essential." Special argument can be made, however, for expenditure planning by families with moderately high incomes. Many years ago Mrs. Abel pointed out that those families are above that income line "where a man earns what he can and spends as he must." "Are they to feel straitened on an income larger than that on which three-fourths of the population live?"[1]

This family has to a considerable degree the power of choice over its expenditures. That is, after meeting the minimum requirements for food, shelter and clothing they

1. Mary Hinman Abel, *Successful Family Life on a Moderate Income* (Philadelphia: J. B. Lippincott Co., 1921), pp. 1–2.

may dispose of the rest of their income as they will, as in adding to the attractions of the table, in buying better dress, in providing more spacious living quarters, or in gaining that feeling of freedom and relief from care which comes from provision against illness or old age; they may help in some form of public welfare or buy books or hear good music. The main thing . . . is that none of these outgoes shall be considered necessities, but as desirable additions which must be weighed against each other since all can not be obtained.

. . . If a line can be drawn between need and desires the family may realize its possession of a surplus to be spent according to choice, and this is the very foundation of that education in comparative values which will raise them in the scale of living. Poverty has been called an automatic standardizer; the outlay is dictated by the absolute needs of life.[2]

WHAT BUDGETING DOES AND DOES NOT ACHIEVE

It is important for many reasons to have clearly in mind what planning expenditures beforehand does and does not achieve. In essence it is the method by which it is sought to insure that the income that becomes available over a period secures what those who benefit from it want most, to prevent the substitution of a good that they deem less essential or that is less desired for one more essential or more desired. It is an attempt over time to maximize the satisfactions derived from the allocation of income among its wide range of alternative uses. The perfect budget is one in which no dollar if moved to another use, thus giving the user command of a larger bundle of some goods and a smaller of another at some time during the period, would enhance the satisfaction derived from the total. The difficulties in the way of achieving this perfection will be discussed later. It is in essence, however, the purpose of all such planning. The decision to spend carries with it the implication that this particular use is more important than any other that could be made then or later.

Budgeting is obviously no magic process that resolves all economic problems of the family. It does not make money income more adequate or market selection more intelligent. It cannot insure that all future financial hazards are adequately met or that the wisest action has been taken to safeguard against them. It is not uniquely designed to promote saving. It aids those who "want to save but can't" only as preplanning tends to rule out expenditures for those things less desired. Nor is it a device that per se brings wisdom in spending or places the level of living qualitatively on a higher plane. Budgeting, in other words, cannot take the place of the long process of cultivation of tastes, development of standards, and acquisition of information concerning needs. A family may be most meticulous in its accounting, most careful in planning its expenditures, and still may be

2. *Ibid.*, pp. 2–3.

living in a manner most objectionable to the person of cultivated taste and informed mind. Budgeting may lead a family to evaluate its standards of consumption, but it does not necessarily do so. It depends upon whether a view of the expenditure pattern as a whole, the relative importance given to various goods, leads to a critical appraisal that would otherwise never have taken place. The fact that budgeting necessitates decision as to the most essential items may lead to a taking thought, perhaps even to a search for information. The budgeting process may make the family conscious of its preferences and bring about deliberation concerning them.

DETERRENTS TO BUDGETING

There are obstacles to budgeting which to an incalculable extent block its adoption as a common family practice. One such obstacle is great uncertainty about the future course of income. Why plan for the future when the likelihood that the plan can be carried out is so uncertain? How plan when an essential element is unknown? The families where budgeting is most prevalent are probably those in receipt of salaries or other income the amount of which is definitely known for some time in advance and which comes in at regular intervals.

As regularity and certainty of income facilitate budgeting, so do regularity and certainty of outlays. It was pointed out in chapter x that the expense of medical and hospital care is nonbudgetable, since the amount to be set aside out of current income is unknown. Fixed, regularly recurring items, payable from current income, are easiest to allow for. Instalment payments are certain; industrial insurance can be paid out of current income. There is evidence of an increase in practices that make budgeting easier. In an English study of wartime spending and saving it was pointed out that the economic arrangements of many families were on a weekly basis.[3] Income was received weekly and payments likewise made weekly—payments for coal, rent, "hire-purchase," insurance, trade-union dues. There were also many deductions by arrangement, as, for income tax and savings, especially National savings (equivalent to our Series E bond payments). Informal arrangements for weekly collection of definite amounts by an appointed person were frequent. Thus there were holiday clubs, Christmas clubs, boot clubs, and even "perm" clubs. In a sense such arrangements made formal budgeting unnecessary, that is, long-term planning and a formidable amount of paperwork. Ignorance of

3. Charles Madge, *Pattern of War-time Spending and Saving* (Cambridge: Cambridge University Press, 1943), p. 41.

what is meant by "budgeting" or its association with elaborate techniques and records clearly is among the reasons for failure to budget.

Attitudes and temperaments must also be reckoned with in accounting for the infrequency of budgeting. There are those who like the role of free spenders. They think of a budget as cramping or limiting. They associate it with penny-pinching and other unpleasant personal traits. There are also some who are emotionally immature so far as financial matters are concerned. They do not want to face what a budget or its accompaniment, account-keeping, discloses. Moreover, a budget is sometimes a device by which a husband attempts to control the spending of a wife, or a wife that of a husband. The budget and the plan for spending become a part of a major or minor disturbance in family relations. Even when this is not the case, budgeting is often associated with an undesired change in expenditures. To make a budget is made synonymous with "Let's reform; let us change radically our manner of living." Touched lightly here are several matters that need further analysis.

WHO DETERMINES HOW THE FAMILY INCOME IS SPENT?

Up to this point expenditure planning has been discussed in rather general terms without asking who determines or should determine expenditure. The unit for which income must provide is usually composed of two or more persons. The income may come from only one or from several persons. When the family includes two or more income recipients, should the total received by all members be budgeted as a whole and who should control its disposition? Should the system be different from that which is suitable for a one-income family? When adult sons and daughters are among the income recipients, their economic independence might be considered a desirable goal. By this standard, having contributed their proportionate or agreed-upon share of the joint household expenses, they would be free agents in the disposition of the remainder. When both husband and wife are income recipients, should this fact alter the system by which financial resources are allocated? If the wife bases her claim to a voice in the disposition of the income on the ground that she contributes a part, or even claims the right completely to control what she earns, and if the husband recognizes her right to a voice only on this ground, the guiding principle thus avowed is that he who contributes should control. Thus in the one-income families authority would rest with the one who contributed the income, usually the husband. Is this principle sound? What is suggested is that the standard to be applied to the two-income family when the two recipients are husband and wife cannot be different from the standard for the family with but one income source.

Any one of several arrangements is possible when the husband is the only income recipient. The wife may not know the amount of his paycheck, business profits, or income derived from other sources. The husband may dole out what the wife is to use, with or without any suggestion as to how she is to use it. He may pay bills she contracts with or without setting definite limits to the amount for each purpose. Since he cannot avoid paying, spending more is then a way of getting more, as cajoling, threats, or favors may be a way of increasing the dole. Since the wife's knowledge of what is too little or too much is necessarily limited, the system does little for the development of her sense of economic responsibility, or for family harmony so far as money matters are concerned. The husband's role is one of authority. He is the generous or nongenerous giver and provider to a degree determined by the amount of the doles or the freedom with which his credit may be used. A second system is to give the wife a regular allowance. This allowance may cover only her personal expenses, or it may cover specified household expenses as well as those of the children. The initial planning then is his: how much to allow her for these purposes. She may then plan the disposition of the amount allowed and he what is retained for other purposes.

A third system is the reverse of the first two. The husband may turn over his pay or other income to the wife, and she may apportion the whole —so much to him for his personal expenses, the remainder to be used as she sees fit. Still a fourth system would be that of joint control, a pooling of income with knowledge by both of amount from all sources. The amount going to each for personal expenses, as well as the pattern for allocation of the remainder as between saving and current use and between different categories of consumption, would be jointly determined. Who pays the bills or who does the buying does not alter the fact of joint control. Along with joint control usually goes the joint checking or savings account. Actually joint control is not so much a matter of certain forms as of a sense of who's deciding, of responsibility, and of agreement. Joint control means complete disclosure of income facts and agreement, even if the agreement is to give one partner a wide range of discretion or the "say" over a wide range of expenditures.

The arguments for the patriarchal system, the husband the lord and master, are several. Since he earned the income, it may seem just that he should control its disposition. The patriarchal system may be harmonious with the roles of husband and wife in other respects, fit their respective temperaments, and make for maximum happiness. It is true that the system fits one type of culture. The question is: Does it fit ours? It fosters the development of a certain type of personality, but is it the type of personality for men or for women that we wish to develop? The husband may assume financial control in some cases because of the economic immaturity and irresponsibility of the wife. The problem would then be how to insure that few lack the requisite maturity and sense of responsibility. With proper training and experience would not this state of arrested childhood become less frequent? There may be born "leaners," but whether they are more frequent among females than among males is unknown.

There is some evidence of the spread of the matriarchal system. Occasionally the assumption of control by the wife is based upon the irresponsibility of the husband. Such an arrangement for this reason is considered, however, a deviation from the norm. Other reasons for the system, for the assumption that the model husband turns over the paycheck to the wife and that she decides upon its disposition, are rarely formulated. It presumably is based in part on the theory that she knows best. She is the expert. Since she does the buying, the decisions as to what to spend money for should be hers. It is the financial equivalent of giving all decisions in regard to the children into her hands. In a sense it is a case of the manager taking over all policy decisions. A similar tendency appears in business and in government as managers and administrative agencies become policy-makers. The system also possibly represents a view as to division of labor. The husband earns the money; the wife spends it. His preoccupation is with the production side of life, hers with consumption.

The system of joint control carries with it certain connotations highly esteemed in our culture: of equality in power and responsibility between the two adults who are husband and wife; of decisions that represent a consensus. The wife may still remain the manager, the buyer, the working housekeeper. Joint control does not mean that the expenditure of every dollar is agreed upon beforehand by both. Actually each may have an area in which he or she has responsibility for decisions, not only for free choice as to items for personal use and enjoyment, but as to those for family use and benefit. The essence of the system is that there is no dominant partner and that both have full knowledge of the financial setting within which decisions are made.

An argument against a system of joint control is that it is based on the false assumption that agreement can be reached. What happens in case of conflict? Must not ultimate and final authority explicitly or implicitly lie in one? Since responsibility for earning lies with the husband, should not that final authority lodge in him? At least for savings or matters that might touch the future financial situation? The family as a way of living, a form of human association, means two personalities, two sets of behavior traits and value systems. One of the adults involved may be wise; the other foolish; one selfish, the other unselfish; one domineering, the other yielding. No "system" alters these facts. Yet the principle behind a system and the resulting practice may work toward desirable goals or the reverse. The problem of arriving harmoniously at a consensus is broader than the one under discussion. Husband and wife are two persons. Every child has two parents. There are many other areas of possible conflict besides those relating to financial matters.

Very little is known concerning the systems of financial control in American families. One can conjecture that age of husband and wife, national origin, education, occupation, size and source of income, would affect what was found. Special inquiry concerning family practices in this respect have recently been made in Great Britain as a part of studies of family spending. One investigator says:

> We have treated family income as a single whole, but in practice it is usually divided into two parts, "Housekeeping Money" and "Pocket-Money." The husband either gives his wife her housekeeping allowance and retains the rest of his earnings for his own private use; or else he may, less commonly, give her the whole of his wage packet receiving back an allowance of pocket money. Obviously much will depend on which of these arrangements is in force. It will decide who is to be the dominant partner in the family economy.[4]

The percentage of men who gave the whole wage packet intact to the wife was small. Concerning this practice, a second investigator observes:

> It does not mean that the wife in those cases is of the domineering type to whom the husband is subservient; oftener it means that the husband cannot be trusted with money and it is done so that he should not be led into temptation by bad company. . . . It remains to be seen whether the husband gets more or less by that arrangement. My guess is that in many cases he gets more. Anyway, this class of person is made up both of model husbands and of notorious mis-spenders who cannot even manage their own pocket money.
>
> At the other extreme are cases where the husband pays his wife very little—even less than a lodger would pay.
>
> But in the majority of cases the husband's money is clearly divided into two parts, with clearly defined obligations incurred by them. Out of her allowance the housewife nearly always pays the rent, light and heat, food consumed at home, all school meals, all clothes for herself and the children, and her own and the children's outings. Her husband's money goes on fares, food out, cigarettes, drink, amusements and other

4. Madge, *op. cit.*, p. 52.

pleasures, his own clothes, sometimes also his savings. But of course the line of division is not always clearly defined, and there is give and take on both sides.

· . . . If it [the housekeeping money] is a fixed sum, its determination is based more often on the lowest level of the husband's fluctuating earnings than on the average—i.e., without counting overtime or nightshifts or extras. But when extra money is earned, the worker gives his wife a treat or allows her something out of his money for extra expenses like clothes; but this is kept apart from regular housekeeping, because the husband would not like the housewife to regard this as her right on which she can rely. The housekeeping money is treated as a sort of guaranteed wages for the housewife, who is free to dispose of it as she wishes, and even save when she can.[5]

CHILDREN AND MONEY

The discussion of who controls and who should control the disposition of the family income would not be complete without raising a question concerning the part children play in that decision. Should they be on the dole or the allowance system? If allowance, at what age should it begin? What should it cover? Should they have complete freedom in its expenditure? Should they have any voice in the disposition of the remainder of the income? A voice or a vote? A thoroughly sound discussion of these and related matters may be found in the book by Dr. and Mrs. Gruenberg, *Parents, Children and Money.*[6] In brief, their position is that children early should receive a fixed allowance, the amount and the number of items which they secure only through the use of this sum increasing with age. Thus they learn the nature of the world in which they live so far as it is affected by money. Only by having a sum which they are free and compelled to apportion do they learn to spend, save, and give. The allowance is neither a reward for good conduct nor pay for work done. Its receipt is not a gift or a favor. It is something they need as they need milk and shoes. Once given, it must be theirs to dispose of; otherwise its purpose is defeated.

They hold further than the children should know the family's financial situation and, as they are able, participate in the problem of allocating it wisely. Thus they may see the basis upon which their share is determined and learn something of the issues involved in deciding upon its total use. Children so trained are unlikely to be irresponsible marriage partners if their emotional development otherwise is sound.

TOOLS AND TECHNIQUES OF BUDGETING

Most discussions of budgeting begin with the problem of tools and techniques—how to do it. They include the kind of forms to use and even

5. F. Zweig, *Labour, Life and Poverty* (London: Victor Gollancz, 1948), pp. 11–14.

6. S. M. and B. C. Gruenberg, *Parents, Children and Money: Learning To Spend, Save and Earn* (New York: Viking Press, 1933).

occasionally give rules to follow in making the allocation. Yet involved in budgeting are the issues previously discussed. Knowledge of what budgeting can and cannot accomplish, decisions as to what funds are to be budgeted and who is to make the decisions, are what might be called the necessary prelude to budgeting. Budgeting, in fact, as a technical process is not highly complicated. Most families could draw up a tentative plan in a short time. Those that file income-tax returns should know what their income was during the past year. Most families can hazard a guess as to what they are likely to receive in the future. Some are required to file estimates of their incomes for the year to come. They know when income from various sources is received. The family also knows its commitments and when they must be met. Most families also know with some degree of exactness many of their usual expenditures for current living. If they have kept accounts, they know them fairly accurately. For some they have records in receipts or on checkbook stubs. For regularly recurring items they can at least reconstruct the story for the last week or month. Families that participate in income and expenditure studies are expected to be able to give an account of their outlays in some detail. If a schedule such as is used in a field study is available, an attempt to fill it in will at least call to mind possible items of expenditure. Most families have also made some decisions as to future new outlays or savings. These too go in the budget.

A budget is a plan for spending and saving each successive increment of income received. If there were to be no set-asides for future spending or payment of debts incurred in the past, the only form required would be that for recording the outlays planned for food and other purposes before the next payday and the sums to be turned over to family members for disbursements not otherwise allowed for, a form for each income period. On this form would also appear the amount added to permanent savings during this period. If each period's income took care of each period's outgo, nothing more would be required. If the largest outlays could come when the income was largest or if the occasional outlays could be staggered so that they could be fairly evenly distributed among income periods and there was nothing left except regularly recurring and fixed, periodic payments, nothing more would be required. This would be a spend-as-you-go, save-as-you-go plan.

Actually the pay-as-you-go system is not always possible because of unevenness of income receipts as between periods or because some desired outlays are so large they cannot be met from current income. Other forms are then desirable: one for recording income and its planned disposition period by period, and one for the plan for building up a reserve fund for future outlays and savings.[7] The latter would show the set-asides planned at each income period for specific purposes, the total being the difference between current outlays and income. When the expenditure is made, it comes from the reserve fund, and future planned set-asides do not include it. Some outlays would require set-asides for three months, others for much longer, depending upon the size of the projected outlay and the amount to be set aside at each income period. If there are debts to be paid which require similar set-asides, a separate form for listing is advisable.

The difficulty in making the budget arises when allotments of income are compared with one another and the grand total with income. Which shall be reduced, enlarged, or kept as it stands? What the tentative budget reveals will vary. Some budgets will show that the big, relatively fixed outlays are "putting the squeeze" on all others. Housing with all its allied costs may make the family feel poor when it comes to other outlays or savings. Other budgets will indicate that it is the multiplicity of small, diverse outlays that swell the total in certain categories. At this point there is no gain in making decisions that will not be adhered to. The result will be a conclusion that there is no use in budgeting. Some fixed costs cannot be immediately changed. When they are changed, however, a totally new budget may be made. Before they are changed, the "play" is largely in the other items.

A decision in regard to allocation of funds means inevitably a decision as to activities and way of living to small or large degree. It may mean keeping away from opportunities for spending, changing forms of recreation, as well as spending within a fixed limit. It may mean dropping entirely some minor or major item of expense and the activity or enjoyment it represented. It may mean a radical alteration of the relatively fixed expenses: giving up expensive schools for children, a car, a vacation of a particular type, membership in a club, the setting-up of a different type of establishment, or change in the insurance program. Many budgeteers make a plan involving an overly ambitious program of saving without changing fixed expense or noting what great alterations in other expenditures would be called for. The budget then is pronounced a failure.

ARE THERE RULES TO FOLLOW?

Many families proposing to budget their incomes promptly seek an "expert," or "authority," who will tell them the proper or "best" allocation as between consumption and savings and the various consumption

7. Household Finance Corporation, 919 North Michigan Avenue, Chicago, Illinois, has developed budget forms based on this principle.

categories. They seek a standard budget for families of their size and income that represents the "right" practice. This will be a vain quest if they seek to find a rule of any validity. What is essentially the same problem has been discussed previously in connection with the determination of the adequacy of money incomes. Rules concerning dietary practice may be given, and rules concerning line, proportion, and color harmony that may be useful in selecting clothes and house furnishings. There are rules concerning the sleeping quarters to be provided and the equipment necessary to serve a formal dinner. There is a literature broad in scope that will throw light on needs and help the family to appraise its consumption standards. The budget adviser may hazard a guess that, with prevailing prices and standards *as they are*, the family is not likely to be satisfied with an allowance for some category as low as it has been set. The adviser may be fairly certain that the family would be better satisfied if it transferred a part of the amount allocated to one purpose to another; or even that, with a food allowance so low and food preferences as they are, it is likely to go short on some essential nutrient. But the purpose of the budget is to maximize the family's satisfaction, taking as given the members' tastes and standards, their income and the prices of goods and services. The family alone can make the necessary decisions. Even if someone could tell the members what they ought to want, the budget so constructed would turn out to be a useless device, since, unless they came to want what they ought to, the plan proposed would not be followed.

The families that look for outside aid in planning their expenditures sometimes ask: How do other families of our composition and income spend their money? Newly formed families may ask this question, since they have no experience to guide them. Families newly come to a particular community may be unfamiliar with prices. They assume that their standard is like that of others of the same economic level and that their allotments, if they knew the price facts, would be about the same as others. The data that would provide this sort of guidance are limited. Income and expenditure studies are not made every year or processed and published immediately. They are not made in all localities, and many localities are averaged together in the published reports. Families of different composition are not always shown separately. Grouped together at each income level may be families with quite different sources of income, income history, and income expectations. The data on other families' expenditures, when available, do not in any case tell a particular family what it ought to spend or save. They can only lead families to ask: Why are we spending so much more or less?

Those who read economic treatises may sometimes find statements therein which might be interpreted as giving the direction they seek for the allocation of their incomes. Boulding, for example, says: "The question of how to spend a given sum in a given time in the best possible way is answered by the equimarginal principle."[8] What is the equimarginal principle? The equimarginal principle is followed when, in dividing a given quantity of anything (time or money) among different uses, the gain that would be realized by transferring a unit into another use is just equal to the loss involved by withdrawing it from any other.[9] In other words, the satisfaction to be derived by the individual or group from the use of income is at its maximum when the satisfaction gained by a change in the allotment of a dollar would not counterbalance that lost by the shift. Who can make this decision? The individual or group in question. In other words, this is an admonition to budget, to weigh and consider alternative uses of income, rather than a guide to follow in budgeting. The "best possible way" of spending a given sum is, by Boulding's principle, get what you want most.

To divide one's income the best way as defined by Boulding is of course a counsel of perfection. The long view and consideration of all alternatives are possible or even desirable only up to a point. Budgeting is a striving to increase satisfactions rather than attaining a total than which there could be no greater. Boulding calls attention to two limitations upon the application of the equimarginal principle: one he calls the "indivisibility of goods"; the other, the "indefiniteness of the budget period." One must buy, he says, one car or two cars, not one-eighth of a car or one and a half cars. We do not and cannot consider buying a dollar's worth more or less of many items in the budget. Further, he points out that many things bought in one budget period (that for which income is allocated) are used in another or many others. One is making a decision as to satisfactions for many years to come. It is also evident that "immunity from excessive brain-wear about the spending of money . . . is worth some leakage of material enjoyment."[10]

Expositions of the equimarginal principle always run in terms of an individual who is budgeting his own income to satisfy his personal wants. Actually the income may be made up of sums from several persons, and in almost all cases the wants of several must in some degree be met. How are allocations between persons and for the joint benefit of several persons

8. Kenneth Boulding, *Economic Analysis* (New York: Harper & Bros., 1941), p. 648.
9. *Ibid.*, pp. 645–46.
10. D. H. Robertson, *Money* (New York: Harcourt, Brace & Co., 1929), p. 5.

made? When one person is making the allocation, does he decide what he wants most for them? Does he decide what satisfaction for one he wants more than for another or for others than for himself? Or does he attempt to discover what others want most? Actually he cannot know the order of preferences of others, since this is shown only by choice itself, and interpersonal comparisons are often said to be impossible. Nor, if the others are children, could they be supposed to act in a wide range of choice like the "rational" human beings who alone exemplify the equimarginal principle in their choosing. Choices for others are clearly either welfare judgments, that is, what is good for them, or judgments concerning their preferences on the basis of the best evidence available. When two or more jointly make the decisions for themselves and for others, there must be a balancing and adjustment of two or more scales of preferences and two or more judgments as to the preferences or what is good for the others involved.

THE DECISION-MAKING PROCESS

In the simple case of an individual attempting to discover what he really wants, or really wants more than something else, what is the nature of the decision-making process? If all acts were without deliberation, this question would not arise; but, if expenditures are to any degree planned, there has been conscious choice. The apportionment of income among alternative uses involves in part decisions as to ends, or the degree to which certain ends shall be attained, and in part decisions as to means. When various consumption goods or services are means to the same end, the choice represents a decision as to their effectiveness for the purpose in relation to their respective costs. If the facts are known, such decisions are easy; the difficult choices are those among ends. The decisions of the business manager are in a sense simple as compared with those of the consumer in allocating his income. The objective of the former is to maximize profits (or minimize losses), and what he compares are the probable dollar results of his decisions in costs and in revenues. The latter must compare diverse types of satisfactions or ends achieved and one over-all "satisfaction" or pattern of living with another.

In spite of the language we often use, the consumer in making his decision does not literally weigh and measure magnitudes of "pleasure," "satisfaction," or "utility." His deliberation must involve consideration of alternatives and result in an ordering of his preferences. What is the nature of this process? John Dewey described deliberation as "a dramatic rehearsal [in imagination] of various competing lines of action. . . . An

experiment in finding out what the various lines of action are really like."
Deliberation is "a tentative trying-out of various courses of action."
"What then is choice? Simply hitting in imagination upon an object,
which furnishes an adequate stimulus."[11]

Hence there is reasonable and unreasonable choice. The object thought of may
simply stimulate some impulse or habit to a pitch of intensity where it is temporarily
irresistible. It then overrides all competitors and secures for itself sole right of way.
The object looms large in imagination; it swells to fill the field. It allows no room for
alternatives; it absorbs us, enraptures us, carries us away, sweeps us off our feet by its
own attractive force. Then choice is arbitrary, unreasonable. But the object thought of
may be one which stimulates us by unifying and harmonizing competing tendencies.
. . . Deliberation is capable of making eliminations and recombinations in projecting
the course of a projected activity. To every shade of imagined circumstance there is
. . . response; and to every complex situation a sensitiveness as to its integrity, a
feeling of whether it does justice to all facts, or overrides some to the advantage of
others. Deliberation is reasonable when so conducted. There may be error in the result,
but it comes from lack of data not from ineptitude in handling them.[12]

CHECKING PLAN WITH PERFORMANCE

When there is a lapse of time between decision and act, the actual
choice made may not be the one previously decided upon. Furthermore,
although such may be the intent, such a decision as to keep outlays during
a period within a prescribed limit may be at the mercy of what happens in
a series of repeated transactions the net effect of which it is difficult to
foresee. Since the plan for expenditures is for a given income period, the
checking of plan with what actually happens must be at the end of that
period. What was a deliberate deviation from plan? Was it justified?
Which deviations were not deliberate? By experience can they be avoided?
In a sense each successive receipt of income can mark a new beginning, an
adjustment to take account of what previously happened or of new facts
concerning income or new estimation of needs or desires. Along with the
plan, preferably in parallel columns, should be space for recording what
actually happened during the period.

Must complete records of expenditures be kept? Daily records, the
most tedious and burdensome of all? There are various devices that reduce
this necessity. Memory, checkstubs, receipts, will fill in part of the
record. Records of deposits and withdrawals from savings or checking
account, in conjunction with changes in cash on hand during the period,
show how the reserve fund stands and whether set-asides and savings are

11. John Dewey, *Human Nature and Conduct* (New York: Henry Holt & Co., 1922), pp.
190–202.

12. *Ibid.*, pp. 193–94.

what was planned. If personal allowances to family members are paid regularly, their use need be recorded and studied only if there is some reason to question their adequacy or know their disposition. If cash for household expenses and food is kept separately from other funds and amounts recorded as taken, the approximate amount used may be easily arrived at. If, in spite of all such devices there are gaps in the financial history of the period, record-keeping is the only way by which it can be filled in. As a result of the picture of actual spending and saving that by various means is obtained, plans for succeeding periods may become more realistic and practice be made to conform more to plan.

CHAPTER XVII

THE COST OF LIVING

THE phrase "cost of living" has been loosely and ambiguously used even by those who are supposed to use words exactly. Studies of family incomes and expenditures were once frequently called studies of the "cost of living." Since the expenditures tended to vary with the family's financial resources, as many different costs of living were found as there were different incomes. This practice has been generally discontinued in this country, and such studies are simply called studies of incomes and expenditures, disbursements, or spending.

Yet there remains widespread the notion that there is something that may properly be called the "cost of living" which varies from place to place and time to time or even from one group to another. When one group is said to have a higher cost of living than another at the same place and time, investigation usually shows that what is higher is not the cost but the standard of living. What the one group customarily buys or its members consider they must possess and enjoy requires a larger expenditure of money. A higher cost of living as distinguished from a higher standard of living means that what is customarily purchased by a particular group costs more than formerly or at one place than another. The cause is primarily difference in price levels. Factors other than price may explain in part why the necessary outlay is greater at one time or place than another. Climate and the amenities provided by nature differ from one place to another. The nature of the industry, the layout of the community, may mean smoke, dirt, noise, inconvenience, ugliness, or the reverse. Distance from work may be greater, the public services fewer, and the outlay necessary to secure what was once or elsewhere free or less costly may be greater. There still remains the fact that, with all these things similar, cost of attaining a given level of living will vary with the prevailing prices of goods and services of various kinds.

MEASUREMENT OF CHANGES IN THE COST OF LIVING

An index that measures changes in prices from time to time has long been regarded as essential for the appraisal of the operation of the economy and for decisions by labor groups, business, and government. The construction of such an index is regarded as a proper governmental service. In this country responsibility for a wholesale price index has been assumed by the Bureau of Labor Statistics as well as for what was formerly called a "cost of living," now a "consumers' price," index that measures changes of appropriate prices in urban communities. The United States Department of Agriculture provides an index of "Prices Paid by Farm Families."

The construction of an index designed to measure changes in the cost of living either in urban or in farm communities presents a variety of difficult problems. Simplest to measure are the changes in the average price of a selected commodity or service in a given community. But we want not simply the measurement of the changes in the prices of items of food, for example, but of all food and similarly for clothing and other major categories of consumption. The prices of some foods will go up, others may go down, and some will change more than others. To arrive at a "food" index, there must be a weighting of the prices reported for food items that will reflect the relative importance of the various foods in the family budget. If the price of pepper doubles, that is relatively unimportant; if the price of eggs or milk doubles, that is a different matter. To discover the relative importance of various items, family budgets must be studied. The index will then specifically relate to the changes in the prices of the items important in the budgets of those studied. To discover the items to be priced and the appropriate weights, field studies were made in 1918–19, in 1934–36, and again early in 1951.

It is not necessary to price all food items to measure the changes in the cost of "food." By study of price movements it can be discovered which move together. Those of importance in the food budget and those from whose price change that of other items can be predicted will be chosen. If the priced items are given the weight of the group they represent as shown by the field study, the change in their prices relative to the base period will be the change in the group. Thus the aggregate cost of all food at the pricing date may be compared with that at the base period.

After indexes for food, clothing, and other major categories of consumption are secured, the next step is to combine them into an over-all cost of living or consumers' price index. Here again weighting is necessary on the basis of the relative importance of the various categories in the total family budget. The weights again are derived from what is shown on the average in the data from the field study. An addition of the current costs of all categories gives an all-items aggregate which may be compared with that in the base period. We have then a cost-of-living index for a particular community or at least for a designated group in that community. In 1950 separate indexes for all items and for the major consumption categories were published for thirty-four cities, and the food index alone for twenty-two additional cities.

To secure a national index, the results for each city must be combined. In making this combination, the index for each city is given a weight based upon its population and that of other cities in the same region and size class. The national index as developed by the Bureau of Labor Statistics was as follows at five-year intervals from 1915 to 1950:

Year	All Items	Food	Apparel	Rent	Fuel, Light, Electricity	Home Furnishings	Miscellaneous
			(1935–39 = 100)*				
1915....	72.5	80.9	71.4	92.9	62.5	63.6	53.6
1920....	143.0	168.8	201.0	120.7	106.9	164.6	100.5
1925....	125.4	132.9	112.4	152.2	115.4	121.5	102.2
1930....	119.4	126.0	112.7	137.5	111.4	108.9	105.1
1935....	98.1	100.4	96.8	94.2	100.2	96.3	98.7
1940....	100.2	96.6	101.7	104.6	99.7	100.5	101.1
1945....	128.6	139.1	145.9	109.5	110.3	145.8	124.1
1950....	171.9	204.5	187.7	131.0	140.6	190.2	156.5

* As a part of a revision of the index following the 1951 field study a new base period, 1946–47, was chosen. The earlier group indexes when linked to the new will provide a complete series back to 1913, the first base period of the index.

There are various special problems in the construction of an index other than those mentioned; for example, in what cities to secure prices, in what retail outlets in each community, whether regular prices only or sale prices as well are to be taken, how often to secure prices, and how many for each item. There is also the question whether the index that measures changes in the cost of the budget of moderate-income families measures also that of low-income or higher-income families. But there are others more basic. In a dynamic society the population shifts so that the communities represented in the study from which the weights or the prices are secured may alter in their relative importance in the national total. Furthermore, the quality of commodities changes; new goods appear; others disappear. Some of the new goods are substitutes for others once used for the same general purpose; others serve entirely new purposes. Tastes and preferences change, and the relative importance of items and groups of items and even of major consumption categories changes. Relative prices may change as well as the general price level, shifting the relative proportions of the goods purchased.

The simplest concept of a cost-of-living index is that it measures the change in the cost of a fixed budget, a fixed market basket of food, for example, due to price changes alone. Thus one might say: "This is what it would cost in 1950 to purchase what wage-earning or moderate-income families in cities purchased on the average in 1915." But even if the articles commonly purchased in 1915 could be priced in 1950, the index might have little usefulness except as a historical fact. The change in prices that is significant currently is the change occurring in those used currently. It is difficult to define what changes the index should show over a long period of time. It is sometimes defined as the increase or decrease in the cost of obtaining the same satisfactions, something in itself difficult to measure.

As there are changes in the nature and quality of the goods available on the market, substitutions must be made in the list of articles priced. The price line, model, or type most representative of current purchase is then taken. If the substitute is of approximately the same grade and serves the same purpose, a linking method is used so that the price change of the substitute rather than that of the one formerly priced is reflected in the index. If, however, consumers have no choice but to buy the new good, the price difference between the old and the new good becomes the price change. To detect and allow for changes in the relative importance of items and groups of items, new studies of family expenditures are necessary and revisions of the index on the basis of the findings. Changes then may be made in the items priced and in the weights used in computing the indexes for the major categories and for the total cost of the budget.

PLACE-TO-PLACE DIFFERENCES

The problem of measuring differences in cost of living between places grows in difficulty as the places compared vary not simply in prices of items offered in both markets but in climate, in customs and standards, in the type of goods found in the markets, and in family size and composition. When on the average the consumption pattern and the goods commonly purchased are the same in two places, the problem is simple. When they are not, either because of differences in relative prices or because of other differences noted or unnoted, no satisfactory method for its solution has been found. Housing in particular presents a problem, since what is available for pricing and commonly occupied in one place may be quite different from that found in another. When a solution of the pricing problem is found, the budget typical of families in *A* may be priced in *B*. This will show how much more or less it would cost to live in *B* as families do in *A*. In fact, families in *B* may not live in that way, and families moving there would abandon their old pattern, thus having in effect a cost of living in *B* different from that indicated by the method of measurement.

THE HIGH COST OF LIVING

When prices in general are rising, the family's economic predicament is described as the high cost of living. The concern is with prices, that important member of the triumvirate whose relation is the essence of each family's economic problem. The other two are, of course, money income and the standard that determines what is urgently desired. When prices in general are rising or the cost of some necessary item, interest in price-making forces quickens, and questions are raised as to why prices are rising, or how prices in some category might be lowered. At all times families have a vital stake in the price level and in price-reducing forces. Economic welfare is measured by real income—what the money income will buy.

Although the truth of the last statement is undisputed, each family seeks in the main to improve its economic position through increase in money income. Although we rely upon this drive to maximize income as our means of allocating our resources to desired uses, of securing improvements in process and techniques, of increasing efficiency and production, there are some undesirable results. Some means of increasing the money income of a few may not only increase the prices that must be paid for their services or products but reduce the volume available and divert investment and employment into less-productive channels. Some benefit from a rapidly rising price level. A further result of the concentration of the attention of individuals and families upon the movement of their own money income is that they are far less concerned with conditions and measures affecting the prices they pay than with those affecting their incomes. They respond quickly to a threat to their own incomes; are zealous and active in promoting measures that might increase them. As income recipients, moreover, each has a special interest in a special source of income, the wage for some service, the fortunes of some industry, the price for some product. A special interest group may become a "pressure group" to sway public opinion or secure legislation to its special advantage. The benefits that might come to families as consumers from a proposed public policy or an altered labor or business practice are diffused, not an immediate, perceptible gain. Each taken by itself affects real income only slightly. The consumer interest, the interest of the family in its real income, is a general as opposed to a special interest. Since everyone is a consumer, there can scarcely be a consumer-interest *group*.

THE COST OF LIVING HISTORICALLY CONSIDERED

The relativity of what we call the high cost of living should at this point be emphasized. The real cost of our food, apparel, housing, any other requirement or source of enjoyment is the hours of labor we must devote to securing it, or, nationally speaking, the proportion of our resources, human or otherwise, we must devote to securing it. From the long view, the cost of the basic necessaries, so defined, has greatly declined. Comparisons of one-month, one-year, or five-year periods with one another are highly important, but the long view gives a perspective which also has its values. Price data in conjunction with money-income data are too limited to tell the story over a long period. Even if price data were available, the construction of an index that would show differences between points far apart in time would present the same problem that we face when we attempt to compare costs between places and communities that are geographically and culturally unlike. The decline in the cost of the basic necessaries is the reverse side of the increase in man-hour productivity.

A history of food-consumption habits would show in specific terms our relative position today as food consumers. To be adequate, such a history would show not only the items occasionally available in the past or available to a few but the customary, all-year-round diet of the generality of people. Such a history would not show the magnitude of the change in the form of a single figure, nor could it adequately show changes in quality. In general, it would reveal a movement toward increased consumption of the more expensive sources of the nutrients and of those foods generally considered palatable or preferable for various reasons. It would show an increased consumption of fresh fruits and vegetables, muscle meat, milk, sweets, coffee, tea and soft drinks, of white wheaten bread instead of the dark, whole-grain bread of our forefathers. It would show a movement from cereal to animal foods.[1]

But what of the cost of this diet? Its cost as measured by the proportion of productive resources devoted to food-getting has notably declined over time. The decline in the proportion of the labor force in agriculture is well known. To the cost in these terms of food-growing must be added of course the cost of providing the tools, as well as of food processing, transporting, assembling, dispersing in retail lots near the point of consumption, and of preparing for use in the home. But after allowance is made for these additional costs, along with deductions for exports and additions for the cost of securing imports, the net result would be as stated. Engel advanced the proposition that the economic welfare of a family and of a nation could be measured by the proportion of the income going for food. What is released

1. See Sir William J. Ashley, *Bread of Our Forefathers* (Oxford: Clarendon Press, 1928); J. C. Drummond and A. Wilbraham, *The Englishman's Food* (London: J. Cape, 1939); R. O. Cummings, *The American and His Food* (Chicago: University of Chicago Press, 1941).

can then go for other things. The significance of a high or increasing cost of food is not necessarily measured by the changes necessitated in the diet. It is equally well measured by the changes that must occur in the consumption of other things if the same diet is enjoyed as before.

According to the Department of Commerce estimates, during the 1940's roughly from about a fourth to three-tenths of the total disposable personal income went for food and beverages of all kinds both alcoholic and nonalcoholic.[2] Apparel, including furs and footwear and the purchased cleaning and repair of such items, has been taking only a little over a tenth. But one should not exclude jewelry, cosmetics, and the like from this category, since they serve the same purpose as many of the clothing expenditures. Adorning and clothing the body *in toto* absorb about an eighth of the disposable personal income. We have very limited information concerning the clothing of past generations. The so-called histories of costume are histories of the style, materials, and ornamentation of the dress of the upper classes. We are fairly certain, however, that the typical wardrobe today includes more items than formerly and that the length of life of most items has decreased because of the increased fragility of the materials, the increased rate of obsolescence, and reduced frequency of patching, alteration, and renovation.

COST OF HOUSING

The cost of housing has been a major source of concern in recent decades. Our situation as housing consumers has repeatedly been compared unfavorably with our situation as consumers of food, clothing, and automobiles. During and immediately following the war when the rate of construction diminished, to the earlier problem was added that of housing shortage, a discrepancy between demand and supply. Before that period, as well as during it and later, the problem was often defined as a discrepancy between need and supply. The first type of shortage is that which exists when some who are able and willing to pay the same prices as others who are renting or owning find no comparable dwellings available on the market at these prices. Negro families are perenially faced with this type of shortage. The second type of shortage is different. It implies that some who should have their own housekeeping units are not able to find any of acceptable kind and quality at prices they can afford to pay. Thus housing as a cost problem is a result of the relationship, previously emphasized, of the three factors—standards, market costs, and family incomes.

2. See U.S. Department of Commerce, *National Income and Product of the United States, 1929–1950* (Washington: Government Printing Office, 1951), Table 30.

Standards for housing include a standard with respect to who should live together in one dwelling, the proper composition of the social family. This determines the estimate of how many housing units are needed. They include also a standard for the house itself, its built-in facilities as well as the construction, amount of space provided, and its division into rooms. Standards for housing, especially urban housing, include also standards for the environment. What is near by may be as important for the health, comfort, and convenience of the family as the nature of the house itself. The site and all it involves in the way of conveniences and amenities or the reverse is a factor to be taken into account in appraising the adequacy of an actual or proposed dwelling unit. The price that families can afford to pay for housing that meets acceptable standards is that which would enable them to have not only such housing but the food, clothing, and other items that they consider essential for their well-being. Widespread failure of the market to provide such housing for large numbers is in essence the housing problem.

The concrete outcome of such a situation in any community is that many families live in houses that do not come up to acceptable standards. Not all the clearly visible defects in housing can be ascribed to high costs or low incomes. In part they are due to defects in design and character of the dwelling that could be corrected at no greater cost. In part also they are due to defects in the community plan and control of land use. Slums, blighted areas, hazards to children at play, noise, dirt, rats, disrepair, firetraps, dark dwellings, inconveniently placed with respect to schools, parks, churches, and markets, are not entirely a function of construction and occupancy costs and the income level. Programs and policies designed to improve housing cannot be narrowed to those which deal only with the dwelling unit itself, either its equipment, size, design, or cost.

Money outlays for housing have been taking close to a tenth of the total disposable money income. In addition, there is the large consumer investment in owned housing. What it represents as an annual occupancy cost is difficult to measure. As home ownership increases, its proportion of the total increases. The Department of Commerce estimates are much lower than those arrived at in the studies of family incomes and expenditures.[3] If the latter estimates are taken, the proportion of the total disposable income, money and nonmoney, represented by housing cost rises

3. In 1941 the Commerce estimate of the occupancy value to owners of their investment in housing was about 17 per cent of the estimated costs of all housing, but it was 34 per cent of the average cost as reported in the Bureau of Labor Statistics study of the incomes and expenditures of families and single consumers for that year.

to close to a seventh. If costs of fuel, light, refrigeration, and water are added, the proportion rises to not far from one-fifth. The cost of housing as well as the outlay necessary for fuel varies considerably with region. The nonfarm families in the northern areas studied in the mid-thirties were devoting on the average nearer one-fourth than one-fifth of their total income to housing, fuel, and the utilities.

COSTS OF DISTRIBUTION

Whatever may have been the general trend over a period that covers a century or more, the question that concerns consumers now is the current level of prices. Are forces in operation that tend to bring down or to move up the prices of food, clothing, or housing? What alterations in business or consumer practices, in market organization, in public policies, would make them available on more favorable terms? The immediate concern is in the price of milk, eggs, oranges, or meat; in the price of cars, shoes, bathtubs, refrigerators, sheets, blankets, haircuts, electricity—every item that makes up the cost of living. One issue of perennial concern with respect to many of these items is the cost of their distribution, that is, those costs incurred after the item takes final shape and form. This cost is usually measured by the share of the dollar spent for the item that is represented by charges other than those for growing, manufacturing, or processing, the "production" costs, as the latter are usually called. For example, it may be found that, of the dollar spent for fresh fruits and vegetables, 65 cents goes on the average at a particular time for their distribution and 35 cents for their "production." If manufacturers or growers take a large responsibility for distribution, what they get will cover both production and distribution costs. If they take little responsibility, others, that is, separate business units, will get the share of the consumer's dollar that represents distribution costs. Many studies have been made to show the farmer's share, the railway's share, or the retailer's share in the consumer's dollar spent for a specific item or groups of items, as well as the part represented by advertising, packaging, storing, and so on.

The increase over time in the proportion of the consumer's dollar that goes for distribution is paralleled by the increase in the proportion of the labor force engaged in the distributive occupations. The reasons for this increase and for some of the differences in distribution costs between items are better understood than they once were. In general, these costs are the corollary of wide markets and specialization. The place of consumption is often far from the place of production. Commodities are packaged, stored, and transported. The first seller is often not the last seller, nor is the first buyer the last buyer. Clearly, in addition to the outlays for growing, making, and processing, there must be those for making the availability of products known, transporting and making them accessible near the place of consumption, keeping them in good condition until the consumer is ready to buy them, and for all the processes incidental to their disposition in retail lots.

The share of the consumer's dollar that goes for distribution is least when the consumer is the active agent in effecting a transfer of goods, and the producer does little except make the article available at the place of production. If the consumer seeks out the producer, buys in such lots and at such intervals and time as reduce all labor and other costs for the producer, the price should be correspondingly close to the costs of production. If the producer does nothing to promote sales, to seek out buyers, to make goods easily accessible, if the consumer pays cash, asks for no fancy wrapping, carries his purchases home or arranges for transportation, certain costs are not included in the price paid. The consumer in effect has substituted his time and energy for his money; he has foregone certain services.

Most producers' sales would obviously be small if they relied upon such transactions. Few consumers for only the most limited range of items could or would secure goods in this way. It would be the very negation of an exchange economy of the type now characteristic. The situation is the reverse of that described. Sellers seek buyers, promote sales, make goods easily accessible, provide transportation, even doorstep delivery, allow purchase on credit, package, and wrap. Consumers increasingly do hand-to-mouth buying at an easily accessible place. This brief analysis, which could be greatly expanded, suggests why distribution costs are as they are as well as some of the factors which reduce them when consumers find it possible and desirable to dispense with certain services or utilities in the bundle for which they pay.

MARKET STRUCTURE

The structure of the market for consumers' goods depends upon the number of buyers and sellers between the first seller (the producer) and the last buyer (the consumer). There is usually at least one, the retailer, but there may be more—the wholesaler, jobber, country buyer, and so on.

The existence of these middlemen, independent business units that are the intermediary buyers and sellers, indicates that the first sellers, the producers, have not found it possible or desirable to take over a large part or all of the distribution of their products. When the producers are small, scattered, and remote from consumers, this is fairly certain to be the case. When they are large, as is the case with many manufacturers of consumers' goods, they are quite likely to build up a sales or distribution department, possibly separately incorporated but owned by the manufacturing company, and to sell directly to the retailer. In few cases do they establish their own retail outlets. As a part of this process they may spend large sums for national advertising to create demand for their product, in particular for their brand. Their sales efforts go also toward inducing retailers to carry their brands, possibly advertise and display them, and promote their sale. As a result of building up a big sales organization they may find it advantageous to distribute products other than those they themselves produce. Thus meat packers may add butter, eggs, and similar products to those that come from their own plants. They may handle a wide range of related or even seemingly unrelated products. The producers of farm products, who are typically small, can singly build up no far-reaching sales organization. Through the use of co-operative associations they may do so, however.[4] Thus the share of the consumer's dollar that the growers of citrus fruits, milk producers, or others get increases, but it is not all strictly for production. Part is for distribution.

The process of integration or concentration of the operations involved in distribution and production under the control of one business unit may take another form. The retailer, the next to the last buyer, may become also the first buyer, sending his agents to the growers and manufacturers at home or abroad, and may even establish or control manufacturing plants. This can happen only if the retailing firm itself is large. There are three well-known forms of mass merchandising at the retail level: the mail-order house, the department store, and the chain. Independent, small retailers may to some extent reach back in the same way through some form of association. The consumers' co-operative associations in some countries have developed to the point where they can operate on the same scale. The retail co-operatives, owned and controlled by consumer-members, in turn form co-operative wholesale societies which may control manufacturing and importing agencies and other sources of supply. Thus the last buyer may in effect be the first buyer, or even in effect the consumer becomes the producer.

A description of market structure is not complete if only the existence or absence of intermediary buyers and sellers is noted. There are business concerns performing marketing services that do not become owners of the

---

4. When acting singly, these small sellers often find they are confronted with only one buyer. The co-operative removes them from this position.

goods with which they deal. They sell a special service such as transportation, storage, or advertising to buyers or sellers. They buy or sell for others on commission. The large-scale marketing units may use the specialized agencies or perform the services in question for themselves. Rarely, however, would they provide their long-distance transportation.

Market structure clearly will vary from one group of commodities to another. It will vary with the character of the commodity, with the scale and other conditions of production, and with the location of consumers. For some commodities transportation costs will be high; for others, storage costs. Some will be extensively advertised, others very little. Distribution costs for consumer goods as a group will clearly exceed those for producer goods. The latter are usually sold directly by the producer to the user in relatively large lots. Relatively large outlays for sales promotion and one middleman, the retailer, are almost certain to be found in the consumer goods market.

CHANGES IN MARKET STRUCTURE

Market structure is not fixed but subject to change. As there is change, there may be resistance to it from those whose interests are adversely affected. As manufacturers take over the distribution of their products, wholesalers and other intermediary buyers and sellers are threatened. Similarly, as large retailing firms move back and take over functions previously performed by others, the latter do not find the change to their liking. A conflict of interest between manufacturers and large distributors arises. The chains would have the manufacturers act as their producing agents if they do not themselves own plants. They would have the products they sell made to their specifications and bear their name or brand. Manufacturers, upon the other hand, may wish retailers in effect to act as their agents, to carry and promote the sale of their brands. They may give only one dealer the right to handle their products and require that he handle these exclusively. They may even set the minimum price at which the retailer may sell, thus restricting price competition among dealers. Forty-five states have legalized such retailer-manufacturer agreements. Congress in 1937 removed these agreements from the ban of the federal antitrust laws and declared them fair methods of competition in any state in which they were legal. Most of these so-called "fair-trade" laws made resale price maintenance binding upon retailers not entering into such an agreement if one of their competitors had done so. The Supreme Court in 1950 held that the federal law did not bind nonsigners, but merely legalized price agreements. In 1952 Congress passed a new law making specific its intent to prevent nonsigners from selling below the manufacturers' minima when such had legally been established in a particular market by agreement with other dealers.

The small independent retailers also see their position threatened by the growth of large retailing units. First it was the mail-order house and the department store that threatened the small-town merchant. Now emphasis is placed upon the competition of the chains. The chain puts a competitor in the same block with the small independent rather than in a city or a central shopping district. The chain form of organization combines in one big business-unit many specialty shops or neighborhood stores. The small independents vigorously promote price-maintenance laws to protect them from the price competition of the chains.

The first question concerning the marketing developments so briefly described is: What has been the effects upon the cost of distribution? The integration of the activities involved in making goods accessible to consumers under the control and management of one business unit clearly has the elements of economy and efficiency. Mass merchandising as illustrated by the chain has its economies. The competition of the chains has also forced greater efficiency upon the independents and has caused them to strive more zealously to provide what the consumer wants to pay for in the way of stock and services. The chains introduced cash-and-carry, self-service, or minimum service as exemplified by the variety stores.

SPECIAL PROBLEM OF THE CHAINS

It is the size of the business units which today loom so large in the retail market that is the major cause for concern. To the extent that their growth is based upon economies made possible by integration and scale of operation which are reflected in price and upon their ability to detect consumer preferences, their presence in the market is a clear-cut buyer gain.[5] But are these economies so great that ultimately the market in some important line will be dominated by a few large concerns, with independents surviving only to serve small, isolated groups or to provide special goods or services which do not lend themselves to mass-merchandising methods? In this connection it must be remembered that size has its own diseconomies and costs and that remote control of far-flung operating units presents special problems. Independent operation also has its special advantages. Further, retailing, unlike most manufacturing processes, re-

5. For a discussion of alleged malpractices of the chains, low wage scales, and the social effects of absentee ownership see J. L. Palmer, "Economic and Social Effects of Chain Stores," *Journal of Business*, II (1929), 272–90.

quires a relatively small amount of capital. It is therefore relatively easy to enter the field, a fact that has often led to the question: Are there too many retailers? Consumers also may form co-operative associations. A price level at which competitors could flourish would be expected to bring both independents and co-operatives quickly into the field.

There is, however, another issue. Is the size of the chains due entirely to economies? Do the large units have certain unfair advantages which may lead to their domination of the market? May the chains by virtue of large financial resources and generally profitable operations undersell the small retailers in one community or neighborhood and, having forced them out of business, remain alone to operate at a higher price level? Does the chain by virtue of its size have an unfair advantage in buying? May it through the size of its potential orders force suppliers to give it preferential prices either directly or by virtue of rebates and allowances? The fear of market domination by this means was behind the Robinson-Patman Act of 1936. This act strengthened the ban on price differentials among buyers of commodities of like grade and quality which cannot be justified by differences in the cost of serving them. If the chains and other large distributors have enjoyed an undue competitive advantage, the enforcement of this act should restrict its operation. Studies have in fact failed to show that the development of the chains has increased the rate at which small independents fail.

The large retailing units, it should be noted, offer competition to and restrain the control over the market of the large manufacturer or producer groups. It has been pointed out that the small independents tend in a sense to become manufacturers' agents, to stock their brands, and to sell at the prices they set. But the mail-order house, the department store, and the chain can put their own brands on the market, thus providing a competition that would otherwise not exist. They have shown themselves more ready than the manufacturers to provide informative labels. Their advertising is more informative and restricted to information alone. There is a problem of size of supplying agents, of producer control of the market, that is far broader than that presented by the growth of large units in the merchandising field.

CHAPTER XVIII

THE COST OF LIVING—*Continued*

EXTENT OF COMPETITION

THE extent to which monopoly in varying degrees and various forms characterizes our markets is a major consumer problem not only in a restricted sense but in the broadest, over-all sense. The allocation of resources, the level of production, the distribution of income in the economy, and the stability of its operations are adversely affected as the market tends to be more and more monopolistic in character. There is a vast economic literature dealing with price when there are many sellers and many buyers and when there is but one or a few of either or both. There has been widespread debate as to whether competition has or has not declined. On the one hand, we have seen the disappearance of the local merchant as the single supplier of the local clientele. A population on wheels, motor driven, expands the trading area and makes for less difference in prices between places. There has been a great increase in variety of products, and the price of one product is tied to the price of that which can be substituted for it. If the price of one rises, its rate of purchase falls off and that of the substitute increases. On the other hand, in many fields the size of the business unit has grown until one or a few firms are the major suppliers. There not only are the industries dominated by one or a few giant concerns but those with a fairly large number of business units which act as one, dividing the market, setting the production quotas, agreeing on price. Not only business but labor may restrict free entry into markets and employments and in selling act as one. The sheltered rather than the free market seems the *sine qua non.*

In a progress report to a special congressional committee set up to study the concentration of economic power in the production and distribution of goods the situation was summarized as follows:[1]

No accurate estimate concerning the extent of competition and monopoly in American markets is justified by the available evidence. . . . The most that can be said today is that competition is far too common to justify the thesis that the competi-

1. U.S. Temporary National Economic Committee, *Investigation of Concentration of Economic Power, Verbatim Record of Proceedings, Hearings, January 15, 1951* (Washington: Bureau of National Affairs, 1941), XIV, 14.

tive system is approaching extinction, and that monopoly is far too common to justify its treatment as an occasional exception to the general rule.

In those industries which appear to be normally competitive, competition is constantly breaking down. Competitors continually seek to limit competition and to obtain for themselves some measure of monopoly power. They enter into agreements governing prices and production. They set up associations to enforce such agreements. They procure the enactment of restrictive legislation. For a time they may succeed in bringing competition under control. But these arrangements, too, are constantly breaking down. Competitors violate the agreements. Associations lack the power to enforce them. New enterprises come into the field. Restrictive statutes are invalidated by the courts or repealed by the legislature. The lines of control are repeatedly broken and reformed.

. . . In those industries that appear at any time to be monopolized, likewise monopoly is constantly tending to break down. Human wants may be satisfied in many different ways. Shifts in consumer demand may rob the monopolist of his market. Invention may develop numerous substitutes for his product.

. . . In those industries where the nature of the product, the market, the supply of materials, and the technology of production is such as to encourage it, competition reasserts itself in the face of collusive agreements and restrictive legislation. In other fields the characteristics of the product, the market, the supply of materials, and the technology of production are conducive to monopoly. But monopoly cannot be attributed to natural factors alone. It is the product of formal agreements and secret understandings; of combinations; intercorporate stockholdings, and interlocking directorates; of the ruthless employment of superior financial resources and bargaining power; of unequal representation before legislatures, courts and administrative agencies; of the exclusion of competitors from markets, materials, and sources of investment funds; of restrictive contracts and discriminatory prices; of coercion, intimidation and violence. It is the product, too, of institutions of property which permit private enterprises to take exclusive title to scarce resources; of franchises, permits, and licenses which confer upon their holders exclusive privileges in the employment of limited facilities and the performance of important services; of patents which grant to their owners the exclusive right to control the use of certain machines and processes and the manufacture and sale of certain goods; of tariffs and State trade barriers which exclude outside producers from domestic markets; of legislation which limits output, fixes minimum prices, and handicaps strong competitors; and of inadequate enforcement, over many years, of the laws that are designed to preserve competition.

The situation clearly defies over-all characterization. What is found in one industry or in connection with one type or class of product may be quite different from what exists in another. Each requires separate study —milk, women's clothes, shoes, automobiles, bathtubs, tin cans, and glass containers.

WHAT IS COMPETITION?

Some general standards for appraisal may be found by asking what competition is and noting its various forms. Competition is a condition from which comes certain behavior and certain results. Clark says, "The essential nature of competition is rivalry in efficient service to the consuming public."[2] All that goes under the name of "competition" could not be so characterized. Competition is limited when there are barriers to the entry of products into markets, of investment and labor into employments. Free entry, however, does not insure competition of those entering. All entering may by collusion or agreement thereafter act as one in determining the level of production and price. Such arrangements may be highly unstable or persist without any firm or group breaking away for many years.

Competition may take the form of search for new techniques of production that will reduce the cost or improve the quality of the product. If the process cannot be kept secret or patented, it will be freely adopted in time by other suppliers. Competition may take the form of the development of a new product. It may be an addition to the line of an already established producer or the basis of a new industry, the products of which compete with others for a share in the consumer's dollar. Any firm may be free to supply the new product, or only the "inventor" may be free to do so. Suppliers of goods that serve the same purpose may differentiate their products by a distinctive name or mark. The competition then is of one brand with another. If there is a difference in the qualities of these products or if consumers so believe, brand competition merges into quality competition or the competition of close substitutes. If few consumers have a brand preference, the branded products are freely substituted for one another, and there can be little difference in price.

Competition is often described as a condition where there are many sellers and many buyers of an identical product. "Many sellers" means so large a number that no one of them can control the rate of production in the industry and therefore price. In that case no firm has incentive to decrease its own production with the hope of selling at a higher price and will increase it if the prevailing price is higher than the additional cost involved. It does not consider whether producing more will "spoil the market." The level of production in the industry will be higher and the price lower under these than under contrary conditions, as is explained at length in all economics textbooks.

Monopoly, like competition, takes many forms and exists in varying degrees. There is the complete monopoly where entry of others is impossible and investment is controlled. The patent right and franchise may give this degree of control as may possession of an essential element in

2. J. M. Clark, *Social Control of Business* (Chicago: University of Chicago Press, 1926), p. 38.

production limited in supply. There is the monopoly where entry of other suppliers cannot be controlled but where all entering agree to act together. There is the degree of monopoly given by a successfully differentiated product with its own distinctive demand. There is the industry with the dominant firm and the one with a few, usually, if supplying consumer goods, characterized by extensive sales promotion. In all cases there remains interproduct competition, the competition of new goods and of substitutes. Instead of looking for "competition" or "monopoly," it is preferable to look, on the one hand, at the extent of control of the supply of a product and, on the other, at the extent of substitution of another product for the one in question as the price difference increases.

PUBLIC POLICY AND THE MONOPOLY PROBLEM

The consumer interest in the maintenance of a free market is brought into sharp focus when the situation with respect to an important element in the cost of living is analyzed. Thurman W. Arnold, when assistant attorney-general and head of the Antitrust Division of the Department of Justice, described the market situation in the housing industry in this fashion.[3]

Unreasonable restraints of trade are, in my opinion, the most conspicuous reason for high construction costs. They appear at every level of the building industry. . . . Producers of building materials have fixed prices either by private arrangement or as the principal activity of trade associations. Owners of patents on building materials have used them to establish restrictive structures of price control, control of sales methods, and limits upon the quantities sold, in direct contradiction of the broad intent of the patent laws to encourage, through inventions, the development and spread of new productive methods. Some of these patent holders have taken advantage of their control over patented products to require their licensees to give them control of unpatented products also. By the use of basing point systems, and zone price systems, various building materials industries have established by formula rigid structure of uniform prices throughout the country; and in some of these industries such price formulas have encouraged the wasteful location of industrial plants and the wasteful shipment of products to great distances. The use of joint selling agencies has been another means by which some of these groups have undertaken to maintain their prices. In some groups the various producers have subscribed to the theory that every member of the industry should have a definite share of whatever business there is to be done, and that no concern should try to get more than its share by price competition. . . .

. . . Various groups of distributors of building materials engage in two kinds of restrictive practice. First, they try to raise the price of their services by establishing a fixed mark-up between the price they pay the manufacturer and the price at which they resell. For this purpose they collusively determine their mark-up or their selling price,

3. *Domestic Commerce*, August 10, 1939, p. 4.

and sometimes agree among themselves to boycott manufacturers who will not cut off supplies from price-cutting distributors.

The second type of restraint by distributors arises from the effort to see to it that all business passes through their hands and that no new methods of distribution are introduced which may dispense with their services. The great weapon in this field is the boycott.

. . . Contractors who erect buildings add their own systems of restraint. Many contracting groups maintain bid depositories in which copies of all bids and estimates are supposed to be filed prior to the award of the contract. . . . Other contractor groups maintain central estimating bureaus which calculate the cost of the job and supply the various contractors with the bids they are to make. In still other groups a central bureau determines the specifications for materials and labor to be included in the bid, and the contractor is expected to apply standard prices and labor rates to these specifications and thereby to arrive at the same bid as everyone else. Some bidding rings determine in advance which contractor is to get the job and arrange their bids so that everyone else bids higher than he. . . .

. . . The building trades unions often participate in these policies of restraint and add new restraints of their own. In recent years they have frequently been used as the strong-arm squads for collusive agreements among contractors, refusing to supply labor where the contractors' ring wishes labor withheld. In other cases the unions themselves have refused to permit the use of new products or processes because of their fear that the new method might make it possible to erect a house with fewer hours of labor than the old. . . .

. . . Such practices crystallize and lead to legislative restraints on trade. Many building regulations are, in reality, protective tariffs. . . .

On top of legislative restrictions are added municipal ordinances designed to restrain competition. They start out from the fact that there must be protection from fire and safeguards of minimum health requirements. They develop into legally established boycotts, particularly relating to walls, roofs, electrical work, and plumbing.

It will be noted from the example given that the government itself may erect trade barriers. By tariff and other forms of tax, by the character of the building code, by license and other requirements, the national, state, or local government may restrict the free entry of products into markets and of persons into employments and otherwise limit competition. The object of many of the governmental barriers is to protect local residents and businesses from the competition of persons and products coming from other communities. The chain-store tax is a special variant of the protectionist policy. Governmental restraints may take the form of product favoritism, of butter, for example, as opposed to oleomargarine. The use of various devices to protect local business and residents from the competition of outsiders became alarmingly widespread in the depression period of the thirties when employment and profit levels were low. The protection of butter against the competition of a substitute long antedates this period. The problem, of course, is to determine when a particular restraint is in the public interest. The use of the power to tax, to license, to inspect, and the use of the police power in general to safeguard public health and safety are the responsibilities of the state. The sheltering of special groups or interests simply to shelter them is not.

The monopolies that government itself creates by granting an exclusive franchise to operate within a certain area must clearly be regulated as to rates, charges, and services if the public interest is to be served. Such franchises are given when a single system best serves consumers and duplication of systems would be extremely wasteful. But the regulation to some degree of a broad class of private enterprises called "public utilities" extends beyond those that are complete monopolies by virtue of a public franchise or otherwise. It includes rail, water, air and motor-carrier transportation; electricity and gas, telephone, telegraph, television, and radio; and even warehouses and in some places milk distribution. The public utility is a common-law concept. Such a business or calling is one providing something so essential that it is said to be vested with a public interest and by old rule of law must serve the public without discrimination at reasonable rates. Such enterprises, the courts hold, are subject to special regulation. Such businesses, it has also been held, may be given special rights such as that of eminent domain—the taking of private property upon payment of fair compensation. Not all such enterprises are monopolies. Those existing are often protected against competition to the degree that others may not enter without the special permission of a public agency. Rates are not always regulated. If sufficient competition is believed to exist to make rates reasonable, they are filed and may not be changed without notice. In other cases, as the railroads, the responsible commission itself determines the rate structure that is fair and reasonable. Rate-fixing presents problems beyond the scope of this discussion. In many countries public ownership has been regarded as preferable.

Patents may be regarded as a kind of franchise, since they give the patentee the exclusive right to use a process or produce a particular good for at least seventeen years. It might plausibly be argued that such a grant should carry with it some regulation of its exercise, but this has not occurred. Recent studies have indicated a need for revision of patent law and procedures. Rather than constituting a device to promote the industrial arts, the right has become a peril to free enterprise, an instrument that frees the grantee from the general law with respect to restrictive practices. It seems reasonable to argue that a license to use should be available to all on the same terms and that the right to exclusive use of a process or sale of a product should not be the right to abstain from using or selling. The latter is by no means unknown. The patentee may not be required to use the process, but after a certain period it should then pass into the public domain. Is seventeen years of exclusive use just that which maximizes invention? Actually in any case a series of changes in design, a staggering of improvements joined with long delays while patents are pending, has often extended the rights given over a much longer period.

ANTIMONOPOLY LEGISLATION

The great problem as yet unsolved lies outside the realm just considered. It is the maintenance of competition in callings and enterprises that are not public utilities or the beneficiaries of patent rights. How prevent "restraints upon trade" and monopolizing or attempts to monopolize as ways of maximizing pay or profit? Under the common law, contracts with these direct purposes as opposed to those having incidentally this result were unenforceable and evidence of criminal conspiracy punishable under the law. The American courts held late in the 1880's that corporations entering into a trust agreement for the purpose of controlling prices, restrictive agreements, and sharing markets lost their corporate charters.

In 1890 Congress passed the Sherman Act, which declared illegal "every contract, combination in the form of trust, or otherwise" in restraint of interstate and foreign trade or commerce. Every person monopolizing or attempting to monopolize, or who shall "combine with or conspire with any other person or persons to monopolize," any part of such trade or commerce was declared guilty of a misdemeanor. The responsibility for the detection and prosecution of violations of this act now rests with the Antitrust Division of the Department of Justice. After over sixty years of antitrust policy the specific application of the broad prohibitions of the act remains uncertain. Prosecutions have been erratic and infrequent. Questions such as the following arise. What specific acts are monopolizing or attempting to do so? Is monopolizing being in a position to do certain things adverse to the public interest, that is, having the power to do them, or is it doing them? Is intent to be examined or the effect of what was done? If criminal action requires that intent be examined, what type of action avoids this question and concentrates upon potential or actual results?

It is clear that zeal and skill in investigation and in bringing action are important elements in making the law effective. The personnel responsible for enforcement affect the results incalculably. It is clear also that the funds appropriated have not been adequate for the task. There is strong argument that the procedures and penalties provided are unsatisfactory. The Department's investigatory powers are insufficient. It has no power to subpoena in order to secure evidence unless criminal proceedings are started involving indictment by a grand jury. Hence there is resort to this action when other procedure may be preferable. The purpose of criminal prosecution is to punish violators so effectively as to act as a deterrent, but the penalties that may be and have been imposed upon corporate offenders have not hurt greatly. For effective public relief, civil suits are also necessary, and, if violation is found, a dissolution order or a decree as to what is not to be done.[4] Such decrees pose the problem of insuring that the orders are carried out.

In 1914 two additions were made to the antitrust statutes, the Federal Trade Commission and the Clayton acts. The former not only declared unfair methods of competition illegal but set up a special agency to investigate and to act when there was reason to believe that such would be in the public interest. After due notice and hearings the commission may order the offender to cease and desist from the unfair practices. In 1938 the prohibitions of the act were amplified to include deceptive acts and practices as well as a special prohibition of false advertising of foods, drugs, devices, and cosmetics. From the commission's experience it had become clear that the major forms of unfair competition were false and deceptive selling practices, especially in connection with consumers' goods. The effectiveness of the prohibitions was increased somewhat also by statutory alterations in the procedures by which the cease-and-desist orders went into effect.

Certain provisions of the Clayton Act are also administered by the Federal Trade Commission. This act with its amendments prohibits price discrimination among purchasers of commodities of like grade and quality and contracts requiring buyers to abstain from using or dealing in the products of the seller's competitor.[5] It also prohibits interlocking directorates among banks with capital assets of $1,000,000 or more. It also prohibits intercorporate stock acquisitions except for investment purposes and, since 1950, the corporate acquisition by other than banks and common carriers of the assets of another corporation. All these prohibitions are qualified by the phrase "where the effect will be substantially to lessen

4. Without trial proceedings the defendant may accept the court order. This is called a "consent decree," prepared on the basis of negotiations between the department and the defendant. Private suits may also be brought for damages resulting from violation of the act or for injunctions against certain trade practices.

5. The Robinson-Patman Act previously referred to was an amendment of the Clayton Act.

competition or tend to create a monopoly," with the result that the changes in practices have been inconsequential.

What power have consumers through their buying practices to reduce their cost of living? They can of course reduce their expenditures by going without something desired, but can they through their buying techniques secure the same satisfactions for less money? There are possibilities of doing so, known and utilized to a limited extent. Consumers reduce their outlay for a given good or service when they search the market and buy each item at the lowest price offer. They also reduce their outlay if they buy an article of lower grade and price when it serves their purpose as adequately as would one of higher grade and price. If they buy exactly the amount required for a given purpose, they avoid waste or uneconomical use of the excess. They reduce the outlay for seasonal commodities by buying in the low-price season. Probably the most important outlay-reducing practice is the comparison of the quality or qualities of competing goods offered at the same or different prices. Only when such comparisons are accurately made, can buyers select the best for the money or the lowest-priced among identical goods.

The extent to which these practices are put into use will depend, on the one hand, upon consumer knowledge and incentive and, on the other, upon the market itself. There are practical limitations upon the degree to which the consumer buyer can explore the market and buy at the lowest price offered. This buyer is often the homemaker. Buying is but one of her tasks. She has many things to buy. How far shall she extend her quest to learn prices? To how many different retail outlets shall she go? Time and energy costs must be considered. It is obvious that only for the items of large unit costs will there be extensive shopping-around. For many items the amount bought at any one time is relatively small, and the money saving from even a large percentage difference in the prices is small.

The problems involved in selecting from among the goods offered at a particular price the one superior in quality, or with the maximum of the qualities desired and the minimum of those undesired, are the most difficult of all encountered in attempts to keep outlays at a minimum. They arise from the fact that neither inspection nor experience reveals all the facts necessary for intelligent choice in the case of many important purchases. The variety of things bought, the infrequency of some purchases, and the fact that the consumer has many tasks besides buying must also be kept in mind. The buyer, it is true, must know what qualities or characteristics to seek or to avoid if she is to evaluate a good or service in terms of the purpose it serves. Intelligent choice is not possible unless this knowledge exists, but buyer education alone will not solve the problem. The buyer's judgment must always be on the basis of facts known, and either misinformation or incomplete disclosure may lead her astray.

DOES THE MARKET FACILITATE INTELLIGENT CHOICE?

One basis for market appraisal is the degree to which it facilitates or deters the adoption of good buying practices. It should be noted that advertising, for example, greatly expands the effective shopping area and facilitates price comparison as do neighborhood and central shopping districts where stores carrying like items are close together. Another matter with wide ramifications which might be explored is the extent to which the market permits each consumer to acquire just the bundle of utilities she wants enough to pay for and does not force her to take those which she would prefer to do without, either because she prefers the money they cost, or does not desire them at all. Rivalry in efficient service to consumers, in part, takes the form of the study of consumer preferences as to characteristics of product, size of container, retailer service, and the like. The fact is, however, that goods and services are provided not for individuals but for groups of individuals. Thus mass production is possible and the economies it brings. Those whose tastes and preferences do not conform to those of a group large enough to make it profitable to serve them must, when they buy, make the best compromise possible.

The tie-in sale clearly defeats the efforts of consumers to reduce outlays by getting and paying for just what is wanted and that only. Such market practices are relatively rare, but, if one cannot get a car without a radio, the effect is the same. One might also prefer to pay for less chromium trim, but this raises the broader issue just discussed of how many want the same thing. The development of the cash-and-carry store and the one with self-service means that those who do not wish to pay for the services dispensed with can reduce their outlays. Similarly, when consumers can take the "returned-goods" privilege or doorstep delivery of milk or dispense with it at a saving, a reduction in the cost of living is possible.

The consumer's ability to select from among goods offered at a particular price the one with the maximum of the qualities desired, that is, her ability to detect and compare differences both in quantity and in qualities, rests also in large part with the market. As that ability increases, product differentiation not based upon characteristics important

362   *The Family in the American Economy*

to consumers lessens and true quality competition increases. Price differences based upon mistaken assumptions as to product differences decrease. The situation conforms more closely to that described as pure and perfect competition. The market that best serves consumers in the respect noted is the one in which there is the minimum of false and deceptive statement about the goods offered and the maximum of information about those qualities and characteristics which are the basis of consumers' evaluations. When false statement and deception are easy to detect, they are likely to be rare, but, when they are not, the sellers may not consider honesty the best policy. When they can be detected, but only with great care and effort, the market is still unsatisfactory. It is not a market that serves the consumer well or facilitates outlay-reducing efforts.

ATTEMPTS TO OUTLAW MISINFORMATION

Legal standardization of weights and measures came early and the inspection and certification of the correctness of the weights and measures used by sellers. As products came to be sold in packages or containers, rather than "in bulk," further action was taken. The baskets, hampers, barrels, and boxes in which fresh fruits were sold were standardized as were milk containers and in some states those for certain other products. The use or manufacture of odd shapes and sizes, deceptive as to quantity, was forbidden. Since 1913 by federal law packaged foods and drugs entering interstate commerce and, since 1938, cosmetics also must carry an appropriate statement concerning quantity. Slack-filling and deceptive shape or construction of containers have also been forbidden. So far as quantity is concerned, the major problems still remaining arise from the odd shapes and sizes of many packaged goods. Price comparisons are virtually impossible when one package of a particular brand contains $5\frac{1}{2}$, another $8\frac{1}{4}$, another 13 ounces, and the packages of another brand another range of odd amounts. Changes in quantity may conceal what are actually changes in price.

Prevention of misinformation or deception concerning quantity is far easier than with respect to quality. Efforts, however, have been made to do so. No food, drug, "device," or cosmetic entering interstate commerce may bear on its label anything in the form of words or otherwise that is "false or misleading in any particular."[6] Many states have imposed the same restriction upon those originating and sold within their borders. Some states extend the prohibitions only to foods. As was previously noted, the Federal Trade Commission Act now prohibits any deceptive

6. "Devices" in this connection are products the purposes of which are similar to those for which drugs are used.

act or practice by firms in interstate commerce. Thus false or deceptive advertising as well as labeling is forbidden. The act also expressly forbids false advertisement to induce directly or indirectly the purchase of food, drugs, devices, or cosmetics. The false advertisement is one which is "misleading in a material respect." No penalty is attached to false advertisement when this is found unless injury to health may result from the customary or prescribed manner of use of the product or the false advertising was *with intent* to defraud or mislead. Otherwise, as with all other deceptive acts or practices, the remedy is a "cease-and-desist" order. Since few advertisements are used indefinitely in the same form, and one deceptive act or practice to induce purchase may be substituted for another, the firm may be more than ready to cease and desist by the time the commission's order is issued. Extensive publicity of the results of the commission's inquiries and findings would be an additional and possibly the most effective deterrent.

The legislation just discussed is intended primarily to prevent false and misleading statements. It prohibits but does not require. The law with a few exceptions is silent in regard to what must be on the label or in the advertisements. The labels of certain drugs containing special narcotic or hypnotic substances, for example, must indicate the quantity thereof and bear the warning "May be habit-forming," and all must carry "adequate directions for use." By virtue of the procedure prescribed for determining and preventing mislabeling, moreover, the labels of foods and drugs not sold under a common or usual name or that recognized in an official compendium but only under a trade or proprietary name, or those that have two or more ingredients, must properly display and describe their ingredients.

The Wool Products Labeling Act passed in 1939 and the Fur Products Labeling Act in 1951 are true labeling acts. The former not only makes false and deceptive labeling of all products containing wool unlawful but requires that the label shall contain information in regard to the nature of the wool content and the percentage thereof. The latter act, in addition to a prohibition of all false and deceptive advertising, specifically forbids misbranding. Misbranding is then defined not only as false or deceptive labeling but failure to affix to the fur product a label showing the name of the animal or animals that produced the fur as set forth in a Fur Products Name Guide issued, after hearings, by the Federal Trade Commission.

HOW SECURE INFORMATIVE LABELING AND ADVERTISING?

If labels and advertisements are to provide the information in regard to the quality and characteristics of goods that will enable the buyer to make price comparisons between brands and varieties, steps to provide it must be voluntarily taken by suppliers. Various public and private agencies have for some time been attempting to promote and assist in such a movement. Action on the part of one supplier is not sufficient. Information provided by one firm facilitates selection among items supplied by this firm. If increase in sales results, other firms might follow the example of the first. But the terms used by one firm to designate quality or characteristic might not have the same meaning as those used by another. One firm's Grade A might not be identical with another's Grade A. On this matter it is essential that suppliers act together. They must agree to speak a common language as they do when they call a given weight a "pound" or a given length a "yard."

Even if all suppliers were willing, informative labeling and advertising would be limited. For some items it is unnecessary, and for others it is not at present technically possible. No information need be given on matters that buyers can and must judge for themselves. The becomingness of a hat is clearly a matter of taste, and inspection of the hat on the wearer will alone give the answer. Further, information can be given about a specific product only if the relevant facts are known. Unless there are reliable and relatively easy methods of test of performance or the extent to which the article has the desired or undesired characteristics, accurate statements cannot be made. Butter-fat content of milk, for example, could be judged only roughly by taste or appearance before the invention of the Babcock test. Similarly it should be noted that prevention of misinformation depends upon the establishment of "standards of identity and quality" and the development of adequate means of "testing" each labeled or advertised article to ascertain conformity with the standard. The extension of informative labeling and advertising depends upon the development of the knowledge and devices that would make it possible.

Such limitations as those mentioned upon the scope of informative labeling and advertising do not explain why useful information that could be given is now absent or why certain designations of grade or quality are misleading rather than helpful. "Large" olives, for example, are the smallest offered for sale, and A-1 plated silverware, the lowest in quality. No. 1 may be highest grade for one food product, and third grade for another. Some have argued that correct and easily recognizable designations of grade would deter purchase of the inferior grades. It would if they were offered at the same prices as the superior, but not if there were a price differential. Inferior cuts of meat are purchased, although the best cuts are also in the market. Grade labeling is not an economic but a technical problem, that is, the issues involved have to do with standards of quality and the adequacy of possible methods of test. Grade labeling, that is, designation of over-all quality, is appropriate in any case for only certain classes of products. For many it is unnecessary if certain essential facts in regard to characteristics are given. Many products also are too complex and the importance of various characteristics to consumers too varied to make over-all quality measurement possible. It may be very important to know the fastness of color and the potential shrinkage of the material in window draperies, but an over-all quality designation would be out of the question.

The question that any seller will ask in this connection, as in others is: What practice or policy will pay? What effect will informative labeling have on sales? On competitive position? Is there large consumer demand for such information? How many consumers could and would use it as a basis for selection? Does the increase in number of those using such testing agencies as Consumers Union and Consumers Research indicate a demand? The question whether information pays and what kinds of information pay leads over into the larger issue of sales-promotion methods and policies. In general, do they tend to be adverse or beneficial to the consumer interest?

SALES PROMOTION

It is often said that one characteristic of market development is that the attention of business firms has increasingly shifted toward selling. Rivalry has taken the form of attempts to increase sales. Aggressive salesmanship has become the watchword. The art of "winning friends and influencing people" is sedulously studied. Being and doing are not enough. We must actively promote what we have to "sell." Sellers must do more than inform. They must also persuade or cajole. They even devise means of getting a favorable response without persuasion. They "make" people buy if that is possible.

The amount and character of the information given by a seller will vary. Every seller may be expected to put his best foot forward whether applying for a job or advertising a product. The extent to which the seller can withhold facts that might have an adverse effect upon sales will differ. False claims that can be quickly detected are unlikely. Those that cannot be readily detected present a temptation especially if buyer and seller are not face to face and no personal responsibility is felt. If the general philosophy is, "Let the buyer beware," or "If he is fool enough to believe it, let him believe it," the selling appeal will be one thing; if it is different, it will be another.

Advertising has become a potent and persuasive method of selling. Some emphasize the glamour, the color, the pleasurable excitement, and hurly-burly it has added to our lives. Others emphasize its economic benefits, its effect upon the level and standard of living, its essential place in the market process in a free-enterprise economy. A means of communication between suppliers of goods and potential buyers is essential. Advertising is potentially a cheap and effective means in terms of persons reached per dollar of outlay. It can reach all who can read, or even all who can listen or look. Some goods sell themselves, but the buyers' knowledge of what is available would be limited if confined to what he sees in the stores or in another's possession. The label discloses information only to those who see the goods. Sales talk in the form of person-to-person communication is the most expensive way of informing the buyer.

How much useful information do advertisements give about the products advertised? The amount found will depend upon what is considered useful. Roughly, advertisements fall into two classes. There are those that are essentially notices that specific items are for sale. Retailers' advertisements are usually of this character. National advertising, that for which the major outlay is made, is quite different. Paid for by the manufacturer, it is essentially designed to create a demand for a specific product, or group of products, or to center it on a particular brand. A large proportion of the dollars spent go toward promoting the sale of a selected list of goods, relatively few in proportion to the kinds and varieties available. The character of the information given about the product will be determined by the probable effect upon sales, since increase or maintenance of sales volume is the purpose for which the advertisement is composed. Since the superlative and the slogan, repeated over and over, bring brand familiarity and are likely to maximize sales, they are familiar features of national advertising.

Since large-scale production is impossible without a large market, the effect of advertising upon volume of sales and hence upon scale of production is often emphasized, and from that the conclusion that advertising reduces unit cost of production and therefore price. The optimum size of a producing unit varies. For manufactured goods which are thus extensively advertised it is relatively large. It does not follow that, as demand increases for all goods or even for all manufactured goods, so does the size of the producing unit and with it the economies of size. Each business unit may have one or many plants, and the optimum size of the business unit in terms of effectiveness of operation varies. From a general rule that advertising if successful reduces unit cost of production of the advertised product, it would follow that, the greater the demand, the lower the minimum average cost whatever the line of production. Thus if demand were sufficient, this minimum would approach or reach zero. Clearly, with given techniques of production, increase in demand will if anything raise rather than lower the minimum unit cost. Its decrease must come from other sources. Increase in demand for one product means, moreover, decrease in demand for another. The resultant effects upon costs in that industry must also be taken into account.

The outlays for sales promotion, of which advertising is a major form, must, it would seem, be viewed in a somewhat different light from those for growing, manufacturing, storing, and transportation. Outlays for advertising are not simply those incurred to provide the amount demanded, but those incurred to alter the amount demanded of a given commodity or service or of one supplier's brand. Without these outlays it is argued there would be less interproduct competition, less incentive to devise new goods or improve old ones, less competition between brands. Without these outlays also there would be a lesser degree of the monopoly which is inherent in product differentiation. A monopolistic differential is possible in the price of a successfully promoted brand, the amount varying with the impact of the competition from and the degree of preference for another supplier's brand.

More serious than the possible effects of advertising upon the cost of living is its possible effect upon consumption standards and habits. It has often been alleged that these effects have been extremely beneficial. Without advertising, it is said, we would have a less dynamic standard of living. New wants would develop more slowly; old wants be less urgent. We would as a group be content with less and more inclined to settle back and take our ease. Advertising also, it is often argued, renders a service to consumers by increasing the want-satisfying power of goods. It does not simply point out their characteristics or make them more alluring but adds values to those already there. The possibilities of this legerdemain are obviously limited. The quality most frequently alleged to have been added is glamour.

It is also argued that advertising has altered our consumption habits to our advantage and has increased the use of many things important to our welfare. This argument has implicit in it a comparison of the relative welfare merits of the widely advertised goods and those without such promotion. If the consumption of one good increases, that of its substitute declines; or, if one gets a larger share of the consumer's dollar, another must get a smaller. If advertising has altered our consumption pattern in beneficial ways, this result has been purely fortuitous. Decisions to make large advertising outlays are not based upon an appraisal of what changes in consumption habits are desirable. The nutritionist's judgment is not sought before the foods and beverages to be widely advertised are chosen. Those for which advertising outlays are negligible may be those the consumption of which should be increased from the nutritive standpoint. Those advertised extensively such as beer, other alcoholic beverages, the "soft" drinks, coffee, and vitamin tablets may improve it the least.

HIGH COST OF LIVING AS A PRODUCT OF MONETARY INFLATION

Everyone is familiar with the sharp and extensive increases in the price of almost everything during and immediately following World War II. Similarly a sharp upward movement coincided with the beginning of military operations in Korea. If the movement of the Consumers' Price Index is studied; a high point will also be noted in 1920. These upward movements of the price level are clearly associated with an extensive movement of resources toward the preparation for or prosecution of military operations. The results that follow such changes in prices need not be elaborated. The money incomes of some are fixed; others lag behind the movement in prices. The real value of savings accounts, bonds, and insurance policies depreciates. The dollars counted on for home purchase, for children's education, for the support of widows and orphans, for old age security, will no longer suffice for the purpose. At the same time others gain. Their money incomes move upward. Commitments to pay can be met in dollars with less purchasing power than those received. There are, in short, "sizable, haphazard and often undesirable shifts in the distribution of wealth and income."[7]

Less sharp and extensive but appreciable movements of the general price level also accompany the fluctuations of business activity; an upward movement in the prosperity period, a sharp decline as depression sets in, with a slow movement upward in the recovery. The falling prices in periods of low levels of production and employment are a matter of concern rather than of rejoicing. Business firms experience great shrinkage in income and many become insolvent. The unemployed and the underemployed have so few dollars that their enhanced purchasing power has little meaning. Only those with fixed income benefit. But incomes of fixed dollar amount may also shrivel or disappear if the claims they represent cannot be met. Assets depreciate in money value or may become worthless.

7. Lester V. Chandler, *An Introduction to Monetary Theory* (New York: Harper & Bros., 1940), p. 15.

In popular usage all sharp increases in price level are called "inflation," that is, prices are inflated. As a matter of fact something else is inflated, and this inflation plays an important part in the movement of prices observed. What is inflated is the supply of money, either currency or checkbook money, which comes into the market as demand for goods and services. If this increase is greater than that of goods and services, an upward movement of prices is inevitable.

It is generally agreed that, whatever other forces may be operative, inflation plays a major part in accelerating a boom and deflation in accentuating a depression. In a boom period, if prices are rising, this fact in itself stimulates spending. Consumers expect that present incomes will continue or rise. They therefore spend freely. They buy freely on the deferred-payment plan. Anticipation of still further advance in prices also stimulates buying. Business concerns in such periods have good profit expectations. They expand operations, possibly plant capacity. Anticipation of further price increase leads to a building-up of inventories. Thus we have many factors making for an increased rate of spending of both liquid assets and income. We have also an increased demand for loans, a demand that lending institutions will find it profitable to meet. Deposits subject to check will increase in response to this demand. Thereby comes an increase in the volume of money.

Banks have it in their power to create money, not currency but checkbook money, the limit set by the required "reserve." This reserve for all banks that are members of the Federal Reserve System is a deposit account subject to check in the Federal Reserve Bank of their district.[8] This reserve or balance of the member-bank with the Federal Reserve Bank must not fall below a specified percentage of its own deposits subject to check, the percentage set by the Board of Governors of the Federal Reserve System under maximums established by Congress. A bank builds up its reserve as it sends in more checks drawn on other banks than other banks send in checks drawn on it. Since these cancel out for the system as a whole, the reserves of the banking *system* increase only as more currency (mainly Federal Reserve notes) comes back than goes out, as net imports of gold into the country increase, as net "advances" by Federal Reserve banks to member-banks increase, as the volume of commercial paper discounted (i.e., sold) by members to the Federal Reserve banks increases, and, more importantly, as the volume of United States government securities sold to the Federal Reserve banks increases.

Both the members and the Federal Reserve banks have large holdings

8. The bulk of the country's deposits are in banks that are members of the system.

of government securities. The major and effective instrument by which the Federal Reserve System can upon its own initiative control the excess reserve of the banking system is by its "open-market" transactions in such securities. By sale it draws down the member-banks' balances in the Federal Reserve banks; by purchase it brings them up. The important fact in relation to the possibility of monetary inflation is that the power of the banking system to increase checkbook money is several times that of the excess reserve, the multiplier depending upon the reserve requirement. In prosperity periods it will use that power, since demand for loans is strong, and it will be profitable to meet it. In depression periods it does not, since the reverse conditions obtain. The Federal Reserve may then put a brake upon the expansion of purchasing power in the form of checkbook currency in periods of boom if it knows when and the extent to do so, but it cannot increase the demand for checkbook money or the use of excess reserve by banks in a depression period.

The upward movement of the price level in a prosperity period may in itself seem to have few adverse consequences. But within the price structure come distortions which operate to check the expansion. Relative prices will alter. Some prices move upward faster than others. The prices that are costs begin to approach product prices more closely. Expansion of productive capacity lessens. Demand for new construction, machinery, and consumer durables lessens. Some of the forces that moved production and employment upward now begin to work in the opposite direction, first slightly, then with greater impact. Some prices resist downward movement, especially wages. Monopolistic prices in general change less than those subject to competition. Both in boom and in depression the change in the less competitive industries and occupations may be in levels of production and employment rather than in prices. In an economy that is getting ready for or engaged in extensive military operations a new factor is added. Expectations of price increases, of shortages, of big government orders for products, will accelerate rate of spending of income and liquid assets. Demand for bank and other credit increases. The characteristic features of a prosperity period or of movement from a depression period, if such there has been, may appear.

But the monetary inflation that characteristically accompanies a war situation comes from another source, the need of the government for greater purchasing power. If this need were fully met by a transfer of funds that would otherwise be spent from citizens to government through taxes or loans, no monetary inflation because of the fiscal needs of the government would occur. The citizens would have fewer dollars to offer for a possibly diminishing stock of goods and services for civilian consumption and the government more for military purposes. It is true that increase in production will lessen the necessity of a cutback in civilian supplies, or, if the increase is sufficient, the economy may provide "guns and butter" too. The latter is unlikely, unless the start comes when production is at a low level with resources unemployed and the war preparation is on a relatively small scale. It is also true that, if other government expenditures for nonmilitary purposes are cut in the amount those for military purposes increase, total need for revenues will not increase. Inspection of the budget would show the degree to which that would be possible or desirable. It is true also that if citizens and firms abstained from spending a sufficiently large proportion of the incomes received, these dollars would not become effective demand. Liquid assets in various forms would increase. Large cash holdings, checking balances as well as Series E bonds, are potential demand, however. Whenever released, their potentiality is realized. Voluntary restraints upon demand for loans or by lending agencies upon their extension also cut down the volume of purchasing power entering the market.

A large, sustained war effort clearly requires increased taxes and borrowing. Purchasing power secured otherwise means monetary inflation, its extent measured by the gap between transfers and government outlays, its short-run effect upon the price level reduced by controls, voluntary and otherwise, and by the increase in production. Open, monetary inflation recognized by everyone as such takes the form of the issue of paper money. The government uses its monetary power to meet its fiscal needs. There are many examples of this procedure. Less open is borrowing from a central bank. In this country this would take the form of sale of new bond or note issues to the Federal Reserve banks. The Treasury, then, has a credit to its account upon which it can draw; the banks have the securities. This power has seldom been utilized, and there is at present a legal limit upon the amount that may be so acquired and held. Instead the member-banks absorb that part of new issues not fully taken by nonbank buyers, with the Federal Reserve System taking whatever steps may be necessary to insure that they still meet reserve requirements. The effect is, however, to create new bank deposits and monetary inflation. World War II was in part financed by this method as other wars have been financed in part by the issue of government paper money.

Banking operations, the fiscal and monetary policies of the government, may seem to some remote from those problems that concern the consumer and the family. Many of those who voice special interest in family and consumer welfare give no attention to the issues suggested in the preceding discussion. By doing so, they often mistake symptoms and results for causes and put their emphasis upon correctives of little effectiveness. They may even advocate the wrong remedies and are unprepared to give intelligent support to policies of basic importance.

CHAPTER XIX

THE STANDARD OF LIVING

AGAIN and again in the preceding chapters reference has been made to the standard of living as a force determining behavior. The degree of striving for advancement in economic position, to maximize income and make it go farther, is in large part explained by the dynamic character of our standard of living. It is the desire for a certain manner of living that accounts for the persistence of small-scale, decentralized households. The standard of living explains the homemaker's use of time and the allocation of money income among alternative uses. The economic necessity that forces married women into the labor force is the relation between the earnings of the husband and the cost of maintaining the standard. The relation between standard and income spells surplus or deficit in the family budget. The adequacy of incomes for family support is measured by the money cost of providing a given level of living. The high cost of living is the high cost of maintaining a given standard.

WHAT IS ONE'S STANDARD OF LIVING?

What exactly is one's standard of living? An excellent definition is that formulated by Devine, who said:

In simplest terms the standard of living means all those things which one insists upon having. It is not merely a collective name for the commodities enjoyed at a given time, but for those which are so related to one another, and so important to the consumer, that if any one of them is lacking forces to restore it are immediately put into action. . . . Elusive and kaleidoscopic though it may be, nevertheless the conception represented by this phrase is a definite and powerful reality. The expression means something to everyone; the thing itself is the controlling force which shapes every life. . . . Each individual has his own standard, determining every choice he makes. Each family has its own, the result of combinations, consolidations, and compromises among the standards of its individual members. Each locality and each nation has its standard, produced by the interplay of an infinite number of economic, social, and psychic forces.[1]

1. E. T. Devine, *The Normal Life* (New York: Macmillan Co., 1924), p. 1. See also *ibid.*, p. 129, where he speaks of "our standard of living—that indefinable force—which is something more than the sum of its parts, something different from any one of them, a power to which we defer unconsciously in every choice we make, and which we frequently invoke to sustain arguments or justify general policies."

373

All those things one insists upon having—the essential values to be sought —make up one's standard of living; in other words, they determine the first things to be secured through the expenditure of time and money.

The perplexing problem in arriving at a clear-cut notion of what exactly is included in a "standard of living" is to differentiate between the things one desires and those things one "insists upon having." It is obvious that in the Western cultures at least there are no limits upon desires. Except possibly in the highest-income groups there are always goods desired but not yet attainable. But there are also the goods most desired in the sense that they will be first secured and last given up; they are the essentials; they are those "so important to the consumer that if any one of them is lacking forces to restore it are immediately put into action." Everyone probably has, more or less consciously formulated, an ideal standard of living, a level toward which he moves as income and other opportunities permit; he has also, again not necessarily consciously formulated, a standard that he insists upon maintaining. To attain the first would be a highly desirable state of economic well-being, to attain the second is essential, and to fall below it is intolerable. The ideal standard includes all those things hoped for. It is a projection of the trend line into the future; it shows direction of change. But there is a standard other than the ideal standard. There is a scale of preferences, a code or plan for material living that satisfies our sense of the necessary, the decent, the tolerable, although it does not represent our ideal.

SIGNIFICANCE OF THE STANDARD OF LIVING

Within the limits set by resources it is the standard of living that determines the character of the real income of the family—the character of the food, clothing, housing, and other goods sought for the amusement or edification of its members. On the one side of the ledger, there are the time and energy spent in production with the attendant disutilities and, it may be, offsetting satisfactions; on the other side, there is an achieved way of living embodying in varying degrees subsistence, health, vigor, comfort, decency, beauty, order, propitiation, recognition, prestige, knowledge, experience, play, self-expression, creation, social intercourse, in the concrete forms approved at the time and place.

Choices of alternative uses of time and money may then be described as attempts to achieve a particular standard of living. Devine calls the standard of living "a power to which we defer unconsciously in every choice we make." Curiously enough it is not only the power that determines our choice but also the power that makes it appear that we have no choice. The family whose money income is barely sufficient to enable it to maintain its customary standard does not feel that it has any freedom of choice in expenditure. Each dollar comes tagged with the purpose for which it must go. It is only when there is a margin between resources, either in time or in money, and the time and money cost of the standard that there is any sense of real freedom of choice. A surplus over and above the cost of necessaries permits optional consumption. A rise in a family's standard of living may therefore paradoxically mean the enjoyment of a greater variety and abundance of goods but at the same time a greater sense of pressure and of limitation upon the power of choice.

THE STANDARD OF LIVING AS AN ATTITUDE
TOWARD A GIVEN MODE OF LIVING

"Standard of living," as that phrase is used here, is not the same as manner of living. Rather "it is an attitude toward, a way of regarding or of judging, a given mode of life."[2] The reality of the existence of standards is most clearly shown in the different attitudes that people may have toward similar modes of living. A study made in 1928 at Yale University by a committee appointed to study the "academic standard of living" contains significant evidence on this point. The families co-operating in the investigation were asked not only to give such data as the amount of their salaries and other income and of their principal expenditures but also a description or characterization of their mode of life. The returns were arranged in fifty-four groups, each group containing families of similar size and economic status. The first group, consisting of husband and wife without children and an income of about $2,000, said that "the level of living possible . . . represents life at the cheapest and barest with nothing over for the emergencies of sickness and childbirth."[3] To secure the proper perspective upon this statement, it should be noted that the incomes of four-fifths of American married couples probably did not then rise above this level unless supplemented by the earnings of wife and children. The Yale instructors said that on $2,500 a "man and wife must live with extreme frugality." Even when the income was $3,000, the group in question felt that "for a man and wife it is life on the simplest plane"; yet not a tenth of American families had this income. At $4,000 the family with young children "must live with extreme economy in the cheapest obtainable apartment." Even at $5,000 they say they "achieve nothing

2. Hazel Kyrk, *A Theory of Consumption* (Boston: Houghton Mifflin Co., 1923), p. 175.
3. Y. Henderson and M. R. Davie, *Incomes and Living Costs of a University Faculty* (New Haven: Yale University Press, 1928), pp. 7–11 for this and subsequent quotations. The dollar incomes given here would be the equivalents of incomes probably 50 per cent higher now.

better than 'hand to mouth living.' " At the $6,000 level "the family containing young children can barely break even," although the "married man with no children may at this level live simply." Even on $7,000 "the family containing two or three young children . . . can make ends meet only by keeping the expenses for service as low as possible," and those with incomes of $8,500 live "on the edge of a deficit." Even at $12,000, while there are children in school, clothing is said to be limited, and "often the life insurance that can be kept up is inadequate."

From the foregoing it is evident how families of a certain group may feel about modes of living that are clearly far beyond those attainable by the majority. It is evident that the expressions, "extreme frugality," "simple living," "hand-to-mouth living," "life at its cheapest and barest," "limited clothing," are entirely relative as used by this group. They describe their mode of living as measured by their standard; they indicate the limitations felt upon their freedom of choice and their optional consumption.

ORIGIN OF OUR STANDARDS

Whence comes this concept of goods essential for a tolerable mode of life, these things we insist upon having? It seems clear that our standards are in large part at least social products; they are part of the current mores.[4] They are folkways with "doctrines of welfare implicit in them."[5] In other words our wants are culture products and represent culture traits. The individual regards them as in part imposed from without and in a sense compelling him to live in a particular way. Everyone is conscious of the obligatory character of some standards of consumption; of the fact that there are penalties for failure to adopt the accepted mode of living of his group. He will lose status and come into disrepute. He will be regarded as "queer" or as violating fundamental rules of conduct. The individual's feeling that he must have the essentials for living according to his standard expresses not only the strength of his individual desire but his sense of social compulsion and the compulsion of his own system of values. The psychologists Murphy and Newcomb say:

The value world of a given organism is the world of objects to which it is fixated. . . . To us the distinction between immediate biological needs and socially derived needs becomes meaningless. The degree of urgency involved in a value when one wants lamb chops and alligator pears and when one wants Stravinsky may be the same. The urgency of the food need may be great; but if we forget the white rat . . . and look squarely at the man, we find that in many cultures the music need may be

4. W. G. Sumner, *Folkways* (Boston: Ginn & Co., 1907), p. 41.
5. *Ibid.*, p. 30.

far more compelling for many persons and at many times, than is the food need. . . .
Granted that the taste for Stravinsky is acquired, so are all other tastes. . . . Since
values cannot possibly exist in separate pigeon holes of the individual but tend to re-
inforce or contend with one another it seems correct to speak of the organization of
values in a system.[6]

This system of values is what is here called a standard of living.

To quote again Murphy and Newcomb: "Individual preferences and
general cultural preferences develop by a process of fixation. The drive is
channeled or canalized in a specific direction characteristic of the person
and his culture."[7] What is the direction characteristic of our culture?
Elizabeth Hoyt has developed the theory that "the great cultures of the
world are distinguished by the degree to which each is dominated by one
particular interest type"[8] and that "the difference between modern
civilized societies and primitive lies not in types of interest, but in the
way these interests are expressed."[9] These interests, she says, may be
divided into the active and the quietistic, the former characterizing the
Western and the latter the Eastern cultures. But these are not the only
great cultural differences. Some may be outward-looking and objective,
others inward-looking and subjective. Ours might typify the former. These
classifications, however, do not indicate the particular interest dominant
in a particular culture, active and outward-looking or the reverse.

There are, she says, four types of interests which, although found
everywhere expressing themselves in diverse ways, are of greatly varying
importance in different cultures. She designates these as the "intellectual," the "technological," the "aesthetic," and the "empathetic." The
first expresses itself in conceiving ideas and systems of thought; the
second in that invention which gives control over one's environment. It is
interest in science applied in life. "In the society we are most familiar
with, our own, the technological interest is far more dominant than the
intellectual."[10] The aesthetic interests she defines as those shown in the
appreciation of what is "graceful, charming, orderly, harmonious or
otherwise conformable to some conception of beauty."[10] The empathetic
interest "arises from the human being's sense of the relationship of his ego
to the cosmos. . . . Empathetic means, by derivation, entering, living or
feeling in something outside of oneself."[11] The four basic interests here

6. Gardner Murphy, Lois Barclay Murphy, and T. M. Newcomb, *Experimental Social
Psychology* (New York: Harper & Bros., 1937), pp. 198–99, 204.
7. *Ibid.*, p. 191.
8. *Consumption in Our Society* (New York: McGraw-Hill Book Co., 1938), p. 23.
9. *Ibid.*, p. 26.
10. *Ibid.*, p. 20.   11. *Ibid.*, pp. 22–23.

briefly described are not the only ones that always and everywhere manifest themselves in various forms. Two others, which she calls the "sensory" and the "social," are dominant and important always and everywhere. But basic differences between cultures are, she argues, accounted for by the dominance there of one or the other of the four—the intellectual, the technological, the aesthetic, the empathetic. The American standard would then reflect the dominant interest in the great culture of which our society is a part.

The acquisition of the values and the compulsions that determine one's standard of life is a part of group life; the standard of living is a behavior pattern or system of values that is the result of a process of precept and example that begins at birth. Furthermore, one not only learns but lives the standard of consumption. The child is fed, clothed, sheltered, according to the ways of the family in which he is born and grows up. Habit and custom, observation of practices and attitudes, and express indoctrination build up the likes, dislikes, desires, and aversions which govern concrete choices of goods. The family is not the only value-building group. Other kinfolk, the neighbors, friends, the school, play their part. As times goes on, the family in fact may lose its potency. Contact with new groups and new ideas may disestablish or modify established habits and customs. Deliberate attempts may be made by schools and advertisers to build up new values. The modifiability of standards fixed in early life varies greatly from group to group and time to time. In some the ways taught by the family always remain paramount; in others the sanction of other groups is more important, and their ways set the standard. Habit and custom may be exceptionally powerful in governing the choices of some consumption goods, as food; with others, as clothing, contemporary influences may govern.

NATURE OF OUR STANDARDS

If the preceding analysis of the origin of our standards is accurate, it follows that standards of living vary not from individual to individual but from time to time, country to country, and class to class. It follows that the prevailing standard of living will reflect not only the resources, skills, and techniques for producing goods that have been worked out by a given group but attitudes and beliefs as well. Bathrooms, cars, television sets, refrigerators, and fresh fruit and vegetables all the year round may be a part of the American standard of living, but so also are certain values —physical health and vigor, cleanliness, conforming to and mixing with the crowd.

There are at least three ways of describing a group's standard of living, and perhaps no picture is complete in which the situation is not presented in these three lights. One way is in terms of the specific commodities and services which the given group struggles to secure, the kind and quantity of its foodstuffs, its clothing, housing, furniture, personal service, reading matter, medical attention, its system of heating and lighting, plumbing and refrigeration. The age of marriage is also a part of the standard, the formal education considered necessary for children, the age at which they go to work, the kind and amount of work expected of the wife.

Another way of describing the standard of living is an account of the way goods and services are assembled and organized for use—the arrangement, the order, the ritual, that are necessary for their enjoyment. Such a picture is necessary if we are to know the standard as it really is. The concrete character of our desires for food and clothing and possibly the larger part of the cost of satisfying them in time and money are not indicated merely by an inventory or record of goods purchased. The money cost of feeding the family is not shown merely by the figures put down in household accounts under the heading "food." As distinct a part of the food standard as the kinds and quantities of foodstuffs considered essential are the rules for preparation and serving, the paraphernalia, the place and times for serving, the appropriate foods for each time, the order in which they are served. In the same way there is a code governing the house and its subdivisions, their use and their furnishings, their order and cleanliness. There is one also for clothing, the kind proper for each age, sex, and occasion; there is a code that determines the appropriate combination of the various garments and the appropriate accessories. Weddings, births, funerals, holidays, and hospitality also are governed by standards of what is essential and appropriate.

The third and most difficult way of describing a standard is to analyze it into the fundamental values sought, as health and vigor, comfort, cleanliness, beauty, prestige, ostentation, play, knowledge, experience, self-expression, creation, social intercourse, propitiation, and recognition. This third way of describing the standard of living of a group is the most difficult and the one most infrequently attempted. A characterization of a standard in these terms constitutes an appraisal or evaluation of it, for each term has an ethical significance for us. When described in the other terms suggested, one may say it is high or low, costs a great deal or very little, is simple or elaborate, old-fashioned or sophisticated. But what it is ethically like comes only from a depiction of the fundamental values sought and secured.

The other side of the fact that standards of living vary from time to time, country to country, and class to class is their striking uniformity from family to family of the same time, country, section, and class. We assume a relatively high degree of uniformity and predictability of consumers' behavior. Given the place, time, economic level, and a few details of family history and composition, a fairly accurate picture of the standard of living can be drawn. Anyone who knows Middletown can describe the food, clothing, housing, and recreation of the families living there. The budgets of the families of the same income and occupation would reveal amazingly similar patterns for the expenditure of time and money.

THE AMERICAN STANDARD OF LIVING

Nothing is more difficult than to see the peculiar characteristics of one's own standard of living. That is so from the nature of the case; the values incorporated here are those we take for granted. It seems self-evident that certain things are necessary and desirable for comfortable, decent living; that families should strive to live in certain ways and should expend their time and money for certain purposes. In fact, the family is scarcely conscious of the ends it strives for in its expenditure or of the ends it actually achieves. Rather it thinks of the specific consumers' goods which are the means to those ends. The goods become ends in themselves, and there is little evaluation or critical appraisal of the ultimate ends achieved. Therefore, to promote both appraisal and understanding, every possible way of analyzing one's own standard should be sought and every device used that would enable one to view it objectively and in contrast with the standards of other groups and other times.

Are there distinctive characteristics of the American standard of living? The phrase is frequently used as though it stood for a unique set of values. Ours is a variant of that which prevails in all Western industrial countries. Yet there is a process called "Americanizing" the foreigner and "Americanizing" Europe. Some say that America is too big and too varied to admit of a characteristic American standard. It is true that each section and each class has to a degree its distinctive standard. But it is significant that modes of living of all groups tend toward a certain pattern. Given income, means of communication, and mobility, they move in a predictable direction, toward that set of values that is the peculiar American standard.

It is possible, as was said earlier, to describe the American standard of living in terms of the per capita or per family consumption of various articles of food and clothing, types of housing, furnishings, and so on.

Interesting comparisons of our consumption of bread, cheese, meat, sugar, oranges, fresh vegetables, automobiles, and bathtubs with that of other countries can be made. Trends in our consumption habits may be noted. It is a commonplace to say after such comparisons that the American standard of living is quantitatively high. That is, the number and variety of goods considered essential are great; the goods customarily used are of relatively high money cost—white bread rather than black, secondary foodstuffs rather than primary—and they include many articles deemed luxuries by other peoples and in former times. Studies of family expenditures also give a picture of the standard of living of particular American groups—farmers, wage-earners, or the professional class as the case may be—in so far as it can be shown by quantitative data.

Statement of the kinds and quantities of commodities and services consumed by a nation or class within that nation is not, however, the only way of describing the standard of living. Characterizations of American life and manners by thoughtful observers in quite other terms are often equally suggestive and illuminating. For example, a generalization rather commonly made is that the American standard of living has the attributes of a *nouveau riche* standard with its emphasis upon quantity rather than quality and upon display of wealth. When we point out either a public building or a private possession, our first or only comment is the cost, it is said. One writer has compared us to peasants pouring into the baron's castle, feasting and gaping. As he scathingly put it: "From the severity and thrift of pioneer life the great mass of our people passed over into elegant circumstances with all the abandon of a crowd of country men coming noisily into the possession of unimagined splendor. Only as we appreciate this epic occurrence can we understand our highly over-stuffed society."[12] It is true that as a people we have come suddenly into wealth, and there is no doubt that here lies the explanation for certain of our tastes and consumption habits.

Other interesting aspects of the American standard are frequently noted. One is that there is in it the notion that to raise one's standard in the quantitative sense is necessary. In five years one must be living in a larger house, with better furniture, a better car, more labor-saving devices, and with more to spend for food and clothes. If not, the standard as a long-time pattern has not been attained. Simply to maintain the status quo is to fall short of the minimum essentials. Another marked characteristic of American consumption habits is their similarity from class to class. Variations are not in kind, merely in degree. This is the result of a

12. C. W. Ferguson, "High Class," *Harper's Magazine*, CLXIV (March, 1932), 450.

democratization process that is the product not only of the social and political structure but of an educational system which was to some extent deliberately planned for this purpose.[13] Class standards of consumption begin to break down as soon as free purchase and sale on the market begin. But in America the assumption has been that the way of living that is good for one is good for all or proper for one is proper for all; and the schools, aided by a host of supplementary agencies for popular education, have set themselves to impart the knowledge of what is good, necessary, and correct. What is here described as a democratization of consumption is by others called an obnoxious standardization of consumption. The American ideal is described by a British economist as "the maximum production and the maximum consumption of the maximum number of standardised articles."[14] To emulate it, he tells his countrymen, would mean a different type of civilization. Mass production, he says, enforces this standardization of consumption.

> Insofar as the individual in his personal consumption shows a desire to depart from the mass standard the tendency will be for a rising price to punish him for his adventurousness, and to drive him back to accepting the standard pattern of consumption. The very heterogeneity of the American population facilitates the shepherding of the consumer: deprived of his old cultural background, any scheme of values already in the ascendant will be accepted by the newcomer: the mobility of the population, itself largely a product of the standardized car and in its turn making the car a standardized one, adds to the chance of a uniform scheme of life being accepted. To the European visitor, it is not the productive, but the consumptive, aspects of American civilization which arouse most astonishment.[15]

One might add that the astonishment is especially great if he comes from a society where there are class distinctions and a high degree of income inequality.

One way of characterizing a standard of living is in terms of the values rated relatively high and those rated relatively low. What according to the American standard is rated relatively high? Formal education certainly goes on that list. Decade by decade the period of compulsory school attendance has been pushed up, and family budgets as a matter of course allow for high-school and college attendance or even beyond. Protection of health—everything promoting physical health, bodily vigor, and longevity—is also undoubtedly on the list of values rated relatively high. This motive without question justifies any expenditure of time and

13. T. S. McMahon, *Social and Economic Standards of Living* (New York: D. C. Heath & Co., 1925), chap. vii.

14. T. E. Gregory, "Is America Prosperous?" *Economica*, No. 28, March, 1938, p. 13.

15. *Ibid.*, pp. 4–5.

money. Physical comfort and bodily cleanliness too, it may be alleged, rank relatively high in the American standard of living. "Americanization," it is quite frankly said at times, means inculcation of our passion for hot water, large and numerous towels, soaps, and other cleansing agents. The physical comfort motif shows itself in the widespread systems of central heating, electric fans, refrigeration, and easy chairs. We submit, it is true, to a great deal of physical discomfort in our clothes, in our overcrowded trains, and overcrowded city life in general, but there are nonetheless clear-cut expressions of the desire for comfortable living.

The American standard rates, it is said, good clothes above good housing, and "smartness" or style in dress and ornament above beauty, durability, or expensiveness. It rates high things that are new in spite of some evidence in architecture and furniture of a homesickness for the past. Hundred per cent Americans also rate high activities of a gregarious nature, a valuation that shows itself especially in leisure-time activities. They enjoy being with the crowd, yelling in unison. In fact, all elements of the standard show high susceptibility to mob movements. What "everybody" has or does must be good.

Labor- and time-saving devices are other goods which are rated high in the American standard: the telephone, the typewriter, the automobile, the water on tap, the electrical devices. If a time-saving appliance exists, that one should have it admits of no argument. Curiously it happens that time-killing devices also rate high. We fear boredom and the possibility of finding time hanging heavy on our hands. To meet these emergencies, to "kill" time or at least to make it pass quickly without producing ennui, we have "light" literature, the movies, the radio, television, the automobile. These goods have other uses, but they are utilized frequently for the purposes noted. Finally, one curious characteristic of the American standard is the place given in it to outlets for superfluous energy, mental and physical. Among these outlets are the uniquely American articles, chewing gum and rocking chairs. To these may be added dancing, smoking, and, again, automobile riding. None of these involves strenuous activity, but each gives a sense of motion or activity that is relaxing and soothing.

No one who reads the above list of values alleged to characterize the American standard of living will agree with it in its entirety. Agreement, however, is not important. What is important is that each one who would understand a standard, his own or another's, attempt such a listing of both the relatively high values and the relatively low and note evidence of the presence or absence of a given characteristic.

It is even more difficult to secure agreement on a list of goods rated relatively low than on a list of those rated relatively high. The reason is that we desire many of the things we rate relatively low and strive for them to a degree. But how much do we desire them? What we want most we insist upon having, even if we must sacrifice other goods to secure it. Among the things that it may be argued with some plausibility American families estimate relatively low is privacy—witness the front porch, the absence of separation walls between lawns and gardens, and the tendency to eliminate or reduce partition walls within the house. Nor is a quiet dwelling place considered a prime essential judging by the extent to which many families endure noise.[16] Current practice in the use of the radio would even suggest that many prefer noise to silence. Compared with other civilizations, it might also be said that we do not greatly desire leisure and that we are relatively uninterested in personal service and in organized religion and its observances.

Most marked of all, perhaps, is the relatively low esteem in which we hold beauty and the arts in general and manifestations of individual taste and judgment. It is good, we think, to conform and to follow rather than to cultivate individual preference. The appeal to what others do is usually effective. What everyone does and has must be desirable. There are two groups of these others whom we follow. One is just "everybody." No one wants to be different and looked at askance. But there is a second group to be followed, those who know and those with whom one wants to be aligned. The elite are the heroes of the moment, the stars of moviedom, the social leaders, the rich, or, nearer home, the leaders in our crowd.

Miss Hoyt makes the acute observation that there are three kinds of emulation in consumption.[17] One is pecuniary emulation, which encourages the choice of expensive goods and services or those that look expensive. A second is fashion emulation, which encourages the choice of what is currently favored by the fashion arbiters; and, third, there is taste emulation, which leads to the choice of what is judged to be in good taste. Taste emulation, she points out, "masquerades as taste itself." Most common in the United States in her opinion is fashion emulation, which is by no means confined to clothes. One of our most important values is to

16. Expenditures to secure privacy and quiet are for what Hawtrey calls "defensive" purposes, to prevent or remedy discomfort or pain. There are many in this category; expenditures to allay the pangs of hunger, to ward off cold, to cure disease. Expenditures to supply positive satisfactions Hawtrey calls "creative." Only the society where there are many creative expenditures can be said to have attained a high state of well-being (R. G. Hawtrey, *The Economic Problem* [New York: Longmans, Green & Co., 1925], chap. xvii).

17. *Op. cit.*, p. 47.

be up to date, not to be old-fashioned or a back number. Of course if one waits long enough either with ideas or possessions, one is likely to be in the swing of things again. One reason for the observed standardization of consumption is this strong and widespread drive to follow the crowd, that is, the crowd that sets the style in a particular respect. Taste emulation is least common, and it is not always easy, she observes, "to separate from fashion emulation . . . for many canons of so-called good taste have a good deal of fashion in them." Taste emulation is found among those who have become conscious that there is something called "good taste" and wish to demonstrate that they have it. They want what they ought to want, with the result that they get form rather than substance. Taste emulation, however, as Miss Hoyt points out, is the least wasteful form of emulation and is "very closely related to the deliberate discipline and control of tastes for the purpose of maximizing satisfactions."[18]

Disapproving opinion of our aesthetic standards could be cited without end. Miss Hoyt says the American people are far behind the ancient Greeks and probably the modern Chinese and Japanese in comprehension of what aesthetic gratification may mean. Our present status with regard to aesthetics may be compared, she says, to the status of Aristotle and Pliny and their fellow Greeks and Romans with regard to nutrition.[19] C. D. Burns, appraising the consumption habits of Western civilizations, pronounces them higher in cleanliness, food, and shelter and lower in beauty of surroundings.[20] Cram, writing in the *American Scholar*, said: "It is indeed a fact that from the dawn of the first great cultures in Egypt, Crete, and Mesopotamia every high civilization in the long sequence has loved beauty, striven toward its creation, . . . and deliberately expressed itself in terms of beauty; every one—except our own."[21]

A statement of things most and least essential in the foregoing terms would rarely if ever be made by an American family. Statements of things desired are usually in terms of specific consumers' goods of appropriate kinds and quantities, with only vaguely felt reference to the ends to which they are the means. Few families deliberately think through their range of preferences; most accept as good that to which they are accustomed or imitate that which is suggested by the behavior of others. In fact, the family that should deliberately decide that it preferred privacy, quiet,

18. *Ibid.*, p. 52.

19. *The Consumption of Wealth* (New York: Macmillan Co., 1928), p. 175.

20. C. D. Burns, *Industry and Civilization* (London: George Allen & Unwin, Ltd., 1925), chap. vii.

21. Ralph Adams Cram, "The Educational Value of Beauty," *American Scholar*, I (1932), 205.

beauty of surroundings, expression of its own individual taste in dress and furnishings, to physical comfort, time-saving and time-killing devices, fashion, and conformity would find it difficult to attain its desires. Food, clothing, housing, and so on come as bundles of those utilities that please groups large enough to provide a profitable market.

CHARACTER OF OUR WANTS

Another attempt to pierce through to the fundamental character of our wants may be made by analyzing the bundle of utilities represented by some familiar consumers' good. Our desire for food would seem to be simple enough, with a definite basis in physiological need. But as F. H. Knight says: "Even our food and clothing in all their concrete content and by far the larger part of their money cost represent social and aesthetic and not biological values."[22] This statement is indisputable in so far as it applies to clothing. In fact, no relation has ever been established between a particular clothing custom or fashion and biological need. There is abundant evidence that it is true also with reference to food. With increase in income the cost of food per calorie steadily rises and the cost per equivalent adult male. What exactly are these families getting for their increased expenditures? Not biological values but "social and aesthetic."

Variations in food habits and in food likes and dislikes from time to time and group to group are due to differences in these social and aesthetic values. They are built up by example, precept, and habit and are correspondingly modifiable. Modification is unpleasant, but there are numerous instances of circumstances making it necessary. Probably no travelers in foreign lands have been compelled to make such adjustments as have the explorers of Arctic regions. Their experiences indicate without question the modifiability of our food likes and dislikes as well as the uncertain basis of our ideas as to what is good for us. Stefansson writes:

Unless it be religion there is no field of human thought where sentiment and prejudice take the place of sound knowledge and logical thinking so completely as in dietetics. It is therefore not surprising that actual experiments with diet, especially those instituted by stern necessity, should yield results contrary to conventional expectations.[23]

Later he says:

Questions frequently are put to me as to whether caribou meat or musk-ox meat or bear meat or seal meat is good eating, and then I struggle with impatience, for underlying the query is a fundamental misunderstanding of human tastes and prejudices in food. A rule with no more exceptions than ordinary rules is that people like the sort

22. "Economic Psychology and the Value Problem," *Quarterly Journal of Economics,* XXXIX (May, 1925), 401.
23. V. Stefannson, *The Friendly Arctic* (New York: Macmillan Co., 1921), p. 191.

of food to which they are accustomed. An American will tell you that he can eat white bread every day but that he gets tired of rice if he eats it more than once or twice a month, while a Chinaman may think that rice is an excellent food for every day but that wheat bread soon palls. An Englishman will tell you that beef is the best meat in the world, while in Iceland or Thibet you will learn that beef is all right now and then, but mutton is the only meat of which you never tire. If a man is brought up on the west coast of Norway or on Prince Edward Island, he thinks that herring and potatoes make the best of all staple diets, while an Iowa farmer likes potatoes well enough but would balk at the herring.[24]

He remarks further:

> When a white man has been a year without salt, it becomes almost as unpalatable to him as it is to the Eskimos or Indians who have never used it. . . . In dealing with Eskimos we have found that those who work on ships or who for any reason are compelled to eat salted food, acquire the salt habit about as quickly as they do the habit of tobacco smoking or that of eating some such strange food as bread. Sugar we found . . . to be peculiarly distasteful to the natives, and even children of no more than four or five objected violently to the taste of candy, sugar, sweet preserves, canned fruit and the like. Eskimo infants too young for formed tastes take to sugar quite as readily as infant children among white people.[25]

> People of European culture have during the last three centuries allowed sugar to usurp almost wholly the field of gustatory delights where fats were once supreme, while yet the phrase "to live on the fat of the land" had a keen appeal to the senses.[26]

NECESSARIES, DECENCIES, AND LUXURIES

As soon as the words "necessary," "decency," and "luxury" are used, appraisal of consumptive choices begins. "Necessaries" and "decencies" are goods that one ought to have. The word "luxury" may have either of two connotations. To one school of thought command over luxuries is a desirable state of affairs; to another a luxury is something one ought not to possess or consume.

Many attempts have been made to formulate objective criteria of the necessary, the decent, or the luxurious expenditure. The list of necessaries certainly would be slight if it were based on our existing scientific knowledge of what is requisite to keep an individual in health and strength. Certainly what the individual himself regards as necessary goes far beyond the physiologically essential. The necessary to him is everything incorporated in the standard; by definition it includes the things felt to be essential, whether essential for health and vigor or for beauty, sociability, morale, or status. Luxuries are the goods beyond; those enjoyed when one goes on a spree; those enjoyed by an economically more fortunate class. They are the goods for which a surplus will be spent and from which the "higher" standard will be made if an advance becomes possible.

24. *Ibid.*, p. 211.   25. *Ibid.*, p. 366.   26. *Ibid.*, p. 232.

The ancients and the medievalists attempted to set up objective tests of what constitutes a luxury; moderns put their attention on what constitutes a necessary. That is, in former days men were concerned with what they ought not to consume; now they wish to know what they should. To the moralists of classical antiquity, the Church Fathers, and most of the medieval writers "luxury" was a term that covered all prodigal uses of goods, all their uses for the gratification of the senses, especially taste and touch, and all use for ostentation. It was the reprehensible opposite of simplicity, of asceticism, of self-denial. This is the code of consumption we associate with Puritanism. Along with it went the concept of the virtue of thrift. Benefits too came from avoidance of soft and luxurious living: self-control, hardiness, moral discipline. Plain living and high thinking went together.

Thoreau was our most notable preacher and practitioner of the code of simplicity and individual independence.

By the words *necessary of life*, I mean whatever of all that man obtains by his own exertions, has been from the first, or by long use has become, so important to human life that few, if any, whether from savageness, or poverty, or philosophy, ever attempt to do without it. . . . Many of the luxuries, and many of the so-called comforts of life, are not only not indispensable, but positive hindrances to the elevation of mankind. . . . What is the nature of the luxury which enervates and destroys nations? Are we sure there is none of it in our own lives? . . . When a man is warmed by the several modes which I have described, what does he want next? Surely not more warmth of the same kind, as more and richer food, larger and more splendid houses, finer and more abundant clothing, more numerous, incessant and hotter fires, and the like. When he has obtained these things which are necessary to life, there is another alternative than to obtain the superfluities, and that is, to adventure in life.[27]

Walden, however, is never on the list of books recommended to those seeking guidance in planning their expenditures, although in it are sections on economy, clothing, shelter, furniture, and philanthropy. There are no rules to be found in it, however. On the contrary he says:

I would not have any one adopt *my* mode of living on any account; for, beside that before he has fairly learned it I may have found out another for myself, I desire that there may be as many different persons in the world as possible, but I would have each one be very careful, to find out and pursue *his* own way, and not his father's or his mother's or his neighbor's instead.[28]

Urwick's test of a luxury was not the character of the good or the purpose it served. He did not emphasize the effect of luxurious expenditure upon the consumer but the effects as he saw them upon other members of society. A luxury by his definition is any expenditure by a given family

27. H. D. Thoreau, *Walden* (New York: Macmillan Co., 1929), pp. 11–15.
28. *Ibid.*, p. 79.

over and above the average amount available for expenditure by all families in the community.[29] Excess funds should either be saved or given away. Thus he adds a third question—How much shall I give to others?— to the two: How much shall I spend? and How much shall I save?

Today, few order their spending on the basis of a philosophy of self-denial, simplicity, or social welfare. Their philosophy is more akin to that expressed by Francis Hackett:

> I believe in materialism. . . . I believe in all the proceeds of a healthy materialism, good cooking, dry houses, dry feet, sewers, drain pipes, hot water, baths, electric lights, automobiles, good roads, bright streets, long vacations away from the village pump, new ideas, fast horses, swift conversation, theatres, operas, orchestras, bands— I believe in them all for everybody. The man who dies without knowing these things may be as exquisite as a saint, and as rich as a poet; but it is in spite of, not because of, his deprivation.[30]

In other words, spending is potentially the route to positive values to the users of the things thus secured. Actually it may be the reverse. We have mastered to high degree the art of production but not that of consumption. Neither those who spend relatively much nor those who spend relatively little understand clearly what they really seek or why they seek what they do.

IMPROVEMENT OF CONSUMPTIVE CHOICES

The first step toward improvement of consumptive choices is the study of their nature and origin. We thus become conscious of "the power to which we defer unconsciously in every choice we make." Those who are able to analyze their own standards of consumption objectively and compare them with others are bound to evaluate. Dangers and safeguards inherent in the origin of the standards appear, and the ends sought through consumption are laid bare. For example, it is obvious that there are both dangers and safeguards in the fact that some of our choices and preferences are the result of habits and attitudes established very early, with only the sanction of custom and the experience of our parents as a basis. We have here the protection inherent in the cumulative experience and wisdom of our forebears as to what is good for us. We have also the danger of mistaken judgments, of limited observation, and of attempts to carry over old rules and regulations into changed situations. This danger is perhaps the one of which we are most aware. Under certain conditions

---

29. E. J. Urwick, *Luxury and Waste of Life* (London: J. M. Dent & Co., 1908), pp. 14–15.

30. *Ireland: A Study in Nationalism* (New York: B. W. Huebsch & Co., 1920), p. 324. Quoted as Foreword to W. H. Hamilton and S. May, *Control of Wages* (New York: G. H. Doran Co., 1923).

and certain auspices we are characteristically ready to try new goods, to abandon customary ways, and to renounce the authority of the past. The school and other agencies set themselves to supplement shortcomings in parental knowledge either of hygiene, of aesthetics, or of social forms and usages.

Of another source of danger we are less aware, but it becomes evident when we note what happens in the great majority of cases when income rises and optional consumption becomes possible. Too often the family sets itself blindly to reproduce the level of living of the next "higher" social group. In a country like this where incomes do rise and where the next "higher" social group is marked as such primarily by its income, the danger of the development of unsound standards is real. The primary difficulty is that nothing truly experimental or creative of new values results from this process of imitation. The second is that the possession and use of a large income is no guaranty of a knowledge of the good life. Leisure and a long purse are sometimes found in conjunction with cultivated tastes and a manner of living that shows some deliberate attempt to discover the goods and activities that enhance comfort and pleasure and enrich experience, but sometimes they are not. A third danger to wise consumptive choices lies in the fact that they are constantly subjected to influences brought to bear by the salesman and advertiser. The danger lies in the inevitable bias. Some goods are not advertised at all, while the merits of others are constantly pressed on our attention. Each advertiser, moreover, attempts by every art he can command to promote the choice of his particular good. The more aware consumers are of this danger and the more certain they are as to what they really want and why, the less important is this threat to wise consumption.

As was suggested in chapter xvi, we may appraise a spending pattern from the standpoint either of the ends sought or of the means selected to achieve given ends. The former is fundamentally a problem of ethics; the latter, of science or art. As consumers we largely take ends for granted, and our questions concern primarily the means to these ends. The formal teaching that is done usually concerns means, rarely if ever the ends. The means are what the consumers want to know—how to be healthy, to live long, to be beautiful, smart, in the mode, to do the correct thing—all the rest of it. The ends are taught indirectly by family, school, church, theater, press; rarely are they examined critically or comprehensively.

Appraisal of consumption standards in terms of ends sought, the interests fulfilled, involves nothing less than deciding what is the good life. A high standard of consumption is nothing less than a high sense of what is worth while doing and having and being in life. As Davenport said: "The consumption of wealth is inextricably interwoven with the most perplexing problems of living. . . . In what aspects is life worth living and why and when? What things in human nature are best to be fed and what best starved?"[31] It can scarcely be said that these questions have been left untouched through the ages. What is wanting is not wise discussion of the issues involved but a linking of the problem of "welfare" broadly conceived with the problem of consumption, and the desire to examine critically the values now intrenched in our standards, and, if necessary, remake our valuations.

But if we assume as we must that certain interests and activities are worth while, what assistance can science or art give us in the selection of the best means to secure the ends sought? We know most in regard to what makes for physical welfare. But there are no standards for housing and dress similar to the standards for food and medical care. Furthermore, the relation between consumptive practices and mental health is still unknown. We do not know what, if anything, is necessary in the way of food, clothing, housing, or recreation in order to have sound minds as well as sound bodies.

The forms of consumption that are socially desirable from the individual standpoint are also in large degree socially desirable. The group as a whole desires that resources be utilized in consumption in such a way as to make for optimum productive efficiency, optimum health, optimum development, and fulness of life at the least social cost. For the long-run social good it is also desirable that the consumptive process constantly lead to the discovery of new values and a rejection of the undesirable. Conflicting with this is the inevitable desire of the group that the individual's consumption pattern conform to the generally accepted concept of welfare.

EDUCATION FOR WISE CONSUMPTION

The outstanding obstacles to the improvement of our standards of consumption are lack of the leisure necessary for cultivation of the arts of consumption and lack of education of the proper kind to offset faulty valuations and build up new ones. There is good reason for the association of leisure at the right time in the right amount with a high standard of consumption. The term "consumption" covers a series of activities as diverse as the term "production"; whatever else they involve, they involve time, and many of those that are most desirable in their contribu-

31. H. J. Davenport, *Outlines of Economic Theory* (New York: Macmillan Co., 1898), p. 330.

tion to experience and human development take the most time. It follows therefore that certain modes of living require certain kinds of leisure. It cannot be the leisure that comes with unemployment, for that means leisure without income and with anxiety. It must be an anticipated, desired leisure for which activities and pursuits can be arranged and planned. Nor can it be a leisure for women only. Consumption is something that cannot be delegated; to discuss it is a contradiction in terms. Not an improvement but a deterioration in standards of consumption occurs in a society where men produce and women consume.

Education for wise consumption is evidently not something that can be reduced to a course of ten or even forty lessons. To be adequate, it must be a planned attempt to co-ordinate the diverse fields of thought that have something to contribute to the shaping of the consumer's standards of choice and to direct what they have to offer to the specific problems involved. It cannot be limited to "food and clothing" or to one sex; it cannot be limited to answering questions and telling consumers what they want to know. It must include the raising of questions—questions of motives, of values, of ends—and, although what consumers want to know is too often merely what are the proper foods, clothes, books, pictures, and ritual, it must not degenerate to the level of a book of etiquette. It will include the giving of all that science knows in regard to human needs and the means of meeting them. It will include the cultivation of the interests, tastes, skills, and aptitudes necessary for creative and pleasurable aesthetic experience. It will promote understanding of the character of our choices, of the forces that are influencing them, the values that are behind them. Above all, indirectly if not directly, it will endeavor to increase discrimination, self-reliance, and independence of judgment on the part of consumers. The consumer must learn to consult his individual need, to form his own judgments, to desire for himself and to respect in others a creative, experimental attitude toward the various means that are offered him for the enhancement of his health and comfort, or the enrichment of his experience.

An editorial in the *Saturday Review of Literature*, dealing mainly, it is true, with the education of the readers of books, suggests the situation also in many other fields. The writer says:

We present the interesting phenomenon (and have for two centuries) of masses of common people fumbling with keys at door after door of civilization. The civilization was once, of course, the property of a class, and that it was a finer and more precious thing than the masses will ever attain to in our times we may readily admit. Yet there they are, fumbling—rich now, ambitious now, determined to eat better, dress better, read better, live better, and even to think better. A social order that makes no provision for such upward striving is unthinkable. . . . And the provision is inevitably standardization. If the wife of a laborer who has become a capitalist proposes to observe the social decencies which accompany even a modest luxury she must have standards— and where there are a hundred thousand such wives standards must be standardized— in books of etiquette if you please. When some millions who have not read beyond the newspapers if there, begin to crave fiction, articles, the magazines that supply them successfully will have to be standardized—have been as a matter of fact, as successfully standardized as a Ford car. . . . What can go in such a magazine and what can not go, are both rigorously defined. . . . The America that is learning to keep its teeth clean, ready pretty good books, preserve reasonably good manners, eat properly prepared food, is the America of *The Saturday Evening Post, The Ladies Home Journal,* the America of public schools and advertisements. . . . You can not begin to civilize all of the people all the time except by broad methods broadly applied. But the ignorant foreign observer and the supercilious native overlook the violent reaction which this wholesale culture, thin, weak, diffuse, naturally sets up. . . . Not merely are the already civilized protesting but through the last of the opening doors the mob are themselves beginning to stream out in a new atmosphere where taste, individualism, self reliance begin to seem the highest good.[32]

A remark made by Mrs. Simkhovitch in her book, *The City Worker's World in America,* is also well worth pondering in this connection. Discussing the demand for the "parlor" not as a living room but as a token of respectability, she says: "The simplicity of ignorance of need and the simplicity of indifference to purely external standards are two very different things. One is at the beginning and the other at the end of a long chain of experiences. . . . We learn to discard rather than to do without."[33]

32. *Saturday Review of Literature,* III (May 14, 1927), 815.
33. Mary K. Simkhovitch, *The City Worker's World in America* (New York: Macmillan Co., 1917), p. 32.

REFERENCES FOR FURTHER READING

CHAPTER I

ANSHEN, RUTH N. (ed.). *The Family: Its Functions and Destiny*, chaps. ix–x. New York: Harper & Bros., 1949.

DAVIS, KINGSLEY. "Children of Divorced Parents: Sociological and Statistical Analysis," *Law and Contemporary Problems*, X (summer, 1949), 700–710.

MEAD, MARGARET. "Some Contrasts and Comparisons from Primitive Society," *Annals of American Academy of Political and Social Science*, CLX (March, 1932), 23–28.

REID, MARGARET G. *Economics of Household Production*, chaps. ii–iii. New York: John Wiley & Sons, 1934.

CHAPTER II

ANSHEN, RUTH N. (ed.). *The Family: Its Functions and Destiny*, chap. xiii.

GLICK, PAUL C. "The Family Cycle," *American Sociological Review*, XII (April, 1947), 164–74.

UNITED STATES BUREAU OF THE CENSUS. *Current Population Reports* (on marital status, fertility, characteristics and composition of households and families, and related topics). (Processed.)

CHAPTER III

KUZNETS, SIMON. *National Income and Its Composition, 1919–1938*, chap. i, pp. 431–34. New York: National Bureau of Economic Research, 1941.

UNITED STATES DEPARTMENT OF COMMERCE. *National Income and Product Statistics, 1929–1950*. Washington: Government Printing Office, 1951.

CHAPTER IV

UNITED STATES BUREAU OF THE CENSUS. *Current Population Reports* (on the labor force; work experience and employment status of the population; marital and family characteristics of the labor force; employment characteristics of households and married persons; income of individuals and families; and related topics). (Processed.)

CHAPTER V

BIGELOW, H. F. *Family Finance*, chap. xvi. Chicago: J. B. Lippincott Co., 1953.

Monthly Labor Review, LXVI (February, 1948), 131–81.

SYDENSTRICKER, E., and KING, W. I. "The Income Cycle in the Life of the Wage Earner," *Public Health Reports*, XXXIX (1924), 2133–40.

UNITED STATES BUREAU OF THE CENSUS. *Current Population Reports* (on incomes of individuals and families). (Processed.)

CHAPTERS VI, VII, AND VIII

BURNS, A. E.; NEAL, A. C.; and WATSON, D. S. *Modern Economics*, pp. 813–21; chap. xxxix; pp. 421–24; 626–27; and 639–47. New York: Harcourt Brace & Co., 1948.

HOYT, ELIZABETH E. *Consumption in Our Society*, chaps. xviii–xix. New York: McGraw-Hill Book Co., 1938.

MYRDAL, ALVA. *Nation and Family*, pp. 48–67. New York: Harper & Bros., 1941.

RATHBONE, ELEANOR. *The Disinherited Family*, chaps. i–iii and viii. London: Allen & Unwin, 1927.

CHAPTERS IX AND X

BADGER, R. E., and GUTHMANN, H. G. *Investment Principles and Practices*, chaps. v–vi, xi, and xxviii–xxx. New York: Prentice-Hall, Inc., 1941.

BIGELOW, H. F. *Family Finance*, chap. xviii and pp. 388–415.

GAGLIARDO, D. *American Social Insurance*, chaps. ii and ix. New York: Harper & Bros., 1949.

JORDAN, D. F., and WILLETT, E. J., *Managing Personal Finances*, chaps. xii and xvii–xviii. New York: Prentice-Hall, Inc., 1951.

CHAPTER XI

BIGELOW, H. F. *Family Finance*, pp. 276–80, 415–31.

GAGLIARDO, D. *American Social Insurance*, chaps. xx–xxi.

GORDIS, PHILIP. *How To Buy Life Insurance*, chaps. xix–xxiii, xxv, xxxi–xxxii, and xxxiv. New York: W. W. Norton & Co., 1947.

JORDAN, D. F., and WILLETT, E. J. *Managing Personal Finances*, chaps. xiii–xiv.

REIGEL, R., and MILLER, J. S. *Insurance Principles and Practices*, chaps. vi and viii–xiv. New York: Prentice-Hall, Inc., 1947).

CHAPTER XII

American Economic Review, XXXVII (May, 1947), 333–66; XLI (May, 1951), 617–96.

BURNS, A. E.; NEAL, A. C.; and WATSON, D. S. *Modern Economics*, chap. xl.

BURNS, E. M. *The American Social Security System*. Boston: Houghton Mifflin Co., 1949. Appropriate topics.

GAGLIARDO, D. *American Social Insurance*, pp. 14–21 and chaps. xviii–xix and xxii.

Social Work Year Book. New York: American Association of Social Workers, 1951. Appropriate topics.

CHAPTER XIII

BORSODI, R. *This Ugly Civilization*, pp. 11–13, 78–128, 161–72, 271–309. New York: Simon & Schuster, 1929.

GILBRETH, L. M. *The Home-maker and Her Job*, chaps. v–vii. New York: D. Appleton & Co., 1927.

KNEELAND, H. "Limitations of Scientific Management in Household Work," *Journal of Home Economics*, XX (May, 1928), 311–14.

REID, M. G. *Economics of Household Production*, chaps. iv–xii.

CHAPTER XIV

KNEELAND, H. "Is the Modern Homemaker a Lady of Leisure?" *Survey*, LXIII (1929), 301–2.

MYRDAL, A. *Nation and Family*, chap. xxiii.

PARSONS, A. B. *Woman's Dilemma*, pp. 173–290. New York: Thomas Y. Crowell Co., 1926.

PUTNAM, E. J. *The Lady*. New York: G. P. Putnam's Sons, 1910.

REID, M. G. *Economics of Household Production*, chaps. xix–xxii.

CHAPTER XV

"Alimony," *Law and Contemporary Problems,* VI (spring, 1939), 188–96, 215–24, 225–35.

FUNIAK, W. Q. DE. *Principles of Community Property.* Chicago: Callaghan & Co., 1943. Appropriate topics.

MADDEN, J. W. *The Law of Persons and Domestic Relations,* chaps. ii–vi. St. Paul: West Publishing Co., 1931.

MANSFIELD, E. *The Legal Rights, Liabilities and Duties of American Women,* pp. 266–94. Salem, Mass., J. P. JEWETT & Co., 1845.

NOSSAMAN, W. L. "The Origin and Incidents of the Community Property System," *New Jersey Law Journal,* LXXI (February 12, 1948), 49.

UNITED STATES WOMEN'S BUREAU. *The Legal Status of Women in the United States.* Bull. No. 157. Washington: Government Printing Office, 1941.

CHAPTER XVI

BIGELOW, H. F. *Family Finance,* chap. xiv.

BONDE, RUTH L. *Management in Daily Living,* pp. 181–92. New York: Macmillan Co., 1944.

GRUENBERG, S. M. and B. C. *Parents, Children and Money: Learning To Spend, Save and Earn.* New York: Viking Press, 1933.

JORDAN, D. F., and WILLETT, E. J. *Managing Personal Finances,* chap. vi.

CHAPTER XVII

COLES, J. V. *The Consumer-Buyer and the Market,* chap. ix. New York: John Wiley & Sons, 1938.

"Cost of Living," *Encyclopaedia Britannica* (1952).

REID, M. G. *Consumers and the Market,* chap. xvi. New York: F. S. Crofts & Co.,1942.

TWENTIETH CENTURY FUND, COMMITTEE ON DISTRIBUTION. *Does Distribution Cost Too Much?,* chaps. 10–11. New York: Twentieth Century Fund, 1939.

UNITED STATES BUREAU OF LABOR STATISTICS. *Changes in Cost of Living in Large Cities in the United States, 1931–41.* Bull. No. 699. Washington: Government Printing Office, 1941.

WRIGHT, C. W. *The Economic History of the United States,* chap. xlv. New York: McGraw-Hill Book Co., 1949.

CHAPTER XVIII

BASTER, A. S. J. *Advertising Reconsidered,* chaps. i–iii. London: P. S. King & Son, 1935.

BORDEN, N. H. *The Economic Effects of Advertising,* pp. 156–89, 843–77. Chicago: Richard D. Irwin, Inc., 1942.

BURNS, A. E.; NEAL, A. C.; WATSON, D. S. *Modern Economics,* pp. 229–48; 268–71.

COLES, J. V. *The Consumer-Buyer and the Market,* pp. 21–33; chaps. xxii–xxxv. New York: John Wiley & Sons, 1938.

"Governmental Marketing Barriers," *Law and Contemporary Problems,* VIII (spring, 1941), 234–91, 301–33, 359–62, 374–81.

HAMILTON, W. H., *et al. Price and Price Policies,* Secs. VI and VIII. New York: McGraw-Hill Book Co., 1938).

REID, M. G. *Consumers and the Market,* chaps. xx–xxvii.

UNITED STATES TEMPORARY NATIONAL ECONOMIC COMMITTEE. *Competition and Monopoly in American Industry,* chaps. i and vi. Monograph No. 21. Washington: Government Printing Office, 1941.

UNITED STATES TEMPORARY NATIONAL ECONOMIC COMMITTEE. *A Study of the Construction and Enforcement of the Federal Antitrust Laws,* pp. 1–3, 86–100. Monograph No. 38. Washington: Government Printing Office, 1941.

CHAPTER XIX

HOYT, ELIZABETH E. *Consumption in Our Society,* chaps. ii–v, xxii–xxiii, and xxxi.

KYRK, HAZEL. *Theory of Consumption,* chaps. viii–xi. Boston: Houghton Mifflin Co., 1923.

INDEX

Abel, Mary Hinman, 323–24
Accidents
  insurance against, 211–14
  rates, 167–71
  see also Workmen's compensation laws
Account keeping, 251, 336–37
Advertising
  effects, 361, 366–68
  information in, 365–66
  legal regulation, 363
Aged persons
  economic status, 57–60
  family status, 25
  see also Old age
Agency
  of fact, 301–2
  of necessity, 300
Agricultural policy, 136–37
Aid to dependent children
  federal participation in, 218–19
  history of, 217–18
  policy issues, 219–20
Alimony, 311–13
Allowances
  to children, 330
  to husband or wife, 327–30
American standard of living, 380–85
"Ammain," 90
Angell, R. C., 314
Annuities, 206–9
Antitrust legislation; see Clayton Act; Federal Trade Commission Act; Sherman Act
Arnold, Thurman W., 355
Asceticism, as consumption standard, 388
Ashley, William J., 138, 343
Assets
  of American families, 187–89
  possible types of, 41–42

Banking system, and inflation, 369–70
Benedict, Ruth, 3
Benefits under Social Security Act, 45, 233; see also Old Age benefits; Survivors' benefits
Bequests, 179; see also Inheritance; Marital property
Birth rate
  changes in, 28–29
  group differences in, 33, 35, 121

and poverty, 120–22
Black, John D., 245–46
Blind, public assistance to, 225
Blue Cross and Blue Shield insurance plans, 212
Booth, Charles, 99
Borsodi, Ralph, 266
Boulding, Kenneth, 334
Bowley, A. L., 99
Bradway, J. S., 176, 314
Breckinridge, S. P., 286
Budgeting, 322–26, 330–34
Budgets, as tools
  in drawing poverty line, 97–98
  for planning expenditures; see Budgeting
  for public welfare administration, 98
Bücher, Karl, 271
Burns, C. D., 385
Burns, E. M., 216–17, 225, 237, 238
Buying practices, 360–62

Cash-surrender value of insurance policies, 202–4
Cassel, Gustav, 246
Chain stores, 349–51
Chamberlain, N. W., 120
Chance, Sir William, 139
Chandler, L. V., 368
Children
  allowances to, 330
  concentration of support burden, 79–81
  distribution by number per family, 30
  of divorced parents, 311–12
  as earners, 57, 59
  employment of mothers, 65–66, 69–71
  family and domicile status, 22–24
  and income adequacy, 103–4
  insurance on, 192–93
  and length of mothers' workweek, 288–89
  and poverty, 120–22
  security of, 6
  and state, 6, 141–44, 150, 217–20, 232
Children's benefits under Social Security Act, 232
Choice
  between alternative uses of income, 332, 335–36
  improvement of, in consumption, 389–93
  between making and buying, 252–54
  see also Decision-making

Civil rights
  as basis of income, 15–16, 215
  income from
    forms, 43
    national total, 54
    number receiving, 45
  see also Transfer payments
Clark, J. M., 255–56, 354
Clayton Act, 359–60
Closed shop, 118
Clothing
  budget for working woman, 124
  changes in, 344
  total national expenditure for, 344
Collective bargaining, 117–20
Common law, marital property under, 298–301
Community property system
  advantages, 316–19
  in American states, 308–9
  definition of community property, 307
  special problems, 309–11
Competition
  conditions characterizing, 354
  extent, 352–53
  forms, 354–55
Concentration
  of business ownership and management, 348–51, 353
  of ownership of wealth, 125–26
  of support of children, 78–81
Construction costs, reasons for high, 355–56
Consumer
  as buyer, 360–61
  interests of, 342
  see also Consumer production; Standard of living
Consumer credit; *see* Debt
Consumer education
  in market selection, 361
  to raise standards, 391–93
Consumer production
  changes in character of, 247–50
  characteristics of modern, 250–51
  differentiation from leisure activities, 244
  efficiency of workers, 258–655
  future, 265–69
  measurement, 48–51
  number of persons engaged in, 243
  overhead costs in, 255–58
Consumers' price index, 339–41
Consumption expenditures
  national total
    for all purposes, 55
    for food, clothing, and housing, 344–46
  planning, 320–26
Consumption levels
  money incomes as measure of, 84–88
  over time, 343–44

Consumption standards, improvement of, 390–93; *see also* Standards of living
Consumption units, 89–90
Contract income, 15–16, 43
Contributors to family income, 56–57, 60–61
Control of expenditures, 326–30
Co-operatives, 348
Cost of living
  changes in, over time, 342–47
  definition, 338–42
  measurement of differences
    from place to place, 341
    from time to time, 338–44
  see also Price levels
Cram, Ralph Adams, 385
Creditors' claims upon marital property, 306, 310–11, 318–19
Cultures, types of, 377–78
Cummings, R. O., 343
Currently insured worker under Social Security Act, 231–32

Daggett, Harriet S., 314, 316, 317
Dalton, Hugh, 127
Davenport, H. J., 284, 391
Davie, M. R., 94, 375
Davis, J. S., 32
Davis, Kingsley, 4, 6
Debt
  amount and kinds outstanding, 189
  as means of making large outlays, 173–74
Deceptive selling practices, 362, 365
Decision-making, in income allocation, 332, 335–36
Delaware, distribution of dependents in, 80–81
Demand guidance by sellers, 390; *see also* Advertising
Democratization of consumption, 123, 382, 392–93
Dependents
  actual, defined, 77–78
  concentration of, 78–81
  presumptive, defined, 60–61
Devine, E. T., 373
Dewey, John, 335–36
Disability insurance
  accident, 211–14
  compulsory under state law for nonoccupational disabilities, 240–42
  providing hospital, surgical, or medical care, 211–12
  providing income, 211, 213–14
  see also Workmen's compensation laws
Disabled, public assistance to, 225–26

Distribution, costs of
effects of chains on, 348, 350
factors determining, 346–47
Dividends paid to insurance policyholders, 196–97
Division of labor between men and women, 271–74
Divorce
effects of, 5, 311–12
legal concept of, 312–13
rate of, 20
Divorced persons
economic status, 75, 102, 311–12
family and domicile status, 24
remarriage, 21
Domestic servants; *see* Household help
Doubling-up, 3, 23–25
Douglas, Dorothy, 78
Dower rights, 299–300, 302, 306–7
Drummond, J. C., 343
Dublin, Louis F., 192

Earners; *see* Family incomes; Employment status
Earnings
reduction in inequality in, 128–30
as source of income, 44–45, 53–54
Education of women, special problems, 276–77
Educational services, as a free good, 156–58
Efficiency
in consumer production, 254–65
definition of, 254–55
forms of, 255
Employers' liability, 227
Employment status
of family members, 61
of population, 58, 60
Emulation, forms of, 384–85
Endowment insurance, 203–4
Engel, Ernst, 89
Equimarginal principle, 334
Equitable separate estates, 303
Estates in entirety, 303
Expenditures; *see* Budgeting; Consumption expenditures; Control of expenditures
Experience rating, 228, 237–38

"Fair-trade" laws; *see* Resale price maintenance
Fairchild, M., 69
Families, American
assets, 188–89
composition, 26–27, 29–30
debts, 189

distribution
by income, 83, 85
by number of children, 29
experience during life-span, 30–31, 104–10
life insurance carried, 205
members with money income, 61–62
size, 27–31
Familism, versus individualism, 13
Family
changes in, 2, 3
as child-rearing unit, 6, 14–15
degree of self-sufficiency, 6–10
economic significance, 5, 15–17
forms, 1
functions, 1, 13–15
identifying characteristics, 1–2, 18
and inequality, 127, 129
in other cultures, 5–10
relation to larger group, 4–5, 12–13
see also Families, American
Family allowances, 141–44
Family heads, 25
Family incomes
adequacy, 98–100
children as contributors, 61–62
components, 46
definition, 37–40
distribution, by size, 83, 85
husbands as contributors, 61–63
studies of, 36–37
wives as contributors, 61–62, 64–74
see also Income; Money income; Non-money income
Family status
of population groups, 22–25
significance, 1, 15–16
Farm families, 32–34, 85
Farm-furnished goods, 48
Farm incomes, 136
Farm policy; *see* Agricultural policy
Fawcett, H., 139
Federal Deposit Insurance Corporation, 186
Federal old age insurance system, 229–32, 234–35
Federal Reserve System, Board of Governors
control of supply of checkbook money, 369–71
survey of consumer finances, 37, 187–88
Federal Securities Act, 187
Federal Trade Commission Act, 359, 362–63
Ferguson, C. W., 381
Fertility of American women, 28, 31, 33, 35; *see also* Birth rate
Food consumption, 343–44
Food stamp plan, 159

Foods, drugs, and cosmetics
 false advertising, 363
 labeling requirements, 362–63
 misbranding, 362–63
Ford, Percy, 99
Fraternal societies as insurers, 195
Free goods and services
 classes, 148–49
 cost and quality, 152–55
 criteria for choosing, 151–52
 family use of, 163–64
 future expansion, 156
 as income redistribution, 146–47
 outlays for, 155
 reasons for providing, 147
 as supplements to money income, 86
 for whom provided, 149–51
Freedom to enter employments and markets, and incomes, 129–30; *see also*
  Restraints on trade; Restrictive practices
Fully insured worker under Social Security
  Act, 230
Funiak, W. L. de, 310
Fur Products Labeling Act, 363

Gallaher, Ruth A., 299
Giffen, Sir Robert, 138
Glick, P. C., 20
Glotz, Gustave, 9
Goldman, Franz, 160
Goode, W. J., 21
Gordis, Philip, 213
Government
 borrowing, inflationary effects of, 371
 expenditures, 155
 regulation
  to protect investors and savers, 186–87
  of public utilities, 357
  and restraints on trade, 356–58
 revenues, sources of, 133–34
 services, classes of, 148–49
Grade labeling, 365
Grant, Robert, 303
Gregory, T. E., 382
Group insurance, 195, 206, 207, 211
Gruenberg, S. M. and B.C., 330

Hackett, Francis, 389
Hanna, F. A., 44–45
Haring, Albert, 176
Hawtrey, R. G., 384
Health insurance; *see* Disability insurance
Health services, as a free good, 159–63
Henderson, Y., 94, 375
Home management
 changes in character, 260–61

compared with business management,
  263
 efficiency, 259–69
 and poverty, 112–14
Homemakers
 assistance received, 282–83, 288
 character of work, 277
 economic contribution, 49–51
 economic status, 275
 efficiency, 258–65
 length of working week, 282–95
 number, 270
 working conditions, 278–79
 see also Consumer production; Home
  Management; Women
Homemaking; *see* Homemakers
Homeownership
 extent of, 189
 as provision for contingencies, 182
Horowitz, Charles, 315
Hospital care
 as a free service, 159–63
 insurance against cost of, 211–12
 unpredictability of expenditures for, 173,
  176–77
Hospital insurance; *see* Disability insurance
Household Finance Corporation, 332
Household help, paid, 280, 282
Household production; *see* Consumer production
Households, 18, 27–29
Housing, 344–46; *see also* Construction
  costs
Hoyt, Elizabeth, 377–78, 384–85
Hughes, G. S., 69, 71
Husbands
 benefits under Social Security Act, 231–
  32
 control over expenditures, 327–29
 responsibility for
  wife's debts, 300–301
  wife's support, 300–302, 306, 310
Hutchinson, E. J., 282

Incentives, to increase efficiency, 263–65
Income
 components, 39–40
 definition, 37–41
 inequality, 83–84
 insecurity, 165–67, 215
 of persons
  by age, 109–10
  by marital status, 64, 102
  by occupation, 106
 taxes; *see* Taxes
 see also Family incomes; Money income; National income; Nonmoney
  income

Index
cost-of-living; *see* Consumers' price index
level of living, 92
of relative economic well-being, 91
Individualism, and family, 13
Individuals not in families
domicile status, 22
income, 83
in population, 21
Industrial accidents
compulsory insurance against risk of; *see* Workmen's compensation
rate of occurrence
Industrial insurance, 195, 197–98
Inequality
in earnings, 128–30
effects of, 126–28
and felt poverty, 125
in income, 82–84
lessening of, 125–30
in ownership, 125–26
Inflation
effects, 368
in peacetime, 369–70
and savers, 187
in wartime, 370–71
Informative labeling, 364–65
Inheritance, 127–28
Insecurity, economic; *see* Income, insecurity of; Risks
Instalment credit, 175–76
Institute of Life Insurance, 192, 193, 210
Insurance
adequacy of, 210–11, 214
cost of, 196
essential features of, 176
when possible, 177, 190
versus saving, 176–77
see also Annuities; Disability insurance; Endowment insurance; Insurance program; Life insurance; Social insurance
Insurance carriers, 190, 194–95, 197, 199
Insurance premiums; *see* Life insurance
Insurance program
and family life-cycle, 191–94, 209–10
ideal, 211
Investment
of savings, 178–79, 181–87
as source of income, 44–45, 125–26
Investment companies, 183–84, 187

Jacobs, A. C., 315, 318
Joint tenancy, 305
Jordan, D. F., 185, 205

Keller, A. G., 1, 271
King, W. I., 90

Kingsbury, S. M., 69
Kinship, economic significance of, 4–6
Kiser, C. V., 122
Kneeland, Hildegarde, 283
Knight, F. H., 125, 386
Kyrk, Hazel, 375

Labeling requirements, 362–63
Labor force
definition, 57
family members in, 62
Labor organizations; *see* Unions
Lady, as ideal economic role, 280
Lang, Frank, 227
Legal reserve of insurance companies, 202
Leisure
differentiated from labor, 245–47
distribution of, and consumption standards, 391–92
Leisure class, women as new, 279–81
Lerner, S. M., 44–45
Level of living, index of, 92; *see also* Consumption levels
Life-expectancy
increase in, 167–68
of mothers versus fathers, 192
Life insurance
adequacy of, 210–11
carriers, 194–95
cash-surrender and loan value of, 202, 204
on children, 192–93
cost, 196–204
on husband, 191–94
kinds purchased, 193, 195, 197, 205
types of policies, 194–96, 199–204
on wife, 191–94
see also Group insurance; Insurance
Limited-payment life insurance, 203–4
Lindahl, E. R., 51
Linford, Alton A., 224
Liquidity of savings, desirability of, 182–83
Loan value of insurance policies, 202–4
Lotka, Alfred J., 192
Luxuries, criteria of, 387–89
Lynd, Robert S. and Helen M., 257

Mackey, Thomas, 138
McMahon, T. S., 382
Madden, J. W., 301
Madge, Charles, 325, 329
Malinowski, Bronislaw, 7
Malthus, T., 121
Management
definition, 258–59
differentiation from performance, 259

Management—*Continued*
  efficiency in, 259–60
  kinds, 260.
Manorial system, family under, 9–10
Manufacturers
  marketing operations of, 348
  relation to retailers, 349
Marital law
  appraisal of, 314–19
  importance of, 297–98
  systems of, 298
Marital property
  under common law, 298–301
  in community-property states, 307–11
  in former common-law states, 303–7
Market, development of free, 10–11
Market aids to consumer buyers, 361–62
Market structure, 347–50
Marriage
  age and rate, 19–20
  effects upon income and property rights;
    see Marital property
Married men
  adequacy of incomes, 102–4
  distribution by number of children. 103
  as earners, 63–64
  family and domicile status, 23–24
  money income, 102
  see also Husbands
Married women
  as earners, 61–62, 64–74, 116–17, 292–
    96
  disabilities under common law, 299–300
  family and domicile status, 23–24
  money income, 102
  see also Wives
Married Women's Property Acts, 303–4
Marshall, L. C., 314
Mason, O. T., 272
Maximizing
  income, 114–16
  satisfactions through income allocation,
    334–35
May, Geoffrey, 314
Mead, Margaret, 6
Medical care
  as free public service, 159–63
  insurance against cost of, 212
  prepayment plans, 212
  unpredictability of expenditures for, 173,
    176–77
Men
  as earners, 57–60
  economic life-history, 276
  income, 102, 106, 108–10
Meriam, Lewis, 234
Middlemen, 347–48
Minimum-wage laws, 135–36

Minnesota, earnings of individuals in, 110
Misbranding, prohibitions of, 362–63
Mitchell, W. C., 50, 51
Money, changes in supply of, 369–70
Money income
  adequacy of, 98–105
  age differences in, 108–10
  distribution by amount, 83, 85
  flow of, in relation to spending, 320–21
  forms, 42–46
  importance, 39–40, 252
  maximizing, 114–16
  as measure of consumption level, 84–88
  nonrecipients, 59–61
  occupational differences in, 106
  range of uses, 320–21
  recipients, 57–61
Monopoly
  extent, 352–53
  forms, 354–55
  labor unions as, 118–19
Monroe, Day, 19, 70
Mothers
  as earners, 65–66, 75–76
  effect of divorce, widowhood, separation,
    75–76
  in families receiving aid to dependent
    children, 219, 220
  fertility, 28, 31–35
  insurance on, 191–92
Mother's pension; *see* Aid to dependent
    children
Müller-Lyer, F. C., 7, 272, 296
Mumford, Lewis, 286
Murphy, Gardner and Lois, 376–77
Myrdal, Alva, 120, 122

National Bureau of Economic Research, 36
National income, 52–53
National Research Council, Committee on
    Food Habits, 95
National Safety Council, 167
National Service Life Insurance, 195, 199
Necessaries, criteria of, 387–88
Needy; *see* Public Assistance
Negro families; *see* Nonwhite families
Newcomb, T. M., 376–77
Nienberg, B. M., 19
Nonfarm families, 32–34, 85
Nonmoney incomes
  fixed nature, 320
  forms, 46–47
  importance, 40, 48, 50–52, 54, 86–87
  reducing to monetary terms, 48–50
Nonwhite families, 34–35, 87, 201, 344
Nossaman, W. L., 310
Nuclear family, 1, 6

Occupational illness, compulsory insurance against risk of, 227–28
Ogburn, W. F., 90
Old age
  provision for
    by individuals, 178, 206–9
    by public measures, 220–25, 229–32
    as risk, 167–69
Old age assistance
  development of program, 220–21
  federal participation, 220–22
  policy questions, 222–23
Old age benefits under Social Security Act, 230–31
Ordinary insurance, 195–96
Overhead costs, in household, 255–58
Overwork of homemakers, methods of reducing, 289–91
Owned homes, estimating occupancy value, 49, 345–46

Packaged goods, and deceptive trade practices, 362
Palmer, J. L., 350
Parents
  benefits under Social Security Act, 232
  responsibility of, for children, 4, 219
  responsibility of children for, 4, 222–24
Patents, public policy concerning, 357–58
Payroll taxes under Social Security Act, 229–30, 235–36
Pechman, J. A., 44–45
Peixotto, J. B., 94
Personal income total in United States, 53–55
Persons not in labor force, 58
Planning expenditures; *see* Expenditures, planning of; Budgeting
Pooling of incomes
  definition, 38
  when occurring, 101
  when undesirable, 326
Poor law; *see* Public assistance; Responsibility of relatives for support of needy
Population
  family and domicile status in United States, 21
  and poverty, 120–21
Poverty
  measurement of extent, 98–104
  persons in, 100, 103, 109, 137–38
  primary versus secondary, 111–12
  standards for identifying, 93–96
Powell, R. R. B., 314
Preliterate groups, family in, 5–8
President's Conference on Home Building

and Home Ownership, Committee on Household Management, 283
Price comparisons, obstacles to, 360–62
Price competition, 354, 360
Price level
  movements of, 368, 370
  relation of, to supply of money, 369
  see also Consumers' price index; Inflation
Prices; *see* Competition; Inflation; Price level
Primary poverty, 111–12
Product differentiation, 354, 367
Production
  definition, 244–47
  for market, development of, 247–49
Public assistance
  forms of, 137
  history of, 138–40
  number receiving, 45
  policy issues, 140–41, 216
Public health measures, as free service, 148, 158
Public schools, use of, 163; *see also* Educational services
Public utilities, 357

Quality competition, 354, 361–62
"Quet," 90

Real income, 342; *see also* Nonmoney income; Money income
Recreational services, as free good, 156, 164
Reid, Margaret G., 246
Requirements, human, 93–96, 124–25; *see also* Necessaries
Resale price maintenance, 349–50
Responsibility of relatives for support of needy, 4, 222–24
Restraints upon trade, 356–58; *see also* Restrictive practices; Sherman Act
Restrictive practices
  and income security, 165
  and inequality, 130
  of labor and business, 355–56
Retailers
  independent, 350–51
  large business units, 348
  place in market structure, 347, 349
  relation to manufacturers, 349
Richards, Ellen H., 244
Risks
  economic, 168–71
  insurable, 176–77
  personal, 166–68
Rivers, W. H. R., 271

Robertson, D. H., 334
Robinson-Patman Act, 351, 359
Rowntree, B. S., 99, 111, 112, 123

Salaried workers, security of, 172
Sales promotion, 365; *see also* Advertising
Saving
  budgeting to insure, 332
  factors determining amount of, 180–81
  motives for, 176–80
Savings
  disposition, 181–87
  protection, 185–87
  total personal, 55
  uses, 177–78
Savings banks, 183–84, 186
Savings and loan associations, 183–84, 186
Scales of income equivalence, 91
Schouler, James, 304
Schultz, T. W., 137
Science, as guide to requirements, 94–95, 391
Scientific management
  definition, 260
  in household, 261–65
Secondary poverty, 111–12
Securities
  corporate
    family ownership of, 188
    as investment for small saver, 184–87
  government
    as investment for small saver, 184
    operations of Federal Reserve Board, 369–71
Security, economic
  of children, 6
  desire for, 165
  ways of increasing, 165–66
  see also Risks
Self-sufficiency
  of extended family, 7, 9
  of manorial households, 8, 9
  of slave households, 9, 10
  of small family, 4, 6–10, 247–49
Separate estates of married persons; *see* Marital property
Separated persons
  economic status, 75
  family and domicile status, 24
Sherman Act, 358–59
Sickness insurance; *see* Disability insurance; Workmen's compensation laws
Simkhovitch, Mary K., 393
Simons, H. C., 132
Single persons
  economic status, 75
  family and domicile status, 23
Slavery, 9–10

Slichter, S. H., 262
Smith, Sir Hubert, 114
Social changes, and the family, 10–12
Social family, 18
Social insurance, contrasted with
  public assistance, 226, 234
  true insurance, 233
Social Security Act
  grants-in-aid under, 217–22, 225–26
  old age and survivors' insurance, 229–36
  and state unemployment compensation, 236
Social security system, 216–17
Stamp, Sir Josiah, 51
Standardization of consumption, 385
Standards
  of consumption, and poverty, 122–24;
    see also Standard of living
  of identity and quality, 364–65
  of living
    as culture products, 377–78
    definition, 373–74, 375
    origin, 376–78
    relation to given mode of living, 375–76
    significance, 373, 374–75
    ways of describing, 379
    see also American standard of living
Stefannson, V., 386–87
Subfamilies, 23–25
Sumner, W. G., 1, 271, 376
Survivors' benefits under Social Security Act, 232
Sydenstricker, E., 90

Taxes
  as deductions from income, 55, 86
  payroll under Social Security Act, 230, 233–34, 235
  personal income, 132–33
  as protectionist policy, 356
  relative importance of various kinds as sources of revenue, 133–34
  in wartime, 371
Tenancy in common, 305
Term insurance, 199–201, 204
Thomas, W. I., 273–74
Thompson, C. B., 260
Thoreau, H. D., 388
Trade barriers; *see* Restraints on trade; Restrictive practices
Transfer payments, 44, 54, 146, 215

Underwork of homemakers, 291–95
Unemployment
  as an economic risk, 169–71
  state compensation laws, 236–40
Unions, 117–20

U.S. Bureau of the Census
  contributors to family income, 56–58,
    63–66, 75–76
  divorce, 20–21
  employment status, 58, 243
  families, 18–19, 26, 28–29, 31
  family status, 21
  fertility, 28–29, 31, 121
  government expenditures, 155
  incomes, 37–38, 46, 83, 85, 102, 106, 108
  labor force, 56, 169–71
  life-expectancy, 168
  marriage, 20–21
  occupations, 106
U.S. Bureau of Human Nutrition and
  Home Economics, 37, 38, 283, 288
U.S. Bureau of Labor Statistics, 37, 39,
  43, 51, 90–91, 97–98, 126, 199, 282,
  339–40
U.S. Bureau of Public Assistance, 219, 220
U.S. Children's Bureau, 73
U.S. Department of Agriculture, 282, 339
U.S. Department of Commerce, 36, 53,
  344, 345
U.S. Federal Security Board, 219
U.S. Government Life Insurance, 195
U.S. National Institute of Health, 160
U.S. National Resources Committee, 37
U.S. Temporary National Economic Com-
  mittee, 46, 198, 352
U.S. Women's Bureau, 70, 298, 303, 304,
  306
Urwick, E. J., 389

Veblen, Thorstein, 128, 273–74
Vinagradoff, Paul, 9
Vocational divide in life of women, 276–77

Wants
  character, 380, 386–87
  origin, 377

Ward, F. W. O., 139
Whelpton, P. K., 122
Whole-life insurance, 199, 202, 204
Widowed persons
  benefits under Social Security Act, 232
  domicile and family status, 22, 24
  economic status, 75, 102
Wigmore, John, 298
Wilbraham, A., 343
Willett, E. F., 185, 205
Williams, Faith, 90
Willoughby, W. W., 299
Wilson, Maud, 289
Wisconsin, components of contract income, 44–45
Wives
  benefits under Social Security Act, 231
  control over expenditures, 327–30
  responsibility
    for family necessaries, 306, 310
    for support of husband, 306
  right to support, 300–301, 310
Women
  as earners, 57–60
  economic life history, 276–77
  education, 276–77
  income, 102
  as new leisure class, 279–81
  not in labor force, 270
  in primitive societies, 271–72
  psychophysical characteristics, 273–74
  under Social Security Act, 236
  tasks allotted, 271–75
Wool Products Labeling Act, 363
Workmen's compensation laws, 226–29
Wright, Carroll D., 116
Wright, David Mc., 165
Wyer, S. S., 52

Zweig, F., 93–96, 329–30